REFORMATION

JOHN M. TODD

REFORMATION

1971
DOUBLEDAY & COMPANY, INC.
GARDEN CITY, NEW YORK

Library of Congress Catalog Card Number 75-157629

Contents

Introduction

In this book I treat the religious revolution known as the Reformation under the following three headings: (1) Its roots deep in the previous history of the Church and in the nature of Christianity itself. (2) The first fifty years of the revolution throughout Europe. (3) Its outcome today. A first chapter is devoted to a detailed definition of the subject. The whole is intended as relevant history, based on the researches of original scholars.

The religion of fifteenth-century Europe had grown in some respects far from the Christianity of the New Testament. Christianity as people understood it, and experienced it in their own lives, often seemed to them inadequately served by current ecclesiastical structure and practice. Cynicism and discontent were widespread. Reform had to come. By 1500, perhaps by 1400, the Reformation was virtually programed—in principle. The detail would depend on the characters of the leaders who emerged and on the nature of their colleagues, their opponents, their circumstances, and on the numerous other enabling factors, political, economic and cultural.

Today the Reformation themes are running their final course within the Roman Catholic Church itself. Among the majority of the other Christian denominations, which were originally inspired by the Reformation, these themes have completed their course. From being divisive the Protestant inspirations have become unifying. The Bible, from being a sign of contradiction, has set the Christian churches on converging courses. But the need to modify and adapt Christian institutions is leading once again to a radical reconsideration of the nature of the biblical revelation and Christian experience. This continuing reformation is the theme of my final chapter.

Before reaching the Reformation proper, the reader may be surprised to find a chapter on the place of the Bible in the centuries preceding the Reformation, and yet another chapter on

Christianity itself as it developed through the whole preceding fifteen centuries. It is the theme of my book that the Reformation is only intelligible, historically, in the light of a long prehistory, that the key to an understanding of the drive which made the Reformation what it was, can only be found in the preceding history of Christianity. At the heart of this theme lies the institutionalization of Christianity, the submission of its "gospel" to the "law" promulgated by the Church. The processes of the organized Church were identified with "God's will," canon law with the gospel. While society at large was growing, culturally, politically and economically, the religious community was unable to develop. A fatal inflexibility prevented it from responding fruitfully to initiatives which emerged from within it.

The more or less "popular" historian has the task of selecting and organizing material, of quite frequent generalization and assessment. Some readers will think they see special pleading actuated by some prejudice or other of mine. Inevitably. There is no such thing as total history or unslanted history. But my own interest is in history as such, and in theology as such. Whatever my prejudices may be, I have no conscious wish to reach any foregone conclusion, but only to present the facts, and the great processes of thought, experience and life as they emerge from the facts. I plead guilty if anyone wishes to chide me for failing to defend some cause or other.

I depend throughout on the works of numerous scholars. In a book of such wide-ranging content as this it would be impossible to footnote every sentence for which I am in fact indebted in some way to another historian. A bibliography would also tell one little. Instead, I have written bibliographical comments on each chapter. These will be found at the end of the book. In the course of them I refer to all books on which I have relied in a more than passing fashion, and try to mention some of the others which I have read. In addition, from time to time, in the text of the book or in occasional footnotes to it I have put a reference when I have relied extensively on some particular book.

I have tried to mediate the work of experts. Similarly as in other branches of human knowledge today, perhaps nearly half of all the historians who have ever lived have lived in the last twenty years—so explosive has been the growth of population and of historical research work. There is no doubt that, as a result, received versions of historical events can get very rapidly out of date. I have certainly been aware that in being able to use relatively recent research in several areas a picture has emerged notably different from that generally accepted. But I have not confined myself to the use of recent works. Forty or fifty years ago, a Christopher Dawson or a Margaret Deanesly did work which has not been superseded and is still closely relevant.

"Revelance" is one of the cliché virtues of our time. But this quality of relevance to our present situation is often the proper aim of that kind of writing which we call *haute vulgarisation*, such as is the present work. I have tried, then, to write relevant history without in any way surrendering those standards of precision and of concrete presentation which were taught me as a university student thirty and more years ago.

J.M.T.

October 19, 1970

CHAPTER 1

The Reformation — Definition

Reformation, Part of a Longer Process

The Reformation is usually treated as a slice of history roughly from 1517 to 1559. It is tempting to do this for two reasons. (1) Great changes in the organization of many Christian communities in Europe, in their ways of worship and in their teaching, were all achieved in that time. The Pope, and the bishops in communion with him, were disowned by large numbers of people who set up the Bible as the ultimate authority for all Christians in all matters of behavior and belief. Newly constituted human authorities were set up to regulate behavior and belief in daily practice. (2) A number of other changes can be made to appear to fit in roughly with this period of time, changes of a cultural, economic and political kind, though many of them in fact date back to long before these changes in religion.

This treatment of the Reformation makes an understanding of it difficult. The religious changes were numerous, sudden and wide-ranging. When they have all been chronicled, and duly linked with the other changes of the day, one is left with a mass of information which is not easy to digest and assess. One wants to know why these changes swept so suddenly and so swiftly across so much of central and northern Europe. It was an age of intense religious belief; one wants to know what it meant to those who took part in this transformation, who experienced it. What relation did it all have with what appear to have been quite numerous previous attempts to achieve something similar to the "Reformation," those of Hus a century before, of Wycliffe, and of earlier movements? And what relation has it to subsequent reforms of the reformed churches, and eventually to the movement of reform in the Roman Catholic Church of the twentieth century?

The clean slice-of-history approach cuts the story short, fore and aft. It assumes that within the chosen dates there was either a self-sufficient religious revolution, or some kind of a total sociological revolution. But neither is true. Both revolutions were part of an ongoing process which has neither a single sudden beginning, nor an abrupt end. The religious changes cannot be looked at just by themselves, in dissociation from the past or from the other cultural changes. But conversely the religious changes were not just part of a great cultural convulsion. The Reformation was a religious event for whose adequate interpretation religious norms cannot be dispensed with.

In this preliminary chapter we summarize first the changes in society which were the enabling context of the religious revolution, and sometimes part of it. We then summarize the essential facts of the religious revolution and its past, with a look to its future, before going back deep into the detail of the prehistory proper of the Reformation in Chapters 2 and 3.

Enabling Factors

1. Printing During the fourteen-fifties Johann Gutenberg of Mainz perfected his invention of printing. By the first decade of the sixteenth century, there were about 150 presses at Venice, which had become the center of printing; every large town in Europe had its press. For the first time information and opinions could be communicated widely and quickly and at length to all who could read. The vast majority of books printed were connected with religion. The printer-publishers produced what people wanted and would buy. As the Reformation events began to include written material, these printers played a major part in enabling it to be disseminated. Erasmus' New Testament in Greek, Tyndale's New Testament in English, Luther's Ninety-Five Theses in Latin are typical examples. The printers produced what they could sell quickly—the great majority did not have large capital, or great banks behind them. An important part of their wares was the Bible. We shall follow that subject in a little detail in Chapter 2. The printers were of course also used by those who wished to defend the established system. But an advantage is held by one who challenges an existing system and it was some time before the defenders' output began to rival that of the challengers.

2. Humanism The Renaissance, as the whole cultural movement of the fifteenth century, originating in Florence in the fourteenth and early fifteenth centuries, is called, was in the first place a fresh and fundamental desire to understand man. Its concerns ran the whole gamut from aesthetics to sex; from metaphorical language in religion to politics. It often took the form of, and was in some senses identical with, a desire to read the literature of ancient Greece and Rome. There was a new consciousness of the value of each individual person, sometimes a specially intense insight into the nature of each man or woman as unique. This insight was patient of development into a special kind of religious respect for every person as the "temple of the Holy Spirit." Or it could develop into a new confidence in man, impatient of religious values. A new freedom was in the air. The Italian humanist and Christian ascetic Pico della Mirandola said: "Man is born his own master in all liberty . . . He can degenerate into a beast or be born anew to become almost like a God."

With the return to ancient texts went a newly enthusiastic determination to return to the text of the Bible, and particularly to the Greek of the New Testament. There is here a direct link with Reformation events. But again distinctions have to be made. The Reformation was not caused in this way. Ultraconservative and authoritarian Spain produced a Greek text of the New Testament, part of the Ximenes Polyglot Bible, superior to that produced by Erasmus. Good texts easily available helped the Reformation, but did not set it off.

Art was a major factor in the Renaissance. Painters had begun in the fourteenth century to present, for the first time since ancient Rome, absolutely lifelike representations of the people in front of them. The ancients had done it in stone. The Italians did it with pigment. The beginnings of this individualism can be traced back to the thirteenth century, when Cimabue, Giotto and others broke loose from the stylized conventions. In the next century Dante envisaged a new spiritual life, *vita nuova*. In the same century Marsilius envisaged a new political structure. Both began to see man as an individual in a new way; in the eyes of God, in the eyes of the state. "Individualism" as a factor is related to "nationalism" and to "anti-clericalism," as well as to "humanism." But it has a longer pedigree, and is an aspect of a fundamental characteristic of the Christian revelation, which is itself embodied in the Reformation insights. This is not so much an enabling factor, as an aspect of the Reformation itself.

3. *Nationalism and Anti-clericalism* Nationalism may be listed as one of the enabling factors in the success of the Reformation.

Likewise anti-clericalism. They were not inseparable but very often they came together in practice. Neither was new. Nationalism is a vague term. To some extent it does no more than refer to a permanent element in all human societies. People identify themselves with their local community, are proud of the community and defend it against competitors and aggressors. As literacy increased, and as the general standard of living rose, people became aware of the community of interests which was slowly emerging in the form of the modern nation-states. But it was the rulers themselves and their senior administrators, more than their subjects, who became most distinctly aware of this. It was they who found themselves encouraged to objectify the Roman papal ecclesiastical authority as competitive or aggressive, endangering their own authority, which they increasingly understood as autonomous and absolute. In the sixteenth century all this was only an aggravation of nationalist and anti-clericalist sentiments already hundreds of years old, among their subjects as well as among the rulers.

Neither nationalism nor anti-clericalism led automatically to Protestantism. In 1516 the king of France made an agreement with the Pope, the Concordat of Bologna, which gave the king control over the appointments of all bishops and many other senior offices in the Church. But this had nothing to do with any kind of reform of the Church or with any kind of revolt from or reform of received doctrine or ecclesiastical authority. It was a matter of international politics. The state in France, as in England and many other places, already had substantial control over Church appointments, one of the previous landmarks in this matter in France being the Pragmatic Sanction of Bourges (1438). The Concordat of Bologna centralized the already extensive state control of the Church in the hands of the king of France, depriving the parliament and the university of certain rights. It certainly meant that the Church had even less ability than before to act from within the state as a competitive body. But the Church in France remained loyal to the traditional norms in all its teaching and worship. A combination of anti-clericalism and nationalism produced no deviation from Catholic norms. This deviation was to come later, from individuals motivated, in a haphazard pattern, by specific religious concerns.

There was a generalized anti-clericalism spread throughout Europe. It was the direct product of reformers both within the

Church and without, from the twelfth century onwards, and of the abuses within the Church against which these reformers protested. This anti-clericalism, which became a permanent characteristic of society and of written reflections on everyday life, undoubtedly played an extremely important part in the Reformation events. It is itself part of the specific religious motivation, or is a product of it. It is not in this sense an external "enabling factor," but a part of the complex of religious factors which make up the Reformation.

4. *Economic Factors* What of the economic factors? Surely there is something here which lies behind the religious concerns and is at the heart of the Reformation. Historians in Eastern Europe have hailed Luther as a great social revolutionary *malgré lui*. All such interpretations of the *malgré lui* variety must be suspect. We must respect the facts in front of us, and set them in turn in their factual context. Luther liked to speak in the language of the people and to emphasize his earthy ancestry, and this has led sometimes to an idea of him as a rural revolutionary. It has no basis in fact. In practice he tended to respect established public authority and to oppose revolutionary attitudes both in the political sphere and the ecclesiastical.

It is difficult to generalize about the economic facts in Europe at the beginning of the sixteenth century. The situation differed very widely. The depletion of the population after the Black Death had largely been made up. Population was now rising, even though bubonic plague still stalked regularly across the Continent. Speaking very generally we can say that a proportion of the peasants had been progressively freeing themselves in some regions from permanent obligations to feudal overlords, and tying themselves instead by an obligation to deliver produce or cash, and this sometimes led more easily to poverty than the old arrangement. In the towns wealth had grown. Discontent in town and country came from the sight of the few idle and overindulgent rich; and the knowledge of the greater freedom and greater prosperity to be gained from riches. The master craftsmen sometimes made harsh arrangements with their apprentices; the property owners sometimes took too much from or gave too little cash to their peasants. The merchant bankers profited increasingly as men came to them for credit.

In Germany there is a real sense in which religious events triggered off economic and political revolt rather than the opposite. The princes as well as the peasants found in young Father Luther's challenge to religious authority a way in to the expression and promotion of their own interests. At Worms, when Luther was being heard by the emperor in 1521 during the Imperial Diet, the peasant's shoe, the *Bundschuh,* signal of revolt, appeared on doors. By 1524 the achievement of substantial changes in the Mass, the disappearance of some religious houses and the virtual overthrow of episcopal authority in some places played some part in encouraging the peasants to revolt. They sensed in Luther a leader. Luther, himself inexperienced in the nuances of public behavior in delicate situations, issued stern pronouncements about social justice which helped to set the revolt off. He had intended the statements for the princes, lecturing them as to their social duties. But peasants saw the corollary, that injustice should be resisted. When the revolt began Luther issued statements in a politically contrary sense, encouraging the princes to put down violent revolt against established public authority, with all the force that was necessary. Luther had no training in and little aptitude for political affairs, but felt bound to respond when he found himself in a position of leadership, and people hung on his words.

These facts illustrate the complex interrelation of economic and religious affairs. There was much discontent and it sometimes expressed itself through religion. There was perhaps a general intuition of a blockage caused by the established masters and rulers, by a kind of "conspiracy" of authority between princes (including the emperor), bishops (including the Pope), the universities, with the merchants and bankers as auxiliaries and the lawyers well represented in all four spheres. These four or five estates were always competing with each other to have the whip hand, but together they did constitute a kind of magisterium of Christendom. From a Marxist point of view there is a case for saying that the educated and monied people ran the show to the disadvantage of the rest. The difficulty with this case is to be able to understand it as anything else than a truism and a tautology. Has there been any human society where it would be impossible to make out such a case? Do not all human societies provide grounds for making this case out quite strongly? Is it possible to envisage a society free of it? We might, however, be able to say that this exploitational aspect was possibly more in evidence than usual. The general speed-up in efficiency partly due to printing, and the incentives connected with increasing trade, with overseas discoveries and later the inflow of new silver, provided more opportunities to make money quickly and to cause injustice and suffering in the process. Also, rise in production was not keeping pace with rise in population.

The picture in England is typically complex. The apprentices in London were ready to riot at any time—but particularly against foreigners who might be taking their living. The two large-scale provincial revolts against Henry VIII were a mixture of religion and politics, with economic injustice present but not to the fore in the demands made by their leaders. And in general the revolutionaries wanted religion not to be changed.

Another discarded hypothesis is that increase in economic activity, particularly trade in towns and across the frontiers relying on complicated arrangements for credit from bankers, in short, "capitalism," was closely connected with the Reformation.[1] But it is now clear that these "capitalist" activities date back to several centuries before the Reformation. More recently another theory has been put forward that after the Reformation the Catholic Counter-Reformation state tended to eject its great merchants who had become Protestants, in a spirit which was less tolerant than the late medieval papal Church had been.[2]

But all one can say is that all such generalizations seem extremely problematical. All sorts of correlations can be found, but what they signify in terms of general cause and effect, motive, intention, personal satisfaction and achievement is much more difficult to say, other than in purely individual terms. The great cities of late medieval Europe were the great cities of the early six-

[1] At one time it was thought that there was a change at the Reformation from the medieval teaching about the taking of interest on money that was loaned. This is not so. Luther and Calvin both gave advice on this matter and, although they do not use all the categories of the medieval casuist, the upshot is the same in the end. Neither orthodox papal theologians nor the reformers defined usury as the sin involved in every transaction of the lending of money at a price. They are concerned rather to suggest formulae which will ensure justice for both parties to the contract. All condemn exploitation of the need of a man for the purpose of making profit simply for its own sake.
[2] H. R. Trevor-Roper, RELIGION, THE REFORMATION AND SOCIAL CHANGE (Macmillan, London, 1967).

teenth century. It was natural that Venice should become a center of printing. Antwerp, the greatest port in northern Europe, might reasonably be expected to attract a variety of interests, and it is not surprising to find Tyndale living there while he undertook his translation of the Bible. It was a strategic point. Merchants had assisted him in London, when the bishop of London failed to do so. And merchants now protected him in Antwerp and took his books when complete into England. Merchants with some crypto-Lollard inclinations were among those who helped to disseminate the Bible in England. But there was a sufficient general interest in religion and in the Bible to explain the rapidity of the dissemination, without having to raise some special theory. The merchants were precisely the people who were in contact with communication and transport. It was sure to be some of their number who would assist.

"Economic factors" is not really a relevant general term here. Some merchants were interested in religion, and in the Bible. They were uniquely well placed to help with the dissemination of books, and of new opinions. It is a question of how it all happened, but hardly begins to touch the "why," which is concerned with what was going on in the minds of merchants who agreed to do this often illegal and often dangerous work. It is impossible to find such a large majority of merchants everywhere involved in opposition to the papal Church and in promotion of innovation to enable us to say that what went on in their minds looks as if it was really a function of their occupation as merchants.

The economic factor, then, to some extent increased the impetus of religious revolution, but could not be said to have been the cause of it. At the time of Wycliffe in England, in the early 1380's, the unrest of the peasants became loosely linked, in a way similar to that in Germany in the sixteenth century, with religious initiatives. But a Peasants' Revolt against poverty and injustice in the fourteenth century was still, just as in the sixteenth century, an affair which might be primarily either economic or political and could be religiously conservative.

As with any movement which threatens the whole structure of state and society, everyone tends to come in on one side or the other. Economic factors are involved along with other factors. But peasants were just as likely to be on the side of the establish-

ment, as in some parts of Switzerland, and in Cornwall and Yorkshire in England, or to be merely indifferent, as they were to be
on the side of religious change, as in Germany. And it is equally
impossible to generalize about other classes in the first three or
four decades of the sixteenth century. The Reformation appeared
in a large number of very different places within a short space
of time. It is impossible to find any common economic factor in
the very wide geographical distribution.

5. *Political Factors* Political factors keep changing all the time.
Generalizations which have sometimes been made about the Reformation being primarily political in motivation will not bear examination. As we have seen in France, state and Church were already closely bound together. One could not change independently
of the other. But where changes in religion happened they did so
because large numbers of people wished them to happen, not
for some relatively superficial political reason. Politics is the art of
the possible, always a very pragmatic affair. As a result it is always
difficult to generalize. We saw how the generally increasing sense
of national identity could lead towards an attitude which might
support the Reformation, but did not in fact always do so. A
detailed example of the unexpected way in which politics affected
the Reformation will show how impossible it is to generalize. In
the autumn of 1518 the Pope and his advisers were pressing very
hard for the arrest and trial of Luther. Then it became clear that
the Emperor Maximilian could not live long. Rome was very
concerned to prevent his grandson, Charles, already ruler of Spain
and the Netherlands, from being elected and thus dominating
Europe. Rome must therefore be particularly careful to woo the
various electors, one of whom was Elector Frederick of Wittenberg
—not only one of the electors but himself also the principal possible alternative candidate to Charles, and Reichsvikar in the interim. The elector, who had already shown himself inclined to protect the young professor, Dr. Luther, of his own young university,
must on no account be upset. The heat was immediately taken
off. A professional speaker of honied words, Cardinal Miltitz was
dispatched from Rome, equipped with the Golden Rose (a sort of
degenerate Nobel peace prize) for Frederick, and later a scarcely
believable offer of a cardinal's hat for a certain young friend of
his, both of course in return for certain considerations. For a whole

crucial year and more Luther was left alone. It is quite possible that this delay saved Luther's life. It certainly enabled Luther to think and act freely, and it can be said to have been a major factor in enabling the Reformation to occur as a Lutheran Reformation, in the years following.

We have seen some of the factors which provided the enabling context of the Reformation. None of them caused it. Until Luther acted, the impetus was lacking actually to cause or to lead a religious revolution. This lack of impetus was identical with the lack of impetus for reform within the Church—reform, which is what Luther hoped he was achieving and which to the end of his life he thought he was achieving. Programs for such reform had been canvassed for a century or more, even by Rome itself, even by such a Pope as the Borgia Alexander VI. The Reformation was indeed part of a great series of social changes. But in themselves the Reformation events, their outcome and subsequent history all have a particular religious significance which is not attributable to anything else, but only to a religious motive and drive.

The Reformation: Definition

The start of the Reformation events is surely rightly taken to be 1517, when Luther issued his theses on indulgences. As an achievement date, after which there is no possibility of reversal but only of a variety of developments, we may take 1559, the date of the Elizabethan Acts of Supremacy and Uniformity, and the date of the return to regular use in England of the Protestant Prayer Book, a date when the Council of Trent had done much of its work. The identifying factor in the Reformation events is that new or reformed Christian communities were founded, that they took the Bible as their immediate norm, under Christ's headship, and that they rejected communion with the traditional Western Church organized as a single body throughout Europe having the Pope, the bishop of Rome at its head. These new or reformed churches believed that the old organized Church had betrayed the Christian faith by departing from the norms found in the Bible and by setting the authority of its own bishops above that of the Bible. Canon law had taken the place of the gospel. This characterization of the reforming movement was nothing new. What was new was that a majority of the population in some parts of Europe eventually accepted it and lined up behind the reformers.

It was the popular response in the third, fourth and fifth decades of the sixteenth century which finally settled the success of the Reformation. Reforms and changes of all kinds, altogether a very great variety of them, but nearly all having in common an insistence on the Bible as their norm, were put forward on an individual basis by priests, scholars and politicians, occasionally by bishops or cardinals. Instead of a small minority response, there was in some places a large minority response, blossoming quickly into an absolute majority response. Religion had become "critical." As with every total social movement, the movement for reform gathered in its wake, and as part of its decisive majority, all sorts of disparate supporters, such as the handful of archaic-style knights who offered their services to Luther in Germany. But the religious issue remained dominant.

When success came, it came quickly. It was spontaneous and entirely unpremeditated and without any general method. When bubbles appear on the surface of a liquid as it comes to the boil, it is impossible to say just where the first bubble was, or the second or third. All one can say is that at one moment the surface was calm and shortly after it is bubbling. So, biologists say, evolutionary changes commonly occur in living organisms when changes in characteristics are leading to the evolution of a new species. The evolution seems to be achieved independently in a large number of different individuals. It is thus that the events which subsequently came to be identified altogether as the Reformation began to happen in many parts of Europe.

The founding of new or newly independent bodies was not the original aim of any of the reformers. At first there was only the wish and intention to change, in the sense of reform, existing communities and organizations. New structures were not envisaged. Luther disowned any such intention to the end of his life, and always disliked the term "Lutheran" since his concern was for Christians and the Christian Church. In England great emphasis was always laid on historical continuity—it was claimed that an unchanging body reformed itself and threw off papal authority and unchristian practices. In Zurich, Geneva and Strasbourg continuity was more difficult to envisage. In that case the emphasis was on the return to the practice of the primitive church.

The widespread positive response of people at large was the primary factor in the success of the Reformation. But what made it precisely a revolution, rather than a peaceful evolution, was the refusal or failure of ecclesiastical authority, in most countries, to respond to any of the calls to reform, or to put into effect any of the numerous reform programs which had been put forward throughout the fifteenth century and the early years of the sixteenth. With massive support behind them the reformers became intransigent. From being a loyal Catholic in 1517 Luther quickly found that he could only make sense of his position by accepting the isolation from Rome and her bishops, and the leadership of all who looked for reform into which the organized Church threw him. From being strongly opposed, for instance, to those who claimed he was another Hus, he came to agree that he was indeed in some ways in agreement with Hus. Roman authority was determined to control everything from Rome, and determined to be the initiator of any reform. Luther's work was assumed from the start to be in the wrong.

The gap between the reformers on the one hand and on the other the Pope, his Curia, and many of the bishops (with great exceptions, all the English episcopate, save two, eventually disowned the Pope though hardly for any great theological reason) grew with astonishing speed after 1521, when Luther was formally outlawed by the Emperor Charles (here a monarch, the emperor himself, sides with the Pope) at Worms, following his excommunication by Rome, the year before. There were some men of great intelligence and flexibility within the Catholic Church who wanted to negotiate whenever possible. Equally so among the reformers; Philip Melanchthon, Luther's young assistant, appointed professor of Greek at Wittenberg in 1518 was always optimistic and attempting to reconcile and unify. But for the most part the chasm between the two parties was obvious, and a realistic view was that they could never meet. Catholic authority was invincibly certain, utterly confident, that the whole visible apparatus of the Church was in principle what God willed it to be, and that to doubt its authority or the rightness of what it did in any way was simply unthinkable. Equally, the reformers, within a very short time after 1521, became quite firmly convinced that God's will was that there should be a church quite different from that which Rome upheld, one based primarily on Scripture. Within a very short time it began to dawn, with a mixture of astonishment, amazement, horror or delight, on everyone of importance throughout Europe that the established order in religion was really being seriously challenged throughout great parts of Christendom. And challenged not in the name of a new religion or of no religion, but in the name of that Christian religion of which the papal Church purported to be the only proper representative, community and organization.

The Prehistory, Character and Continuation of the Reformation

To understand this cataclysm we need to know its prehistory, and something of the "forerunners."

The Reformation was not merely a sudden cataclysm. And if we are to understand these forerunners, *a fortiori* we have also to try to understand the religious drive of Christianity itself, both of which we do in Chapter 3. In a way this will be the weakest link in the book. How to present an objective picture of the appeal of the Christian gospel, as it spread through Europe from the first century onwards? It cannot be done in so short a space. But something must be indicated here to enable us to understand the drive which perennially set men and women searching for some more authentic understanding of Christianity. To leave a blank, an empty space would be unpardonable in a book which attempts to provide a complete though concise popular conspectus of the Reformation. Without this we would provide only a record of that which mattered least both to those who took part in the Reformation, and to those who defended the traditional Church.

The Western Church inherited from imperial Rome the legal, or canonical, approach to religion, both to belief and to morals. The centralized and legalistic approach finally became dominant, formed in a monarchical pattern, in the reign of Pope Gregory VII (Hildebrand), during 1073–85. The first strongly biblical reactions to the official Church appeared within a century. The Waldensians may be said to have typified something that Gregory wanted above all to banish from the Church. They had been preceded and accompanied by many movements, including the Manichean Cathari and others less well documented and less lasting. And they were followed by very many similar movements, some of which, like that of St. Francis, were able to remain within the organized body, while others were declared heretical. The appearance of these movements heightened the conviction of ecclesiastical authority that in general they should be opposed, and eventually the Inquisition was established in the thirteenth century.

Means of canonical enforcement became easier with time; and with it grew the sheer emphasis on law. And so also the reaction to it. In the late fourteenth century Wycliffe in England, and at the turn of the century Hus in Bohemia, the country of the Czechs, provoked quite massive movements, similar in their basic orientation (back to the Bible, use of the vernacular, modification of the priesthood and sacramental life) to the Reformation of the sixteenth century. The Lollards, Wycliffe's followers after his death, continued as an underground movement after their suppression. The Hussite movement was never suppressed and remained as a running sore in Europe, an invitation to future rebels, a sign that they might succeed.

Wycliffe had glimpsed one inadequacy of the Church, Hus another. Luther imprinted his own personality on the Reformation when it eventually occurred. It was part of the reason for his particular emergence that he had plumbed some of the depths of personal religious experience, and that he was concerned with the central matter of man's relationship with God. All his writings flow directly from his own Christian belief in the gospel, in Christ as the Redeemer of men, from his understanding of the total faith demanded, and from his intense concern for the life of ordinary Christians. The characters of the Swiss Zwingli, much more of Calvin from northeastern France, and then of a group of men in England, notably Cranmer, and then again of others ranging from Bucer in Strasbourg to Knox in Scotland, gave the Reformation a further distinctive character.

It is of the greatest significance that the contrast between law and gospel, between ecclesiastical authority and Scripture, is that which gives all these reforms their principal motivational identity. It was this same contrast which lay at the heart of the majority of all the previous attempts at reform.

The foundation of new bodies and the throwing off of papal and often of episcopal authority by continuing Christian communities with the intention of enabling them to live not by canon law but by the gospel caused a sharp reaction in the old Church, which gradually became identified as "Roman," "papal" and eventually "Roman Catholic," or finally just "Catholic." At the Council of Trent (1545–63) many reforms were put into effect, but the papal Church also further emphasized and defined the legal and organizational character of its Christian purpose and commitment. The spiritual was tied even more directly than before to disciplinary and canonical norms. For instance, it further confirmed private aural confession, first imposed on all members of the Church as of obligation at the very least once a year at the Fourth Lateran Council in 1215. It is important to point out that Tridentine (adjective meaning "of Trent") canon law need not in itself be interpreted very strictly. But bishops, priests and educated laity tended to interpret it in the strictest possible fashion. Confession of sins at least once a year was an obligation. But only "mortal sins" had to be confessed. It is quite easy to argue (as is done today by some Roman Catholics) that people do not often commit mortal sins, and that frequent confession (once a month, or once a week), which became conventional throughout the Church (once a day in the strictest circles of vowed religions), is not only not necessary but is a hindrance. But the Roman Catholic Church as a whole tended to see canonical obligations of this kind, viewed in the strictest sense, as an essential characteristic of their Church.

It is also proper to realize that all the new or reorganized Christian bodies set up pastoral norms to which they usually tied their members very strictly. Calvin's complaint was that Catholics were much too lax; the citizens of Strasbourg and of Geneva, at least from time to time, had their lives very rigorously orientated (within living memory the United States of America forbade the sale of alcohol). But the special point about the Catholic norms is related to the claim of the papal Church, in effect of its Pope and bishops, to be the sole and absolute authority on all matters of faith and morals for all Christians throughout the world, and to have the right, by the fiat of Jesus Christ, who had founded the Church, to speak for God to all Christians, and expect absolute obedience on pain of excommunication and the grave danger of everlasting punishment. Such a threat somehow always carried a more scandalous and horrific weight even than when Calvin spoke of the destiny of the predestined damned.

If history is to be a living discipline a book of this kind cannot be written as though we did not know what happened afterwards. Here, above all, the "slice of history" technique can become a kind of *trahison des clercs*. The Reformation went on reverberating through four centuries with seemingly never-ending effect. The reformers thought in terms of a church always needing reform, always standing under God's judgment—the judgment of Scripture and of history. Their principles led also for several centuries to a greater and greater fragmentation of Christian communities as each person or group of persons thought they understood the true significance of Scripture and the proper course for Christian behavior personally and communally. But the process eventually ceased and began to go into reverse in Europe, and in parts of America and Asia; though in Africa and elsewhere the impetus of fragmentation continued.

As the drive towards a new reunification began to gather impetus, the old Church itself also began to stir. Suddenly in the 1960's it revealed an astonishing intention to take into itself much of what had been done in the reformed churches. The Second Vatican Council ends our story. On our own premise, that the drive behind Christianity is perennial, the story has no ending. The point to which we have arrived today involves an intense interest among all Christians as to what happened at the Reformation. It is towards a popular clarification of this that the present book is directed.

CHAPTER 2

The Bible, from the Eleventh
to the Sixteenth Century

Status of the Bible

Christianity has as its only original source document the Bible.
All practice of Christianity must in some way be squared with
the Bible.

The significance of the Bible at the Reformation may be seen
by contrasting: (1) The control of the text by ecclesiastical authority and its limited circulation prior to the Reformation. (2) The
great popularity of the Bible after the Reformation. The control
of the text in its Latin, Greek and Hebrew texts, and in translations
from those texts into European languages, played an important
part in the orientation and limitation of the Church's life in the
fifteenth and preceding centuries throughout most of Europe. When
the events of the Reformation led to a substantial lifting of control
throughout Europe both for those who broke away from the papal
Church, and in considerable though lesser measure, for Catholics,
the Bible immediately became very popular. It has remained a
best seller among books in every European language, and hundreds
of others, throughout the four and a half centuries since that time.

To understand the unique part played by the Bible in the
Reformation it is necessary first to understand fully the unique
place of the Bible in the Christian religion, whatever may be the
precise interpretation placed upon its words by any Christian
group or individual. It is the nature of the Bible as history which
in the end lifts it out of the run of other religious literature. The
Bible teaches a right way of living, and a right way of knowing
God, only as part of the history it tells. It records a long series
of historical events which culminate in the life and death and
resurrection of Jesus Christ, and then records events in the lives
of his followers in the half-century or so after his death, together

with letters written by several of his followers to the communities they founded.

This life, death and resurrection of Jesus are themselves placed in the center of the teaching about the right way of living and knowing God. "I am the way, the truth and the life." The teaching proclaims that this man was "perfect" man, was one with God, was his Son, was inspired by his Spirit. "Who sees me sees the Father." Developing these and many other statements in the New Testament, Christian teachers drew from them the doctrine of the threefold God, the "Blessed Trinity," the Father, Son and Holy Spirit. Jesus is the incarnation of the Son, the Word of God, the second person of the threefold God.

The New Testament describes how Jesus gave his followers forms of remembrance and renewal which would bring him continually back into their lives. These were sacramental ritual actions, centered round a particular sacrament most commonly known by the Greek word "Eucharist," meaning thanksgiving.

Reference to the Bible as "history" does not imply any judgment about the precise accuracy of any item in it, or about the kind of history which it is. The point is simply that it has a historical form, that when recording historical events its content is broadly consonant with historical fact as known from other sources, that this history leads up to the life, death and resurrection of Jesus of Nazareth, and culminates in the community of his followers who set out to tell others about him. The Bible identifies Christianity with these events as recorded by the primitive Church, and as understood by it. Christians have understood in various ways the declaration that the Bible is inspired by God. But whatever is said about this, there can be no doubt that the Bible plays in Christianity a part more important than any document plays in any other religion, simply because it claims to record a series of events entirely unique, which if true in the sense stated must be in some sense the center of human history.

The Bible is a major influence common to all the Reformation events. If a reformer wanted a standard by which to justify his teaching, he turned to the Bible. "He deceives himself who anticipates long prosperity to any kingdom which is not ruled by the sceptre of God, that is, by his divine word. For the heavenly oracle is infallible which has declared that where there is no vision the people perish," wrote Calvin in his prefatory address to the king of France in his *Institutes of the Christian Religion,* first published in 1536. Equally, when the reformers wished to denounce the old traditions they turned to Scripture. Calvin again wrote in the same preface about Catholics: "The true religion which is delivered in the Scriptures, and which all ought to hold, they readily permit both themselves and others to be ignorant of, to neglect and despise: and they deem it of little moment what each man believes concerning God and Christ, or disbelieves, providing he submits to the judgment of the Church with what they call implicit faith. . . . Why, then, do they war for the Mass, purgatory, pilgrimages, and similar follies, with such fierceness and acerbity, that though they cannot prove one of them from the word of God, they deny godliness can be safe without faith in these things—faith drawn out if I may so express it, to its utmost stretch?"

What was the most common rallying cry? "Return to the Word of God," or something similar was in effect the most frequently heard symbol of the initiatives taken by reformers in the sixteenth century all over Europe. Luther wrote: "The Spirit is nowhere more present and alive than in his own sacred writings . . . We must let Scripture have the chief place and be its own truest, simplest and clearest interpreter . . . I want Scripture alone to rule, and not to be interpreted according to my spirit or that of any other man, but to be understood in its own light (*per seipsum*) and according to its own Spirit."[1]

A great spate of vernacular translations of the Bible in nearly all European languages accompanied the events of the Reformation. The publication of these translations was part and parcel of the Reformation, both cause and consequence of the initiative taken by the reformers and their followers.

The Bible and the Scholars

What was the situation of the Bible up till 1516? Who read it or heard it read? In what languages? When? Manuscripts of the complete Bible were available to the higher clergy and serious students in the Latin Vulgate version of St. Jerome in universities,

---

[1] A famous statement of Luther's in 1519, quoted here in the English given by P. S. Watson in his Introduction to the translation of Luther's *Commentary on Galatians* (James Clarke, London, 1953).

larger monasteries and priories, and in cathedral libraries, and were occasionally in the hands of sovereigns and those at court, throughout Europe. The original-language versions, Greek and Hebrew, were not forbidden to serious students authorized by ecclesiastical authority. But until 1516 these students might have to make strenuous efforts to be able to consult the Greek. The Greek version was in use, as it always had been, at Byzantium. But there were certainly few copies of the Septuagint (the Greek Old Testament) or the Greek New Testament to be found in Europe up till about 1300, though it was not entirely unknown. In the fourteenth and fifteenth centuries things were perhaps a little, but not much, easier in spite of the decree of the Council of Vienne (1311–12) that chairs of Greek and oriental languages should be set up and endowed in the principal schools and universities of Europe.

The contrast with Byzantium is striking. There "the highest title was professor of the Gospel."[2] In the West scholars preferred to work on the Old Testament and to follow Hebrew rather than Greek studies. The New Testament was very largely left aside as a quarry of texts for the theologian. "The roots of this preference for Hebrew lie deep in medieval Latin psychology. Something must be allowed for the actual physical obstacles that a westerner had to encounter if he wanted to become proficient in Greek. He would have to make the journey to Byzantium or to southern Italy or Sicily, while he could learn Hebrew from the Jew next door. But the translators of Aristotle from Greek managed to surmount the expense and inconvenience involved in their enterprise. So we need to look further. The preference was implicit in the Christian tradition as it was received by Western scholars. It came to them via Jerome from Origen, who had consulted Jews and who had not dared to extend his researches on the text from the Old to the New Testament." Hebrew had a special attraction, along with the people who spoke it. "Here was a people which spoke the language of Moses and observed the Law and had a vast store of traditions about Bible history."

Reluctance to study the New Testament is relevant to this present attempt to describe the prehistory of the Reformation. The reluctance, running over many centuries, probably played

[2] Beryl Smalley, *The Study of the Bible in the Middle Ages* (Basil Blackwell, Oxford, 1952), second edition, from which the next quotation is also taken.

its part in the general inadequacy of the official Church in the
sixteenth century. Certainly from the mid-twelfth century onwards
reformers, who sometimes became heretics, often turned first to
the Gospels. In itself the reluctance made a great gap in Christian
life, for the New Testament is the only source of knowledge about
Jesus Christ and his followers. There was perhaps a general
recognition that since this material is at the very fount of the
Christian religion and of the highest truth, the Church could
only speak of it from its highest places. The failure was thus,
possibly, in part a function of the increasingly centralized and
authoritarian organization of the Church. Instead of facing the
challenging and very difficult ideals of the gospel it was easier
and safer for the scholar to continue with the old tradition of
commenting on the Psalter, a tradition going straight back into
Christianity's own prehistory, for it was from the Jewish rites
that the practice of reciting or singing the Psalms came to have
such a substantial place in the Christian liturgy. And after the
Psalter, it was easier to take part in that massive work of sifting
the literal and three other, allegorical, moral and spiritual, senses
in three Old Testament groups of books, the prophets, the historical
books and the sapiential books. Then if a scholar turned to the
New Testament, it was often to the Revelation of St. John,
again well away from the factual fount. The Gospels were left
to authority and to preachers of sermons, St. Paul to the theologians.
To some extent it can be said that the Bible tended thus to
be sterilized. When it was most extensively studied, its specifically Christian message tended to be assumed at second hand
from doctrine rather than received direct from the gospel.

The Vulgate, then, was freely available to the cultured, and it
would not be too difficult to study the Old Testament in the
Hebrew. But for the most part Greek was not to be had. The
student and scholar alike must be content with the New Testament in Latin, until during the second half of the fifteenth century a general enthusiasm for the Greco-Roman culture began
to spread through the universities of Europe, culminating for
biblical studies, in the publication by Erasmus of *Novum Instrumentum* (1516), the New Testament in a complete newly edited
Greek text, and in the polyglot version of Cardinal Ximenes in
Spain, published in 1522 (though partly in print eight years earlier).

But right up to this time all study of the Bible, except in

Latin, tended to be suspect. In the last century and a half before the Reformation, the situation was aggravated by rapidly increasing literacy. Censorship became more effective in some places; suspicion and persecution became more frequent. The most notable example of this occurs right at the start of the Reformation. Between 1513 and 1520 a movement was fomented in Germany to end all study of Hebrew in the German universities, and an attempt was made entirely to discredit the greatest Hebraist of the age, Reuchlin. Perhaps nothing indicates more starkly the ineptitude of the sixteenth-century Church than that anti-Semitism was able to motivate a movement for the destruction of all Hebrew books and the complete cessation of study of the Hebrew Bible. A kind of barbaric despair seems to be written across the Church's face in this horrible movement.

The Bible and the Rest of the Church

What of the ordinary parish priest and his flock? What of the nuns? For most of the five centuries before the Reformation the great majority of lay people could not read. For much of the time in some parts, many parish priests were illiterate. Where some lay people were able to read, excerpts or paraphrases from the Bible were sometimes available to a few of them in written form in the vernacular in the fourteenth and fifteenth centuries. These manuscripts might commonly contain some or all of the Psalms, perhaps the Revelation of St. John, the Book of Tobit, something from the Gospels; or it might be a "General History" or a "Biblical History," incorporating much from the Pentateuch. By the fifteenth century some manuscript of this kind might be in the hands of most monks, friars and nuns who made an effort to obtain one.

For the great majority of lay people, nuns, religious brothers, junior monks and friars, and parish priests, the excerpts from the Bible read in Latin at Mass, usually followed by a vernacular sermon, were the only regular channels through which they knew the Bible. These excerpts were for the most part, one from the letters ("Epistles") in the New Testament, and the other from one of the four Gospels in the New Testament. Occasionally the first reading was from the Old Testament. Virtually everyone went to church and heard these excerpts read out from the

Mass books each Sunday and each feast day; additional passages would be heard at times such as Passiontide and Easter (commemorating the crucifixion and resurrection of Jesus), and at Christmas. The priest was expected to draw out, in a vernacular sermon, teaching to be found in or from these biblical passages; this would involve giving the sense of the passage though not a translation. There seems to have been no tradition of reading out the excerpts in a vernacular translation. The priest in giving the sense of the passage might provide one of the allegorical explanations, and might apply it also to the everyday lives of people. Usually he would be dependent on his knowledge of Latin if he was to do the latter, since he would need to know more or less accurately the literal meaning of the text. However, manuscripts of translated Epistles and Gospels from the thirteenth century, and at the end of the period, printed editions of them were available to a few priests in some parts of Europe. Preaching itself lapsed from time to time. Numerous complaints are made about this by reformers before and at the time of the Reformation. Such complaints came often from churchmen who remained within the Church and saw the importance of the sermon as the only means of instructing people. "Faith comes by hearing," as St. Paul said. St. Bernardino told his congregation in Siena in 1427, a hundred years before the Reformation, that it was more important to hear the sermon than be present for the rest of the Mass. If one of the two had to be missed for some good reason (minding the baby or whatever), then it was better to miss the rest of Mass. He said: "All you have and know comes from God's word; and, as a general rule, what we hold concerning the faith of Jesus comes through preaching alone; nor will the faith ever fail, so long as it shall be preached." He sounds exactly like a sixteenth-century reformer.

It is a reasonable conclusion that the ordinary member of a parish, in town and country, throughout Europe, got to know some two hundred or so passages from Scripture in the Latin. He or she would understand the meaning either not at all in some cases, or perhaps more or less obscurely, in most cases, having some glimmering of the meaning of the Latin from long attention to explanations in sermons, and in the absence of many other authoritative and formal communications reaching them at any time. The majority of priests, and not a few bishops, knew little more of the Bible than the ordinary people to whom they read out the passages. Some did not understand the Latin.

What of the complete or nearly complete vernacular versions? It is possible to make a wide generalization that such versions were occasionally tolerated in widely varying degrees in different parts of Europe, but that they were all liable to cause suspicion and to be considered dangerous for the ordinary laity and priests, while being unnecessary for the scholar. Some detail will be found later in this chapter under the two sections: *Some Translations and Their Use Outlawed*, and the following section, *Some Translations and Their Use Not Outlawed*. Preceding these two sections we consider *The Control of Translations*. Together these sections provide a key to a complicated situation: (1) The formal policy of the Church's central government was to discourage translations generally, and usually to forbid it in particular. (2) The unofficial practice of local churches was often to tolerate it among the faithful where it was beginning to come into some small use among the literate. (3) Reformers were more assiduous in making translations than others, and their efforts succeeded both in encouraging people to read the Bible and in some parts, though not all, in bringing down violent penalties on all who did so from both the local and the central Church authorities.

By the sixteenth century we can say that the position was anomalous. In some parts of the Church, particularly Poland and Eastern Europe, in Scandinavia, in the British Isles, Spain and parts of southern France and southern Italy, and some but by no means all areas elsewhere in Italy, France and Germany, the Bible was certainly not available in the only language they understood to some priests and most nuns and lay people. Here, then, was a religion whose principal reference document was not easily available, as regards the great majority of its content, to most of those who believed and practiced it. In an overwhelmingly illiterate society this would be inevitable. But sixteenth-century Europe could not be described as overwhelmingly illiterate. What had happened was that rough rules, drawn up for an earlier, more primitive society had been elevated into sharp canonical laws in a society for which they were inappropriate. Part of the anomaly was that, as we shall see, in some towns, the Bible had in fact become quite freely available and authority did not take action against its use. This availability of the Bible in some parts of Germany and France and some parts of Italy constitutes much the smaller part of the picture.

The Control of Translations

The origin of the control of the language in which the Bible might be read in the Western Church during the Middle Ages, along with the control of many other aspects of the Church's life, may be said to lie with Hildebrand, Pope Gregory VII, although the tradition was already present as early as St. Jerome. In the developing society of Europe at that time, when kings and rulers of all kinds were exercising closer control over their subjects, protecting them and taxing them, a stronger and more centralized ecclesiastical organization was to be expected. It was the age of William the Conqueror, with his dominions of England and Sicily, as well as his homeland in Normandy, itself only a second homeland since his people were Norsemen from Scandinavia. Added to this general movement towards some centralization, was the Roman legislative tradition which the Church had inherited from the empire. Decree from the center was the normal way of governing. The toleration by the Roman Empire in its early days of the cultures and laws of its various peoples was forgotten, and only the later dictatorial and centralized bureaucracy was remembered and inherited. So the Church used codified laws, as distinct from a method of equity, the working out of norms through practical experience and the local solution, the method of the incipient civilizations of northern Europe.

A logical part of Hildebrand's plan was that for worship, including reading of the Bible, only Latin should be used. The occasion which historians point to as the origin of a specific policy concerns relations between Rome and the Church in a part of Eastern Europe. Slavonic had been used for Scripture and liturgy in Moravia. St. Methodius obtained permission for this from Pope John VIII about 879. This was rescinded a few years later by Pope Stephen V though possibly the practice continued. In any case a further petition was sent in the eleventh century by King Vratislaus of Bohemia to Hildebrand, for the liturgy in Slavonic. The refusal which came back to him in a letter of 1079 from the Pope was no doubt actuated by the consideration that the use of Slavonic would tend to draw the Christians of Eastern Europe towards the Eastern Church, centered in Byzantium, since the liturgy was sung in that language in neighboring Bulgaria; Latin would help to cement Moravia's bond with Rome. There had also been pressure from German lands. Hildebrand's reply contained an opinion, and a statement of policy, which was quoted as normative at the Council of Trent, five hundred years later, for opposing the free circulation of the Bible in the vernacular among the faithful: ". . . it has pleased almighty God that holy scripture should be a secret in certain places, lest, if it were plainly apparent to all men, perchance it would be little esteemed and be subject to disrespect; or it might be falsely understood by those of mediocre learning and lead to error." Even though translations may have been used in the past, this must not be seen as a precedent, "since the primitive Church allowed many things to pass unheeded, which, after Christianity had grown stronger and when religion was increasing, were corrected by subtle examination. Wherefore we forbid what you have so imprudently demanded of the authority of St. Peter, and we command you to resist this strange rashness with all your might, to the honour of almighty God."

Here then in a clear Roman letter we have an enunciation of a formal ecclesiastical policy of protecting the faithful from the erroneous ideas which might arise in their minds if they were allowed free access to Scripture without scholarly doctrinal guidance. The policy contrasts with that of the Eastern Church, which on the whole regarded the inspirational nature of the biblical text as a recommendation rather than a danger; Byzantium never felt the need to follow Roman legal precedents, confident of their own culture. The Roman policy lingered on into the first part of the twentieth century in the practice of Roman Catholic episcopal authority not to grant approbation, the "imprimatur" ("it may be printed") to translations from the Bible which had no guiding notes published with them. The directly contradictory policy of Protestantism lingered on also. The British and Foreign Bible Society, the principal world society for the propagation of the Bible was still in the 1960's pledged to limit itself to the pure text of the Bible, devoid of any ancillary material. Both policies appear to be in the process of abandonment at the time of writing.

Some Translations and Their Use Outlawed—c.1100–c.1380

The suspicion that free access to the text of the Bible might lead to heretical ideas, and to an attitude of insubordination, to a measure of social and political disturbance received some justification soon after the death of Pope Gregory VII. We still know surprisingly little about the origin of many European vernacular versions of the Bible, but not long after Gregory VII had issued his letter to Moravia, there were Cathari and Waldensians in the southern part of what is now France, sometimes called Languedoc, and they were making translations of the Bible.

The Cathari were Manicheans; their belief in a dualistic form of Christianity, the whole created world being evil and unredeemable, had followers in Eastern Europe from about the fourth century, and had always been rejected by the great majority of Christians, and by ecclesiastical authority. Historians are not in agreement about the precise time of their appearance in southern France and northern Italy. But they were certainly there by 1150, and perhaps much earlier. They used vernacular versions of parts of the Bible, particularly the Gospel of St. John.

Peter Waldo, a French merchant, experienced a conversion of heart in Lyons some time about the year 1176. Just thirty years before St. Francis, Waldo began to follow the gospel literally in its call to poverty. Very soon he was encouraging followers to read excerpts from the Bible in translation, and to teach others. They read the Gospels. In the first place these were often the pieces used each Sunday at Mass. From an early time they were also reading the Revelation of St. John and drawing a variety of conclusions from its highly symbolical and elusive text.

There is occasional evidence of similar events far back into the previous centuries. But it is only with Waldo and the Cathari that we have sufficient documentation to be sure, in principle, if not in much detail, what occurred. It seems to have been a strange chance that conversions to the Manichean doctrines were taking place in southern France just when Waldo also began to take his own initiatives. The Cathari and the followers of Waldo encouraged and influenced each other. Cathari took to the study of Scripture more widely as a result of influence from the Waldensians.

It seems almost certain that it was the Waldensians themselves who took the initiative and that translations of some, and quite probably the whole, of the Bible into Provençal (Languedoc), Catalan, Tuscan Italian, German, and perhaps French (*langue d'oïl*) were due to them. The German version possibly became the source version for the numerous translations which appeared in Germany in subsequent centuries, when the German language became the major growing point in Europe of a popular demand for the translated Bible. But meanwhile, approximately 1150–1250, translation was going on in the Mediterranean coastal area and north of it, from northern Spain to northern Italy. The existence in this area of rapidly growing vernacular means of communication, the emergence of new languages, perhaps made possible a growth in consciousness and in understanding, which led to the new attempts to live Christianity literally, and so also to the attempts to translate the Bible.

The official Church made some rather small attempts to hold Waldo and his followers within the bounds of the orthodox corpus of belief and organization. They were not successful. The Bible translation and reading practiced by the Waldensians appeared to the local churches to be an attempt to encroach on the domain of the priest. Waldo was eventually declared guilty of promoting heresy. Sharp definition of church membership led rapidly to the stigmatization of large numbers of men and women as heretics, Cathari and Waldensians indifferently, and to their persecution, finally and most notably in the Albigensian Crusade. The degree to which personal study of the Bible became at this time, in the opinion of authority, synonymous with heresy, that is, with opposition to Christian truth, is shown by words of Etienne de Bourbon, one of the inquisitors in the South of France during the thirteenth century:

> The signs by which heretics may be known are first their presumptuous and unwarrantable usurpation of the office of preaching, and teaching of holy doctrine . . . and especially of the gospels and other books of the New Testament, which they learn firmly by heart in the vernacular, and mumble the one to the other. [He tells how he had seen a young

cowherd who had learned by heart forty of the Sunday
Gospels in his own language, as a result of living in the
same house as a Waldensian.] I have seen some lay people
who were so imbued with their teaching, that they could
repeat by heart much of the evangelists, as for instance
Matthew or Luke, and especially those things which are said
of the instruction and words of the Lord, so that they would
hardly miss a word here but repeat them in order; which
matter I relate because of their diligence in evil, and the
negligence of catholics in good, for very many are so unmind-
ful of their soul and their salvation, that they scarcely know
their Paternoster or Credo, or teach them to their families.

It was considered a terrible evil to know the Gospels by heart.
Erasmus' dream of the plowboy and the cowherd reciting Scripture at work seems to have come true some three hundred years
before he wrote about it!

The Synod of Toulouse issued the following decree in 1229:
"Lay people shall not have books of scripture, except the psalter
and the divine office: and they shall not have these books in
the vulgar tongue. Moreover we prohibit that lay people should
be permitted to have books of the Old or New Testament, except
perchance any should wish from devotion to have a psalter, or
a breviary for the divine office, or have the hours of the Blessed
Virgin: but we most strictly prohibit their having even the afore-
said books translated into the vulgar tongue."

This decision set a precedent for decisions and action in other
countries, especially northern Spain, where the Waldensians had
made converts. In 1233 James I of Aragon at the provincial
Synod of Tarragona promulgated twenty-six decrees, of which
the first read: "No man shall possess books of the Old or New
Testmant in Romance. And if any possess such, let him hand
them over to the episcopal see to be burnt within eight days
of the publication of this constitution; and whosoever shall not
do thus, be he clerk or layman, shall be held suspect of heresy,
until he shall have purged himself." By the following century
informal communities of unmarried lay people, both of men and
women respectively wishing to follow a simple Christian way of
life together, began to arise, called beguinages. They wanted
the Bible and wanted it in their own language. In 1317 another
Synod of Tarragona issued an edict that Beguines should not

have "theological books in the vulgar tongue, except books which contain only prayers."

We take this story up again in this chapter with Wycliffe and Hus, and in the following chapter. Generally, in spite of such an incident as a paternal inquiry by Pope Innocent III in 1199 about the Waldensian translations, in practice translation of the Bible aroused suspicion, and nowhere received even a limited or implied approval from authority during the twelfth, thirteenth and fourteenth centuries.

Some Translations and Their Use Not Outlawed—Before 1401

Throughout Europe, as soon as a local language was available at all, there were attempts, in monasteries or at court to put some Scripture into the vernacular. At first, it would often be a matter of presenting the subject in the traditional verse of the minstrel or court poet. Caedmon's work in the seventh century in England is of this kind. He is followed by Cynewulf and the author of *The Dream of the Rood;* by the scholar Alcuin; by King Alfred and St. Aelfric. There was never any question of making a complete formal translation, but of giving the sense and adapting particular texts of the Vulgate, a process which did involve giving quite long passages in translation, many others summarized, and all subject to comment, and interpretation, often of a highly imaginative and esoteric kind. A more methodical approach was shown when, in about the tenth century, a manuscript of the Lindisfarne Gospels had a vernacular gloss written in over the Latin text. One of the earliest manuscripts in France is an octosyllabic verse of about the year 1000 on the Passion narrative. German manuscripts start with the renaissance of Charlemagne, when Alcuin came from England. But we should not forget that, many centuries before, as soon as the Goths had arrived to attack the northern boundaries of the Roman Empire, they were converted in large numbers and a Gothic Bible was in existence as early as the fourth century. The first Italian manuscripts are as late as the thirteenth century, owing to the late development of the language. Spanish manuscripts are few and later but much research remains to be done, as also in Italy.

We have seen that in the eleventh century Pope Gregory VII provided a precedent for disapproval of translations of Scripture.

The policy which this precedent implied was not always imple-
mented, but with only a few exceptions was adhered to in principle by subsequent Popes. Local churches did not always imple-
ment it by any means. For every Waldensian indicted, and for
every translation of Scripture destroyed, hundreds went free. In
southern France the Waldensians were identified as heretics, and
bracketed with the Cathari. But their influence spread far throughout Europe from this point. Elsewhere than in southern France
and parts of Spain, perhaps owing to their relatively small numbers, they were left free more often than not; or perhaps they
simply escaped the notice of authority. Whatever the truth
of this, they translated Scripture, and their versions in German,
French, Tuscan Italian, Catalan, and Provençal seem often to
have escaped censorship, although the historical picture is still
obscure in many details. Of the early Italian versions of the
Bible, Kenelm Forster, writing in the *Cambridge History of the
Bible*, says: "It is probable—not proved—that the first Italian
versions were the work of Waldensian heretics or near-heretics,
whether missionaries from France or, as would be more likely,
Italians affected by their preaching, and it is then not impossible
that the Italian Bible, and particularly the New Testament, was
put together under heretical influence originating north of the
Alps." He points out that this thirteenth-century translation
is not doctrinally tendentious and he puts forward no other alternative hypothesis for the origin of the Italian Bible. Something
similar seems likely to have been true of other early vernacular
versions of the Bible in the western and central European mainland in the twelfth, thirteenth and fourteenth centuries. In most
cases there was already some demand, and some primitive tradition of vernacular Scripture in rhymed or adapted styles, with
which the Waldensian impulse was able to link up. Complete
translations had been made into German by the fourteenth century; and probably also into Provençal and Catalan.

Generally we may say that many initiatives in translating
Scripture during the twelfth and thirteenth century are known
to historians, that these initiatives came from below, from individual laymen or priests. In many cases authority seems either
not to have known about them or else to have tolerated them. We
can say certainly that authority never initiated the translations
and that many of them were neither outlawed nor approved.

Along with what were definitely translations, of the Psalter, Proverbs, Job, Tobit, the Gospels, or of the Pentateuch, and occasionally of all the Bible, went a continuation of the minstrel tradition of providing Bible histories in rhyme, or some conventional literary form. The best known of the vernacular Bible histories was the French *Bible Historiale,* of Guyart des Moulins (1295), a translation of Comestor's *Historia Scholastica.* It is a mixture of translations of the Vulgate text with narrative summaries and commentary. Similar histories existed in German and Spanish.

England was a special case, in that Anglo-Norman gradually replaced the Anglo-Saxon vernacular in most parts during the decades following 1066. It was only in the fourteenth century that the new vernacular became available. Translations of the Psalter (by the hermit ex-university man Richard Rolle) and of the Gospels and Revelation of St. John begin to appear towards the middle of the century along with a general movement of mysticism and devotion similar to that already widespread in northern Europe. Before the end of the fourteenth century Walter Hilton, another university man turned hermit, had written *The Scale of Perfection,* William Langland the priest poet had written *The Visions of Piers Plowman* and Chaucer *The Canterbury Tales.* The latter has quotations from or references to every section of the Bible. *Piers Plowman,* written from a less sophisticated point of view, provides a deeply felt Christian commentary on the contemporary world, the Fair Field full of Folk.

We have in Chaucer and Langland evidence as to what the Bible could mean to the well-educated, and the slightly educated men of the day. William Langland provides us with a multiple echo in his *Piers Plowman,* for he is both a man of strong personal faith and one whose education as cleric did not lead on to much further study. But he uses in his poem the four different senses that the medieval scholars distinguished in their commentaries on Scripture. He did this as an artist and created a glowing symbol of faith and life, a many-faceted work of art. When a medieval scholar writes on the Bible and expounds the literal sense, the allegorical sense, the tropological or moral sense, and the religious sense, we may find it very abstract and artificial—but with Langland it all makes good artistic sense. There is the plain meaning of the story about the good Samaritan. There is its allegorical meaning, in which the traveler can be mankind, and the inn the Church. There is an application of this to our lives. And finally there is a religious or anagogical sense, where an identity may be found between the Samaritan, Piers, Christ and God. But often the relevance of Langland's shorter scriptural quotations will not be as easy as that. Only a scholar with a knowledge of traditional medieval exegesis, often very far from the literal or more obvious possible allegorical senses, will understand them.

In Langland we notice the same kind of subjective mystical approach as is to be found in the early Anglo-Saxon poems, fed on a piety which is partially rooted in the Bible, particularly the Passion. But we have to beware of a false romanticism here. True mysticism is ascetic and demanding. Langland had a hard life. His vision was hardly romantic for him. Along with his piercing faith went a piercing sense of the real brutalities of life, and of man's nature. They came from experience.

No complete translations of the Bible or anything like it existed in England before the Wycliffe translation of about 1384. Chaucer and Langland may both have had access to this translation: John of Gaunt was the patron both of Chaucer, (nephew of his third wife) and of Wycliffe. But Langland probably wrote nothing after that time and Chaucer does not seem to have been aware that anything extraordinary had happened. They had been used to the idea of partial versions of Scripture, either adaptations, or excerpts translated in French, or as the latest thing, in English. Langland in his description of "Do Well," describes him as having distributed his wealth, entered a religious order, and made a rendering of the Bible. It was fashionable to want a vernacular version. For both authors Latin was the key to a professional understanding of religion and of the Scriptures, Latin, of which Langland had an imperfect grasp. Chaucer is more difficult as a character than Langland because more sophisticated. He tells a tale with professional objectivity. Christian faith on the one hand inspires the noble figure of the poor parson, and on the other is the stock in trade of the ignoble pardoner and of others who use it to exploit people and accumulate wealth. Chaucer's own faith is hardly in doubt, but we can say that while his knowledge of the Bible is extensive, it does not have the same inspirational function as in *Piers Plowman*. It is subject, as with *Piers Plowman*, to the same (to us) fantastic exegesis. At the end of *The Canterbury Tales* Chaucer writes of his wish to retract any evil thing he has written.

It was and still is a tradition for Christians in their will to beg forgiveness for any wrong they have done to others. Chaucer was following a convention when he wrote what are called his retractions. It was not really a formal "retraction" in our sense. It was a pious gesture, sincere certainly, but not the sort of awestruck fruit of remorse which the word retraction might conjure up. Chaucer starts by asking those who are pleased by what he has written to "thank Our Lord Jesus Christ for it, from whom proceeds all understanding and goodness." Then he apologizes for anything that may displease. Finally, "I beseech you meekly for the mercy of God to pray for me, that Christ have mercy on me and forgive me my sins: and especially for my translations and enditings of worldly vanities, which I revoke in my retractions: as are the book of Troilus . . . The Tales of Canterbury, those that tend towards sin . . . and many a lecherous lay; that Christ in his mercy forgive me the sin." It was an honest statement set in a usual convention, useful evidence of the Christianity which was Chaucer's, rooted in the Bible.

Walter Hilton, writing about 1370–80, advised his readers to read the Gospels before they proceed to meditation, saying that it would kindle the fire of love in the soul and enable it to pray. He recommended the Latin Gospels, nothing else apparently being available to his knowledge.

During the fourteenth century in France and Germany translations of the Bible text continued to flourish. It is possible that the first complete German translation was in existence by 1300, or earlier. It is likely that this was due to the Waldensians. A synod was held at Trier in 1231 for the purpose of suppressing heresy and vernacular translations, but it seems certain that in the following hundred years editions of vernacular texts of parts or all of the Bible escaped censorship and were read by some religious, men and women, and by some laymen. In the Netherlands, and in the Rhineland, the houses of Beghards and Beguines, lay people living in community but not under vows, were increasing and Bible reading was a staple part of their spiritual fare. At the end of the fourteenth century the Brothers of the Common Life gained formal recognition of their right to read the Scripture in the vernacular, by a gathering of Cologne

lawyers, convened by themselves. Translation also continued in
Spain and Italy, though not to the same extent as in France and
Germany. In many places we should note that the Jews played
some part in putting the Old Testament into the vernacular,
their activity being greatest in Spain, where the inquisitors were
also greatly worried about it.

Little seems to be known of vernacular movements in Eastern
Europe, Scandinavia and Ireland. The *Cambridge History of the
Bible* is entirely silent about vernacular translation in these areas
before the sixteenth-century Reformation.

We can say then that before the reaction of authority to
Wycliffe and Hus, that is, until approximately 1401, we have
an ambivalent situation. The practice of the Holy See in dis-
couraging translations of Scripture can hardly have been unknown
to the bishops of the more important towns in Europe. Heresy
continued to appear sometimes in connection with the vernacular
translations. But heresy had not been a major preoccupation since
the Albigensian Crusade against the Cathari. Many translations
went unopposed, even though none had any official approval.

Wycliffe and Hus

The association of heresy with the translation of the Bible was
emphatically underlined by the series of events in England connected with John Wycliffe at Oxford University and with the
translation of the Bible which was in the first place due to his
initiative. He was a gifted theologian, and a philosopher of the
"realist" or Platonist school. He came to the conclusion that men
have a right to their possessions directly from God. In theory,
then, they owed no allegiance directly to any man. Convenience
might lead to all sorts of arrangements and these might be necessary politically, but at root there was only allegiance to God. It
followed forcibly that every man, being God's tenant, ought to
have direct access to the book which spoke of God. Wycliffe
carried many at Oxford with him at first. His patron as we have
seen was the revered John of Gaunt, uncle of the king.

It seems morally certain that some translation of the complete
Bible would have been made in England about this time, whether
or not Wycliffe had appeared. Translations existed by now in a
number of languages on the European mainland. English was

now available as a fully articulated language. Translations of some small parts of the Bible had already appeared. The works of Hilton, Richard Rolle, Dame Juliana, Langland, Chaucer and others were being circulated. Educated people were now using English instead of or as well as French.

Wycliffe had an "ultra-realist" view of the Bible, which he regarded as a Platonic exemplar existing in the mind of God before the Creation, a book which was of equal sanction throughout. His theories about property also meant that he thought the Bible should be available to the ordinary man. These theories triggered off an attempt which was notably successful as far as accuracy is concerned. The translation was made at Oxford, probably in the years 1380–84.

Wycliffe's theological and political teaching was condemned at a Council held at Blackfriars, Holborn, by Archbishop Courtenay in 1382. Wycliffe had to retire to Lutterworth till his death two years later. But the fact that the Bible was being translated seems not to have been considered worthy of condemnation in itself. Authority was concerned, rather, with the fact that in the same year Wycliffe had presented to Parliament seven propositions urging the gradual confiscation of all clerical property by special taxation. The year before, the Peasants' Revolt had alerted the authorities to all potentially inflammable political events, and to the need to protect ecclesiastical property and authority. Neither Wycliffe's death in 1384 nor his condemnation seem to have affected the proliferation of his doctrines or of the translated Bible through his followers. They soon became known as Lollards, "mutterers" or "mumblers," referring to their repetition of biblical passages. The translation was copied many times and was widely circulated, so that when authority eventually moved against it, it was too late; the Wycliffe Bible was possessed and read by many from that time until the Bible was translated again in the next century by Tyndale and Coverdale. More than five hundred Wycliffe manuscripts still survive.

In 1401 political authority was sufficiently concerned about the possibly revolutionary influence of heretics to have the act *De Haeretico Comburendo* passed by Parliament. Heretics were to be burned by the secular authority once a Church court had found them guilty. There is a myth that men were barbarically cruel in medieval times to a degree not experienced today. But it would not be difficult to defend another thesis, that men have become progressively more cruel each century as time goes on. This formal decision by the government of England to kill heretics by burning them to death would have to be noted as one of the stages of a notable increase in cruelty.

In 1408 the Constitutions of Oxford were issued by a provincial council held in Oxford by Archbishop Arundel. The most important of these for our purpose was the seventh:

"Also since it is dangerous, as St Jerome witnesses, to translate the text of holy scripture from one language into another, because in such translations the same meaning is not easily retained in all particulars: even as St Jerome, although he was inspired, confessed that he had often erred in this matter: therefore we decree and ordain that no one shall in future translate on his own authority any text of holy scripture into the English tongue or into any other tongue, by way of book, booklet or treatise. Nor shall any man read this kind of book, booklet or treatise, now recently composed in the time of John Wycliffe, or later, or any that shall be composed in future, in whole or part, publicly or secretly, under penalty of the greater excommunication, until that translation shall be recognised and approved by the diocesan of the place, or if the matter demand it, by a provincial council."

Thus Hildebrand's policy was applied to England. The first heretic was burned in England in 1401. Wycliffe's remains were eventually disinterred in 1428, burned and thrown into the nearby river. Later in the century Joan of Arc was a victim of the new zeal for burning heretics.

Following to some extent, but by no means entirely, in Wycliffe's footsteps was John Hus of Prague. More even than Wycliffe he made the Bible his ultimate authority. His teaching encouraged lay people to translate and read the Bible. A Czech version of the Gospels was already in existence, for Wycliffe wrote, referring to Anne of Bohemia, the wife of Richard II: "If it is lawful for the noble Queen of England, the sister of the Emperor, to have the gospel written in three languages, that is in Czech, and in German and Latin, it would savour of the pride of Lucifer to call her a heretic for such a reason as this."

The burning of Hus as a heretic immediately subsequent to his condemnation at the Council of Constance (1415) further emphasized the connection between heresy and Bible reading. Jean

Gerson, chancellor of Paris University in 1395, put the case against vernacular translation at the council. He was a man of outstanding personality and ability, and was by no means always on the conservative side in all questions—he was a conciliarist, considered that an erring Pope could be deposed, and indeed helped the council to depose John XXIII. But on the matter of the Bible he was fanatically opposed to all translation, preserving the traditional elitist position of the theologian. Although he was himself critical of his fellow theologians—"they frequently invent for themselves technical terms uncomprehensible to other doctors and masters"—yet he was sure that they must provide explanations of the biblical text, and that it must not be left to the untutored laymen: "Now this use of holy scripture by modern men, as if holy scripture should be believed in its bare text without the help of any interpretation or explanation, is a kind of use which is attended by grave dangers and scandals . . . Moreover, the errors of the Beghards and the Poor Men of Lyons and the like have sprung from this pestiferous root, and do daily increase: because there are many lay people who have a translation of the Bible into the vulgar tongue, to the great prejudice and scandal of catholic truth, and it is proposed in the scheme of reform that this should be abolished." This was part of Gerson's submission at the Council of Constance (1415, published 1417), in which he was opposing the Hussite demand for communion under both kinds for the laity. He also wrote of the "presumptuous curiosity, and singularity" which tended to accompany use of the vernacular Bible; and he spoke of the danger of bad translations—as with medicine badly used, it is better not to have it at all than use it badly.

The Demand for the Bible in the Fifteenth Century

In the 150 years between 1348 and 1506, fifteen universities were founded in central Europe alone, as follows: Prague, 1348; Cracow, 1364; Vienna, 1386; Cologne, 1388; Erfurt, 1392; Würzburg, 1402; Leipzig, 1409; Rostock, 1409; Greifswald, 1456; Freiburg in Trier, 1457; Basel, 1460; Ingolstadt, 1472; Tübingen, 1477; Wittenberg, 1502; Frankfurt-ân-der-Oder, 1506. Along with this intellectual growth went a religious and spiritual development centered on the Rhineland and the Netherlands. This was the growing point of demand for the Bible. The Brothers of the Common Life,

founded by Gerard Groote (d. 1384), were probably the first to
gain a somewhat grudging agreement of authority to their promotion of Bible reading by lay people, as we have seen. The
Brothers were also referred to under the generic name of the
Devotio Moderna. There is a hint of the Renaissance here.
"Modern" man is thinking of his own individual progress in the
spiritual life, and is conscious of definite needs—such as a Bible in
the language he uses every day.

The Bible was widely read in Germany and the Netherlands,
but only at or after the turn of the fifteenth century is it possible
to find overt recommendations to read it. "Have you some pious
books? Read them on Sunday after the sermon after supper in the
family. No one should be without a copy of the gospel in his
house."[3]

In Italy, particularly in Florence, and particularly with the encouragement of the Dominican friars, use of the Scriptures was a
commonly unnoticed part of the Renaissance flowering. It is also
particularly remarkable that in Italy there seems to be practically
no evidence of any substantial hindrance by ecclesiastical authority to the making or the use of these translations. Nowhere
else in Europe was it so easy to read Scripture in the vernacular
without fear of the suspicion it might arouse as it was in Florence.
But here as everywhere there is no record of official approval.

In England developments similar to those on the Continent were
largely prevented by the fairly severe regime of regular persecution mounted against the Lollards. Suspicion tended to fall on
anyone inclined towards a biblically inspired spiritual life. There
were Lollards scattered about in many parts of the country,
from Coventry, east, south and west. In Bristol, the Thames
Valley, Kent and East Anglia there were definite concentrations
of them. The ecclesiastical authorities proceeded against them
throughout most of the century. There was something like a lull
in the middle of the century. John A. F. Thomson in *The Later
Lollards* (Oxford University Press, London, 1965) records no
processes between 1440 and 1462. But for the rest of the century,
before and after those dates, there is a record of convictions,
executions and burnings or recantations. Very often those pro-

[3] Basel Plenary, 1514, quoted by Margaret Deanesly in *The Lollard Bible*
(Cambridge University Press, London, 1920/1966).

ceeded against possessed copies of parts of the Bible in English, and this is set down automatically as grounds for suspicion regardless of the nature of the translation. Possession of Scripture in translation implied heresy and almost invariably led to conviction. Thomson's book makes it clear that in parts of the country there must have been an underground network of people who had copies of one or another of the Gospels or other parts of the New or Old Testament which were passed round. Isolated Lollards might appear almost anywhere in the South and Midlands. By the beginning of the sixteenth century the numbers of Lollards had almost certainly begun to increase again, and they had spread far into the North. Recent research tends to confirm the impression given in the late sixteenth-century Protestant *Book of Martyrs* by John Foxe that Lollardy was widespread and eventually joined hands with Lutheran teaching from the Continent, though Lollardy itself never had a refined theology of that kind.

Wycliffe's Bible (it was a second translation, probably done by Purvey; Wycliffe may have had no part in it) had already spread quite widely by the time of the regulations (1408) forbidding both it and any new translations unless authorized by authority. When it was copied, Wycliffe's glosses and introduction were not always included, and the Bible was in the hands of loyal Catholics from time to time in the ensuing century and beyond, without their realizing its origin. This occurred to Sir Thomas More, who spoke of a vernacular Bible at the Charterhouse at Sheen, without realizing that it was Wycliffe's translation. We refer below to the situation in England on the eve of the Reformation and to the inhibiting ignorance of the immediate past which was part of the situation.

In Spain Boniface Ferrer (d. 1417) translated the whole Bible into Valencian, whether or not relying on previous translation is not known. The absence of any surviving manuscripts, apart from a single page, seems to indicate that ecclesiastical and political disapproval was very effective. But much research still remains to be done in Spain.

In 1446 Johann Gensfleisch of Gutenberg began to print his first pages. In 1456 came the first printed Latin Bible, and ten years later began a spate of Bibles in the German and French languages, but all without any ecclesiastical permission or ap-

probation.[4] None of these Bibles were produced by the Cloister
presses, which everywhere were turning out devotional books required by their customers. Sometimes these Bibles omitted the
name of the printer—and no printer would want such a major
work not to advertise the face of his expertise unless there was
some danger attached to such advertisement. The truth about
these Bibles is clear. There was an eager market for them. But
the Church still officially disapproved of translations. More Bibles
would have been produced if this policy had not still been in
force. In Mainz in 1486 the archbishop issued an edict to discourage vernacular translation. This was normal.

England on the Eve of the Reformation

In England, as we have seen, the Constitutions of Oxford
envisaged controlled translation but succeeded in making England
the one country where no more translation was done until the
1520's. Tyndale began his translation then and left the country
in 1524 to be able to complete and print it. The theory of the
Constitutions of 1408 was that translations could be made if
permission was first sought and granted; likewise, the reading of
them. But in practice the processes against heretics frightened off
anyone who might have thought of making the attempt. The
difference between theory and fact is shown up very clearly in a

[4] The first printed vernacular Bible was the German Bible of Johann Mentel
manufactured at Strasbourg in 1466. Another edition was produced by Heinrich Eggestein at Strasbourg in 1470. A third was produced at Augsburg.
Altogether eighteen different German Bibles are known up to 1522. Four
of them are in Low German, similar to Dutch. The language and translation technique of the Mentel Bible suggest that the work of translation
was originally done about 1300, probably by Waldensians. The first French
vernacular Bible was printed in Lyons by Barthelemy Buyer in 1474. King
Charles VIII ordered a new French Bible to be made and this was printed
in Paris by Antoine Verard in 1496. In Spain Ferrer's Valencian Bible
was printed in 1478 but no copies remain. Translations of the Psalter and
the Gospels into Castilian escaped the Inquisition as late as 1512, but not
thereafter. In Bohemia Hus's Bible was printed in 1488 partly at the expense
of the civic authority, and under their auspices. Another Slavonic Bible
was published in 1506 in Venice, where the great Aldus had made himself
the first printer in Europe. Venice had become the most important of all
printing centers. As early as 1471 Malermi's Italian Bible was printed there.
Malermi was a Camaldolese monk, and his Bible went into ten editions
before 1500. Its origin is almost certainly a Waldensian translation. Other
languages had to wait for a vernacular version till after the Reformation.

work of Sir Thomas More. More himself was unaware of the facts as historians now know them, and somewhat bewildered himself by the apparent contradiction of theory by fact. The constitutions seemed to him to imply, by their statement that the Bible might be read in the vernacular (permission being given by the local bishop), that an orthodox translation existed and that manuscript copies and perhaps later printed copies actually existed. But we now know that this was not so. All that existed before Wycliffe's Bible was a very small number of vernacular manuscripts of the Psalter, Gospels and the Revelation of St. John, apart from the ancient Anglo-Saxon manuscripts, which no one but scholars could understand.

The situation as it appeared to educated man in the 1520's is brought amusingly before our eyes by part of the dialogue in Sir Thomas More's own book *Dialogue against Tyndale* (1529). More puts into the mouth of one called the Messenger the ideas which might be expected to be held by the educated man in the street. The Messenger suspects "that the clergy, though the law serve them not therefore, do yet indeed take all translations out of every layman's hand. And sometime, with those that be burned or convicted of heresy, they burn the English Bible without respect, be the translation old or new, bad or good."[5] The immediate reference here is to the fact that Tyndale's New Testament was burned at Paul's Cross in 1526. At the beginning of the dialogue, the Messenger makes the general charge that the burning and "all this gear is done but only to stop men's mouths, and to put every man to silence that would speak anything of the faults of the clergy." In the course of the book More explains that the law is clear enough (the 1408 constitutions) that translations may be made, with permission, and equally so the reading of them. And he says that he has himself seen translations of the Bible—but he makes no claim that these were to be found at all widely, or read, nor says how many such translations he has seen. More sums the matter up, and allows the Messenger to remain

[5] This and the following excerpts are from the edition published by Eyre and Spottiswoode in 1927. This provides a facsimile copy of the original 1557 edition, together also with the text in modern English, though this involves, in fact, very little change indeed from the original, only it is easier to read, being set in a modern type face, and abbreviations are adjusted.

unanswered as to his main accusation, that as a matter of fact, the Bible is not in people's hands.

The Messenger speaks: "Sir, yet for all this, can I see no cause why the clergy should keep the bible out of laymen's hands, that can know no more but their mother tongue.

"I had went [thought], quod I, that I had proved you plainly that they keep it not from them. For I have shewed you that they keep none from them but such translation as be either not yet approved for good or such as be already reproved for nought, as Wycliffe's was, and Tyndale's. For as for other old ones, that were before Wycliffe's days, remain lawful, and be in some folks hand had and read."

These were in fact those copies of the Wycliffe translation which More had no way of knowing to be Wycliffe's, and which he assumed must date back to some time before him.

"Ye say well, quod he. But yet, as women say somewhat, it was alway that the cat winked when her eye was out. Surely so is it not for nought that the English Bible is in so few hands when so many would so fain have it."

More agrees to this. He says that the bishops probably fear that people may be wanting the Scripture in English for the wrong, heretical reasons. But More says he doesn't think this a good reason. "Whosoever would of their malice or folly take harm of that thing that is of itself ordained to do all men good, I would never, for the avoiding of their harm, take from other the profit which they might take, and nothing deserve to lose." More then goes on to a lengthy discussion about the way in which an English Bible should be made available. The Messenger wants it freely available for everyone, to be purchased. But More wants the bishop to pay for the printing, and then to license those to read the Bible whom he considers "honest, sad and virtuous," telling them to use it reverently with humble heart and lowly mind, "rather seeking therein occasion of devotion than of discussion." The translation is to be handed back to the bishop at the death of the person concerned.

More, for all his humanity, candor, culture and religion, remains paternalist, and insensitive apparently to the dangers of the abuse of power by ecclesiastical authority when so much discretion is given to it. However, he never glosses over the facts of a case. The Messenger remains essentially unanswered as to his basic contention: "It is not for nought that the English Bible is in so few hands when so many would so fain have it." That was the situation in England in 1529.

Two Great Bibles and the Spate of New Translations

We did not have room for a complete list of the printed vernacular texts of the Bible in French and German before 1529. It is all the more impossible to provide an exhaustive list of editions of the Bible in the main European languages in the decades subsequent to that date. We shall restrict ourselves largely to providing some sort of picture by listing the better-known editions. But first we must refer to two famous Bibles, Erasmus' Greek New Testament, and the Ximenes Polyglot Bible, which stand commandingly at the very watershed of the age. They are fruits of the medieval Church at its best combined with the scholarship of the Renaissance. They are also signs of a world to come where a policy of censorship would no longer be acceptable.

In 1516 Erasmus published *Novum Instrumentum,* a new Greek text of the New Testament, set beside a translation of it into Latin. It was a tool which was very soon being widely used by scholars and reformers alike. It was in the hands of Luther two years after publication, and brought forcibly to his attention, for instance, the fact that the words usually translated by "do penance" were better translated by "change your heart" or "repent." At this time there was no particular sign that ecclesiastical authority would lose control of the situation, and it is important to see this publication of Erasmus' in the context of the much more ambitious but strangely doomed project in Spain.

By 1516 another new Greek text of the New Testament had already been in print for two years, though in the private possession of Cardinal Ximenes at his University of Alcalá. It was part of his project for a polyglot Bible including original language versions of the Old and New Testament, eventually known as the Complutensian Polyglot Bible. The New Testament was done first and was completed by 1514, but held back until the rest of the Bible should be ready. All was complete by 1517, but was not released for publication until 1522 for reasons which are still not all clear.

This polyglot Bible and the New Testament of Erasmus have a

common inspiration—that of Lorenzo Valla (d. 1457), the Italian humanist and philologist one of whose works Erasmus had edited and published. About 1470 a nineteen-year-old Spaniard, Antonio de Nebrija, was traveling in Italy seeking "to restore to Spain the old Latin writers for many centuries in oblivion in Spain,"[6] as he said himself. He discovered Valla, and as a result was able to introduce "to Spain the grammatical principles and methods of exposition proposed by Valla . . . Nebrija was in effect both the Valla of Spain and the forerunner of Erasmus in those aims which are commonly believed to be uniquely Erasmusian." Nebrija held that critical examination of the ancient manuscripts, and careful philological methods, were necessary for the establishment of a text of Scripture which would be as accurate as possible. He taught at the University of Salamanca but his teaching was eventually considered too advanced and in 1512 Cardinal Ximenes appointed him to a chair at the university which he, Ximenes, had founded at Alcalá.

Cardinal Francisco Ximenes de Cisneros, Archbishop of Toledo, Primate of Spain, and regent of state during two interregna (1506–7 and 1516–17), was a remarkable man, ascetic, Franciscan monk, priest, scholar, reformer, statesman. He founded the University at Alcalá de Henares (then known as Complutum, giving the name Complutensian to the Bible) for the purpose of providing the clergy with a better education. It became a center for Greek studies, and Ximenes' project for a Bible in the original language was instituted. Nebrija assisted in the preparation of the Greek text. Volume V, the New Testament, was complete and printed in 1514. It provided a Greek text alongside the Vulgate. The other four volumes were completed in 1517. The Greek version of the Old Testament (the Septuagint, made in the third century), was printed in the inner columns of both pages, with an interlinear Latin crib for the majority of scholars, who still could not read Greek. There were two other columns on each page. The outer column had the Hebrew. The middle columns of each page carried the Latin of St. Jerome's Vulgate—which the Church had taken as the only authentic text for so many centuries. Room,

[6] Quoted by Basil Hall in his *The Trilingual College of San Ildefonso and the Making of the Complutensian Polyglot Bible*, No. 5 of *Studies in Church History*, (E. J. Brill, Leiden, 1969), from which the next quotation also comes.

was left at the foot of the pages of the Pentateuch (the first five books of the Old Testament) for the Targum, a version in Aramaic (the derivative from Hebrew which Jesus spoke) made in about A.D. 100, in a long line across the page. The prefaces of St. Jerome were included, also prologues to Pope Leo X and to the reader. There were many aids to the construing of the Greek and Hebrew, including a dictionary of Hebrew words superior to that produced by Reuchlin in Germany.

Within little over half a century of its invention in Europe one of the masterpieces of printing had been produced. But perhaps it might be truer to say that the editors and printers were still dominated by the glory of the manually written and decorated book. As we shall never see the like again of those vintage motorcars, still based on the design of horse-drawn carriages, so we are not likely to see anything quite like this Bible again. In one respect it did show an absolute climax of printing, for its Greek face is said never to have been bettered (Basil Hall, agreeing with Victor Scholderer's judgment in *Greek Printing Types,* 1927).

Ximenes received the last volume in 1517 from the printers and said he had never done anything better. A few months later he died. The Spanish-Flemish court arrived soon afterwards and impounded all his goods, preventing the university from issuing the Bible. The presentation copy in the Vatican Library was entered there in December 1521. The date on the finally published work was March 1520. About 600 copies were sold from about 1523 onwards at a price of six and a half ducats. Many were lost in the sinking of a Spanish ship on its way to Italy.

It is a symbol of the paralysis of the old Church structure held inactive by its masters, that this magnificent Bible became a museum piece. Into it had been poured the best Greek, the best Hebrew and the best philology of the age. It could have been a primary tool for the development of a lively Christianity. Instead, it was virtually suppressed for six years (nine years for the New Testament); the subsequent failure to reprint it led to its disappearance until an edition was made in Antwerp many decades later. For the generality of scholars Erasmus' text was the only Greek text they knew. Working quite on his own, with little encouragement, and not infrequent discouragements and even threats, he had produced a new printed version of the Greek

New Testament which enabled men to penetrate into its meaning as never before.

It was Erasmus' Latin translation of his new Greek text which came into the hands of people all over Europe. This and his Greek text, reprinted five times in new editions, the last in 1535, were in the universities all over Europe and were used as norms for the numerous translations that were then undertaken into the vernacular languages of the Continent. Erasmus had appropriately named it *Novum Instrumentum,* although this title was taken as provocative by many conservatives.

Luther had already begun to think about a new translation of the Bible into German about this time. His enforced inactivity, 1521–22, provided him with the necessary opportunity. Relying largely on Erasmus' work but also on previous translations he completed a translation of the New Testament into German which was published in 1522. The Old Testament took another twelve years, and was the joint product under his chairmanship of a committee of lecturers at the University of Wittenberg.

In England William Tyndale had begun sometime about 1522 to start on a translation of the New Testament into English. A priest, graduate of Oxford who also studied at Cambridge, Tyndale was the pure scholar, individualist, ascetic. He seems to have been largely indifferent to anything but the Bible, and preaching of the truth he found in it. He was a difficult man and never found it easy to make any friends. But he was not lacking in charity; two days in the week, in Antwerp at a later date, he gave up entirely to helping those in trouble, using money which was surplus from the subsidy sent him from merchants in England. These merchants were part of a network sometimes called the Christian Brethren and certainly connected with Lollards, all of whom helped Tyndale and other early Protestants abroad, and assisted in the rapid dissemination of Tyndale's Bible, and other Protestant books. It was these merchants who had been the first to befriend and encourage Tyndale in London in his project of translating the Bible when he was unable to find a patron. In 1523 Cuthbert Tunstall, Bishop of London, declined to take him into his service, and Tyndale stayed with a merchant, Humphrey Monmouth. In 1524 he went to Hamburg and thence to Wittenberg University. He began to have his New Testament printed in Cologne in 1525. Interrupted by a local censor who had been tipped off by spies of Henry VIII, still entirely papalist, he had the printing completed at Worms. Thousands of copies began to stream into England, and the success with which these copies evaded the watchers at the ports, forewarned as they were, and the ease with which they were distributed and sold make clear the existence both of a substantial market and of a means (not only unauthorized by, but in despite of, ecclesiastical authority) of reaching it. Six thousand copies are said to have been issued in the first twelve months. Further revised editions were published in 1526, 1534, 1535.

Tyndale then set to work to learn Hebrew and translate the Old Testament, residing at Antwerp for the rest of his life. By the time of his violent death in 1535—kidnaped by an Englishman, hanged and burned by the Netherlands imperial government—he had completed a translation of the Pentateuch and of some other parts of the rest. With him at one time or another were George Joye, John Rogers and Miles Coverdale, future translators of the Bible. And it was Tyndale's translation which remained the basis of all their work, including the Great Bible of 1539, prepared by Coverdale under instructions from the Chancellor Thomas Cromwell. Tyndale's translation also provides the substantial basis for the Roman Catholic Rheims New Testament of 1582, the Roman Catholic Douay Old Testament of 1609, and the Authorized Version, of James I, of the whole Bible of 1611. All over Europe it is a similar story.[7]

---

[7] Between 1520 and 1530 appeared versions of the New Testament in Swedish and Danish; in Magyar by Jan Sylvester; and in French by Lefèvre, a version which survived for three hundred years and more, and was completed as a whole Bible by 1530. A Bible was printed in Prague in 1529. In Poland at Cracow a translation of Ecclesiastes was published in 1522. Between 1530 and 1540, versions of the four Gospels and of the Psalter were produced in Polish, and of the New Testament in Icelandic. New editions appeared in Italian, and one of these was the first vernacular Bible at all with an official dedication to a cardinal; this was an edition published in Antwerp in 1538 and addressed to the cardinal of Mantua; the version used was one already well known, by Brucioli. Between 1540 and 1550 appeared complete translations of the Bible in Danish (Christian III's Bible, published by Christian Pedersen, Canon of Lund, 1550), in Swedish (the great Vasa Bible of the brothers Petri), and in Czech by Bishop Jan Augusta. A New Testament in Finnish was made by Agricola in 1548. Eck published a "Catholic" version of the Bible in German in 1530, but it did not catch on and Catholics used Luther's version (with corrections). No Spanish vernacular Bibles were made inside the country till the eighteenth century, though a market existed and was supplied by editions from the Netherlands and England.

The Bible had become divisive. The Council of Trent retained the formal papal ban on the use of translations unless there were notes or commentary to ensure correct interpretation and general warnings about the possible danger of reading the Bible. Those not in communion with Rome, though divided about many other things, remained substantially united in their belief that the Bible was the norm for all Christians, incomparably more important than tradition or Church authority. As time went on attitudes of both parties gradually softened or became more adapted to evident fact. Today the Bible has largely ceased to be divisive and is judged by many to be the instrument par excellence for the reconciliation of Christians to each other. This is largely due to a recognition by all men of the historical nature of the Bible, and of the validity of universal frames of reference as relevant to an understanding of it. The books of the Bible were written at particular times by particular people. If it contains, as Christians believe, the revelation of the most important events in history then it should be studied with all the care available from every human science. Catholics and Protestants (and Jews and Muslims in the case of the Old Testament) are united in a search for truth, which is not different from man's search for truth in any other sphere. They are still divided on interpretation. But the unitary nature of truth is bringing them together at this level as well as at the purely historical and scientific level. At the same time, the nature of the Bible as "revelation" is necessarily being submitted increasingly to rigorous examination from outside the Church. Again both the inheritors of the Reformation and Roman Catholics are today generally united in welcoming this challenge.

CHAPTER 3

Christianity, Religion of Reformation, from the Primitive Church to the Sixteenth Century

The great majority of Christians prior to the Reformation and for some centuries after it could not read. Their religion was something which came to them by spoken word and by symbol, in their families, and in communal religious activities, churchgoing and other more general celebrations. In church they saw pictures on the walls, and they heard words, and took part sometimes in their recitation. From the time in any country when a common vernacular language came to be established a number of people began to want to read what the priest read out, to understand more of the gospel, of the Bible, of the story of the world. Some had a motive of curiosity. Some had a motive of religion. Most no doubt had both motives. Some were in monasteries or friaries, some were merchants, some courtiers or part of the noble families. Some were ordinary people who had persuaded someone to teach them to read. Our concern is with those who, once launched on this way, began to wish very strongly to be able to penetrate further into the meaning of religion, and therefore to be able to read the Bible. For some of these in some parts of Europe during some of the time there was not much sense that they were doing anything disapproved of by authority. But in many places in the case of lay people, there was some sense that they were invading the things which belonged to the priest. Some tension was set up between their wish to penetrate more deeply into their religion by means of reading about it in their own language and the established conventions by which the Bible was in Latin and read by the priest, and explained by him at second hand, or else explained in books of biblical histories and rhymes. We need to try to specify this tension as exactly as possible. Sociologically we have class barriers which might be given various special descriptions; no doubt various degrees of psychological and economic motivation could be assumed in various cases. But taken all over, the numerous cases where individuals and communities were defying convention or authority, whether to a moderate degree as perhaps with the Brothers of the Common Life in the late fourteenth century in the Netherlands, or to a very great degree in the case of the Waldensians in Provence in the early thirteenth century, manifest only one common motivation. We are driven back to find a common religious motivation among all those who wanted to read the Bible, whether this involved much or little opposition to Church authority, or none at all, as in the case of those who did this in late fourteenth-century Florence with the encouragement of Dominican friars. This religious motivation was identical with the religious motivation which ran through all society and kept the Church as a whole alive. What was it? How did it work?

The literature which we have to consult, along with architecture, art and music, suggests that the answer is something like a kind of mysticism. And this is not to take an elitist view. In their attendance at Mass, in their eucharistic communion at Mass, in the other sacramental occasions and pious practices, ordinary people evidently found a religious dimension which was deeply satisfying to them. They found authenticity in the traditional description of the Mass as a sacrament of unity with Jesus Christ and with each other. A devotion to Christ crucified was part of the culture and one of the deepest experiences of the age. Religious rites were for them symbolical of that unity with God which they found in prayer, in their inmost beings, in intercourse with their fellow men and women. This is to express it in ideal terms. And an abstract sentence cannot convey the actuality, with all its failures and betrayals on the one hand and its ecstasy on the other. Let us look at some witnesses.

A thirteenth-century folk lament from the hill country of Urbino brings something of the reality which suffused Christian life in all countries. The last verse sings:

Plange lo bene, plange lo male
plange la gente tucta ad uguale
mort'e lo rege celestiale
e no de morte sua naturale.

> Weep, O sad, weep, O gay,
> Weep, O folk of everyday
> Heaven's King in mortal fray
> Violently has passed away.

And Jacopone da Todi from the same century:

> *Clama la lengua e 'l core*
> *Amore! Amore! Amore!*
> *Chi tace el tuo dolzore*
> *Lo cor li sia crepato*

> My tongue, my heart, are crying,
> My love! My love! My love!
> If I should cease my sighing,
> My heart will split. My love!

The piety, the deep religious conviction lying behind these words was expressed and re-expressed often in the following two centuries, in the countries further north, usually in less violently lyrical language. While there was much emphasis on death and sin there was also much emphasis on joy. In England one could quote passim from *The Cloud of Unknowing*, Margery Kempe, *Piers Plowman*, Richard Rolle, Walter Hilton, but we take a passage from *The Revelations of Divine Love*, written by the nun of Norwich, Juliana, who probably became an anchoress and lived immured in a cottage beside a bridge in Norwich, c.1370, where people brought her food, and came for advice, and asked her prayers. Her words take us to the other extreme of religious expression, measured and philosophical even though visionary in the contemporary way. "I saw that if the blessed Trinity could have made man's soul better, fairer, nobler than he did, he cannot have been, as he was, fully satisfied with the making of his soul. And he wills that our hearts be lifted high above earthly depths and empty sorrows and rejoice in him." The serious concerns of the age were all anchored back in religion. Later in this chapter we shall see the gradual building-up of a tension between this religion as experienced and lived by people, and the ecclesiastical organization. But first we must trace back the pedigree of the religious drive.

Although during the eighth, ninth and tenth centuries, written records are few, they are sufficient along with other records and those of all other centuries for us to be able to say that there had always been a more or less intense religious experience among Christians, and that this always issued in an altruistic concern for each other and for the whole human community. The original witnesses to these things we find in numerous statements of the New Testament writers. It is clear that they all in their very different ways believed they had had experience of something and someone of a kind not known to man before that time, something unique.

St. Paul was the first to put anything down on papyrus about his conversion to the religion he had persecuted—but it was not so much conversion to a religion as conversion by and to a person, Jesus, in whom he saw the real fulfillment of the religion of his upbringing and early life, which in this sense he never abjured. A little later the four authors of the Gospels set down what they knew of the life of Jesus—the same story told for four different purposes, sometimes overlapping, sometimes complementing, sometimes confusing one another. They all saw in him the Messiah which the Jewish people had expected for so long, and they all saw in him, following on from that, the Messiah or Savior who had come to the whole world. They saw him as one who "saves" and "changes" people, directing them away from evil and towards good. He gives them spiritual health. He binds together in a single body all who believe in him. His life is the central fact of the whole history of human experience. He speaks the word of love, and is the "Word of God," "Son" of God, whom he addresses as "Father." He has now sent his "Holy Spirit" to help and guide Christians. He has left a form of worship, the repetition of his taking of bread and wine the night before he was crucified, giving this to his friends as his body and his blood offered for them.

The drive which led St. Paul and the other New Testament writers to write down what they knew of Jesus, also collected great numbers of people to this new religion, "the way," or Christianity, as it came to be called. Any satisfactory historical explanation of how Christianity came to dominate the empire, leaving all other religions behind, must, I think, advert to the specifically religious dimension of history. Trevor-Roper (*The Rise of Christian Europe*) explains that this domination was due to the success of Christianity in converting the peasants, and that because of this "it was proof against persecution . . . it could not be stamped out." But one must ask why it was that Christianity was successful in the rural areas as well as in the towns. And why did it not get drawn into the syncretistic mass of oriental sects and mystery religions of the Roman Empire? "It survived because it possessed a system of ecclesiastical organization and a principle of social authority that distinguished it from all other religious bodies of the age." So explains Christopher Dawson in *The Making of Europe,* who goes on to point out that Christians regarded their Church as the New Israel, "a chosen race, a royal priesthood, a consecrated nation, a people set apart," to quote St. Peter, who was quoting Isaiah and Exodus. He continues, relevantly: "This holy society was a theocracy inspired and governed by the Holy Spirit, and its rulers, the apostles, were the representatives not of the community but of the Christ, who had chosen them and transmitted to them His divine authority. This conception of a divine apostolic authority remained as the foundation of ecclesiastical order in the post-apostolic period. The 'overseers' and elders, who were the rulers of the local churches, were regarded as the successors of the apostles, and the churches that were of direct apostolic origin enjoyed a peculiar prestige and authority among the rest."

There is a religious dimension in history; religious factors sometimes override all others. Its sheer authenticity as a religion, as spiritual truth, is the only possible principal explanation for the rise of Christianity, as for the success of some other religions at other times in other places. Of course there are always a hundred enabling factors, and factors of confusion and abuse, magic and superstition. All human situations are immensely complex, even the simplest, because the human make-up is immensely complex. But the absence of anything like a sufficient non-religious historical cause for the rise of Christianity does simplify that situation and point to the one obvious reason.

This may all seem a long way from the Reformation. It is not. For one of the underlying contentions of this book is that the Reformation was a religious event, primarily. To carry this statement through convincingly we have to establish or assume the fact at all of religious events, and the particular nature of those religious events which are Christian. As we implied in the first chapter, this must be largely assumption. But at least the factual basis for this assumption can be made plain. This assumption (or establishment of fact) is grounded first in the New Testament witness, a substantial collection of documents. Second, we point to the rise of Christianity as a religious event. Thirdly, we point to the constant personal witness, from the earliest times, to a unique experience and its effect.

At this point we turn to a single major witness. He is important for three reasons. He has had an intense experience of the nature of Christian conversion. He has had detailed experience of the difficulty of retaining within one body and one organization all those who call themselves Christian, the difficulty which was to defeat everyone in the sixteenth century. Thirdly, his writings were to be read at a crucial moment by the man who started the Reformation events.

St. Augustine

Augustine of Hippo, a native of the north coast of Africa, born of a Christian mother and a pagan father about the year 354, an agnostic for a time, a Manichean also for a time, lecturer in philosophy at universities in Africa and Italy, was converted to Christianity, and then became a Christian leader, a bishop responsible for organization and for administration of the rules as well as for inspiring Christians and teaching the gospel to them. Here is Augustine speaking from his heart in a way which has set its deepest seal on Christianity in the West. It comes from his *Confessions:*

"Even if I would not confess to You, what could be hidden in me, O Lord, from You to whose eyes the deepest depth of man's conscience lies bare? I should only be hiding You from myself, not myself from You. But now that my groaning is witness that I am displeasing to myself, You shine unto me and I delight in You and love You and yearn for You, so that I am ashamed of what I am and renounce myself and choose You and please neither You nor myself save in You. To You then, O Lord, I am laid bare for what I am. And I have said with what profit I confess to You. For my confession is not by bodily words, or bodily cries, but with the words of the soul and the upward crying of my thought, which Your ear knows. For when I am wicked, confession to You simply means being displeased at myself; when I am good, confession to You simply means not attributing my goodness to myself: for You, O Lord, bless the just man, but first You turn him from ungodliness to justice. And so my confession, O my God, in Your sight is made silently, for if it makes no sound, yet it cries aloud in my heart. For whatever good I offer to men, You have heard from me before I utter it: and whatever good You hear from me, You have first spoken to me." (*Confessions*, Book X, 2 [Sheed and Ward, New York, 1964].)

God was the inner principle of his life and of all life. God was at the same time intensely personal, he was the Word, Jesus, Truth, to be spoken to, confided in. Augustine is a witness to the authenticity of religion and to the particular nature of the Christian religion. For Augustine religion is this intense life of union with God which is also a tension between himself and "You," or "Truth." One may ask whether in writing his *Confessions*, Augustine was not really being didactic, was really writing for others. Indeed this is true and he says so more than once in the course of the *Confessions:* "But to whom am I telling this? Not to Thee, O My God, but in Thy presence I am telling it to my own kind, to the race of men, or rather to that small part of the human race that may come upon these writings. And to what purpose do I tell? Simply that I and any other who may read may realize out of what depths we must cry to Thee. For nothing is more surely heard by Thee than a heart that confesses Thee and a life in Thy faith."

But Augustine's life was not simply that of the mystic dévot, ex-agnostic, convert, university man. How does he measure up as a bishop? What has he to say about those in his day who found that their consciences would not be accommodated within the organization?

"Often too the divine Providence allows even good men to be driven out of the Christian communion by the all too factious dissensions of carnally minded men. And if they bear this ignominy or injury patiently for the sake of the peace of the Church, and do not give occasion to any new heresies or schisms, they will teach men, with what true affection and sincere charity God must be served. The intention of such men is either to return when the storms are stilled; or if this be not allowed them, whether because the same storm persists or because their return may give rise to a similar or more violent one, they hold to the will to have regard for the good of those very men, owing to whose violences and disturbances they had withdrawn, and, without setting up any separate sect, to the day of their death defend and by their witness support that faith which they know to be preached in the Catholic Church. These the Father, who sees in secret, crowns in secret. Men such as these are seldom seen; yet examples are not wanting; indeed there are more than might be thought."[1]

The situation for which St. Augustine was writing was not that of the sixteenth-century Reformation, or that of the twentieth-century Protestant and Roman Catholic Churches. But his words are useful. They refer to the tension which is always likely to exist within voluntary but highly organized communities, and particularly those with a religious purpose. Augustine's words are also important because they establish his opinion that a man may not only be in good Christian faith and be outside the visible organization of the Church, but that this may even be his right place, and that it may certainly be God's will that he be outside the organization. Augustine gives reasons and attaches to his opinion the rider that such a man would not set up any separate sect. But the fact remains that he does not identify membership of the organization in an absolute fashion with good Christian faith.

The Pedigree of Reform

It is worth lingering on this point, for the internal problems of all Western churches from the eleventh century onwards to the present day are related to the claims which the Roman Catholic Church has frequently, and other churches have occasionally put forward, to be in effect bodies that have the exclusive guidance of God's Spirit, and outside the bounds of whose membership a man cannot be a Christian. It is possible to trace something in this attitude to the very great reverence which Augustine himself had for the Church. This reverence became articulated during our last nine centuries in those typically legal and organizational terms which in some sense are the genius of Western man, but which when used autocratically by religious bodies leave no room for the understanding shown by Augustine in the passage quoted. Man's plans are never perfect and even when made in the name of God

[1] *De Vera Religione*, VI, 10–11; cited by Erich Przywara in *An Augustine Synthesis* (Sheed and Ward, London and New York, 1936), p. 276.

and religion can be unworthily motivated and carried out inhumanly. It is impossible logically to impute to every authoritative action of an ecclesiastical authority the plenitude of the gospel, and it is probable that some such actions in all ages will cause mortal offense to Christian conscience.

There has always been a tension between the idea of a Christian community subject purely to the Holy Spirit as it inspires individuals, or groups of them, and the idea of a Christian community which as a group of human beings must have some generally understood and obligatory rules and organization. Individuals or groups have repeatedly rejected the existing organization of a Christian church in the name of gospel truth to set up a new organization supposedly entirely true to the gospel, subject exclusively to its word and to the guidance of the Holy Spirit, only to find that within a few years another structured society has come into being, against which a new set of individuals wishes to revolt on the same grounds as those which led to this society itself. The claims of conscience amount in the end to that independence, or freedom of initiative, which lies at the heart of human action. History is littered with the deaths of those who prefer in one cause or another to do what they believe to be right and risk penal, perhaps mortal, consequences rather than obey a law in actions which they consider to be sinful or in some absolute way a denial of truth or of humanity or of Deity. The problem is not confined to religious bodies. It may be said to reach its most acute crisis there. But a similar crisis is liable to arise in any human group which claims to provide a total environment and explanation of human life, such as any totalitarian polity.

The most honored Christian theologians, and those most consistently referred to, have always insisted that revealed truth cannot be adequately contained within some formula. The gospel is a revelation, a communication to particular men and women. It must be preached. So there must be preachers. And these preachers must not rely exclusively on any formula, as if the gospel were so much mathematics. But in that case some room needs to be left for what St. Paul called charismata, spiritual capacities which are not something the Church can produce in her members at will. God is not bound even by his own Church. Room must be left for what Judaism knew as prophets. The prophets were often persecuted, but they were recognized as prophets, and their office was recognized. St. Paul could hardly be said to have encouraged the appearance of charismata in his Christian converts, but he certainly recognized them and left some place for them, albeit controlled. The nearest the Western Church came to recognizing prophets and to providing a place for charismata is in its process of canonization of saints. But of course this always happens after their death! And there was good sense in a system which insisted that the holier a man is the more easily should he fit himself to the demands of an organization. But the crucial crunch came just here, because the demands might be the inappropriately un-christian demands of a corrupted official who had reached his position by unworthy means. There is a good case then for the holy man to say that God has given him work to do and that he does not intend to allow a man to stop him.

"Love and do what you will" would seem to be most consonant with the Christian gospel. And it is striking that this saying was originated by St. Augustine. But one needs perhaps to comment that it is easy to make a hortatory remark of this kind when one knows very well that a fairly rigid organization is holding the whole community together and that in practice "do what you will" is kept within severe bounds by the local parish priest or bishop. Perhaps, conversely, only a Catholic in the full organizational tradition needed to make such a remark as "Love and do what you will," in order to compensate for the obligatory nature of some of his religious life.

From the earliest times there has been a reaction in the name of "religion" against the organized Church, whose functionaries, like any other men, are always sure to have sufficient failings for an opposition to be able to justify itself. The reformers of the sixteenth century never knew enough history to be able to trace their own pedigree, except in a highly selective fashion. At first they hardly knew they had one. When they did recognize it, they understood it in a semi-apocalyptic prophetic sense, history firmly subordinate to theology. But the historian can now observe throughout all the centuries previous to the Reformation reactions against the organiza-tion which have too much in common for them not to be definitive, in reverse, of a character in ecclesiastical organization, and in themselves typical of an authentically religious reaction to it. "It is not the identity of answers but the similarity of the questions

which makes the categorizing of Forerunners valid and necessary."[2]
He can also observe in the later half of these centuries a continuity
in the reaction, and its growth, which shows one reformer standing
on the shoulders of one who went before. Of course all this can
be exaggerated. We must never forget that Luther, Zwingli, Calvin, Cromwell, Cranmer, Bucer, while they knew a good deal of
the early Fathers only knew a little about the centuries immediately
preceding themselves, and this was true of all previous medieval
reformers. But the achievements of previous reformers had created
attitudes and assumptions which were then built into the whole
social situation; and Luther did increasingly identify himself as the
last of a line of reformers.

In the fifteenth century there was a religious anti-clericalism
spread throughout Europe. There was a general assumption about
the possibly corrupt practices of some or many of those who had
gained high ecclesiastical office. There was a generally cynical
attitude among the intelligentsia towards all forms of "pardons,"
"indulgences," "relics," etc. On the other hand there was a general
inclination to praise anyone who was truly poor and had chosen
this poverty in the name of Christ. The Mass, the Bible, the
offices of priest, bishop and Pope were held in reverence. These
attitudes can be found, for instance, throughout *The Canterbury
Tales* and *Piers Plowman*. It seems not to have occurred to anyone
in the normal way of life, that the system as it stood might be
overthrown and another put in its stead. Yet the system was
challenged perennially by heretics; and, although this challenge
itself was not taken seriously, it left a result. Those who had
attempted to follow the gospel closely on their own initiative and
had become heretics, or had remained within the Church as
reformers, or become founders of orders, or just lesser men who
had spoken out against customs at variance as they thought with the
Gospels, had all left their mark. Generalized social attitudes were
gradually built up, and provided not so much a mere enabling
context for the sixteenth-century reformers, as a growing social
and religious consensus on which the Reformation was actually
based. The historian needs to record something of the pedigree of
these attitudes.

[2] H. A. Oberman, *Forerunners of the Reformation* (Lutterworth, London;
Holt, Rinehart and Winston, New York; 1967).

In one sense the Church's legal and organizational methods are themselves a complete explanation of the Reformation. We have seen that such forms in religion are sure to provoke a reaction, genuine and spiritual. "Heresy," then, and eventually religious revolution, sociologically, is simply a function of an imposed orthodoxy. The establishment of rigid religious norms, supported by a comprehensive canon law, made heresy inevitable. If norms are established in this way, there will be deviations from them. Heresies often did not become polemical or rebellious, and were not distinctively "heretical" until authority had made its excluding pronouncement.[3]

From the twelfth century onwards it is possible to trace a continuous line of reformers, some of whom became heretics, some of whom remained within the organization of the Church and its sacramental communion. One of the earliest of these reformers was perhaps the most important of all in that his followers became very numerous and continued in existence till the Reformation and indeed to the present day. This was Peter Waldo, whose Waldensian followers were responsible for so much of the early translations of the Bible. But before we describe this phenomenon and the following events, we have to say something about the reformers scattered about in place and time in the previous four centuries. We have also, first of all, to say something about the one other very substantial heretical movement prior to and contemporary with Waldo, which, however, declined thereafter and was extinct by the time of the Reformation itself, that of the Cathari or Manicheans.

The Manicheans

The Manicheans have some importance for us, because they survived in one form or another through the centuries from about 350, and from the tenth to the end of the thirteenth century attracted religious reformers and rebels and large numbers of ordinary people to their movement, also because in the first century of their movement, they had an influence on the mainstream of Christian development in the West, and are partially responsible

---

[3] See Gordon Leff, *Heresy in the Later Middle Ages*, 2 vols. (Manchester University Press, Manchester; Barnes and Noble, New York; 1967), passim.

for a certain dualistic attitude which has remained a traditional part of Christianity.

Part of the Manichean doctrine was that there is a religious elite with a special knowledge (*gnosis*). This linked in origin with early Christian Gnostics. One of the greatest early Christian thinkers, Origen, thought that the salvation of the simple believer was a different thing from that of the "elect." This idea became the core of a "Gnostic" movement which claimed that some people had a special knowledge, distinct from and superior to the mere faith (*pistis*) of the ordinary Christian. This Gnostic tradition was taken up by Mani in Persia, in Ctesiphon about 242. Mani was first a Zoroastrian, but subsequently came to call himself an "Apostle of Jesus Christ." For him Light is God, Darkness is all Creation. Some part of the Light has become imprisoned in each man. Marriage is evil in that it institutionalizes the process of imprisoning more and more of the Light in the Darkness. Casual sex is bad, but slightly less so. There was a small hierarchy of the elite (*perfecti*) and a vast congregation of hearers (*credenti*). Of its early theory and practice Steven Runciman writes : "All killing, even of animals, was forbidden. . . . Considerable numbers of believers wandered about refusing to work. . . . refusing to notice secular regulations, living on the charity of others, and exercising a vast influence on the whole community." Augustine was a Manichean from the age of twenty-four, between 378 and 383. Something of the Manichean dualistic pessimism about man entered Christianity through him and others at this time, and earlier. There is plenty of "dualistic pessimism" in the gospel. But the particular point at which the Manichean approach bit into Christianity concerns the use of the sexual impulse. Manicheans had an attitude, not simply of realistic pessimism (which can be quite Christian—Jesus "knew what is in man"), but of entire hopelessness about sex (not apparently on account of the strength of the impulse but because of its results —more people). This sense of hopelessness about sex does seem to have entered the Christian tradition from them at this time. It seems to have been transposed from a theological and sociological judgment about the resultant increase of population (of more or less evil human beings) to a moral and psychological judgment concerning its irresistible and degrading nature. This attitude to sex is not found in the Old Testament, and hardly in the New. It is certainly contradictory of the traditional Judaic delight in the large family and in the works of creation, and of the same factors in the New Testament. The new suspicious attitude towards the sexual impulse seems to have become almost an official part of Christianity as time went on. Full theoretical dualism, however, was always resisted and was seen as fundamentally contradictory of the gospel message. Augustine turned from Manicheanism to find in the gospel an offer of salvation for the whole man, even though he remained emotionally pessimistic about the sexual relation.

A thoroughgoing dualistic tradition survived in Eastern Europe for many centuries, flowering in the Paulicians, the Bogomils, the Patarines and others. Runciman writes of the Bogomil heresy in the tenth century in Bulgaria: "The Bogomil heresy was born amidst peasants whose physical misery made them conscious of the wickedness of things. The Christianity imposed upon them by their masters seemed alien and without comfort. The creed of the Paulicians, settled nearby, was fitter, it taught a simple Dualism and explained the misery of the world. An unknown priest called Bogomil adapted it for the Slavs, damping its militarism into a more formidable passive resistance. But as time went on the new faith developed; the heretics came into touch with the Messalians, who gave them access to all the wealth of Orientalised Gnostic tradition. And thus a new Christianity was founded, based on early Christian legend and Eastern Dualism, and answering to the needs of the medieval peasantry to become very soon one of the greatest religions of Europe." This was in the middle of the tenth century.[4]

Between about the middle of the eleventh century and the middle of the twelfth century, perhaps not until nearly 1150—the scholars are not agreed—the Manicheans, or the Cathari (the name for the "perfect" within the movement) arrived in Europe and spread across what is now southern France. Runciman again deserves to be quoted: "So it was that one great confederate Dualist Church arose, stretching from the Black Sea to Biscay. In all the countries into which it spread, its successes were made by political conditions, by circumstances of racial politics, of class politics and of personal politics. But for the social condition of the

[4] The original source material is very meager. Research and discussion continue. Some historians say the European Cathari could be independent and indigenous.

peasants of Bulgaria, but for the diplomatic conditions of Bosnia, midway between Eastern and Western Christendom, and but for the rapacity of certain great nobles of Languedoc, stimulated by the vulnerability of an inadequate Catholic hierarchy, the Dualists might have remained in obscurity. But the political impulse was not everything. Behind it there was a steady spiritual teaching, a definite religion, that developed and declined as most religions do, but that embodied a constant Tradition."

Two or three centuries previous to this time Christianity seemed to be mortally threatened by Islam, creeping up over the Pyrenees, into the Italian coastal areas, into Eastern Europe. Now it was threatened from within. The fact that the Manichean movement could gather so many followers was doubtless to an important extent indicative of political and economic conditions as Runciman says. And it is useful to know this. But the tradition itself is sufficiently close to Christianity, using the New Testament as it did, thriving on Christian sources, its followers being converts from Christianity, for us not to dismiss it as irrelevant to our theme. Here was a religion which made it seem possible to put some of the extreme statements of the gospel into some sort of literal practice. The sixteenth-century Reformation took part of its inspiration from just such a wish to put the gospel into practice without compromise.

The appeal of St. John's Gospel perhaps found its first popular appreciation when the Cathari in southern France translated it. It has also been suggested that the general environment which enabled St. Francis to turn to the natural world and personify it—Brother Sun, Sister Water, Brother Fire, Mother Earth and Sister Death—owes something to the widespread influence of Catharist ideas, in particular that of metempsychosis. This was the doctrine by which a soul unworthy of release at death was reincarnated in some other living body. On the other hand, the Manichean doctrine of the evil nature of all Creation led to the practice of the *endura*, the practice of starvation to death, and it was the absence of all hope which finally killed this religion. It is worth listening again to words from the final paragraph of Runciman's book.

"The Christian heresy of Dualism . . . died without issue, before the sword of the Turks and the fire of the Dominicans. It was not an ignoble religion. It taught the value of the fundamental virtues;

it faced with courage the anxious question of evil. But it was a religion of pessimism. It held out no hope for individual men and their salvation. Mankind should die out, that the imprisoned fragments of Godhead should return to their home. It was a religion without hope, and such a religion cannot survive unless it be helped artificially. For Hope is a necessary part of religion. Faith and charity are not enough . . . Confident of the truth of their cause, but in no expectation of their own salvation, its children went uncomplaining to the stake, and their hopeless faith was burnt with them."

Rome was so concerned with the extent of the heresy that when it would yield to the preaching neither of St. Bernard nor of St. Dominic a "crusade" was called. War was declared on the Albigensians and the heresy destroyed in Europe by Christian soldiers, supported by the Dominican friar preachers.

Peter Waldo, His Predecessors and His Successors

Manicheanism arrived in Western Europe perhaps only twenty years before Peter Waldo took his first steps towards a literal implementation of the gospel, perhaps a good deal longer. We cannot be sure of the exact date, partly because for four centuries there had been stray reformers of one kind and another—they demanded a more exact following of poverty, or rejected ecclesiastical authority on account of luxurious living, and took the Bible and the Holy Spirit as their authority, or rejected the sacraments, or a combination of some of these. Various reformers of the eleventh and twelfth centuries have some Manichean characteristics, but these characteristics are not conclusive. Some abstained from eating meat, as the Manicheans did.

The records of these quite numerous protests have led a recent author to categorize them under four headings: Reformists, Eccentrics, Catharists and Reactionaries.[5] As with the Manicheans, according to Runciman's reckoning, it is impossible to deny that an important part of the motive of these earlier religious innovators and dissenters may really have been social or economic—on the other hand evidence from other ages does not make it particularly likely that this was often or ever a dominant motive. The least

[5] J. B. Russell, *Dissent and Reform in the Early Middle Ages* (University of California Press, Berkeley, 1965).

attractive aspect in some cases is when they demanded reverence for themselves as saints. Such is the case of Aldebert, of whom we know from St. Boniface. It is noteworthy how relatively gently the Church dealt with such people in the eighth, ninth and tenth centuries. Very seldom was there any physical duress or punishment such as occurred in the later, more "civilized" times. Aldebert frequently failed to toe the line. He was simply summoned again to appear and explain himself.

It seems impossible to make any generalization about these early reformers and dissenters other than the negative statement that no individual secured a following comparable with that of Peter Waldo or of the Manicheans in the twelfth century. Doubtless, however, they prepared the ground for the latter in the sense that when the latter appeared, religious innovation from below in the name of poverty and simplicity and of some kind of gnosis or special inspiration was not something entirely new.

From the twelfth to the sixteenth century the majority of heretics were concerned with a return to the precepts of the gospel through a life of poverty or to a life of simplicity and preaching, all based on the Bible. They wished to reform the Church, in particular to expel undue luxury, in the later centuries criticizing priests and bishops for drawing income from more than one cure or see (pluralism) and for being absent from their duties, and for buying their office (simony). It was only subsequent to condemnation by authority that a heresy commonly took on an anti-sacerdotal character. None of the principal sects except the Cathari was initially heretical, nor did they owe their distinctiveness to the imprint of an original heresiarch with the exception of Wycliffe. Only subsequent to its condemnation did a group begin to exaggerate its preaching to the extent of contradiction of common teaching, and to regard their members as Christ's true apostles and their struggle against authority as part of a wider struggle between the forces of Christ and Antichrist. But by a circular process the authorities began to be suspicious of any movement which showed certain characteristics: "appeal to the bible and to the evangelical virtues of poverty and humility became or was treated as a challenge to the church."[6] These generalizations are important for us. By the sixteenth century the process was more or less instan-

[6] Leff, Op. cit. The next two quotations also come from this work, to which I am also indebted for insights in this and the previous section.

taneous. Thus Luther was recognized from the start as virtually a heretic just because he appealed to the Bible at the same time as criticizing financial profit made from popular religious activities and propounding new theological theses—an unknown German Augustinian friar had no right to such views.

Heretics had much in common with the most thoughtful among orthodox Christians. Society at large was exercised by a moral concern with simony, worldliness and wealth in general. Heresies arose "over the recurrent need to find new modes of living and to remedy existing ones. Hence there was a convergence between heresy and orthodoxy; it is not too much to say that from the later twelfth century onwards all the most prominent heretical movements—centred on poverty, prophecy, the mystical search for God, the nature of the church—bore directly upon the major intellectual and doctrinal themes; the preoccupations among the learned found a resonance, albeit often distorted, in popular religious life."

Within the bounds of orthodoxy reforming motives had resulted in the foundation of new and more strict religious orders. One, the Camaldolese, was an order virtually for hermits. The Carthusians and the Cistercians were founded by Benedictine monks as a reaction from what seemed to them to be a fall from the rule and from the ideals in many of the monasteries of St. Benedict. St. Bernard was abbot of the first Cistercian monastery soon after its foundation. Many other reforms of monasticism, and new versions of the vowed religious life were initiated by monks. The reforming drive would become more problematical for the Church when initiated by laymen, although as we shall see, in the next century one such survived and became more famous than any other Christian movement. The twelfth-century Waldo, however, failed to remain within the organizational bounds.

In a sense heresies were a sign precisely of the vitality of Christianity, and in that sense of the Church. Life was Christian from top to bottom, through and through. And this did not mean some kind of complacent in-turned indifference to life. The buildings, the paintings, the manuscripts and the literature of the later Middle Ages rank as one of the great human achievements, seen as a whole, almost a single work of art in itself, in such a way that we can refer to the Duecento—the thirteenth century in Italy—and know a whole world knit into one. And yet it was in this century that heresy first became really notorious and the Inquisition was set up. During this century heresy became endemic in parts of Europe, and the Bible was translated into a number of languages.

Three men may be mentioned who are less obscure than the reformers of previous centuries but did not reach the achievement of Waldo. Peter of Bruis (d. 1126), Arnold of Brescia (d. 1155) and Ugo Speroni (d. after 1174). Peter attracted a considerable following, called the Petrobrusians; he rejected churches, clergy and sacraments. He died, apparently lynched, being burned by a crowd in Provence, near the Abbey of St. Gilles. Arnold denounced the wealth of the clergy, and helped to found a commune in Rome. He was violently killed in Rome by order of Frederick Barbarossa. (Leff says he was burned; David Knowles [*The Middle Ages*] says he was hanged. Both are right perhaps.) Ugo was an Italian lawyer heretic, constantly in collision with authority.

About 1176 Peter Waldo took a decision, similar to the decision taken thirty years later by St. Francis, to sell what he had and to try to follow the pattern of poverty seen in the life and teachings of Jesus Christ as it is described in the Bible. A rich merchant of Lyons, he settled two daughters in convents and left home. Followers soon gathered and the group were given formal consideration at the Third Lateran Council in 1179. Pope Alexander III approved their vow of poverty, but made their freedom to preach subject to the local clergy's approval. This proved to be their undoing. In 1181 the bishop of Lyons prohibited them from expounding Scripture. They were made to feel persecuted, and they began to talk about obeying God rather than man. Three years later they were condemned by Pope Lucius III at the Council of Verona, along with the Patarines of Lombardy and the Arnoldists. The excommunication of the Waldensians and their expulsion from Lyons led to a rapid dissemination of the group, though only quite gradually to their growth as a formidably heretical group. One branch joined for a time in Milan with another similar group, the Humiliati, whom Innocent III constituted as an order in the Church in 1199. The Humiliati continued to live in their own homes, while many Waldensians seem to have kept on the move. This new group in Milan became a separate group known as the Poor Men of Lombardy. Innocent III also formed a group of Waldensians under Durandus of Huesca in southern France into the Catholic Poor, in 1207. But the antagonism of the local church was too much for them, as for previous groups.

Durandus and his companions were taken to be heretics on account of their living on alms and their preaching. They were finally banned by Innocent IV in 1247. A remnant of them entered the Augustinian Hermits in 1256. Innocent III had recognized yet another group in 1210, pledged to vagrant poverty under Bernard Primus. It seems to have vanished quite swiftly.

It is significant that the one great witness to the power of religion who stands up above all others in the Middle Ages was yet another layman dedicated to poverty and simplicity, and remaining a simple "brother" in the order he founded. Francis Bernardone of Assisi, son of a prosperous cloth merchant, found himself taking the gospel seriously. He had always been nauseated at the sight of the lepers, and, like everyone else before a cure was found in the twentieth century, was terrified of the disease. Increasingly he felt this to be unworthy of a Christian. One day he got off his horse, gave the begging leper in front of him some money and kissed his hand. About this time he fell silent at a banquet and his friends asked him if he had fallen in love and he said that he had done so, with someone nobler, richer and lovelier than any other. It was Lady Poverty.

He had a dream that God was asking him to build up his church. The chapel of San Damiano had a hole in the roof. Francis took a bale of cloth from his father's store, sold it and took the money to the priest there. He then retired for several weeks to a cave to pray. His father caught up with him and eventually asked the bishop to help him bring the young man to heel. The bishop ordered Francis to hand back the money to his father. Francis agreed—and said "you'd better have my clothes too," and removed them. Standing there naked he symbolizes the whole complex of reform, simplicity and poverty. The bishop's servants brought a rough tunic to cover him. Francis went off to rebuild San Damiano and lived by begging. As he built he sang. One day the text at Mass struck him: "Provide yourselves with no gold or silver, not even with a few coppers for your purses, with no haversack for the journey or spare tunic or footwear or a staff." His way of life attracted two others, who became Brother Bernard and Brother Peter. The three of them wondered what was the will of God for them. The story is that they opened the gospel three times and found these three texts: "If you wish to be perfect, go and sell what you own and give the money to the poor, and you will have treasure in heaven"; "And he told them that they should take nothing for the journey"; "If anyone wants to be a follower of mine let him renounce himself." Fifteen years later Francis had five thousand followers. By the end of the century there were thirty-five thousand Franciscans. "Sister Poverty" exercised a fascination which is still most powerful today. The life and writings of St. Francis (and by association his town of Assisi) still draw men. Most men recognize the ideals Francis set down as simply impossible for them to act out literally. Yet few who read of them fail to sense the attraction. St. Francis lived a life of extreme poverty and penance. Whatever may be the meaning of it, his hands and feet became marked as in the manner of one who has been crucified, marked with what came to be called the stigmata. He died at the age of about forty-five, worn out by fasting. His life tells us something of the attraction which all other reformers were able to exercise when they turned to that call to simplicity and poverty which lies at the heart of the gospel. Francis sang this *Song of the Sun* when he was ill, half blind, after a night of pain and joy toward the end of his life. This song seems almost certainly to be one of many that Francis did compose himself, though we no longer have the tune:

> Most high almighty good Lord,
> Yours are praise, glory, honor and every blessing,
> To you alone, most high, do they belong,
> And no man is worthy to speak your name.
>
> Praise to you, my Lord, with all your creatures,
> Especially Sir Brother Sun,
> Who brings the day, through whom you bring light,
> Who is beautiful and radiant with a great splendor;
> Of thee, most high, he is a sign.

And the song continues with, Sister Moon, Brother Wind, Sister Water, Brother Fire, Mother Earth, Sister Death.

Innocent III had said he would allow no further religious orders to be founded. He had already relented over St. Dominic. The *poverello* soon got under his skin. Francis was no mere provincial. His short life included a visit to the Middle East to the crusading armies in order to try to mediate between them and Islam. He succeeded in reducing the incidence of war between towns in Umbria. It is difficult not to view the story of Francis as myth.

But in fact his life is of outstanding historical importance. It reveals precisely that religious dimension without a recognition of which history cannot be written properly. He reveals both the power of the reforming movements and the power of Christianity within its conventional structure. His life speaks with an insistence like that of the gospel; it has that element of protest, of single-mindedness, conversion, simplicity—in fact of charity, of faith and hope—which will lie at the heart of the sixteenth-century Reformation as of all genuine Christianity.

The line between heresy and orthodox piety was by no means clear-cut. Papal policy was not tyrannically insensitive. The local church was commonly more prejudiced than Roman authority. No doubt some of those who were eventually condemned could not accept any kind of a minimum of teaching such as would have kept them in communion with the papal Church. It seems almost impossible to make an accurate assessment here. The impulse towards poverty and simplicity and towards a deepened spiritual or mystical life was tremendously strong. At first the attitude of authority was not as hard and fast as it was to become later. But later Pope Gregory IX regularized various inquisitional procedures already being operated and the Inquisition became a part of the Church's armory. It tended to treat Cathari and Waldensians as indistinguishable, thereby throwing the two movements into each other's arms. The Waldensians took on some of the esoteric dogmatism of the Cathari. They took over the Cathar last rite, the *consolamentum,* during which a copy of the Gospel of St. John was laid on the head of the dying person. Anyone who recovered was thereafter one of the "perfect." This streak of esoteric ritualism was not typical of the Waldensians, who have some claim to be called proto-Protestants. They took the Bible as their authority and generally tended to object to the Cathar priesthood. They accepted baptism but not the other sacraments.

The Waldensians eventually spread to many parts of Europe, from the Polish border to the Pyrenees and into Spain but not into England. The parallel between them and the followers of St. Francis is striking. Both groups spread with great rapidity through Europe. In both cases the attraction was simplicity and poverty, mirroring the gospel text. The history of the Franciscan order during its first century is important here. There was continual

controversy in it about the nature of the poverty on which the
order was based. Francis had written a rule for his first few
followers; it was personal, simple, ascetic. Like the gospel, it could
not be followed to the letter by more than a handful of people
round the leader. But the Church had to do something about the
35,000 followers. The refusal of ecclesiastical authority to allow an
outright following of total poverty as an ideal, in the way recommended by Francis and by Jesus in the gospel, led to breakaway groups, notably the Fraticelli in central and southern Italy
and in Sicily and the Michaelists, or Fraticelli de opinione.

Within a short time the Waldensians became sufficiently
numerous and widespread and sufficiently much of a missionary
body to need to have a general conference. This they held at
Bergamo in 1218. The points they discussed were baptism, which
they upheld; work or manual labor, which was not to be undertaken by the perfecti (the title taken over from the Cathari);
marriage, which they disapproved of for the perfecti. Sinners
could not consecrate the Eucharist—in time they accepted the
doctrine that any just man may celebrate the Eucharist. It is a
measure of their power that they were able to hold this council
at Bergamo. In practice the papal Church was not yet an organization that automatically persecuted anyone who organized
themselves as Christians outside the established structure. The
Waldensians were clearly tolerated in practice by civil and
ecclesiastical authority or they could not have held this council.
They and their work of Bible translation spread far and wide
across Europe.

Two other groups need to be mentioned. The Flagellants, first
appearing in Perugia, only forty miles from Assisi, in 1260, took
up the ascetic theme in the Gospels, which we have seen already
in the Cathari and Waldensians, and in St. Francis. They traveled
around, giving public displays of self-flagellation as penance for
men's sins. They were condemned as heretical many times by
various bishops. They were often linked with Joachism. People
inspired by the prophecies of Joachim of Fiore were found throughout the Church and probably in most of the heretical groups.
Preaching at the end of the twelfth century Joachim, abbot of
a Cistercian monastery in Calabria, left it to found a new order,
preached the opening of the third era of the Holy Spirit (the
first, that of the Father, from Creation till A.D. 1; the second, that

of the Son, till about 1260) and the need to prepare for it. His warnings and prophecies together with a real insight into Christianity, and an understanding of the linear, rather than cyclical, nature of history recommended him to many people for many centuries. The apocalyptic, prophetic, eschatological, millennial factors in the Bible were taken up by him, and found a ready ear. It is difficult to predicate a distinctive influence just because it ranged so widely. Christians see "judgment" in calamities. Joachim's words were a comfort in a world of calamities, the mechanisms of which were in so many cases not known.

The Flagellants and Joachists grew more extreme and more numerous; and authority tended to get more rigorous. For instance: ". . . Baptism by blood (the act of flagellation) had replaced all penance and the other sacraments. . . . The barefooted monks of Joachim's vision had given way to the scourged bodies of the Flagellants. . . . Under the inquisitor, Henry of Schönfeld, who was dispatched there, the sect was hunted out at Sangerhausen between 1414 and 1416. His first visitation resulted in well over 100 persons being burned at Sangerhausen. . . . Survivors still remained . . . Three hundred were discovered at Sangerhausen. Penances were imposed upon those who repented; the others were handed over to the secular arm. But, after the inquisitor had departed, the princes gathered them together and had them all burned . . ." (Leff, p. 493.)

But this is to look far ahead, a hundred and fifty years. The thirteenth century is dominated by St. Francis, totally poor, totally obedient, the first known stigmatic, founder of a movement which failed to survive with anything like its original character, prophetic sign of the need for more flexible structures in the Church.

The Fourteenth Century, the Beginning of the Breakup

Through all the movements of reform and protest, whether aimed specifically to return to apostolic simplicity and poverty, or to reform the Church, or to return to the Bible, or to reject the priesthood and sacraments, ran a thread of that desire for God, for union with him, which was at the heart of Christianity. During the fourteenth century this motive inspired a great new movement of mysticism. It did not start suddenly anywhere; it inherited much from the great men of the past, including St. Bernard, St. Augustine, and the Neoplatonist Denis the Areopagite. Dominican friars, members of the Order of Preachers founded by St. Dominic, were in the forefront of the movement. Most famous was Thomas Aquinas, philosopher and theologian; his thought revolved ultimately round the nature of man as created by and for God, and round the incarnation of the Word of God. Dominicans of the next two generations in some sense stand on his shoulders in their mystical explorations, notably three Rhineland preachers, Eckhart, followed by Tauler and Suso. Many convents in the Rhineland and in the Low Countries became centers of mystical prayer. They and their Dominican teachers were accused from time to time of pantheism, or of too great a passivity in their explanation of the Christian life. This was inevitable in any systematic intellectual attempt to understand how man can become united with God. Ruysbroeck in the Low Countries was another, perhaps the greatest, of these mystical teachers. In England there was a similar flowering.

This orthodox mystical movement had its heretical counterpart in a movement called The Free Spirit, which purported to enable a man to die to himself so completely that he was no longer involved with the actions of the body.[7] The orthodox expression of initiation into Christianity first proposed by St. Paul was that in baptism a man goes down into the waters of death with the crucified Christ, a death to oneself, to rise again a new man, clothed with the risen Christ. Similar expressions were used by the devotees of The Free Spirit to justify the idea that when a man had passed through a mystical death he was detached from all the actions of his body and could allow it to do as it wished in matters of eating, sexual desire, and all other bodily functions and impulses.

The orthodox and the heretical met in the new movement of lay people living in small communities of men or of women called Beghards and Beguines. These were people who wished to live a religious life but without taking vows. They worked at weaving or teaching or nursing or copying books, and sometimes kept regular hours of devotion and a certain religious discipline in their houses. These were most numerous at first in the Rhineland, where the mystical movement arose. From there they spread out widely

[7] This description of The Free Spirit depends on Leff, who is not accepted by all historians.

through Europe, though not into England. In some places they fell into the hands of devotees of The Free Spirit. In other places they remained quite orthodox. In most places they were enthusiastic, as we saw in the previous chapter, to read the Scriptures in their own language.

In the Netherlands in the last two decades of the century the movement which we have already referred to, the Devotio Moderna grew up—the Brothers of the Common Life, founded by Gerhard Groote at Deventer and the Austin canons at Windesheim, one of whom was Thomas à Kempis, author of *The Imitation of Christ*. They wanted to get away from the long liturgical rites, from elaborate theology, and to live instead a simple life of work and prayer, encouraging a rather individualistic piety. "A community of the Common Life," says David Knowles, "stands halfway between a medieval friary and a devout Puritan or Quaker household of the sixteenth or seventeenth century."[8] They usually settled in a town where they could be of service to the community. The work they did most commonly was to copy books for the universities. All this movement remained orthodox and in communion with Rome. Both Erasmus and Luther, as a young boy for a year, were to be taught by the Brothers.

All these developments at the grass roots tended not to be accompanied by appropriate developments in the bureaucracy, through the whole range of ecclesiastical organizational procedures. We have already seen the misjudged attempt in many parts of Europe to discourage or prevent by force the reading of Scripture in the vernacular, by those who could read but did not know Latin. The same lack of vision is found in many other spheres, or perhaps rather the failure of authority to act on the vision of spiritual leaders. The Church became hamstrung by its belief that everything must be done by means of a rigid legal structure, working always from the top downwards—a system parallel to but in fact much more strict than the structure of empire, nation and commune. The occasional lay person who emerged as a power in the Church, such as St. Catherine of Siena or St. Francis, was looked on as a strange exception. The laity as a whole were the sheep, to be fed and fleeced, as

[8] *The Middle Ages*, Vol. II of *The Christian Centuries* (Darton, Longman and Todd, London; McGraw-Hill, New York; 1969).

many a medieval joke had it. In the social, the political and economic spheres the continuity of village and town owed a great deal to local common sense, organization and leadership. The Church had nothing but its parish guilds as some kind of a grass roots community where people might take an initiative. There was nothing in the Church comparable with the movements by which serfs were gaining their "freedom" in some places, towns becoming self-governing in others. The laity and junior clergy continued often to be treated by their superiors like the serfs of the early Middle Ages.

Forms of teaching and general attitudes suitable to the Dark Ages were no longer appropriate to the emerging society. Not always very close to the gospel, some of these had become enshrined in canon law and in received theological categories, and were very difficult to adapt. The concept of the "treasury of merits" amassed by Christ and saints, although in origin an attempt to express the unity and mutual interdependence of all Christians living and dead round Christ, became an abuse when the Church claimed to be able to pay out spiritual goods from this treasury in terms of "indulgences," which in practice could be bought, and which in practice contributed to the financial treasury on which the bureaucracy lived. Again there is the idea of the religious life as a better life than that of the layman, and of the bishop's life as "perfect," a blend of contemplation and activity in a life entirely dedicated to being the shepherd of Christ's flock. We have already seen what so many Christians really felt about the gospel, from their response to St. Francis and to the Waldensians.

How could people think of the bishop as living a "perfect" life when many of the men who were put into this office were palpably unsuitable, arriving there by virtue of bribery and the will of the local ruler, when the Pope was "exiled" at Avignon, guest of the king of Naples? It is not, however, a matter primarily of the poor quality of these men, but of the fact that the organization and its theological suppositions left the laity and the junior clergy as a kind of "also ran," subjects to be administered. A significant proportion of this laity were becoming increasingly aware of themselves as Christians, each of them having a vocation, or at least a spiritual destiny. The general critical attitude to every official part of the Church is sharply illustrated by the attitude of Gerson to his sisters, whom he advised not to become nuns, but to follow a devout life at home. To another he wrote: "I dare not advise you to enter a monastery." Here is one of the great intellectuals of the end of the fourteenth and beginning of the fifteenth century, chancellor of the University of Paris, hammer of Hus, showing himself to be deeply skeptical about the true spiritual worth of one of the central pillars of the whole structure. He would have been the last to deny that contemplation of God, prayer, and the spiritual life, were the essential basis of Christian life. But was it often to be found in the religious houses, where above all, in theory, were to be seen those who professed to be specially dedicated to it? He thought not, apparently. He also boasted of having encouraged no more than one man to become a priest, which is echoed by the plea of Thomas More in the sixteenth century for fewer priests and better.

The bases of society were already beginning to be recognized as inevitably to some extent democratic—the voice of the king has the force of law because the people will it, as one formula had it. Ecclesiastical authority set its face rigorously against any such attitude in Church affairs, in spite of theories of canonists such as Hostiensis (thirteenth century), who traced authority in the Church back to its own corporate nature. And this was a major factor in increasing the quantity and quality of the reformers. Only in the twentieth century has the papal Church finally begun to abandon its autocratic attitude in the revolution to be seen in the texts of the Second Vatican Council, where some of what the reformers began to fight for in the early part of the sixteenth century is now found transposed to fit with a developed Catholicism.

The Church had become a kind of super-state. Instead of its great skill in the realms of the law, finance and administration being put at the service of its spiritual purposes, this skill began to be exercised in its own right and to provide the primary criteria. On all occasions the book that lay ready to be consulted was the book of canon law. This was more practical than an attitude which supposed that every problem could find an answer immediately by consulting texts from Scripture. But ultimately canon law derived its own authority from a faith that Scripture spoke of revealed truth. It was necessary, then, for all ecclesiastical problems to be resolved in the light of the whole of this scriptural faith. And it was necessary to realize that canon law was no more than a necessary means of providing a set of rules or norms, which would always be in need of modification. In practice finance began to dominate; law was its tool and a theology of ecclesiastical authority its justification. At the same time the Pope and his administration, along with that of many bishops, began to fall under various degrees of pressure and control from secular states, the Pope himself living at Avignon, and this at the very time when the papacy had just issued its most stunning claim to jurisdiction over all men and over all their affairs in the bull *Unam Sanctam* (1302), issued by Pope Boniface VIII. Its failure to find general acceptance led to a mounting number of decrees of excommunication. The system was unable to digest the thinkers who now began to appear, thinkers who were beginning to insist on a certain autonomy for their disciplines.

Marsilius and Ockham

Marsilius of Padua made manuscripts of his *Defensor Pacis* public in 1324, at first anonymously. It had a great influence from that time onwards until the present day. Wycliffe and Hus read it. Sixteenth-century thinkers and politicians were influenced by it more greatly still. Marsilius' work was perhaps the first methodical attempt to rethink the whole nature of the Church as a body. Knowles describes his mind as being like an oxy-acetylene flame cutting through the whole fabric of society. Marsilius' first point was the fundamental one that the Church is a spiritual body and was not intended by its founder to wield coercive power. He wants the Pope (as also the emperor) to be a constitutional monarch. Marsilius read the Gospels and the rest of the New Testament and some other meager historical materials to try to see what the Church was really like in its origin. He came to the conclusion that Peter's position was purely personal, that his status had not been transmitted to the Pope as Christ's vicar; that there was only one head of the Church, Christ; and that to be bishop of Rome was that and no more. He denied the customary interpretation of the classic gospel text: "Thou art Peter, and on this rock I will found my church." He said that the rock was not Peter, but Christ. The papacy was a purely human institution. The Bible was the source of all truth. The Church he saw as a *congregatio fidelium,* the gathering of believers; ultimate ecclesiastical authority resided therein. "It is indeed remarkable," he wrote, "if we are obliged to believe the authority of the glossators rather than Christ, whoever be that glossator, even a saint."

Marsilius was closely involved in politics, and had one moment of glory in 1328, when as adviser on religion to the Emperor Lewis IV he took part in the election by the Roman people of an anti-pope to replace John XXII, whom they declared heretical. John XXII had declared five years earlier that it was heretical to believe that Christ owned no property. But the Pope prevailed. Marsilius was excommunicated, and died many years later, protected by the emperor, but as yet little known.

Marsilius took his theories to a far extremity and said that ecclesiastics should be as "slaves" *in forma servi existens* towards society. All power should be in civil hands. The Church would have no rights. Knowles says his theory reduces the Church to "a department of state or a kind of religious guild." From another point of view Marsilius might be seen to be a man far ahead of his time, for in the twentieth century no one asks for any kind of power for the Church—it is up to the Church whether its activities make it into a mere guild or a great body spiritually and practically effective.

In the fourteenth century it seems that the immediate effect of Marsilius was to add further to the record of moral protest against the worldly Church. And he raised this protest up to a new plane by providing a large-scale rationale for it in the form of alternative proposals. He is the first substantial sign that the endemic Waldensian type of reform proposed in the name of the Bible and of poverty was to be taken up by the scholars in the name of truth and given a full theological and philosophical justification. Nine hundred years had gone by since Augustine. Once again it was becoming possible to stand back and take a calm view of what authority may call schism or heresy. Marsilius prepared the way for a new assessment by providing an optimistic prospect of how relations between Church and state might be better organized.

Ockham, like Marsilius, took refuge with the emperor when he found himself censured by John XXII. He was involved in the controversy about property and took the side of the extreme, and schismatic, Franciscans, who wished to follow the original rule of

St. Francis. He followed Marsilius in denying the divine institution of the papacy and insisted, again like Marsilius, that the Church was the community of the faithful not just the clergy. Ockham was a logician in the first place. He had a very wide influence on the universities during his life and for the following century. He cut through all general concepts and ideas, propounding a nominalism which was a philosophy of extreme economy. It was based on a kind of agnostic epistemology—words are simply conveniences of the moment, and have no general reference. God and the world of theology are a law unto themselves. Thought about God has no relation to thought about the world. As with Marsilius the practical outcome was the predominance of the contemporary political setup, whatever it may be. The state was the beneficiary. But Ockham was less revolutionary than Marsilius, less interested in political theory. He was concerned to keep a balance of influence between religion and secular authority.

Marsilius and Ockham had an important influence along with many other lesser and subsequent writers in building up the body of thought eventually to be called conciliarist, which considered that a general council of the Church was its ultimate authority and that such a council might depose a Pope. Eventually it did depose a counter-pope, or anti-pope, at the Council of Constance (1415). As a part of the gradual build-up towards the sixteenth-century Reformation they are of great importance. But Ockham had gone further. He questioned the status of the institutional aspect of the Church, whether the operating authority be Pope or council. The majority vote is as doubtful a guarantee of orthodoxy as is hierarchy. His doctrine points towards an idea of the Church which includes all the living and all the faithful of past ages, back to Abel.

In the thirteenth century within the Church's structure and community, as Christian and reformer, St. Francis was strikingly greater than any of the reformers who were excommunicated. His devotion to unity and his loyalty to the Pope were entirely integral with his own ideals. Again in this fourteenth century a figure arose profoundly critical of much that went on in the Church, and like Francis one of the greatest figures of all history, but also like Francis loyal to the traditional community. A native of Florence in the early fourteenth century, and later banished from his own city, the poet Dante Alighieri was nothing if not critical.

In his famous poem *The Divine Comedy* he meets many famous churchmen, in hell, in purgatory and occasionally in heaven. Entitling a poem *La Vita Nuova,* he conjures up a whole world of spiritual and intellectual light—the beginning of the Renaissance. His political vision in *De Monarchia* is of a single world polity and a single ruler (the emperor)—a courageous vision in a fragmented political world. It has been called more an epitaph than a prophecy. There is more to it than that. But in one sense Dante is the end of an age. He is the last of the unquestioned spiritual giants of the medieval world to remain utterly loyal to the papal Church. After that the sands begin to run out. By the end of the fourteenth century rival Popes were excommunicating one another, undermining the credibility of the claim to be Vicar of Christ, doubling the burden of taxation on the Church in some places.

Wycliffe and Hus—The First Real Challenge

Marsilius and Ockham presented the first substantial intellectual criticism of the received systems; they were hardly as yet a challenge. In every previous century intellectual initiatives and innovations tended to be rejected. But the issues had not become mortal. The writings of Aquinas were at one point condemned by the University of Paris, along with Aristotle. Similarly in the previous century Abelard was opposed. But for Abelard and Aquinas these were rather personal occasions between them and their particular opponents, Abelard opposed by an abbot, St. Bernard; Aquinas, by the university authorities at Paris. It was not a matter of a head-on collision with the Church as such. With Marsilius and Ockham, it began to look something very like a head-on collision; but it takes two to make a quarrel, and in affairs of this kind it takes two parties to make a heretical movement of one of them. Neither Marsilius nor Ockham raised up followers immediately to the extent of a party which might challenge the Church on principle.

Until Wycliffe and Hus, the only challenges in this sense had come from grass roots movements, from the more or less uneducated, of which the Waldensian movement is the type. No intellectual had as yet arisen to lead a Bible-centered, anti-sacerdotal movement which would damn the Pope and the bishops as "Antichrist."

John Wycliffe, Oxford don, was the first portent of religious revolution on the full scale, as the unwitting founder of two movements (of Lollards in England, and Hussite followers in Bohemia) who took him as a symbol of their revolt. During his life little of this appeared. There were two condemnations of his teaching. The second and most definite, which drove him from Oxford, was only two years before his death. He died in 1384 while hearing Mass.

We have already said something about his teaching when referring to his translation of the Bible. Here we must refer to his public image, which was what really mattered. The time was just ripe for someone of his status, with his denunciation of obvious abuses in the Church, his confident and strange metaphysics, his initiative in getting the Bible translated.

What gave Wycliffe his importance was not really the specifically heretical nature of his writings; they reposed on a philosophy so strange that it was hardly likely to recommend itself to anyone else much, and it did not. It was the combination of factors which made him attractive and influential. His denunciation of worldly priests, bishops and Popes was perhaps the most virulent of all time—at any rate equaling that of Martin Luther. Much of Christendom was feeling the need to give vent to similar feelings. The fact that this denunciation should come from a typical academic with a mind able to construct an intellectual system helped to give his denunciations a special status. We shall see something a little similar happening in the case of Luther. Bitter and sincere prophesying by a learned don can sometimes be a very explosive factor. Wycliffe's theory about the Eucharist was only another scholastic attempt to explain the reality behind the theory of transubstantiation, not to deny that reality. And his theory of grace is not very relevant compared with his views of the Church and of the Bible which supported his denunciations. These theories led to an elevation of the Bible, and denunciation of Church authority which are precursors of the sixteenth-century Protestant theology. Wycliffe had a theory of the predestined damned, very similar to that of Calvin, and denounced indulgences like Luther.

It was a form of extreme Platonism that supported Wycliffe's proto-Protestantism. There was a Church laid up in heaven, perfect exemplar; and from this standpoint the deplorable nature of its current realization on earth was only too obvious. From this Platonic height one then jumps to an exercise in elementary logic which can be used to show that mankind is divided up into those whom God knows will be saved and those whom he knows will be damned (the *presciti*, Wycliffe called them). Now, any of the priests and bishops, even the Pope himself may be among these *presciti*. It will be well therefore not to be willing to obey them thoughtlessly; and they are in any case already self-condemned by their wealth and their luxurious living. Wycliffe suggests the elect are themselves nearly as good as priests. And Christ is really the head of the Church "the chief Abbot"; the Pope has usurped his place. For us on earth we have God's word in the form of the Bible. So we end up with a direct comfrontation between the Bible and the pretensions of the hierarchy, which is described as Antichrist. In practice, Wycliffe turns to the civil state to discipline the Church and to run it when its members are not worthy, again anticipating the sixteenth-century Reformation and providing a theory for a practice which is as characteristic of the Middle Ages as it is of the sixteenth century.

The raising of the Bible to the place of complete authority led, as we have seen, to an encouragement of those who wanted to have it fully translated. And it set a tradition of reverence for Scripture in England which became the backbone of Lollardy in the fifteenth century and was carried through into the national culture. The denunciation of the worldly clergy was what appealed to Hus, who was probably also fascinated by the great corpus of the rest of Wycliffe's writings, although he always held himself uncommitted to them as a whole, including his explanation of the Eucharist. But Wycliffe's independence and courage, and his preaching of return to apostolic poverty became a symbol of what Hus felt must be done about the Church in Bohemia.

Hus was one of the mildest of reformers and one who proved the inability of ecclesiastical authority to cope, when he got himself burned by them in 1415—practically for nothing of great importance. He began to preach reform in Prague in 1402. His principal subject was the need for a clergy purified and relieved of the burden of property. Hussitism was prophetic. Prague was with Hus—the people, the king, the university. If he had remained in

Bohemia he would never have suffered death at the hands of authority. This was a national religious reformation movement a hundred years before the Reformation proper began. In general Hus was fighting the same battles as the sixteenth-century reformers. But he lacked the opportunity of Luther and Calvin to produce a reformed theology. Hus's movement prevailed eventually, though only after his death. For a short time there was a compromise between the Church in Bohemia on the one hand and the emperor and Rome on the other. But the Church in Bohemia became virtually an independent national church from about the middle of the fifteenth century. This was in no sense Hus's intention, just as it was not the original intention of Luther, or of Zwingli, to erect separate Christian communions on a national or regional basis. Like the great majority of all other reformers Hus, Luther and Zwingli wished to reform the Church. When excommunicated, they or their movements had eventually to accept the logic of the situation, and their protest was simplified into one of "gospel" against "law," and then led on to the need for new law. The phenomenon of Hus confirms the impression which until the fifteenth century is only a suggestion that the canonical definition of Church membership along with the idea of a sovereign (whether Pope or council) whose actions have for all practical purposes the sanction of divine authority not so different from a pagan oracle, is unworkable and is always seen by some Christians to be contradictory of the Christianity which it is intended to serve.

The ultimate issue between Hus and ecclesiastical authority can be summed up in the same way as the ultimate issue between Luther and the other sixteenth-century reformers on the one hand and the papal Church on the other—that of gospel against law. The whole event of the Bohemian religious rebellion and the achievement of a national church, for a short time in ambivalent communion with Rome in the fifteenth century, is important. For this, more than any other event, makes nonsense of the historical isolation of the sixteenth-century Reformation. Leff reasonably suggests that if printing had been available the Bohemian reformation might have triggered off further reforms all over Europe. And at this point we may well remember also the conviction of one of the best known of the historians of the late medieval Church: "It is scarcely doubtful that the unity of Christendom was preserved till the sixteenth century only by force. Had lay people in the thirteenth century been allowed the right to read the gospels for themselves, or exposed to the temptation to do so, and had they generally been able to read, re-interpretation would inevitably have followed, and Christendom would have been divided in that century instead of the sixteenth." (Margaret Deanesly in *The Lollard Bible*.) By the fifteenth century the evidence is widespread that access to the Bible tended to lead a person to the conviction that the ecclesiastical organization of the papal Church was not in accord with the gospel. And already some of the other enabling factors outlined in the first chapter were in operation. A strong national and anti-clerical sense was part of the Bohemian or rather the Czech scene. And Hus himself assisted the full emergence of the Czech language.

Hus is sometimes described as a kind of second fiddle to Wycliffe. The truth could hardly be more badly misrepresented. Wycliffe was an eccentric, a genius perhaps, an academic, but a man with such a strange theological system that he could not be expected to have any substantial following. Nor did he have one. Wycliffe became famous because he inspired the translation of the Bible and left behind him a breach in the ecclesiastical establishment which provided opportunity for a general movement of dissent, ironically among the same poor and simple who had joined the Waldensians. Although Wycliffe did inspire Hus and became for him a kind of symbol of integrity and independence, Hus did not in fact propagate Wycliffe's complete philosophical system in all its extremism, nor did he propagate his theological views, in particular not Wycliffe's eucharistic theory. Hus did have in common with Wycliffe, as with virtually all other reformers, protest against abuses in the Church.

In 1360 Emperor Charles IV, also king of Bohemia, had called in Conrad of Waldhausen to preach against abuses in the Church. The situation seems to have been even worse than in other parts of Europe. Probably half of all the land was owned by the Church, and another quarter by the king. Simony, and the laxity of monks and friars due to excessive wealth, were denounced by Waldhausen. He was joined in 1363 by Milíč of Kromeriz who repented of having gained a canonry by simony, and turned to a life of asceticism and preaching. Milíč in turn had a more important disciple, Matthew of Janov. He wrote a five-volume *Regulae Veteris et Novi Testamenti*. The foundations of his system were the Bible and the sacraments. There was an apocalyptic note in all three preachers, and it was part of their system to try to identify the Antichrist. Their belief that a kind of crisis of evil was present in their day was illustrated by the Great Schism, Pope and anti-pope opposing one another; and the scandal of a divided papacy was an important influence, as indeed it was on many other preachers throughout Europe. Janov recommended frequent communion for both lay people and priests. He was the most important of a band of reformers and preachers who provided the circumstances for Hus's own rise to fame.

Hus studied at Prague University from 1386 to 1396. He was ordained priest in 1401 and became dean of the Faculty of Arts in 1401. In 1402 he became rector and preacher at the Bethlehem Chapel in Prague. This chapel had been founded by a Prague merchant, Wenceslas Kriz, precisely to promote preaching in the vernacular. Hus was not an original thinker, and it was doubtless the virtuosity of Wycliffe's writing which attracted him. There was perhaps also a certain glamour attaching to these writings from the far northwestern university, which had been the subject of a local condemnation; and King Charles IV's daughter, Anne, had been queen of England, wife of King Richard II. It is important to note that no definitive condemnation of Wycliffe as a heretic was promulgated until the Council of Constance, at which Hus himself suffered.

The first showdown in Prague was in 1403, when the University Chapter voted a condemnation of forty-five articles taken from Wycliffe's writing. The voting was three to one. The three votes were those of the representatives from the three "German" nations, Bavaria, Silesia and Poland. The one in support of Wycliffe was the Czech vote. The vote stimulated interest and aroused national sentiment.

Hus's preaching was largely against what he regarded as immoral behavior, the sexual immorality of and the financial exactions by the clergy. Other preachers and reformers went further on than he did, and their words gradually became attributed to him, since he was regarded as a leader. It was part of the tragedy of Hus's life that he was continually being charged with saying what he never said. The crowning irony is the history book cliché that he put forward the demand for communion under both kinds for the laity, incurring the description "Utraquist" (from the Latin for "both"). In fact he only considered this matter during the last few months of his life, in prison, giving it a qualified approval. But in any case it is not an opinion for which a man could be branded a heretic. Hus was first attacked in 1408, and was declared to have said that any priest performing offices for money was a heretic, and that he would gladly be where Wycliffe was; and he was charged generally with defaming the clergy. There was also reference to Wycliffe's eucharistic theory of remanence, that the bread and the wine remain totally bread and wine even though they are also the sacrament of Christ's body and blood. This theory occurs nowhere in Hus's writings. A further attack was made in the following year and various theories, similar to some Waldensian theories, were attributed to him, that a priest in mortal sin cannot consecrate at the Eucharist. This again is not an opinion attributable to Hus. The Germans at the university tended to be anti-Hus. The politics of the whole scene, with many international reverberations, were complicated. King Wenceslas came in on Hus's side and reduced the effect of the German vote. The Germans then left the university in a body in 1409, and the University of Leipzig was founded largely as a result. Hus was appointed rector of the University of Prague. Zbynek, Archbishop of Prague, was opposed to Hus and to his work at the Chapel of Bethlehem. He got one of the new rival Popes (Alexander V, elected June 25, 1409) to issue a bull confirming his decrees against the possession of Wycliffe's writings, also to ban all preaching outside cathedral, monastic and parochial churches—phrased to exclude the Chapel of Bethlehem. Giving effect to this bull in the summer of 1410, the archbishop decreed the burning of seventeen books of Wycliffe's, and a ban on possessing them.

The whole university protested. Hus pointed out that there is no theological sense in burning philosophical works, a description which applied to many of Wycliffe's. At this point Hus took his crucial step of disobedience to established authority. He had been forbidden to preach. He continued preaching. From this point on he is beginning to be aligned with the previous anti-sacerdotal reformers, and with the sixteenth-century reformers, in fact with "gospel" against "law." And it is from this time that he began to work out his own position, which he eventually set down in his

De Ecclesia and other writings during 1412–15. In his *Exposition of the Decalogue* (1413) he wrote: "The Word of God says: 'preach the word to all the world,'" and assured his readers that ecclesiastical superiors cannot exact obedience on this issue "except in such matters in which you are bound by obedience to God." In another reply to charges made against him in 1413 he said that while the Pope had primacy on earth, Christ was the sole head of the Church, and that some Popes had been heretics. At the time of writing there were three claimants to the papal throne. The Church might be without a Pope but the Bible was the law to which all must submit, Pope included. Hus never opposed the papal episcopal and sacerdotal Church on principle. But he wished to subject it to the judgment of Scripture. He is here a pupil of Ockham and Wycliffe and a proto-Protestant.

Eventually Hus's case reached a new Council of the Church at Constance in 1414. He welcomed the opportunity to defend himself. Wycliffe was still the central trouble; and while Hus never preached Wycliffe's doctrine on the Eucharist he did come closer to his general denunciations of Church practice, especially in the matter of indulgences. And it is highly significant that this matter, for so long the cause of popular complaint and disillusion (see Chaucer's "The Pardoner's Tale"), itself to be the touch-point of Luther's explosion, should also have been one of the principal causes which brought Hus's own affair to a sharp conclusion. Pope John XXIII had issued a bull of indulgence in 1411 to all those who supported a war he was fighting against the king of Naples. The collecting of the money and the granting of indulgences was farmed out to various people in Bohemia. Hus denounced the indulgence when the pardoners arrived in Prague in May 1412. This he did in Latin treatises in the university, and in Czech from the pulpit of Bethlehem.

Although Hus had been excommunicated several times, he was assured by the emperor that he might have a safe conduct to the Council of Constance, and that the excommunication would be lifted. But within weeks of his arrival at Constance Hus was imprisoned and was eventually condemned and burned after a number of confrontations with his accusers. Ultimately the charges against him were based on his refusal to accept Church authority. His accusers, Gerson and D'Ailly, had, three months previously, taken a principal part in the deposition of Pope John XXIII on March 29 at this same Council of Constance. It was pointed out by Hus that he was being condemned for supporting a theory which had just been put into effect by his accusers.

Hus was taken by surprise at the duplicity of the Church and imperial authorities in agreeing to hear his case, and then imprisoning him, also at their refusal actually to hear his case. His accusers were only interested, in principle, in accusing and demanding a recantation. They modified the accusations gradually, as they began to realize that Hus never had said most of the things he was accused of. But they were really not interested in a debate. They simply wanted to condemn or pardon. But this was exactly the aspect of the Church which Hus was not prepared to accept— this was for God to do, to judge, and to condemn or to pardon. An almost exclusively canonical or legal approach was taken to him at the Council of Constance. It did not occur apparently to Hus's accusers that the New Testament criteria might not be recognizable in their attitude. One hundred and three years later the same considerations apply to Luther's meeting with Cajetan. Luther would have little opportunity to put his theology or his criticisms, and was unable to believe that Cajetan, a man of great intelligence, was really not willing to follow an argument where it led. But his task was to judge, and so to enable the Church to condemn or pardon. The meeting was traumatic for Luther. Like Hus he drew the conclusion—these men could not be accepted as God's men, in the absolute kind of sense which they demanded.

The burning of Hus and, nearly a year after, of his companion Jerome, set Bohemia by the ears. The nation was united behind Hus's followers. Wars followed. The Emperor Sigismund attempted to impose orthodoxy on the Church there and to discipline those who insisted on communion in both kinds. Crusades were launched against the country. The moderation of Hus himself soon disappeared among many of his followers, who founded a movement in a new town which they called Tabor. After many wars and arguments some sort of an agreement was come to at the Council of Basel. It was finally ratified in July 1436 at a joint Bohemian and Moravian Diet by the Emperor Sigismund. Communion was now finally allowed in both kinds; but in one kind for those who preferred to have it thus. Priests were to have no hereditary property but the Church retained its existing property. The agreement was a compromise, and for the Taborites largely a defeat. Preaching was to be confined to ordained priests and worthy deacons. The Taborites had wanted to modify the Mass and the sacraments. However, the Bohemian Church had by now established a reformed tradition, with the Bible, not a bishop, in the place of ultimate authority. In spite of the new agreement, it was impossible to hold Bohemia as a whole within the organization of the papal Church. By the end of the century there was little contact between Bohemia and Rome. The great majority of the nation followed the national religious settlement, which was Utraquist and not recognized by Rome. A further large group emerged, the Unity of the Brotherhood, anti-sacerdotal and, like the Lollards in England, what one might call proto-Protestant. They survived into the eighteenth century as the quietest Moravian Brethren. The process of events in Bohemia was thus typical of the process of events a hundred years later throughout Europe, when in so many countries after the first revolt, a second followed in the name of religion, against the newly established Protestant Church authorities.

The Fifteenth Century

Throughout the one hundred and two years from the burning of Hus until Luther's publication of his Ninety-Five Theses a religious revolution was to be expected. It occurred in Bohemia. Possibly only the absence of the means of swift communication prevented it from spreading. All the ingredients of the sixteenth-century Reformation, except for the existence of the printing press, were present and active throughout the century. The numerous enabling factors which were outlined in Chapter 1 were gradually becoming more favorable towards religious change. And gradually the religious issues themselves became more pressing. Everywhere heretics continued to appear, to be condemned and burned. The Lollards had become important in England within a short time after Wycliffe's death. A group of them were members of the House of Commons in the reign of Richard II, and in 1395 they formulated "Twelve Conclusions" which enable us to speak of them accurately as proto-Protestants. Dickens[9] says that this manifesto "condemns the subordination of the English Church to Rome, together with transubstantiation, clerical celibacy and its untoward moral consequences, the consecration of physical objects (as akin to necromancy), prayers for the dead, pilgrimages, images and the excessive preoccupation of the Church with the arts and crafts. In addition it denounces the work of prelates as temporal rulers and judges, declares all forms of warfare contrary to the teaching of the New Testament and denies that confession to a priest is necessary for salvation."

The Reformation in England was to draw strongly on a generalized underground assent to these propositions, in spite of more than a hundred years of persecution of these Bible-reading Lollards.

It was a cumulative process. Eventually massive support would be available, all unconscious of itself, for any leader who might arise to challenge the whole religious structure. In 1516 Aleander, the papal nuncio to Germany, prophetically reported to his masters that all Germany was only waiting for a leader to arise to enable it to turn against Rome. Resentment against abuses grew steadily during the century. The papacy became more authoritarian, victoriously anti-conciliar, decadent and occasionally repentant, and aggressively secular both in its artistic patronage and in its political activity. The piety of ordinary folk waxed as strong as ever, and increasingly biblical, going underground where necessary, as in England. Theology, affected by all these influences, progressed towards that point where radical reaffirmations would be possible in a way that would be strikingly relevant to the abuses, to the decadent papacy and to the resurgent piety.

The abuses had become part and parcel of the system—nepotism, pluralism, the buying of ecclesiastical office to provide income for the Roman Curia, and the reduction of all questions to matters of law and finance. The literacy of the clergy, if it increased at all, lagged behind the increasing literacy of the laity. The sheer inadequacy of the clergy was widely admitted and commented on. We have already seen what so orthodox a figure as Gerson thought of the current standards of religion in monasteries and friaries. More than a hundred years later, in 1537, the papalist authors of a reform plan *Consilium de Emen-*

[9] A. G. Dickens, *The English Reformation* (Batsford, London; Schocken Books, Inc., New York; 1966), p. 24.

denda Ecclesia, recommended the closing of most religious houses. A twentieth-century historian who has studied the religious orders in England comes to the conclusion that the majority were so mediocre, and a few so outrightly bad, and so few really fervent that reformation of them was impossible to envisage as a practical policy.[10]

Anti-clericalism and sheer cynicism about every official religious procedure was to be found everywhere. Reform plans were endlessly put forward. But any kind of improvement was blocked by vested interests, which could always argue that their interests were those of the Church and that regular procedures must not be disturbed. Thus pluralists, priests and bishops, who received the income from pastoral offices none of which they fulfilled themselves, had they been challenged, would have argued that they were doing more important work, active on behalf of the Church in court circles, or elsewhere. Their income was used for a good purpose, and they could see little wrong in the procedure by which they paid some other person to do the work of the office concerned. Indeed the work and the fee they handed to other priests were gratefully received, for there were too many priests available for too little work. One cause of this superfluity of priests was that privilege attracted men to the priesthood, protected as they were by the Church courts. Today people who live on the dividends from shares in commercial operations can argue that they use their wealth to the benefit of the community, perhaps providing employment, perhaps doing valuable unpaid work. But the argument appears worthless if 90 per cent of the population in the same region have barely enough to eat or wear and are often unable to find any work to do. Eventually the 90 per cent may take matters into their own hands, in order to change a situation which many have recognized as unjust but which no one has succeeded in altering just because the changes needed are so considerable and would involve such disruption. So it was in the fifteenth century with the whole structure of the Church. The evil of pluralism was obvious and frequently described, the remedies equally so. But no one had the will to embark methodically on such a vast metamorphosis as was required. Eventually violence would obtrude.

[10] David Knowles, *The Religious Orders in England,* Vol. III (Cambridge University Press, London, 1959).

The picture is never entirely black and white. While abuses of all kinds were widespread there were also many successes in living up to the ideals of the gospel. Daily life still involved a tough piety, of the kind described in *Piers Plowman*—the ideal of charity towards Christ in one's neighbor, an intuition of joy and glory in religious song, building, and painting; in the family and the religious house sometimes were to be found Bible reading and intense prayer. The Christian motive and inspiration was still running strongly. The inadequacy of the clergy was counteracted by special missions and sermons, sometimes by famous preachers, though these were sometimes perhaps more emotive than truly religious. Vincent Ferrer preached widely all over Europe always in Spanish to vast enthusiastic crowds. Not all monasteries and friaries were bad. Houses of contemplative prayer lived up to their ideals. We can still boast, for the Carthusians, in the twentieth century, that they have never been reformed because they never needed to be reformed. Here was a strong Christian drive. It made possible the criticism and religious revolution of the Reformation.

Awareness of the need for reform often went to the heart of the matter, in its insistence on personal as well as institutional reform. That reform was to start with people themselves was emphasized by the man to whom the Borgia Pope, Alexander VI (d. 1503), entrusted the task of drawing up a plan of reform, Oliviero Carafa: "The first thing is that our hearts be cleansed within us." And he picks up a famous theme of St. Bernard which was again being repeated constantly by Roman Catholic reformers during the Second Vatican Council (1962–65). "Let the Pope realise that he is the successor of Peter, not of the Emperor Constantine, and that Peter was commissioned by our Lord to feed his sheep." Carafa was emphasizing that the business of the Church was essentially spiritual and should not concern itself primarily with temporal things. Rome was particularly sensitive on this matter just when Carafa was writing, because Lorenzo Valla had demonstrated in 1440 that the so-called Donation of Constantine was a forgery. This document purported to be a bequest by the Emperor Constantine (early fourth century) of his power and responsibility to the Pope, making the Pope in effect the temporal as well as the spiritual master of the world. As well as Valla, Bishop Pecock in England, and the Swiss Cardinal Nicholas of Cusa had come to a similar conclusion about the falsity of the "Donation," though without the rigorous proof which had been given by Valla.

When the Emperor Constantine was converted and Christianity became the official religion of the Roman Empire, from that time on the Church had a privileged position. As an institution it became for some centuries the primary structure and was itself the creator of Christendom, of medieval Europe. When European civilization began to develop its own momentum the privileged place of the Church could seem seriously anomalous, and, as we have seen, reformers and heretics began to contrast the gospel ideal with the life followed by the priests, bishops and Pope. St. Bernard summed it up writing to the Pope: "As far as you are concerned I hear of nothing but awards and 'laws.' All this, as well as claims to prestige and riches, goes back to Constantine not to Peter."

It was a very real dilemma. Christians had become the creators of culture, of politics, of economics and law. The Church had become an empire. An act of something like decolonialization was needed and was almost impossibly difficult. That difficulty still dogs nearly all Christian churches today. The Reformation in the end made little difference. Only the left-wing radical Christian communities sometimes succeeded in being truly poor and without privilege. Some reformed churches became state churches; others claimed status of one kind and another. Only at the Second Vatican Council did the Roman Catholic Church finally turn away from the policy of seeking special privilege for itself wherever possible. Only then was the doctrine formally disowned that "error has no right" and that the Catholic must ask for privilege for itself and deny it to others. Only in the nineteenth and twentieth centuries did the papal Church gradually disown the policy of being a state just like other states, a polity to deal and be dealt with on a par with other polities. And today in practice this policy has still only been modified, not completely abandoned.

Carafa reminded Pope Alexander VI that a Pope is surrounded by flatterers and is liable never to hear the truth about himself. Carafa's reform report was preceded and followed by many similar reform reports, none of which were effective. Nicholas of Cusa along with Domenico Domenichi presented recommendations to the famous humanist Pope Pius II (1458–64). They spoke firmly of the need to "transform all Christians, beginning with the Pope, into the likeness of Christ," and the prelates must start to seek not their own advantage but the kingdom of God. But it had all been said before by Cardinal Capranica in his *Advisamenta super*

Reformatione Papae et Romanae Curiae to Pope Nicholas V (1447–55). And it would all be said again in the reign of Julius II (1503–13), whose Venetian advisers became closely aware of the Church's missionary task and the difficulty she would have in undertaking it with the inadequate clergy (only 2 per cent, they said, could understand the Latin of the liturgy) and laity of the day.

The apocalyptic and prophetic factor continued to influence people very strongly throughout the fifteenth century, bypassing perhaps only some of the relatively small number of people influenced by the literary renaissance at that time. For the rest, many people were always ready to find a new kind of revelation in any catastrophe, or success, or in the person of any reformer, any leader. Among the less educated this continued to take the kind of form which we have already described as Joachism. Theologians thought also in terms, established by St. Augustine, of a line of virtue coming from Abel, and a line leading to Antichrist coming from Cain. There was always an attraction in looking for someone or something as the Antichrist. And it was perhaps a kind of terrifying temptation to admit the possibility that this Antichrist might be in Rome. This identification eventually made by Luther and other reformers led on to a permanent obsession in Protestantism generally with "the scarlet woman" which tended to tie Protestantism back to a medieval apocalyptic. The obsession was simply the exact reversal of an absolute and autocratic claim that the Pope was "Christ's vicar on earth." The claim in its crudest form, and its reversal, both seem to be coming in the twentieth century to the end of their history. But the apocalyptic approach, in general, is receiving a new lease of life, albeit inverted, in the claim of "secularist" theology to see all events as God's work.

There was plenty of apocalypticism in the fifteenth century. A document called *Reformatio Sigismundi* was widely read through Europe—it purported to be a revelation made to the Emperor Sigismund, also king of Bavaria (1410–37), that he should "prepare a road for the coming of the divine order because all the written law lacks righteousness. But it is not given to you to bring this yourself. . . ." Hus, whose name meant Goose, said, while he was in prison that they might be going to roast him but that after him would come a swan whom they would be unable to catch. This prophetic vein was taken seriously, or at least was adverted to as part of a significant historical and theological plan. Luther referred to this prophecy of Hus's when making his reply to the imperial edict at the Diet of Augsburg (1530).

This apocalyptic dimension goes hand in hand with the more or less suspicious, frightened and "spooky" atmosphere which was still a normal, partially pre-Christian semi-pagan ingredient of everyday life. Luther's mother believed that a witch had killed one of her babies. It links up with the obsessional concept of Roman authority as virtually equivalent to divine authority and with the willingness to torture and burn heretics. We find the bizarre association of the Renaissance with the world when Savonarola was burned in the great piazza at Florence. The great new cathredral with its famous dome by Brunelleschi had been built at Florence, where the Renaissance had its roots a hundred years before. In this town where the Dominican friars had been influential for a long while, emerged the strange new reformer. Fr. Savonarola, O.P., summoned the populace to abandon the pleasures of life and to burn their profane books and ornaments, destroy their pagan works of art, and turn to God. He spoke of visions and prophesied like an Old Testament prophet. Eventually he was hanged, and then burned, in the middle of the piazza at Florence in 1498, having been turned over to the "secular arm" by the ecclesiastical authorities, who had found him guilty of being a schismatic and a heretic. He had been throwing out condemnations of everyone from the Pope downward and claimed to be inspired directly by the Holy Spirit. It is very difficult to unravel the truth of the affair, to know how much Savonarola was perhaps mentally unbalanced, how much he practiced deliberate deception, how much truth there was in his confession (written after torture) that he invented his visions, how much of the real saint there was in him. Many did and do revere him as a saint—Philip Neri had a picture of him with a square halo. The new civilization and humanism of the Renaissance stood cheek by jowl with this barbaric hanging and burning in the middle of its own piazza, to be seen in a famous picture. No one could really say what were the rights and wrongs of the matter and they cannot do so today. Pope Alexander VI wrote some very patient letters to Savonarola, while continuing in his private life to deserve the denunciation Savonarola lavished on him.

In 1377 the papacy's exile in Avignon ended. In 1417 the scandal of schism and competing Popes was brought to an end by the Council of Constance. The following council at Basel, 1438, at first attempting to subordinate the Pope to itself, eventually submitted to the Pope, who moved it to Ferrara and then to Florence, where a superficial unity with the Eastern Church was agreed to and the end of the West–East schism announced. The conciliar movement was, as a movement, over. The papacy proceeded rapidly to resume its previous power and status. In 1460 Pope Pius II at the Council of Mantua issued the bull *Execrabilis,* in which appeals by any person or institution from the Pope to a future council were forbidden. The edict was regarded with detachment, unconcern, disinterest at the time. But it became a landmark. The authoritarian policy set by *Unam Sanctam* was re-established. Pius issued a call to a crusade against the Turk at the same Council of Mantua, although his humanist past had led him also to hope for some kind of reconciliation between Christianity and Islam, and, at the instigation of the Swiss Cardinal Nicholas of Cusa, who had been studying the Koran, to send a letter to Mahomed suggesting some kind of co-operation. Pius II had previously been known as Aeneas Sylvius Piccolimini. A Renaissance scholar and a libertine, he had written his autobiography in classical style, and supported conciliarism at Basel. His swift change to traditional papal autocracy leads us to one key to the nature of the papacy's revival. It was a matter of bureaucracy. The papacy was becoming a medium-sized political power. Its income from foreign taxes and the sale of indulgences and offices grew strongly through the century. The army accounted for the single biggest item of expenditure in the annual budget. There was increasing rivalry between rival families for election to the sovereignty of this "power."

Meanwhile in the Renaissance was brewing a really threatening twofold attack on the Church. On the one hand the autonomy of human sciences was leading to the growth of a world of skepticism, which would hold itself somewhat aloof from the official Church. It would have its most influential representatives in Erasmus in the first half of the sixteenth century, and Montaigne in the second half. But more important were the actual achievements of these sciences. As we have seen Lorenzo Valla proved conclusively that the Donation of Constantine was a forgery. Other decretals were also exposed. His science of philology was seized on by the leaders of the movement for a more rigorous study of the Bible. This was really the beginning of a battle which still today seems not to have been finally concluded, between the findings of science and the *ipse dixit* of ecclesiastical authority. Dean Colet returned to England in 1496 from a visit to Italy imbued with excitement just as Linacre, the English royal physician, had done a few years before, bringing the latest discoveries in medicine and natural science. Erasmus was about to start his journeying between France, Italy, the Lowlands, England and Switzerland, studying Valla and preparing for his work on the Fathers and the New Testament. By the end of the fifteenth century and early on in the next, Renaissance ideals and Christianity fused in such a man as Pico della Mirandola, who turned away from skepticism to an ascetic life and was not abashed when his only reward for some exciting religious propositions he put forward was to be told he was a heretic. The official Church was prepared to welcome and commission the Renaissance artist, sculptor or architect; but the Renaissance thinker came too near the bone. The trouble here was the same that we have seen throughout these four centuries. Theology's search for truth based on the revelation of the New Testament and respect for the search and conclusions reached by previous generations, was overborne by canonical procedures which took the definitions of Popes and councils as definitive and final interpretations of Scripture for all time. To see this crystallizing we turn back again to Gerson. Talking of Scripture he wrote:

"The literal sense . . . once decided and determined in decrees and decretals and conciliar books must be regarded as *theologia* and as belonging to Holy Scripture no less than the Apostolic Symbol."[11] When the ordinary people began to read the Bible for the first time, there was clearly going to be tension between the literal meaning of the text, as the grammar made it clear to such people, and the "literal" meaning established by the Church. Already Marsilius had challenged the Church's "literal" meaning when he contradicted the official interpretation of "Thou art Peter . . ." The Old Testament was the happy hunting ground of the medieval exegete—it was often not easy to establish for certain what the original Hebrew words meant; next to nothing was known about the background; so it was not difficult to turn the whole of the Old Testament into a "shadow" of the New Testament. Gerson declared roundly that the literal sense of the Old Testament was revealed by Christ. Until then apparently its words did not per-

[11] Quotation from Gerson in *From Shadow to Promise* by J. S. Preus (Harvard University Press, 1969).

form the normal function of words. It was on this point that Luther was to make one of his lesser-known breakthroughs, when he began to interpret the Psalms as religious discourse in its own right.

As well as the respective influences of Scripture and tradition, other theological topics central to the Reformation were being discussed in the fifteenth century—justification, and the relation of grace and free will. This latter problem appeared under the heading of semi-Pelagianism. This is the name given to theology which, without really meaning to, in fact allows man's own initiative to slip in front of God's grace, which St. Paul had taught to be the only and exclusive cause and origin of our salvation and our good works. This is a more difficult and profound topic than may at first appear. It is necessary to clear the mind first of all the ways in which man does take a free initiative, does make a free choice in his everyday life. This is not at issue. Man has free will—we are not arguing about determinism. We are talking theology, not philosophy, and are concerned solely about man's salvation, his conversion in this world to a life lived for God, doing God's will. Even then we may still get very tangled by the need for man to "appropriate" grace by his act of faith, to co-operate with the grace given. Is he not choosing his salvation in this act of appropriation? Theologians would say that even this act of faith is made possible by prevenient grace. Then there is always a temptation to say that man's good works are meritorious and in some way he therefore deserves this grace. The heavy emphasis on external acts during the latter half of the Middle Ages, on sacramental acts bringing grace *ex opere operato* (grace being infused into the subject by the very action of the sacrament itself, so long as he presented no obstacle—almost a kind of white magic), and on such activities as gaining indulgences (often by a cash payment) led to a practical emphasis on merit of this kind. Theologians were bothered by what seemed to be the psychological realities, that a man did make and must make some effort of his own, and to cover this they coined the phrase "to do what was in him" (*facere quod in se est*). Expounding the fifteenth-century theologian, Oberman writes (in *The Harvest of Medieval Theology*) that "this *facere quod in se est* is first *de congruo* rewarded with the infusion of grace." Still apparently interpreting Biel he writes: "the *viator* never knows whether he is actually in a state of grace, or perhaps has unconsciously committed a mortal sin." This is really legalism overriding theology. For while certain specified acts may be described objectively as "mortal sins," such actions cannot be described as actual mortal sins when a person commits them without full intention, and they would not therefore remove a man from the state of grace if committed unconsciously. Nominalist theology tended to be an intellectual exercise far removed from a full analysis of personal life. The kingpin of nominalism was that theology was a law to itself, and was something separate from philosophy and all other sciences.

Various aspects of the Mass were discussed throughout the medieval period. Two problems were dominant. First, what did Jesus mean and what did he do when he said "This is my body"? The question was always posed as a kind of challenge to belief: How could he give his body as food, and what actually was this action? "Transubstantiation" was a word coined to describe in terms of current philosophy and natural science the change in the bread and wine which it was believed Jesus had referred to. The second problem was connected with the nature of the Mass as "sacrifice" and "oblation." The Epistle to the Hebrews had said that Jesus had made the one and only necessary sacrifice for all time. Theologians had got themselves into a tangle, and theologians on the whole are perhaps still in it. In the Mass, they said, Jesus is present in his sacrifical form, but the Mass itself is also a sacrificial offering. This insistence on the nature of the Mass as something to be done as a good thing in its own right, apart from or at least as well as in its function of sacramental communion, was to be the jumping-off point of the criticisms of many reformers. Oberman writes of Biel: "we must conclude that with all due appreciation for his efforts to *distinguish* the two offerings, Biel does not suceed in showing their *unity*. . . . for Biel the sacrifice of the Mass remains a second sacrifice, proferred *ad provocandum dei misericordiam*— only historically related to the sacrifice of Christ on the cross."

Research continues on these fifteenth-century theologians. They do not comprise the core of Reformation prehistory. They are only part and parcel of the whole fifteenth-century story of the Church, failing to reform itself, and failing to release itself and evolve from its cultural and theological cradle, pegged down by legal precedents, and law books, giving to the papacy a status and an authority it did not act up to. The theology became more important in later ages, when historians and theologians looked back and tried to make a completely rational and integral picture of all that happened at the Reformation. But in fact the theological scene is very complex and in no sense clear-cut either in the fifteenth century or among the reformers whom we shall study. The concern about what Jesus did at the Last Supper became among the reformers themselves an even more controversial matter than before. In the fifteenth century the crucial matter was the inability of the Church to grow, and to allow room on the one hand for charisma, on the other for science. Fire could no longer contain them! It would have been possible for the Church to understand and to encourage the change of emphasis from *memento mori* to *memento vivere*. And from such a position it would have been possible to resist the amorality of a Machiavelli. The official Church did neither. Charisma and science were to break out and find themselves new permanent homes.

CHAPTER 4

Luther and the Reformation
Throughout Europe to 1532

The Program

The Reformation was programed. It is not just hindsight that enables us to say that there would be some kind of a breakdown of
the ecclesiastical structure. This inevitable breakdown had its roots
in the whole previous history of the Church. It would be motivated
by the same religious drive that had always motivated Christians.
And it would have the roots of its destructive and reforming purposes deep in the previous four centuries in the numerous attempts
to return to the Christianity of the Gospels.

The calls for reform of abuses and corrupt practices together
with a summons to greater simplicity and poverty had become
such a commonplace that an endemic anti-clericalism threw the
whole of the Church's officialdom into disrespect, even while many
people retained an intense devotion and religious sense. Indeed it
was partly through this devotion and sense of religion that a reform
could come. Translation and reading of the Bible had become
more and more widespread in parts of the Netherlands, France
and the German states, and a few towns in Italy. In other parts
persecution of those who wished to read the Bible in their own
tongue, particularly in England and Spain, had become quite
intense, but without achieving anything like final suppression of it.
The spread of a habit of reading spiritual and mystical books was
influenced by and helped to encourage the growing individual
self-consciousness of educated men and women. This in its turn
enabled them increasingly to look with a certain objective judgment at the Church's sacramental, canonical and pious practices.
All this along with what we called the enabling factors, that is,

printing, the humanist Renaissance with special reference to the critique of biblical and other received texts, economic factors, nationalism, and sometimes other political factors, had brought Christendom to the point where the ecclesiastical machinery and structure could be challenged—and when challenged would collapse dramatically in some places. By 1517 this situation had obtained essentially for some decades, and in some particulars for a century and more. Possibly only the absence of printing had prevented the Bohemian revolt from spreading throughout the Church. But even with the printing presses available a leader was still necessary, not just a theory or a program. In Luther the theory and eventually a program found a soul afire.

The power behind Luther's initiative was theology, and the courage of a man who is driven on by an insight he cannot deny. He did not object to indulgences just because they were an abuse. He posed the objection at the theological level. And this theological level itself involved a new combination of factors: an appeal to Scripture, an "Augustinian" attack on the current scholastic philosophical approach, a practical and pastoral application to everyday situations, all fired with his own psychological and spiritual drive. Here was the power: Luther's own disillusion, from his own personal experience, with accepted theories and with pastoral practice. The anguish he suffered drove him on to the spiritual solution which was then translated into practical terms for others. The practical bent was crucial. Luther became appalled at the third-rate spiritual lives which were the result of people treating indulgences as more important than sacraments, and in effect free passes to heaven for themselves and the deceased. Nothing like this could be found in the New Testament.

There was little in Luther of the medieval reformer's cliché of recall to simplicity and poverty. Yet the assumption of the need for this recall among people generally was important for his success. A large factor in his success was the welcome he had from ordinary people. Luther's was not the brilliant scheme of a political adviser such as Marsilius of Padua, nor the clever intellectual philosophy of an Ockham, nor the strange way-out theology of a Wycliffe. Luther's theology was always close enough to tradition to be taken seriously by everyone. It was rooted in a very wide and entirely professional knowledge of Scripture. He was able to deal with the conventional four senses in which Scripture was normally interpreted and discard them in favor of the one overmastering idea of God's Word speaking to me, to you—just as with Augustine. His thought was rooted also in traditional sacramental theology and practice, and in the German mystical tradition. His theology of the cross comes straight from the gospel and the Rhineland mystics. This hard spiritual vision, born of experience and prayer and hard work, was then given a practical orientation which knew just where the abuses really bit and why the rejection of them meant a fundamental rebirth of the whole Christian community. Four centuries of failed reformers had prepared something like a perfect seedbed among the people.

Along with this powerful combination of factors went others at the crucial moment: Erasmus' new version of the New Testament; the German disgust with Roman influence, which encouraged nationalist forces in Germany, from the knights to the peasants, to join with Luther; available printers. Luther's own small-farming and incipiently bourgeois background enabled those with economic resentments to feel glad to join forces with him. Here the history book cliché is surely just right. Luther did light the bonfire which had been built over many previous years. But like many bonfires it needed some special and highly inflammable fuel to get its sometimes damp contents fully alight. We shall have to look in detail at this fuel—Luther's characteristic theology—and the public actions which resulted from it.

This chapter follows Luther's life through from the beginning to 1532. His childhood years are not unimportant, for we want to know what sort of man this was, what sort of an identity this man had, through whom the Reformation was begun and carried through. The Reformation in its early stages and even right up to the present day was and is strongly marked by the characteristic experience of Martin Luther, just as the whole character of Western Christianity has been marked by the personal experience of Augustine. Although Luther himself remained living at Wittenberg for the entire span of time from 1512 to his death in 1546, and traveled only occasionally to meetings elsewhere in the German states and never further afield (the solitary journey to Rome as a young friar was 1510–11), yet the character of his writings and his experience, of his life, was to be deeply etched on the Reformation in all other countries. The printing presses carried his writings to them. It was the nature of his experience, his ability to express it and relate it to theology, to the New Testament and daily life, in both a critical and an affirmative sense which so frequently fired the imagination of other men and women, in northern, central and parts of southern Europe. The speed with which the Reformation events occurred was something quite new in Europe. Never before had established institutions and procedures changed so widely, rapidly and radically. To enable us to see this as nearly as possible as it occurred we call a halt several times in the course of Luther's life and survey Reformation events as they developed concurrently throughout the rest of Europe. If the reader wishes, he can skip the halts and read through Luther's life as a whole; and then go back and read through the remaining intervening sections. The material was written as it is printed, in order to get a kind of "stereo" effect, to convey the significance of what happened, the effect which we described in the first chapter as being similar to that when a new species emerges not from one pair but more or less simultaneously from a great number of pairs. But there is nothing sacred about the order of the pages of a history book, and there is no reason why the reader might not gain more from abandoning the printed order. The main point is that within two decades of Luther's first important public action in 1517, the religious changes known to us as the Reformation were taking place very widely in northern and central Europe.

Martin, Child, Student, Young Friar

Martin Luther was sent away to school by his parents at the age of thirteen. We know only too little about his life at boarding school, and even less about his infancy and early childhood. His father, Hans Luther (or Luder as it was then spelled) had interests at the time of Martin's birth in a number of copper mines and in a copper foundry, within another fifteen years becoming the owner of at least six mines and two foundries, also having a seat on the town council at Mansfeld. Martin's grandfather was a small farmer, and Hans had decided to move out into mining shortly before he married. He worked in the mine himself at first. We know little of Frau Margaret Luther. Some portraits of her show a striking likeness between her and her son Martin. Luther's strong piety, his love of traditional Church services, his attachment to Church music, were perhaps due to his mother's strong religious sense. He was baptized less than twenty-four hours after birth in the local parish church. Both parents treated the boy strictly, according to Luther's statements in later life, so much so as to leave something like a permanent grudge against this treatment, though Luther used to distinguish between his parents, whom he loved, and their behavior to him, which he said was due to social convention. He had an ambivalent relationship with his father, fearing and wishing to please him. His father was ambitious for his son, and had plans for him to become a lawyer; he was not pleased when Martin decided to become a friar. He made tiresome remarks at the dinner party in the priory after Luther's ordination. An entire book has been written about the relationship between Luther and his father—built up on a small number of remarks in Luther's writings.[1] It serves a useful purpose in making us look carefully at Luther's early life.

Luther is certainly one of those "great men" of history who while they benefited from exceptionally appropriate circumstances, raising them ever higher and higher in a mounting wave of causes all in need of a symbol and a leader, were also men with a special, perhaps quasi-pathological, mentality. In such men one sees perhaps a psychological power akin to that found in mental illness. There was a drive in Luther which might seem at times to tend towards the psychopathic—one thinks of his reactions of sadness and joy, and the general moodiness. Or it may be that one can see a drive of the kind related to anxiety neurosis or else connected with sublimation of the sexual and emotive life. It is impossible to make up anything like a completely convincing clinical diagnosis of some specific condition in Luther's case. There are too many unsubstantiated hypotheses. But events which did take place are sufficient to enable us to see a man certainly driven exceptionally fiercely at times. And equally there is sufficient written evidence for us to know that there was a difficult relationship between Luther and his father. Luther tells us that in his early life as a friar he found himself plagued by anxiety, always nagged by the feeling

[1] Erik H. Erikson, *Young Man Luther* (Faber and Faber, London; W. W. Norton, New York; 1958).

of guilt, fearing God, finding the crucifix to hang over him like a threat, overwhelmed by a sense of his own sinfulness. This took on a quasi-pathological dimension, with attendant physical symptoms, sweating and constipation. Luther allowed his own daily regime to be dominated by his immediate cares and sometimes had to shut himself up in his room for hours to recite the offices, to which a priest was bound but which he had omitted for a day or two and was canonically bound to make up for. It is reasonable to see Luther's relationship with his father as one of the factors lying behind all this, and predisposing him towards that need to find a total simplified theology of justification by faith, where actions were not to count as merit or demerit.

This is the far limit of what can reasonably be said about Luther's psychopathology. Against it, or at least beside it, go a number of other factors. Notably, as has been pointed out,[2] Luther made and kept many friends during the crucial years. He was also given posts of responsibility in ascending importance year by year. Neither of these things would have been likely to have happened to anyone at all noticeably odd or unbalanced.

When he first went away to school at twelve and a half to the cathedral town of Magdeburg young Martin was probably conscious that his parents expected good results. Not many parents would send their child off at this age, when he could be of substantial help at work. Martin helped to earn something for his schooling by the accepted convention of joining a small choir which sang in the streets and begged. At Magdeburg young Martin was taught by the Brothers of the Common Life, who may have helped the boy towards a life of interior prayer. Martin was only there for a year, and we do not know how strong the influence of the Brothers was; but their quiet pious regime chimes in with Luther's preference later. All that Luther recorded in later life about this year was the great impression made on him by an aristocrat turned ascetic who used to beg in the streets, Prince William of Anhalt. Luther says that although not old in years the noble penitent who "begged bread in God's name . . . was the picture of death, mere skin and bones." The boy lodged with one of the officials of the archbishop.

[2] See Jared Wicks, *Man Yearning for Grace* (Corpus Books, Washington, D.C., 1968).

A year later his parents decided to send Martin to another school, this time to Eisenach, site of the Wartburg castle, some fifty or sixty miles away. Frau Luther had an aunt there. Martin lodged first at the school, and then with a pious family who were friendly with the Franciscans in the town. Luther earned something for his keep by looking after a younger son of the family where he stayed. He was on good terms with the head of his school, John Trebonius, also with one of the teachers, Wiegand Guldennapf. Luther was apparently happy here, speaking afterwards of the "good city of Eisenach."

When he was seventeen and a half, in 1501, Luther moved on to the University of Erfurt. It was only thirty-five miles from Eisenach. While at the university, as at the school at Eisenach, Luther did not specially distinguish himself, though he did very well in his finals, coming second out of seventeen for his master's degree at the university in 1505. Luther was then 21.

One of the moods to which he had become accustomed gripped Luther a few months after this while he was waiting to start on a post-graduate course in law. He was given to introverted depressions. A fellow student had died recently. The exam pressure was off, and the future held nothing special—a course in law, and then a career in that profession. Luther speaks later of the "*tentatio tristitiae*," temptation towards sadness, which gripped him at the time. It is a significant memory. Sadness, in this Latin term, is akin to self-pity and despair. It is not surprising that Luther turned to thoughts of religious vows, of life in a monastery or friary, as a way to make sure he made the best of his life, and as a way out of this despair. For the despair had a strong religious dimension in it; he wondered how he could ever measure up to the perfection demanded by God. Soon after he began his course in law, things seem to have come to a head. Luther went home for a week or so. The reason for this we do not know. It was an odd thing to do soon after the course had started. He used to do the journey on foot. On his way back to the university he was caught by a thunderstorm, lightning struck close by him and he fell to the ground, at the same time uttering a spontaneous prayer begging for his life to be saved and vowing to enter a monastery. It was probably the climax of weeks or months, perhaps years of pondering.

Fifteen days later Luther was admitted as a postulant to the Augustinian friary, having held a farewell party with his friends on the previous evening. The Augustinian house had a high reputation in the town for its regularity and the sincere nature of its observance, being perhaps the best thought of among a plethora of such houses, for there was a Benedictine, a Carthusian, a Dominican, a Franciscan and a Servite house in the small town. That was on July 17, 1505. As soon as his father heard, he sent an angry letter cutting his son off from "all paternal grace and favour," since he had hoped Martin would have a fine career in the law and make a respectable and wealthy marriage. A little later another letter came saying that his father resigned himself to Martin's decision though "with reluctance and sadness."

As at school and in the university, so also in the monastery there is nothing recorded to indicate that Luther attracted special attention. It seems highly probable that he lived an exemplary, at any rate a normal life as a novice and then as a young ordinand preparing to receive the priesthood. Luther wrote later, "I know from my own experience, and that of many others, how peaceful and quiet Satan is wont to be in one's first years as a religious or priest." The sheer security of the community, the rule, the regular life, is profoundly comforting. There is nothing much to go wrong. There is time to pray without the feeling that something else ought to be being done. For Luther no doubt the community and its prior provided in a specially effective way a substitute family and a substitute father, in the short term a great relief.

On May 2, 1507, at the age of twenty-three years and six months, Brother Martin was ordained priest and became Father Martin. From that day his father abandoned the second person singular and began to use the second person plural to address him, respecting the office of the priesthood. Luther had been in the friary nineteen months.

This day of his ordination was a climactic day for Luther as for all others in this situation. Looking back on it fourteen years later he recorded the emotions of that day and the worrying experiences he had. On starting to recite the Canon of the Mass, the central eucharistic prayer, he said that he was overwhelmed by a realization of the majesty of God. This prayer in the Roman rite begins in earnest after the preface (which is technically part of it) and the

Sanctus. The celebrant then continues, *"Te igitur clementissime Pater* [Therefore, most merciful Father] . . ."; the celebrant is launched on the prayer to God, which leads eventually into the section recalling the Last Supper, and the words of Jesus, "This is my body," and "This is my blood." Luther says: "At these words I was stupefied and terror-stricken. I thought to myself, 'With what tongue shall I address such Majesty, seeing that all men ought to tremble in the presence of even an earthly prince? Who am I, that I should lift up my eyes or raise my hands to the divine Majesty? The angels surround him. At his nod the earth trembles. And shall I, a miserable little pygmy, say I want this, I ask for that? For I am dust and ashes and full of sin and I am speaking to the living, eternal and true God.'"

If this experience was part of a neurosis relating to his father, the force of it at this crucial moment might indeed have been terrifying. It certainly seems to have been neurotic, for Luther selected from the prayer just that which fitted his mood, omitting the greater part. Even these opening words refer to God the Father as *clementissime*—very merciful. And they go straight on, *"per Jesum Christum, Filium tuum, Dominum nostrum* [through Jesus Christ, your Son, our Lord]." In Christian prayer God is usually addressed "through Jesus." It is understood that Jesus is the way to God in all senses. God is no longer the unspeakable Yahweh of the Old Testament, ineffable, the one whose name should not be spoken. He is the Father whose Son has shared all our troubles. But Luther ignores this. It is certainly true that in spite of the formula which appeared in almost every prayer, the frightening aspect of God had tended to be dominant in popular piety. The New Testament was studied less than the old—as we shall see, Luther himself was to soak himself first in the Psalms, and take them for his first lecture course, a common practice. Even the crucifix had about it shades of the Last Judgment, "the Four Last Things"—Death, Judgment, Heaven and Hell. However we account for it, we cannot ignore Luther's description. He remembered being overwhelmed and stopping for a moment while he recovered himself. It is an important point in a life where the ultimate realities and the directive influences are all religious.

Luther's father was present with a band of companions, come on horseback. The actual day of the ordination had been fixed to suit their convenience. Luther, still so young, may certainly have felt so very much the "little boy" before this band of well-to-do citizens. His father had presented the friary with a substantial sum of money. To add to Luther's troubles, at the festive meal following the Mass his father brought up the matter of his vow in the thunderstorm, twitted his son with the suggestion that perhaps it was the devil or a pixie and not God who had inspired him, and further reminded his son that a son should honor and obey his father. This must have seemed rather ill timed. It is not surprising that Luther remembered it all so clearly. We may see the incident as one little psychological predisposing milestone on the road towards the statement of justification through faith alone, and the rejection of all meritorious works as of any significance in God's eyes.

From the time of his ordination in April 1507 till the following October, young Father Luther continued his study of theology in the friary and in the university at Erfurt. Under Father Nathin he studied the standard theology book, *The Sentences* of Peter Lombard, the twelfth-century anthology of biblical texts and excerpts from the Fathers. He also read theologians of the fourteenth and fifteenth centuries, Biel, D'Ailly and Ockham, while following the normal attendance in choir and no doubt having other duties in the friary. In the autumn of 1508 his superiors sent Luther to the friary at Wittenberg. A post had to be filled at the six-year-old university there, that of lecturer in philosophy. Luther could fulfill the obligations, while continuing his own studies. In the spring of 1509 he gained his Baccalaureus Biblicus at Wittenberg, and was given responsibility for lecturing on the Bible. In the autumn Luther passed the final university examination, which made him *sententiarius,* a degree entitling him to lecture on theology using *The Sentences.* With this we come in the autumn of 1509 to the moment when substantial firsthand evidence is available about Luther's development in the form of his own written comments in the margins of the great book which he used for lecturing to students.

Before we take Luther's story forward any further and look in detail at the first stirrings in Luther's mind of those thoughts and experiences which eventually led to his own characteristic theology and to the Reformation we shall make the first of our halts to survey the scene in Europe.

Europe 1509

In the rest of Europe perhaps the most important event of 1509 was the crowning of Henry VIII as king of England, "a full blooded seventeen year old on whom Nature had showered apparently every gift."[3] The reports of foreigners resident in London were unanimous about his astonishing looks, his fine body, his love of clothes, his addiction to exercise and his expertise at games of every kind. Hunting, tennis, throwing the spear, hawking, cards, dancing—whatever it was, Henry tired the others out and was ready for another meal and a further bout of some other recreation. Above all he was good at jousting and tilting. He was a gifted musician and composed a number of Masses, enjoyed talking theology and learning about the latest discoveries in astronomy. He had several languages, and learned some Greek. So it goes on. Name it, Henry has it or does it. He now married twenty-two-year-old Catherine of Aragon, Spanish widow of his older brother Arthur, who had died of consumption seven years before at the age of fifteen (the marriage almost certainly not consummated). Eighteen days after his accession they went together from the Tower of London through the city to Westminster to be crowned.

Activity against heretics was still strongly apparent in England. In 1506 or 1507 Bishop Smyth dealt with over sixty in Amersham and over twenty at Buckingham. There were abjurations in 1508. In 1510 Bishop Fitzjames of London prosecuted forty offenders. The London chroniclers reported a steady succession of offenders doing penance or going to the stake throughout the reign of Henry VII. Heretics were part of the daily scene. There were a lot of them. Some of the opinions for which they died were held in a more general form widely in society, so that many observers commented on the bitter anti-clericalism of London and of Parliament. It was one of the king's tasks in the first fifteen years of his reign to try to mediate between Church and state, Church and society, encouraging each to keep the peace. It is notable that after more than a hundred years of continuous cruel persecution, heretics seemed to be bolder and more numerous than ever, and this

[3] J. Scarisbrick, *Henry VIII* (Eyre and Spottiswoode, London; University of California Press, U.S.A.; 1968), p. 13.

without any kind of inspiration from anywhere except their own religious sense, their conscience and what traditions, including principally reading Scripture, existed in the religious underground of the day. It was this that was to make possible the so wide dissemination of Tyndale's Bible, and eventually to inspire many people of all classes to support the Reformation.

For the moment the accession was of no special import. Luther could not have been interested. Through the rest of Europe, events continued to presage some kind of eventual universal religious reform, but nothing of special significance was afoot. Maximilian was still the emperor "the last of the knights," unable to do much about the emerging consciousness of so many new polities, whether those of the countries to the east and the north, Hungary, Bohemia, Poland, Denmark, Sweden and Finland, or of towns and regions in France, Switzerland and northern Italy. He was aware of this fragmentation and tried to form the German states into a more definite unity. He had hoped by his marriage to unite Burgundy to the empire. He fancied himself as Pope at one time. (So also Henry VIII took himself seriously as being in the lists for emperor when Maximilian died ten years later.) The king of France and the Pope were the other two sovereigns who took part in a kaleidoscope of negotiations, alliances and wars. Charles VIII of France conquered Naples in 1495, as successor to an extinct line of Anjou. It was won back for Spain in 1504. In northern Italy, Milan changed hands regularly. Pope Julius II (1503–13) was a warrior Pope who led his armies into northern Italy to subdue Venice or France in order to ensure the greater security of the papal territories. He himself led his armies in battle. His energy also had an outlet in the commissioning of the great architects, sculptors and painters at the Vatican in Rome. Bramante started work on St. Peter's. Michelangelo painted the ceiling of the Sistine Chapel. Raphael painted his frescoes in the papal apartments. To pay for this work Julius established the fateful Jubilee Indulgence (1510)—eventually to be preached in districts not far from Wittenberg in 1517 and to attract the patronage of the citizens from that town, who then flourished their "pardons" in the confessional at home. Permission had to be given by the local ruler for these indulgences to be preached, and they were by no means always welcome, in that they competed with local church taxation and money raising. The Jubilee Indulgence was not preached in Spain at all. Under Ferdinand and Isabella Spanish national unity and religious uniformity were part of a strict regime. The Inquisition persecuted converted Jews. Conquered Moors were forcibly converted. At the same time Cardinal Ximenes followed an enlightened policy in training the clergy, which led to the famous Polyglot Bible project.

In France the biblical revival had already led to several editions of the Bible in French. Lefèvre published a new edition and more accurate translation of the Psalter in this year 1509, the *Psalterium Quintuplex*, the Psalter in three ancient and two modern languages, which was in Luther's hands four years later when lecturing on the Psalms to the undergraduates and Augustinian students at Wittenberg.

Events and movements were gestating, and when we reach our next halting point in Luther's life, 1516–17, there will be great signs of powerful influences, and new trends, though still nothing which would allow one to foresee the vast upheaval. In 1509 we may allow ourselves the fiction of saying there was something like a calm before the storm. Life is never calm for everyone and never all calm for anyone. We have seen various factors disturbing the surface and the depths at this time. But none were specially remarkable and none reached Luther. One thing we might remark is the absence of any signs of the humanist Renaissance in Luther's life at this stage. Erfurt had its own circle of humanists, influenced by the German Celtis. But it was another six years before Luther was to have his brief passion for humanism and signed himself Eleutherius. But humanism does lead us to one man who was already beginning to make his mark in Europe. We must look at his life in detail before following Luther through his first crucial seven years of life as a theology lecturer.

Erasmus

Desiderius Erasmus was forty-four in 1509, when Luther, in his twenty-sixth year, was about to begin his first public lecture as Sententiarius. Erasmus had spent his life studying, and only in the previous few years had begun to publish anything. We know that the Greek New Testament was to come in seven years' time, and thereafter many editions of the Fathers. They were the fruit of most of a lifetime's work. In 1509 he was beginning to become well known to the elite, and to be heard about by a wider circle. In 1500 he had published a collection of 800 excerpts from Latin authors under the title *Adagia*. By 1507 he had studied Greek and was able to add quotations in that language to a fine new edition printed by Aldus Manutius in Venice (1508), where Erasmus stayed with him and attended the printing personally. In the intervening time he had published two other important works.

His *Enchiridion Militis Christiani* (Handbook of the Christian Soldier) (1503), Erasmus says was written at the request of a woman who asked him through a third party to write something in an effort to reform her dissolute husband, himself a friend of Erasmus, and a man, as Erasmus says, who was "no one's enemy so much as his own." It is primarily a moralistic work, and secondarily a scriptural work. Erasmus frequently abjures his reader to seek only Christ, "have Christ always in your sight as the only mark of all your living and conversation." He makes various criticisms of monks and friars, and avoids theological terms. The absence of reference to grace and to the sacraments, and the presence of animated criticism of the contemporary Church make it possible to present the book as a kind of proto-Protestant manifesto. But careful examination of the book itself, and of the rest of Erasmus' life make such an interpretation unhistorical. The book is directed towards the moral reform of a particular person. It is the work of a man educated by the Brothers of the Common Life and a member of the Augustinians, whom we would expect to play down the formal aspects of religion, and concentrate on the interior life and on moral purpose and behavior just as the book does. The criticisms of the Church which occur in it are a commonplace of the late Middle Ages. Erasmus has the gift of setting them down in a suitably sharp and readable style. This book was destined to a wide popularity partly for its criticism of clerical abuse but much more for its pastoral advice. It was used by many for "spiritual reading," and was perhaps more welcome to some people than that famous work of the previous century from the same tradition, *Of the Imitation of Christ*, because it was full of a commonsense expression of the daily reality of world and Church. Translations were made of it into English (1518), Czech (1519), German (1520), Dutch (1523), Spanish (1526), French (1529),

Portuguese (1541), Italian (1542) and Polish (1585). In 1509 it was known only to a few.

The other book so far published at this time by Erasmus was his first really important piece of intellectual work, an edition of the *Adnotationes* on the New Testament of Lorenzo Valla, of which Erasmus had seen a manuscript at the Premonstratensian monastery at Louvain. Louis Bouyer has called this book "probably the most crucial book Erasmus ever read."[4] He says that Erasmus found in it the key to the reconciliation of the diverse elements in his upbringing and experience and to their future development. Valla had died as long ago as 1457, but his work had outlined a new philological method which enabled a scholar to approach a text, in this case the text of the New Testament, critically, with a view to trying to establish a correct text, and the meaning originally intended. Erasmus published this in 1505.

When he met Colet at Oxford during his visit to England in 1499 Erasmus got an invigorating firsthand whiff of Italian humanism, for Colet was just back from a visit to Italy and was imbued with a new realization of what a knowledge of Greek and a careful examination of the text of Scripture might reveal. Colet gave Erasmus confidence too on account of his ascetic life and high principles. Three years later, in 1502 Erasmus wrote the first versions of one of his New Testament paraphrases, that on the Epistle to the Romans with a commentary. Then after reading Valla and a second visit to England, he went on to a trial work in the form of a new Latin version of the Epistles and Gospels in 1506. And sometime then he began firmly to envisage editing a fresh edition in Greek of the New Testament. It was then he was able at last to travel to Italy, the land of the Renaissance, being paid to take charge of two English boys and their tutor.

As a man Desiderius Erasmus was a loner. His father was possibly a priest. The date of his birth is uncertain, 1466 or 1469, the place, unknown. His parents were both dead before he was sixteen. After school with the Brothers of the Common Life, when he was seventeen or eighteen, his guardian persuaded him to enter the house of the Augustinian canons at Steyn. He was

[4] In his chapter in *The Cambridge History of the Bible*, ed. G. W. H. Lampe, Vol. II (Cambridge University Press, 1969).

ordained priest and remained there until he was about twenty-eight, when he asked to be allowed to leave the monastery temporarily. He became secretary for a short time to the bishop of Cambrai, who allowed him after a few months to go to Paris to study at the university. Erasmus obtained a doctor's degree in theology and taught pupils in order to earn enough to keep himself. Then in 1499 came the visit to England, which may be said to have given his life a definite direction. In later years he obtained formal and permanent permission to be absent from his religious house. During his first visit to England, however, he stayed with the Austin canons at Oxford. In later years the connection was disregarded and Erasmus wore lay clothes. He never ceased, however, to be a devout Catholic. Contrary to statements in many textbooks, an old friend who was a priest was staying with him when he died,[5] and there is no evidence at all for suppositions that have sometimes been made that he ceased to frequent the sacraments.

Erasmus met the young English lawyer Thomas More, then just twenty-one years old, on his visit to England in 1499, and then again in 1506. The two became very friendly. During the first stay More introduced Erasmus to the boy who would be Henry VIII on a spontaneous visit one afternoon. Erasmus retained all his life a considerable respect for Henry's ability, his understanding of religious matters and wish to follow a right way through the calls for translation of Scripture and reform generally. During his journeyings in 1509 Erasmus thought much of his friend whom he was going to see shortly on a third visit, and got into the mood for English witticisms. Combined with the humanist air of Venice, where he had been staying with Aldus, as we saw, the thought of More led him to pass the time by writing notes for a *jeu d'esprit*, his *Encomium Moriae*, *The Praise of Folly* or "The Praise of More" if the *i* is omitted from *Moriae*.

To stay with Aldus meant taking part in a house party. Erasmus shared a room with young Aleander, later to be a leading member of the Pope's diplomatic corps, responsible for publishing the excommunication of Luther and of informing Rome over many

[5] See "La Muerte de Erasmo" in *Miscellanea Giovanni Mercati*, Vol. IV, 1946, referred to on p. 274 of W. E. Campbell, *Erasmus, Tyndale and More* (Eyre and Spottiswoode, London, 1946; Bruce, New York, 1949).

years about the situation in Germany. Erasmus' connections from this time on became very numerous. He met virtually everyone of importance, and at one time or another was revered by every one of them. At Aldus' house he found the regime very difficult —no breakfast, midday meal at two or later, an evening meal at ten or so. And he did not get enough meat. In the end he ate in his own room.

While waiting for his books to arrive in England he completed the *Encomium Moriae* and read it to More, and they all had a great laugh. It was all badinage. And yet it was serious too. Erasmus had been upset by the sight of the warlike Pope Julius entering Bologna in state. His book spoke searingly of the warlike activities of the followers of the Prince of Peace. It also spoke disparagingly of the deplorable state of the lives of many priests, monks and friars, as well as the perennial folly of mankind always taking himself too seriously. All is recited by Folly herself, in the manner of a classical conceit. The work was not very important, intended to amuse as well as to act the gadfly. But this short work is the easiest to read of all Erasmus' works and it became then, and more so later, a cause for people to think of its author as a mere superficial denigrator. Jedin (in *A History of the Council of Trent*) sees in the book "the grin of the sceptic." There are parts which can incline one to envisage such a grin behind the words. But then one must look at the causes, and it is necessary to admit that the antics of churchmen were sufficient excuse for an occasional recreational hour in which the claims of the theologians, and of Christians of all sorts, are matched astringently against the daily realities. The Gospels, after all, record that Jesus did this quite often. The record of Erasmus' life does not allow us to suppose that his purpose was merely to exploit his own literary gifts and his situation while holding cynically aloof. Search for truth and a new passion for at least a basic minimum of objective fact in religion never leaves him. At the same time it is certainly clear that Erasmus thought theology very largely a waste of time, while, however, remaining adamantly loyal to the Catholic Church and to all the essential practices and beliefs as traditionally formulated. By isolating the anti-theological facet in his writing it is possible to speak of him as a "dissolvent" influence, an adjective Knowles uses about him (and about Ockham).

Erasmus' eventual achievement gave him an authority second to none in Europe by the third decade of the century. And it is possible that people took the words of his *Encomium Moriae* (published probably in 1511, in Latin) more seriously than they were intended. Erasmus never departs from a more or less urbane manner. It is perhaps this apparent superiority of manner, so much quieter than that of Luther and many others, which strangely irritates historians still, so that few histories of the Reformation seem to be judged complete without a number of more or less irrelevant digs at Erasmus. But we must hear Folly speak, because so many people read the book, and it played its important "enabling" part in preparing people for the destructive side of the Reformation, inevitable but as yet still awaiting the great executive himself. It is this book which led people to say that Erasmus laid the egg that Luther hatched—a highly misleading summary of immediate pre-Reformation history! But we must see what led to it. Here is Folly talking about the theologians:

St Paul, no question, had a full measure of faith; yet when he lays down faith to be the substance of things not seen, these men carp at it for an imperfect definition, and would undertake to teach the apostles better logic . . . The primitive disciples were very frequent in administering the holy sacrament, breaking bread from house to house; yet should they be asked the *Terminus a quo* and the *Terminus ad quem*, the nature of transubstantiation, the manner how one body can be in several places at the same time . . . were they asked these and several other confused queries I do not believe they could answer so readily as our mincing schoolmen nowadays take a pride to do. They were well acquainted with the Virgin Mary, yet none of them undertook to prove that she was preserved immaculate from original sin, as some of our divines very hotly contend for . . . They worshipped in the spirit, following their master's injunction, God is a spirit and they which worship him, must worship him in spirit, and in truth; yet it does not appear that it was ever revealed to them how divine adoration should be paid at the same time to our Saviour in heaven, and to his picture below on a wall, drawn with two fingers held out, a bald crown, and a circle round his head. [Erasmus adds to these thoughts:] To reconcile these intricacies to an appearance of reason requires three score years' experience in metaphysics.

Metaphysics was of course the bane of the nominalists, who were still the most powerful school of philosophers. Erasmus liked them no more than the others, but he possibly inherited from them, as Luther did, an almost automatic assumption that metaphysics was something to be despised. His book written in the name of Folly is moderate by contemporary standards. And Erasmus is able to call in Ecclesiastes and Jeremiah to back up Folly in her belief that "Wise men of the nations are altogether brutish and foolish," or that "Vanity of vanities, all is vanity." In a few years' time Luther will be objecting to the inadequate nature of Erasmus' criticisms. They do not go far enough.

Erasmus wrote as a man of his times, but the historian can also see that he was heir to all the discontents and protests, all the progress and promise, which we have surveyed. He was heir to all that stream of reformers who were impatient with a priesthood that tended towards a semi-magical superstition in its practice of the sacraments, and who wished to return to the spiritual note that rings out so clearly in the New Testament. He was heir to those like Marsilius who wished the organized Church to mind its own spiritual business—an attitude which was also consonant with the mystics of the Rhineland, and the movements in the Netherlands.

The humanist movement was an intellectual and aesthetic movement begun in Florence, in the fourteenth century. Through it all was the growing sense of a new understanding of man, and a belief that science could reveal all there was to be known. Erasmus was heir above all to nearly two centuries of thought along these lines. It did not reject traditional asceticism. It did not reject the accepted sacramental practice. But it wished for purification, simplification, reform in the light of the new knowledge. In particular as the new knowledge reached a special point in its historical and philological aspect, it suggested more care in the study of Scripture.

Erasmus stayed in England almost continuously from the end of 1509 for over four years, and it was during this time that he resided for about two years at St. Catherine's College, Cambridge, teaching Greek, and studying in preparation for his editions of the New Testament and of Jerome, the years during which Luther was giving his first lectures in the priory at Erfurt.

Young Doctor Luther's Discovery

Having attained the status of Sententiarius at Wittenberg, the young priest Luther was recalled unexpectedly to the priory at Erfurt to teach theology to the young students there. At first Erfurt University was disinclined to recognize the degree given by upstart Wittenberg; however, they relented. In January 1510 there was a violent riot in the town at Erfurt by apprentices and small craftsmen against high taxation. The troubles continued through the spring. The old library was burned down. In June the head of the town council was executed. Luther expressed his disgust with the lack of discipline, as befitted the son of a town councilor.

Luther was lecturing on *The Sentences* of Peter Lombard, the normal theology course. He made notes in the margin of the copy he used, and this we have. He was also reading Augustine's *On the Trinity, The City of God,* and some other small works. Again the margins provide firsthand evidence of what was going on in Luther's mind.[6] It is not too much to say that the marks of an original theologian are already clearly to be seen. He is noticeably free, from the start, from acceptance of the usual contemporary nominalist structure. When he speaks of God as "ineffable" and "transcendent," the emphasis is not on the nominalist logical concept, but on something personal, religious and theological, as in Augustine or Bernard. He is inevitably using traditional theological terms, and one of these is significant. "Grace" is the enabling force of all good actions. Prevenient grace motivates and underpins all man's life. Wicks writes, giving many detailed references for this view: "Thus it is prevenient grace that gives to our life its character of ever new response to a call, to an inclination, to the urging to advance. To sin is to refuse this call and so to let the dragging force of concupiscence become dominant. Thus the Christian man, as Luther views him, lives under two influences, prevenient grace and an unruly and disobedient flesh. It is grace

[6] The best guide to this is Chapter 2 of Wicks, *Man Yearning for Grace.*

that makes him able and effectively free; it makes him the responsible agent who can assent to move ahead but who can also stand still under the inertial pull of the flesh." All this can also be found in Aquinas, who himself had been influenced by Augustine more than by any other. Luther's theology is orthodox, pious and intelligent.

On March 17, 1509, Father Martin wrote to Johannes Braun about his longing to take up theology seriously, adding in a characteristic Augustinian vein, "But God is God. Man often, nay always, is mistaken in his own judgment. Here is God's place. May he rule us sweetly and for ever." Gordon Rupp[7] selects from the writings of the early years the phrase *"Coram Deo* [Before God, or In God's Presence]" as their keynote. He and Wicks both comment on the young priest's preference for speaking of the Holy Spirit directly rather than of an Aristotelian "habitus," a category he finds inappropriate, when speaking of love. Aristotle and all other philosophers come in for a great deal of harsh criticism. This is Luther's first Augustinian period—". . . in the beginning I devoured Augustine." He was getting his first strong desire to master Scripture study, and was beginning to learn Hebrew.

After one year of this teaching and study Father Martin was sent on a five-month journey with another priest on behalf of the priory. The local "provincial" superior, Staupitz, was trying to bring other Augustinian houses into the same group as that of the Erfurt house. Erfurt was "reformed," and Staupitz was keen to spread the reform. But Erfurt and others were jealous of their status as reformed and preferred not to be joined by others. They decided to appeal against the decision of Staupitz. This meant a journey to Halle, to Nuremberg and then on to Rome. The 1500-mile journey there and back all on foot took Luther and his companion about five months, with a few weeks in Rome in the middle. It was wintry weather and Rome itself was cold and wet. Luther was interested in the various kinds of country and agriculture on the way. On the approach to Rome he was overcome with emotion and knelt down at his first sight of the city, Rome the eternal, Rome the city of the Pope, Vicar of Christ. "I threw myself on the ground and said, 'Blessed art thou, Holy Rome.'" He did the rounds of the basilicas and the *scala sancta,* and wished

[7] In *The Righteousness of God* (Hodden and Stoughton, London, 1953).

that his parents were already dead so that he could bail them out of purgatory with all the indulgences he was earning.

Erfurt priory's appeal was disallowed. As soon as Luther got back the reformed houses sent off another couple of priests to appeal again. This and the previous appeal had in fact been "out of order" in that no appeals were officially permitted in the circumstances concerned. Staupitz continued with his attempt to put the reform amalgamation through. The Erfurt house continued to resist—except for two of its members, whose names were Father John Lang, and Father Martin Luther. These two felt that the opposition to ecclesiastical authority was going too far. It is an interesting and typical example of Luther's characteristic approach. He is not a revolutionary by nature, and prefers to support authority where the subject does not concern some fundamental matter of conscience. The tension at Erfurt was apparently considerable and Staupitz brought the two men across to his own house at Wittenberg. It was a crucial decision. Staupitz had plans for young Luther and set him to get a doctorate at the university. At twenty-eight Luther became doctor of theology and was appointed sub-prior and master of studies in the priory. That was in 1512. A year later he began formal lectures in Wittenberg University. Father Martin was doing very well.

Luther's subject for this first university course was the Psalms. The course went on from 1513 to 1515. He got Grunenberg the printer at Wittenberg to produce a large edition of the Psalms for him with plenty of room to write his glosses in the margin—in effect the preparatory notes for his lectures. This precious book may still be studied by scholars, all but the last two pages. Luther also had a copy of the 1509 *Psalterium Quintuplex* of Lefèvre. There is another precious book in existence with longer theological comments written by Luther at this time—his *Scholiae,* and *Excursus.* About the time of the end of the course in 1515 he was appointed preacher in the parish church at Wittenberg. He began to preach there on Sundays and feast days to the townsfolk and continued to do so till the end of his life. Here was a further opportunity to develop his thought, this time in a pastoral and practical direction. It was a post he always treasured. He was also made district superior about this time of the local group of Augustinian houses. In this capacity he sent John Lang to be superior of the house at Erfurt. Here was a third post giving him authority at an early age.

After the course on the Psalms came a course on the Letter to the Romans, which occupied the academic year 1515–16; then followed a course on the Letter to the Galatians, which lasted till March 1517, when he started on the Letter to the Hebrews, which took him till March 1518, covering the period of the publication of the Indulgence Theses and the first months of incipient fame.

These nine years from 1509 to 1518 were crucial, nine years of studying, lecturing, preaching, and latterly of steadily rising administrative and pastoral responsibilities. During them Luther went through times of great personal anguish, and bouts of depression. He found no relief from attacks, temptations, *Anfechtungen* of acute despair, in any of the usual remedies. Spiritually and psychologically the crisis was sometimes extreme. But he did find some help in the text of the Bbile. He read Augustine and found him better fare than recent theologians like Biel. He read one of the German mystics, Tauler, and found a "theology of the cross" which fitted with the gospel. And slowly or suddenly, it does not matter which, nor does the exact date or dates matter greatly for our purposes, he understood that "God does everything." Staupitz helped him, as we shall see, towards this. But the personal and theological realization came in a moment of understanding. He could stop worrying. He need only believe. "The just man lives by faith."

This insight meant a great release. There is nothing, after all, that a man *must* do. For no action of ours can justify us in God's eyes. God justifies the believer. No need to worry any more about the unbridgeable chasm between man and God. Only trust the Father. The old law emphasizes the chasm. The man without faith must live by the law and obey it, he has no other way. So also citizens must obey the state and children their parents. But the Christian has another righteousness which is none of his work. And the Church therefore must not set up a new structure of obligations, things which have to be done, actions which can gain merit.

We are at the heart here of the drive, the energy, the seemingly endless resources of the Protestant Reformation. Psychologically there was a double aspect to this new-found freedom. There was the inner effect, what Freud would call a release from the super-ego—no more anxious attempts to satisfy an inner relentless and unappeasable lawgiver. There was the outer effect—the Church's laws could be treated, as indeed so many had always treated them, with a certain flexibility or altogether rejected, but now not for reasons of slackness and mediocrity but because they were seen in a new perspective. This is not to say that there is any evidence that Luther was anything other than a scrupulously correct Catholic until he became convinced years later that the authority of the Pope and those in communion with him was not necessarily to be accepted in the traditional way. But immediately he was able to tame his obsession with the need to confess his sins very frequently just as Staupitz indeed had advised him to tame it.

Luther's new insight was based on the text of Romans 1:16 & 17: "For I am not ashamed of the Good News: it is the power of God saving all who have faith—Jews first, but Greeks as well —since this is what reveals the justice of God to us: it shows how faith leads to faith, or as scripture says: The upright man finds life through faith." This is St. Paul's way of summing up the gospel message. Why, then, was Luther's repetition of it not accepted by ecclesiastical authority? The question in fact is ill put, because when Luther first began to put this phraseology at the heart of his lectures and of his sermons there was no opposition from authority. There were many discussions at the university and in the priory. But the majority in both places found no heresy and were won over by the exposition of the young professor. Luther had been drawing on Augustine and on German mystical writing and was not considered out of line.

Let us listen to Luther himself expounding his insight, first at the end of his life, and then in his commentary on Galatians. In the last year of his life a Latin edition of Luther's works was being prepared at Wittenberg. He was asked to write a preface. He made it autobiographical. We need to be cautious of Luther describing something that happened twenty-five or more years previously. However, the following excerpts, while being a high-lighted version of events described by a middle-aged man looking back on the time of his early manhood, are yet not far from the reality as we have it from writings at the time and not long after: "I had been seized with a strong desire of understanding Paul in the Letter to the Romans. . . . One word held me up until now. . . . I hated this word *Justitia Dei* which by the use and consent of all doctors I was taught to understand philosophically as that formal or active justice with which God is just, and punishes unjust sinners. For however irreproachably I lived as a monk, I felt myself in the presence of God to be a sinner with a most unquiet conscience nor could I trust that I had pleased him with my satisfaction. I did not love, nay, rather I hated this just God who punished sinners and if not with 'open blasphemy' certainly with huge murmuring I was angry with God. . . . At last God being merciful, as I meditated day and night on the connection of the words, namely, 'the Justice of God is revealed in it as it is written "the just shall live by Faith"' there I began to understand the Justice of God as that by which the just lives by the gift of God, namely by faith. . . . This immediately made me feel as though reborn, and as though I had entered through open gates into paradise itself. From then on the whole face of scripture appeared different. I ran through the scriptures then as memory served and found the same analogy in other words, as the work of God that which God works in us. Power of God with which he makes us strong, wisdom of God, with which he makes us wise, fortitude of God, salvation of God, glory of God."

The same teaching may be read in other words in Luther's introduction to his Commentary on the Letter to the Galatians (as in many other parts of his writings): "The afflicted and troubled conscience has no remedy against despair and eternal death unless it takes hold of the promise of grace freely in Christ, that is to say, this passive righteousness of faith, or Christian righteousness. Which if it can apprehend, then may it be at peace and say boldly: 'I seek not the active or working righteousness, although I know that I ought to have it, and also to fulfil it. But even if I had it and did fulfil it, even so I cannot put my trust in it nor dare I set it against the judgment of God. Thus I abandon myself from all active righteousness, both of my own and of God's law, and embrace only that passive righteousness, which is the righteousness of grace, mercy and forgiveness of sins. In short the righteousness of Christ and of the Holy Spirit; which we do not do, but suffer; and have not but receive; God the Father freely giving it to us through Jesus Christ.'"

This teaching has a twofold significance. First, it repeats St. Paul's teaching that the Christian is not bound any longer by the law of the Old Testament (he was referring to circumcision, which Jewish Christians were trying to insist on for all Christians) but is now to live a life of love, motivated by Christ. Luther transposed this teaching to the contemporary situation. For the law of the Old Testament he substitutes the law of the Roman Church, which, Luther is saying, has wrongly taken upon itself to command the keeping of all sorts of laws and the doing of all sorts of actions as pleasing to God, whereas the New Testament tells Christians not to live by fulfilling various prescribed laws of behavior but by the grace of Christ. What particularly concerned Luther personally at this time was the aspect of judgment on those who failed to keep the laws. He had been overwhelmed for many years by the current emphasis on judgment after death, and acutely aware that since he never lived up perfectly to the ideals set before him he could never be quite sure about his motives or whether he really was in a state of sin and was incurring the judgment of a just God. He would often ask a priest to hear his confession just before celebrating Mass. It was therefore a vast relief to him when he understood that the New Testament did not encourage such an attitude but preached a complete trust in God. The believer was justified, simply, in his faith. Good works were not required of him, but they would flow from his life of faith. God's justice, as he said, is not a justice of judgment but a justice by which he makes us just.

It was a simple answer to a profound trouble. There had been discussions between theologians in the fifteenth century about the nature of "justification" as about most other theological topics. But no one would have prophesied that this particular subject would be the one to set Europe alight, the one which could sum up all the centuries of dissent. Its ability to do this lay partly in its return to something which was at the heart of Christian teaching in the primitive Church, and partly in that it spoke profoundly to the current psychological condition. Luther's statement that he had always understood "justice" as retributive relates to the fifteenth-century theologians—this is how Biel speaks of it. And it is typical also of the obsession with the "Last Judgment" and hell, so frequently depicted by artists. But Luther's idea was not new. His exposition of "justice" is in fact also that of Augustine, and occurred in a sentence from Augustine in *The Sentences* of Peter Lombard: "The love of God is said to be spread in our hearts, not because God loves us, but because he makes us his lovers: just as the justice of God is that by which we are made just by his gift." Conceptually speaking, Luther's exposition was not new, much less unorthodox. But Luther presented it in a new light and himself added his almost obsessive condemnation of "good works" as meritorious.

In his exposition of the Psalms in these first lectures at the university Luther found the old methods of the fourfold interpretation of Scripture too arid—as many others had done in recent years. As he struggled with his own troubles, the Psalms chimed in with his mood. He concentrated on the "tropological" or moral sense, in a Christological direction. But he did not try to interpret the Psalms simply as something foretelling Christ. Rather, the words with which the psalmist addressed God, could be used by the Christian to address Christ—which in fact is a description of what had been done in Christian public prayer from the very beginning. Luther wanted to enter into the actual experience of the psalmist in his struggles. He began to find an analogy between contemporary Christians and the people of God in the Old Testament. "The faithful synagogue" becomes a kind of model and norm for the church. Joseph Lortz writes perceptively:

> It is highly significant that the point at which Luther struck up his lifelong association with the Bible did not lie in the New Testament. It was not the accounts of the Gospels that first moved him and from which he sought light to illuminate the dark night of his soul. It was the psalter, those theological-poetical books with their intensely experiential portrayal of a man struggling for and with God, with the majesty of God. Next in his preference came St. Paul's theology of sin, grace and redemption.[8]

Luther found that the text of the Bible was for him really the word of God. It inspired; when believed in, it saved. Here was a new context for Christian life—and a new context for Christian rites. The reading or hearing of Scripture came to be something like a primary sacrament. It would no longer be possible to see the seven sacraments of the Church as the only means of grace, or as a grace given *ex opere operato,* by the very action of the minister. Luther's teaching is beginning to lay emphasis on the faith of the believer, to throw the whole of Christian life back

[8] *The Reformation in Germany* (Darton, Longman and Todd, London; Herder and Herder, New York; 1968), Vol. I.

onto the essentials which the great theologians had always seen to be its basis. All sacramental theology had assumed a "faithful" Christian—but the element of faith had been reduced in practice almost to nil. In "Christendom" it was assumed that all men were Christians. The act of faith was forgotten. Luther was reviving the essential foundation on which a sacramental life could be built. "Your faith has made you whole."

Some of Luther's animadversions in his marginalia at this time refer to the controversy among the Augustinian priories. He attacked those who put their faith in "works" and "observances"— a reference to the reformed "observant" group. As we have seen, Luther had become disillusioned with the "observant" camp of those in his own priory at Erfurt. He takes the "observants" as typical of the "good works" theology which he wishes to castigate.

Luther gradually carried the priory at Wittenberg and the university with him, gaining, as we saw, various promotions by 1515. He was approved. Staupitz found a young man both deeply spiritual and capable of hard and good intellectual work. His spiritual troubles were not unlike what his own had been, scruples about not being as perfect as some impossible ideal. He did everything he could for young Luther, sometimes laughing at him, sometimes being very serious and intimate. Luther always said later that Staupitz had been at the origin of his insight. Staupitz told Luther he had had the same experiences over confession, and told Luther not to go to confession unless he had some real good sins to confess—such as murdering his father! At another time he told Luther, "God is not angry with you, but you are angry with God!" At one time Staupitz confessed that he was beaten and he could no longer understand Luther's trouble, which made Luther feel he was in some kind of a very special position, enough to make him despair, but also a challenge to which he responded. In practice Staupitz stood by Luther in crucial days now and in the future. Through Staupitz Luther also received something of the German mystical tradition.

Everything was conspiring to push Luther forward. At Wittenberg, up the far other end of the one-street town was the castle, residence of Frederick "the Wise," Elector of Saxony, elector already a very long time, since 1486. In 1502 he had succeeded in founding the university at Wittenberg, thereby raising the status of his town, which until then was famous only for its smells and its privilege of selling salt to the region around—and the elector's vast collection of relics, including a piece of the burning bush of Moses, nine thorns from the cross, stalks of hay and straw on which the Christ child lay, some of the virgin's milk, and a whole baby (one of those murdered by Herod)—a sort of Tussaud's chamber of horrors, but all with indulgences attached to them, obtainable for cash. These 5000 objects provided an excellent income for the elector and "spiritual privileges" for the inhabitants of Wittenberg and district.

Elector Frederick was destined to play a very important part in Luther's life. Up to 1518 the significant thing is that Frederick's personal assistant, Spalatin, was a fan of Luther's. He was really bowled over by the young friar, university lecturer, preacher. In 1513 he wrote of Father Martin that he "is an excellent man and scholar whose judgment I value very highly." In 1515 Spalatin was consulting Luther frequently about the university when Frederick had decisions to make. Luther was already forming in his mind the contours of how he thought a truly Christian university should be built up, and would share his insights with Spalatin. In 1516 he wrote to Spalatin: "If you take delight in pure and solid theology in the German language, a theology very similar to that of the ancients, get the sermons of John Tauler . . . Taste therefore and see how sweet is the Lord, where formerly you have seen how bitter is whatever is of ourselves." Tauler was one of the fourteenth-century Rhineland mystics. Luther was drinking at a main stream of mystical development. Tauler preaches inner self-annihilation, and union with the "Nothing" of which Dionysius spoke when he defined God as "no thing." He teaches detachment from all spiritual gifts and experiences as well as from earthly. Luther surely owes something of his out-and-out rejection of works of all kinds to Tauler's absolute following of the gospel recommendation to total self-abnegation. Luther was to simplify it, transpose it, make it homely, but there is something of "totality" about his teaching which ties back to Tauler. "Children, this true self-abasement sinks down into the innermost divine abyss and loses itself entirely, being truly lost to the world and self. *Abyssus, abyssum invocat,* 'deep calleth unto deep,'" wrote Tauler. There was also a book in

the same tradition called *Theologia Deutsch*, which further influenced Luther.

In the margin of his copy of Tauler's sermon Luther jotted down
a well-known couplet (so Wicks tells us); *"Quidquid habes meriti,
praevenetrix gratia donat; Nil Deus in nobis praeter sua dona
coronat* [Whatever of merit you have, prevenient grace gives it;
God crowns nothing in us except his own gifts]." Technically
this is important. The phrase "prevenient grace" is really effective in enabling a theologian to avoid semi-Pelagianism. Everything good which man does proceeds from this anterior movement
of God in him, of the Spirit, of grace, so that by definition there
is nothing good which he actually *initiates*. His response to grace
is itself grace-inspired. All man can do is to reject, to turn aside.
As Augustine so often says, sin alone is the only action which
man can claim to be his own. Luther was using the well-established
technical theology to express his grasp of the need to oppose all
kinds of neo-semi-Pelagianism, to give it the full title some authors
prefer.

In September 1516 Luther helped his pupil Bartholomew Bernhardi to defend his thesis that man can do nothing pleasing to God
without grace—a subject doubtless suggested to the pupil by the
lectures of Luther, his theology lecturer. The thesis rejected
Duns Scotus, Ockham, D'Ailly and Biel in favor of Augustine.
So convincing was his exposition, or so riling to Karlstadt, arch-
deacon of the castle church and dean of the faculty of theology,
that he went off to Leipzig and purchased a complete edition of
Augustine—certain that Luther and his pupil could not be right
in rejecting the theologians he had always known and honored.
Instead, Karlstadt was converted by Augustine and became a
disciple of Luther's. The event was typical of many other such.

A few weeks later, on All Saints' Eve, October 31, 1516,
Luther was responsible as usual for the sermon in the parish
church. On the following day many of the citizens would be
going for their annual visit to the castle to see the relics and obtain
a plenary indulgence. Luther preached about repentance, and
attacked the idea of indulgences. He said that he feared indulgences militated against true repentance, "the inner penitence
of the heart which should pervade the whole life of the believer."
Then he came to his great point, fruit of his own harrowing

personal struggle: "one who feels remorse for his sins does not try to evade punishment, but rather actually longs for punishment." This is a new dynamic presentation of Christian asceticism. Luther had been taught ascetic practices, particularly fasting. But he turns this long-standing ascetic tradition nicely to criticize the common practice of trying to buy a way out of the punishments of purgatory for oneself or someone else.

Luther's sharp, glinting, penetrating eyes watched the crowds swarming to get their indulgences. He felt sick at the distance between this so-called religion and that which he found in the New Testament.

The mechanical running after indulgences upset him as it had Hus—and as, just as this very time, it was also upsetting Zwingli in Einsiedeln. What has this to do with the gospel of Jesus Christ—or for that matter with religion as any theologian defined it? Little or nothing, he could honestly reply. Three hundred years previously Aquinas had defended indulgences but ended up by admitting that "other works of satisfaction are more meritorious with respect to our essential reward" and this "reward" he refers to as "infinitely better than the remission of temporal punishment"—evidently when it came to essentials the theologian did not have much to say for indulgences.

By now Luther was lecturing on Galatians, which later in life he referred to as his Katie von Bora (his wife) among the books of the Bible, his favorite. Three times during his life he lectured at length on it at Wittenberg. The version which we know is that of 1531, translated and introduced by the bishop of London in 1575, and re-edited and published in 1953. Its theme fitted Luther's needs perfectly. The Jewish Christians had been trying to insist that all converts must keep the Jewish law, first becoming circumcised, as a necessary part of being a Christian. For Paul this circumcision is no longer of any value. It was never more than a sign. What he asks of his Christians is "circumcision of the heart." Even Abraham, he says, was only justified because he had faith in God. St. Paul wrote: "Don't you see that it is those who rely on faith who are the sons of Abraham?" and "Everyone who accepts circumcision is obliged to keep the whole Law. But if you do look to the Law to make you justified, then you have separated yourselves from Christ, and have fallen from grace.

Christians are told by the Spirit to look to faith for those rewards that righteousness hopes for, since in Jesus Christ whether you are circumcised or not makes no matter—what does matter is having faith." Luther's characteristic theology is rooted directly in Paul. These first lectures on Galatians during the autumn and winter of 1516–17 must have led him on into a great certainty about his principal thesis.

By the spring of 1517 Luther was well set on his characteristic biblical theology. But he certainly had no inkling of an idea that he would one day be numbered among the "heretics." He was carrying Wittenberg with him. Just now Karlstadt, the dean of theology, quite converted, published 151 Augustinian theses. Luther was a promising young Augustinian with perhaps quite a career in front of him. This year he had his first printed piece published. It was a pastoral commentary on the seven penitential psalms. And about this time he wrote a famous letter to a friend which is often quoted, saying that Aristotle and his like are entirely banished from the university and that now it is all the Bible and Augustine, and no one wishes to study any more in the old way. His academic and his pastoral interests go hand in hand.

With these interests, and completely sustaining them, driving them on not indeed as "interests" but as overwhelming "concerns" went Luther's inner compulsion. Call it a prophetic impulse, a psychological obsession, an inner necessity—there is no denying that a single-minded drive had captured him, a drive which was also harmonious with a well-worked-out intellectual scheme. And yet it was not a "scheme," and hardly "worked out." It was a response to events, and it was being worked out all the time. The drive had come from the personal experience of a terrible desolation when faced with the impossibility of living by the norms originally set by religion, and with his personal discovery of the need for total "faith," and total reliance on God. All the spiritual, biblical, intellectual, reforming drives of the last four centuries were at last caught up in the devastating experience and ability of a single man, funneling out through him at great pressure—in the unlikeliest of places, Germany's junior university, in the person of a fairly ordinary sort of Augustinian priest, whose ordinariness was soon to prove that it could draw to him half the ordinary population of Germany, for it was a vehicle for the "extraordinary," not in the Renaissance sense of Neoplatonism or astrology, or aesthetics, or science or humanism, but in the most traditional "extraordinary" thing known to Europeans, the teaching of Jesus Christ, found in the New Testament.

Europe 1516

1516 is on the very brink of the thunderstorm, itself still under the horizon. Although there are signs of unrest no one, least of all young Father Martin, could have forecast that the circulation of some university theses of his on indulgences in Wittenberg would, within four years, have led him to develop his theology into bitterly critical diatribes against Rome, that it would have set a great part of Germany by the ears, ready to reject the ecclesiastical authority of Rome, and be causing deep concern and interest in many other parts of Europe. Yet it is untrue to suggest that there was not an expectation that some religious revolt of a large kind might occur. For a hundred years perceptive observers had declared it to be inevitable. At this very time the papal nuncio to Germany, Aleander, wrote to the Pope that many people were only waiting for the right man to arise and enable them to defy Rome.

In 1512 the Fifth Lateran Council had opened in Rome. We have already seen that Roman circles were perhaps more conscious than any others of the need for reform. The official opening sermon given by Giles of Viterbo, General of the Augustinian Order, on May 10, bore further witness to this realization of the urgent need, and underlines also the apocalyptic dimension which accompanied this realization. In the opening of the council he felt that it was at last possible to say that the hour of reform had come. Giles said that in the past he himself had been used to announce that the Church would be stricken by strife and sword but that it would also be reformed (*"emendatio"* is the word used). "It seems appropriate that the same man who said that all this would happen should also testify that it has now been fulfilled." He praises the custom of holding councils and says that the Church's health needs them. It is clear that he is not thinking there is any need for doctrinal reform, except in so far as heresies might arise as a result of the poor health of the Church itself. The abuses he evidently believed were at last to be suppressed.

In 1517 the council concluded, having made all the usual gestures about the need for reform but having achieved nothing. The failure was inevitable. The council had been called by Julius II partly as a counteraction to Louis XII's pseudo-Council of Pisa, also with the need to combat the Turkish threat in mind. Like the "Turks," reform, *emendatio* was always on the agenda. But unlike the Turkish threat, reform could be indefinitely adjourned.

Erasmus published his Greek New Testament and his edition of Jerome in this year, 1516; also his *Institutio Principis Christiani,* which he dedicated to the sixteen-year-old Charles, ruler of Castile and the Netherlands, three years later to be emperor. It was a plea for peace and for the encouragement of learning. Both Erasmus and More were deeply concerned with the general state of the world.

Erasmus was getting well known as a critic, and earning himself a band of enemies. In this year 1516, Thomas More wrote a letter defending Erasmus against the accusations of one Canon Dorpius, a professor at Louvain. The canon had attacked Erasmus for daring to think there could be a better text of the Bible than the Latin Vulgate, also for criticizing the theologians. More's reply has a special interest in that he was a middle-of-the-road man, and his defense of Erasmus is the kind of thing that many others were certainly thinking. He is speaking against academic theology and philosophy. "I cannot hear it said that these minute questionings are more useful than the knowledge of the sacred writings to the flock for which Christ died. If you merely contend that these things are worth study, I will not deny it; but if you put them on a level with the discourses of the ancient Fathers, I cannot listen to you. . . . I do not think you will question that whatever is necessary to salvation is communicated to us in the first place from the sacred Scriptures then from the ancient interpreters, and by traditional customs handed down through the ancient Fathers from hand to hand, and finally, by the sacred definitions of the Church. If in addition to all this, these acute disputants have curiously discovered anything, though I grant it may be convenient and useful, yet I think it belongs to the class of things without which it is possible to live." More says the ancients are neglected because people think "there is nowhere any honey to be found except in the hives of the Summists."

Canon Dorpius avowed himself convinced and retracted his criticism.

More had recently been lured from his law and his books reluctantly into public life. In 1515, being under-sheriff of London, he went as the representative of the City Merchants in an embassy to Flanders, to talk with representatives of Charles. It was during this time that he wrote *Utopia*. Like Erasmus, More could see no virtue in wars which were fought for little more than reputation, which is what Henry's occasional laborious sorties onto the Continent seemed to be. The jockeying and maneuvering included at one point a brief issued by Pope Julius on 20 March 1512 stripping the "schismatic" Louis XII of his title "Most Christian King of France," and conferring that title on Henry VIII. The brief bestowed the kingdom of France on Henry and promised him coronation as king of France. The *condition* of all this was that Louis was to be defeated. Until then the brief would be kept secret! These events have little relevance for the Reformation except in so far as in a purely accidental and haphazard fashion they may chance to help one cause or another. It is impossible to argue any general theory either that international events assisted the Protestant Reformation or that they enabled many parts of Europe to remain Catholic. Both these things happened in various places, but haphazardly. Perhaps it would be better to say that in neither case did political events have a deciding influence. As we have already seen, the new king of France, Francis I (1515–47), made an agreement with the Pope, the Concordat of Bologna, by which the appointment of bishops in France was virtually in the total control of that king. Yet France remained Catholic, and this agreement cannot by any stretch of the imagination be made to seem to be part of the Reformation.

An event in London at this time is evidence of the sort of sharp discontent that was to make the Reformation possible. Erasmus and More and their circle felt strongly about the futility of scholastic philosophy, and the need for a return to the Bible. A much wider circle of people were in a general way resentful against the clergy. The resentment covered a complete spectrum of human concern from the privileges of clergy before the law—all ordained men could claim to be tried for a large number of offenses not before the ordinary courts but before special clergy courts—to the fact that so many of them failed to order their lives by the high standards set, the monks and friars in particular failing to keep their rule of poverty, and often many other items of their rule, such as celibacy, obedience and enclosure. The generalized anti-clericalism was always ready to burst forth, and did so in the affair of Richard Hunne (1514–15).

Hunne, a merchant tailor and freeman of the City of London, had a quarrel with his local clergy about fees for baptizing his baby. He became very angry and sued them for slander, eventually bringing an action for an offense by the clergy against the great Praemunire Statute of 1393, which threatened forfeiture of goods against anyone introducing papal bulls into the country. The bishop of London, Fitzjames, tried to stop this by arresting Hunne and having his house searched. A Wycliffite Bible was found in it. Then suddenly, after a day of examination by Fitzjames at Fulham, Hunne was found hanged in his cell. The rights and wrongs have never been solved. It may have been suicide—More thought it was. The populace were convinced it was murder, inspired by the antagonism of the bishop and clergy. The city was tense for months after this.

The law of England, as of other countries, had assumed for hundreds of years that the Pope's laws might be interfering with the king's laws. Church and state joined hands to rule, but they competed in many spheres of life. As elsewhere in the Church the bishops were well aware both of the need for reform and of the threatening nature of the widespread anti-clericalism which surfaced in the Hunne affair. In January 1510 Warham, the archbishop of Canterbury, had called a provincial council. His summons dwelt on the hostile attitude of the laity towards priests and bishops. Colet's opening sermon echoed all the admissions we have heard already so much of from Roman sources. He was evidently aware of a general resentment about the protection given to priests by the Church courts. "Ye will have the church's liberty, and not be drawn before secular judge, and that also is right . . . but if ye desire this liberty, first unloose yourself from the wordly bondage." A reform committee was set up, which included Colet and John Fisher, bishop of Rochester, but nothing substantial emerged—typical were three new rules against simoniacs, unruly stipendiary priests, and improper clerical costume.

Before we leave England, we may notice that in this year 1516 at Oxford and Cambridge were two men who were going to have a very great influence on future affairs. Cranmer went to Cambridge in the first years of the century and took his B.A. in 1511, aged twenty-two, coming thirty-second in a list of forty-two. Other names to become famous later were also in the list: Latimer (Bishop of Worcester 1535–39) was eighth. Cranmer took an M.A. in 1514, having studied Greek and Hebrew at a time when Erasmus was at Cambridge. He became a fellow of Jesus College. Then he married, sacrificing what promised to be a normal comfortable clerical career. It was an odd decision. Normally dons were content to have a concubine or mistress. Cranmer's wife died along with her first baby. Then a second very unusual event occurred—his old college took him back as a fellow (records show no other example for two hundred years of such a readmission of a widower). There he stayed. We shall meet him again many years later.

William Tyndale, two or three years younger than Cranmer, had taken his B.A. at Magdalen Hall, Oxford, in 1512, and M.A. three years later. Sometime about then he was ordained priest, perhaps a year later, in 1516.

In Switzerland too something was gestating, though again it was of no great public interest as yet. In 1516 Ulrich Zwingli was vicar and preacher at Einsiedeln, where the great Benedictine abbey attracted large numbers of pilgrims. As with Luther, in this same year, and as with Hus just over a hundred years before, it was indulgences that stung him into action. They were particularly in evidence at this pilgrimage center. Apart from a love of music, there was very little in common between Zwingli and Luther. Almost any problem one might name, they would approach differently. But these two priests had one virtue in common, a sincere and sensitive approach to their pastoral work. And this brought them both up against the use of indulgences, which tended so clearly to devalue the practice of religion, valuing it indeed with a cash payment.

Zwingli was born on the first day of 1484, in the village of Wildhaus, high up east of Zurich, just fifty days after the birth of Luther. His father was the mayor. His uncle, parish priest, and dean of Wesen, taught him Latin. Like Luther, Zwingli was sent away to school, first at Basel, then to Berne; then to the University of Vienna. He went on to study at the University of Basel. At Basel, as well as at Vienna, Zwingli learned to be a humanist. At

Basel he was influenced by Thomas Wyttenbach, a teacher of the *via antiqua*. The world of classical Greece and Rome remained of permanent delight to him. The last evening of his life was spent in Zurich watching a performance in Greek arranged by himself of a play by Aristophanes. Zwingli had no idea that he would die in battle the next day, but this last evening remains a useful symbol of the man, so different from most of the other reformers, all of them closer to the popular idea of religious fanaticism. Zwingli was the nearest any of them came to the position of Erasmus.

Nothing particular is known about Zwingli's motives for becoming a priest. But it would be a very normal sort of choice for a man in his position. His first appointment was as parish priest to the village of Glarus. There he went in 1507, with his books and his music. He continued his education on his own account. He spent nine years there. In the course of it, he had twice to go as chaplain with Swiss mercenaries who were fighting the battles of the emperor. He was present at the battle of Marignano, 1515, where Swiss troops fighting for the emperor suffered disaster at the hands of the French. Zwingli became a bitter opponent of the mercenary system, though by no means of war itself. He wrote a poem at this time called *The Labyrinth* criticizing power politics: "Is this what Christ taught us?" he cried. But the population round Glarus depended for a living on the mercenary system. Zwingli looked for another post, and found one at Einsiedeln.

In this year, 1516, Zwingli wrote a letter to Erasmus which seems to indicate a definite stage in his life. It was a fulsome letter of devotion, saying that Erasmus had said Bible reading would be a help in sexual difficulties and that Zwingli had found it to be such. Zwingli said in his letter that Christ was the sole mediator between man and God and that Scripture and the Fathers are the sole foundation of faith. He was aligning himself with humanist theology. He had no idea that it would lead him in a few years to a revolution in religion.

Also in this year occurred the protest by Zwingli about the waging of war by the Christian mercenaries. Now he protested, like so many before and after, about indulgences. He was shocked into this by the indulgence preacher Bernadino Samson. Zwingli was supported, for the moment, by the administrator of the minster chapter at Einsiedeln, Diebold von Geroldseck, and had possibly been encouraged by the bishop of Constance. The subject always brought an admission from any fair-minded person that current practice was indefensible. But as in the case of all practices of long standing, with very widespread financial implications, the sheer difficulty of finding any immediate practical alternative inhibited opposition from most of those in a position of authority. A prophet is needed to incite a general public determination to have done with something that everyone knows to be wrong. Zwingli suggested some reforms. But they were not taken up. No doubt his protest created much less shock to those around him than would Luther's theses of the following year or his All Saints' Day sermon of this year. For Zwingli lacked the violent emotional involvement of Luther. However, his sincerity may have helped to recommend him for his next post in 1518 at the Great Minster in Zurich, as "people's priest," or parish priest. Zwingli was recommended for this post by his friend Myconius (Oswald Geisshussler) who, although younger than Zwingli, was already master of the cathedral school, and a burgess of the city.

In 1516 Calvin was seven years old, living with his parents in the cathedral town of Noyon northeast of Paris. But elsewhere in France the biblical and reforming movement was advancing. Guillaume Briçonnet, appointed bishop of Meaux in 1515, set about a program of reform in his diocese inviting Lefèvre, editor of the *Psalterium Quintuplex*, and translator of the Epistles of St. Paul to join him, also Gerard Roussel and Guillaume Farel. In 1512 Lefèvre had published a commentary on the epistles emphasizing justification by faith.

In the German universities the movement against Reuchlin was at its height. The leading Hebraist and Greek scholar in Germany, Reuchlin was inspired by the Italian humanist movement, Pico della Mirandola in particular. He attracted the animosity of a converted Jew, Pfefferkorn, and of the Dominicans of Cologne, and of others concerned for strict orthodoxy. The campaign roused the scorn of all those who saw in Italian humanism, and in the works of Erasmus in particular, a way forward for the Church. This scorn was bitterly expressed in a lampoon entitled *Letters of Obscure Men*, one of whose authors was Ulrich von Hutten, humanist, knight, degenerate. Both the Jewish anti-Semitic campaign and the opposition to it are significant for their violence, and for their apparent failure to set the problem at a respectable level of intellectual inquiry. Sweetness perhaps came out of it all in some way. Reuchlin's book defending himself was burned. But he survived, and his great-nephew, Melanchthon (Greek transposition of his name Schwarzerd), became a living synthesis of much of the best in both the humanist Renaissance and in Luther's reformed theology, being made professor of Greek at Wittenberg in 1518 and staying there to become Luther's right-hand man till the end of his life, one of the preachers at Luther's funeral.

Into the Forum

In 1516 as All Saints' Day drew near Father Martin had felt he must make some protest in the name of religion, and of theology, against the reliance on indulgences expressed so strongly by those who visited the relics in the castle. In 1517 things were apparently little changed. But a further event had made Martin more worried. A Dominican friar had been preaching in the district not far from Wittenberg, outside the elector's territory. His name was Tetzel, and his task was to collect money for the building of St. Peter's in Rome, and to provide indulgences for those who took part in the good work of making a cash contribution. Many of the Wittenbergers had been visiting the preacher. In the confessional they gave Father Martin to understand that what really mattered was the indulgence, and that little emphasis need be placed on the specifically sacramental action—their sincere confessions of their sins, sorrow for them, a determination to do better in future, and the absolution which the priest gave in the name of Christ, but which he could also withhold if he judged the penitent insincere. They seemed to imply that the confessor could not withhold absolution from someone holding a pardon from Tetzel.

One of the three sample sermons which Tetzel drew up for use by parish priests is of interest. It makes quite clear that the faithful must go to confession and must be contrite if they are to gain the benefit of the indulgence. But so much depends on how such things are said, and the whole context. In the same sermon Tetzel makes statements about the "time" to be spent in purgatory for sins. He also implies that most people commit mortal sins regularly. It was this kind of preaching that stirred the people up, made them put such confidence in the act of contributing to the building fund and getting an indulgence certificate, and gave Luther so deeply to think. It was, after all, not very dissimilar to the kind of thing so castigated in the Pharisees by Jesus in the gospel. Tetzel's sermon runs:

> Let them (the sheep) be aware that for any mortal sin there is need to do penance for seven years after confession and contrition, either in this life or in purgatory. How many mortal sins are committed in a day, how many in a week, how many in a year, how many in a whole lifetime? They are all but infinite and they have to undergo an infinite penalty in the flaming punishment of purgatory. And yet in virtue of these confessional letters, you shall be able to gain, once in a life, full pardon of the penalties due up to that time . . . Again whenever you are willing to confess, gain as well a similar remission . . . and finally at the moment of death a plenary indulgence . . . etc.

It was always emphasized that the indulgence could by an act of prayer be gained not for oneself but for a soul in purgatory. There was a little jingle.

> So soon as the coin in box does ring
> The soul from purgatory does spring.

Illustrations survive which show the great money chest and various grades of indulgence certificates displayed on a banner.

It was all rather exciting. In any place or time of highly charged religious emotion it is very difficult to judge the rights and wrongs of the matter. For Luther he was sure this was not how the gospel was meant to be preached, nor did he find it consonant with the Church's own teaching about faith and grace.

A quite secondary but still important point was the more or less gross scandal attached to the whole operation. It is noteworthy that this is only referred to briefly in Luther's protest, which is pastoral and theological. But his protest takes its place in a world where the general public opinion of churchmen was very low. Centuries of protesters had done their work in forming public opinion. The scandals themselves had only got larger. In this case half of all the money collected by Tetzel was paid straight to the German and international bankers, the Fuggers, liquidating a debt owed them by the local archbishop of Mainz. He had incurred this debt when paying a large fee to the Roman Curia for his post as archbishop, for which he was below the canonical age, and for which he was ineligible because of other ecclesiastical offices which he already held and wished to retain. Of the other half of the money some went to support Tetzel and his servant at a high standard of living. The balance went to pay the architect, masons and quarrymen, and others involved in the erection of Bramante's great basilica still standing in Rome.

As All Saints' Day drew near Luther was preparing a protest which he would send to his bishop and his archbishop, thus acting according to correct procedure. He drew up a set of theses (as yet unnumbered). It was a hypothetical theological statement, propositions for debate, intended to lead to a better definition and practice of indulgences, fitting better with the gospel and theology.

Indulgences themselves were not attacked. ("He who speaks against the truth of apostolic pardons let him be anathema and cursed. But he who exercises zeal against the wanton licence of the pardon-merchants, let him be blessed." Numbers 71 and 72, as subsequently numbered.) It was typically the kind of thing which Luther would expect to debate at university level so that the truth of the matter could be thrashed out. With the theses, which we shall refer to from now on as the Ninety-Five Theses, Luther sent a letter to the archbishop. He also enclosed a further detailed theological rationale.

Many years later Melanchthon declared that Luther nailed the theses up on the church door at Wittenberg. There is no other good evidence for this statement, and much against it. Melanchthon had a notoriously bad memory, and was not resident at Wittenberg at the time. On the whole it seems unlikely that this supposedly famous historical action ever occurred. Luther delayed a fortnight or so before sending copies of the theses to other university friends in Germany. Publicity came when these friends began to show them to other friends, and when printers in Leipzig, Nuremberg and Basel published them without Luther's permission. When these things happened there began to be something of a stir. Was there a new Savonarola, albeit a less violent one, arising in Germany? Some people feared for the small-town friar, feared that he was asking for trouble. Big protests, well justified, made by little people tend to attract excessive attention from authority, so that they may be blotted out before too much public attention is focused on them. And Goliath can be enraged by David. Something of this sort began to happen in this case. By next spring, 1518, there was tension in the air. The elector tried to persuade Luther, through Spalatin, not to travel to the meeting of the Augustinians at Heidelberg, where he was due as district superior to consult with other superiors at one of the Order's regular reunions. The elector was concerned for his safety. Men sometimes disappeared mysteriously.

Letters which went to and fro at this time show that Luther saw himself as a quite minor person, wishing to debate this subject at university level at Wittenberg, as he had in 1516, but hoping now to get views from beyond Wittenberg itself. He proceeded with care and circumspection in what he wrote throughout 1517 and 1518.

Sometime probably in November 1517 Luther received a letter from Spalatin asking him why the court of the elector had not received a copy of his latest theses, since he understood they were being discussed. Luther's reply is extant: "I did not want my theses to come into the hands of our illustrious prince-elector or of anyone from the court until those who are criticised in the theses had received copies. They must not think that the theses were ordered or supported by the prince-elector." The people criticized by implication are presumably his own bishop of Brandenburg, Hieronymus, and Albert, Archbishop and Elector of Mainz, to whom, as we have seen, the theses were sent in the first place. Luther wanted to make the protest exclusively on his own responsibility.

In the absence of any reply from the bishop or archbishop, Luther sent a few copies to friends. It is quite clear that their reaction was totally unexpected by Luther. He wanted a debate, a university discussion. But it was not for nothing that he had been struggling his way for six years or so through the Psalms, Galatians and Romans, and formulating a reinvigorated biblical theology, Christological, pastorally orientated. All this showed through in the theses, and immediately excited those who read them. They saw straight away that this was something more than a routine protest. Today a man will go to a photo-copying

machine when what looks to him like an important and influential document comes to his hand. These friends of Luther's
rushed to their equivalent, the local printer. They wanted others
to be able to see these theses. Ulrich von Dinsted, a Wittenberg
canon at the castle sent a handwritten copy to his friend, a lawyer
Christoph Scheurl in Nuremberg, who had the theses translated
into German and printed. "I am most grateful to have received
Martin's theses . . ." he wrote. He sent copies of the Latin and
German printed version from Nuremberg to Luther, saying that
he was disappointed not to have received the theses from Luther
himself in the first place.

Luther's reply of March 5, 1518, is enlightening: "You are
surprised that I did not send them to you. But I did not want
to circulate them widely. I only intended to submit them to a
few close friends for discussion, and if they disapproved of the
theses, to suppress them. I wanted to publish them, only if they
met with approval. But now they are being printed and spread
everywhere far beyond my expectation, a result that I regret. It
is not that I am against telling people the truth, in fact that is
alone what I want, but this is not the proper way to instruct
the people. For I have doubts about some of the theses, and
others I would have put much differently and more cogently,
and some I would have omitted, had I known what was to
come. Still, the spread of my theses shows what people everywhere really think of indulgences, although they conceal their
thoughts 'out of fear of the Jews.' Therefore, I had to write out
proofs for my theses, but I do not yet have permission to publish
these." On this same date, March 5, 1518, Erasmus sent a copy
of the theses to Thomas More in England. About this time
Dürer wrote to Luther thanking him for his action, and the
bishop of Merseburg said he was glad to see someone exposing
Tetzel.

Luther's reference to "proofs" for his theses is to the *Resolutiones*
about indulgences which he sent to his bishop, in February 1518
with a long letter asking for permission to publish them on
account of the public controversy then arising. Luther waited
obediently till the bishop gave permission and then published
them in August 1518.

Luther's letter to the Pope in May of the same year is also
important: ". . . I am at a loss, indeed, to know why it is fated

that these particular theses of mine and no others, whether of mine or of any other teachers, should have spread throughout almost the entire country. They were made public at the University of Wittenberg, and intended only for this university. They were made public in such a manner that it seems incredible that all and sundry could understand them. They are theses; they are neither teachings nor doctrines; as is customary, they are cast in obscure and ambiguous language. If I could have foreseen what would happen, I should certainly have done my part to see that they were more fully intelligible. . . . Wherefore, Holy Father, I fling myself prostrate at the feet of your Holiness with all that I am and all that I have. Revive, kill, call, recall, approve, reprove, as it pleases you. I shall acknowledge your voice as the voice of Christ who is enthroned in you, and who speaks through you. If I merit death, I shall not refuse to die. For the earth is the Lord's and the fulness thereof. He is blessed for ever. Amen, and may He have you for ever in his keeping."

The text of the Ninety-Five Theses set hearts and minds alight. We must examine the text. The opening contains the words "Our Lord and Master, Jesus Christ, when he said *Poenitentiam agite*, willed that the whole life of the faithful should be repentance." If one is truly repentant, says Luther, he should not want to evade whatever punishment is his due. Indulgences are basically selfish. This opening was powerful—it sent the reader to look up the New Testament if he could find a copy. It tied in with deep religious sentiment and conscience. It also tied in with the Church's traditional sacramental practice. The traditional practice and doctrine involved confession of sins, for which one was given a "penance" to do (it might only be a prayer to say); and the sinner understood that although the sin was forgiven, he might not necessarily be fit for heaven and might need to undergo "purgation" in purgatory after death. It was further understood that a man might during the rest of his life become more worthy, more fit for heaven, and so avoid some or all of the purgatorial fires. Theologians spoke of the "good works" which might be done and lead to this same desired result. They failed sometimes to observe that everything really depended on motive and intention, and that good works, without charity, to use St. Paul's understanding of the matter, are useless. Further, to interpret a money payment as a "good work" may on some or many occasions be stretching the term "good work" far beyond its original meaning.

So these opening words of the theses certainly represented a very widespread understanding of the unavoidably spiritual nature of all true religion, and of the devaluation of this to be found in much official religion, and particularly in the practice of granting indulgences, and particularly when they were granted in return for money badly needed by prelates for paying their debts, or for starting a crusade or even building a church. The public feeling on this had been growing, as we have seen, for centuries. In Germany disillusion and irritation was now at a more intense level than ever before.

Theses 5–7 denied the Pope's power to remit purgatorial penalties to come (as distinct from present penances imposed), and Theses 8–29 denied the same power over souls already in purgatory. In part the subject argued here is a highly technical theological matter. But from another point of view, and that the most important for our purposes, the theses were again turning to a fundamental religious insight. Theology was struggling towards its clarification in the following way. When a man had done something he knew to be wrong, he needed to admit to himself that he had sinned. When he admitted to it and turned to God, he was forgiven. The Church's rites, it could be said, aimed at an objective expression of this truth. In such a context questions about penance, punishment, retribution were important but secondary matters. Generally there was likely to be a strong response to such a return to an emphasis on the fundamental religious truths. Involving as it did, a denial of some of the spiritual power claimed by the Pope, it automatically raised a favorable attitude in the minds of many.

Popular preaching of indulgences was at odds with theology. The Church had always avoided any absolute statement of the Church's power to release souls from purgatory. Roman Catholic plenary indulgences have always been stated (when it comes to absolutely formal official teaching) as working by means of prayer, and not by means of "the keys," not by means of any power given the Church by Christ. And it is difficult to see how the Church could ever claim any jurisdiction beyond death. Excommunication, for instance, has always been excommunication from the earthly community of the faithful, with the purpose of causing repentance, return and eventual salvation.

Theses 30–40 continue in a similar way with the fundamental matter of repentance from sin. But Luther introduces here a very important new idea. When a man repents, not only is he immediately forgiven, but he is also absolved from undergoing any punishment. In effect this involves the abolition of purgatory, for which there is no longer any purpose. The Protestant denial of purgatory has its origin in this section of the theses. It is an important symbol of the difference between traditional Catholic teaching, which saw man as being able to, and needing to, become slowly a better man, to progress in sanctity, with its corollary of purgatorial cleansing after death, and on the other hand the Lutheran idea of a salvation which, once accepted and appropriated by faith, is total, and immediate. Luther finds a continuing use for indulgences in this section by saying: "The Pope's remission and distribution are in no way to be despised, since, as I have said, they are a declaration of divine forgiveness." This is a good example of the fact that these theses contained a large number of hypotheses which were intended for discussion at academic level. Luther was a loyal Catholic, and was trying to find a positive way of maintaining his severe criticisms of indulgences without abolishing them altogether. But he does not compromise: "Those who believe that they can be sure of their salvation because they have purchased an indulgence will fall into eternal damnation together with their teachers."

Theses 41–52 again go driving into the fundamental religious dimension, and give Luther the opportunity to refer to the kind of "good work" he believes a follower of Christ will do, not to gain merit, but because as a believer he cannot help it. To fail to help a poor man in order to buy an indulgence incurs God's wrath. "Christians must be taught ['*Christiani docendi*' rings out many times in the theses] that it is not the Pope's intention that the purchase of indulgence is in any way comparable with works of mercy." "Christians must be taught that if the Pope knew the demands made by the pardon preachers he would prefer to have St. Peter's basilica reduced to ashes than built with the skin, flesh and bones of his sheep."

Theses 53–80 turn to the gospel. Numbers 53–55 are blunt in their implied criticism of Luther's archbishop, and all ecclesiastical

authorities, in the policies they follow in permitting indulgences
to be preached. He says that they are enemies of Christ who
forbid all other preaching while the indulgence is being preached
in a town or district. This is what was always done. In order to
ensure the best possible spiritual and financial return, all other
sermons were to cease during the visit of the indulgence preachers.
Luther sees here a direct competition between the preaching of the
gospel as such and the preaching of indulgences.

Theses 81–91 become more polemical, and pose some tough
questions, of a kind which might, in the course of a debate, be
thoroughly refuted, or might lead to some previously unforeseen
theological developments. "Why does not the Pope empty purgatory for the sake of holy charity . . . if he redeems an infinite
number of souls for the sake of sordid money for building a
basilica, the most trivial of causes?" "Why do requiems and
anniversaries of the departed continue, and why does he not
return or allow to be returned the benefices established on their
behalf, since it is now wrong to pray for those redeemed? The
last few theses (92–95) return to the original opening theme,
and reveal that although the Latin language and general form
implied academic discussion, Luther's overriding concern was for
the true preaching of the gospel, a pastoral concern rooted in
daily experience:

92. Away with all those prophets who say to the people
of Christ: "Peace! Peace!" where there is no peace.

93. Let all these prophets take this right action and say to
the people of Christ: "Cross! Cross!" . . .

94. Christians must be exhorted to follow Christ, their head,
with complete devotion through punishment, through death,
through hell.

95. In this way let them have confidence that they will
enter heaven through many tribulations, rather than through
a false assurance of peace.

By the spring it was clear to Luther that the theses had spread
far and wide across Europe, and nothing he could do would reverse
the controversy. He had written them partly out of a determination
to get something done about a gross public scandal; partly out of a
determination to try to get the theology of the matter advanced;
partly out of pastoral concern and a wish to get the subject of

the true naure of the Christian religion for the ordinary person into general discussion. But the theses themselves were not well adapted, in his opinion, for translation and wide dissemination; also even in Latin they did not express as well as might be, his own theological thought. About the latter we have seen already he wrote a new treatise, the *Resolutiones*, which he sent to his bishop, and which outlined a reform program as well. But over indulgences themselves Luther felt he must make his position clear publicly, and he took a very important step. He wrote and published in German a *Sermon on Indulgences and Grace*. This pushed things much further ahead much faster. Its position was specific and forthright; and it was printed and bought and read very widely indeed. Twelve editions appeared during 1518 in Wittenberg, Leipzig, Augsburg, Nuremberg and Basel. It was read widely by people generally, and made Luther's name and style directly known to them for the first time. It went further than before in the direction of making the Bible the only norm. The Scriptures, he says, only require the sinner to have a genuine repentance and resolution to bear the cross of Christ, and to do the true works of satisfaction. What are these works? (1) Those that "belong to the soul, such as prayer and the reading, meditating, hearing and preaching of God's word." (2) Everything that leads to mortification of the old Adam. (3) Works of love and mercy towards one's neighbor. Then he gives direct personal advice to ordinary people simply to ignore indulgences: "My will, my prayer, my advice is that no one buy indulgences any more, for it is neither meritorious nor a work of obedience, but on the contrary, a temptation to throw off due obedience. Whether the poor souls can be released from purgatory by means of indulgences, I do not know, but I do not believe it. Nor has the church as yet decided anything concerning it. In any case, you will be quite safe if you pray for her and work for her in other ways. It bothers me very little that those whose profit is curtailed by these truths revile me as a heretic. Those who behave thus only prove that they are ignorant numbskulls who have never even smelled the bible, nor ever read the church fathers, and have never understood their own teachers; for if they had, they would know that no one should be called heretic until he has been heard and convicted of his error." The harsh and aggressive tone which first appeared in purely private marginalia had not been moderated for the public.

Luther's local bishop agreed that this sermon should be published; later he agreed also that the *Resolutiones* should be published. Not long after this Luther went to the meetings at Heidelberg to which we have already referred. There he was invited by the provincial superior of the order, his friend and mentor Staupitz, to speak. Luther delivered a sketch of his basic theology, and won over a majority of those present. Its theme was the Pauline theology of the Law condemning us; Grace, saving us; and the way to this salvation, Christ. His attack is always aimed at the idea that man can of his own power do anything to save himself. "Grace is given to heal the spiritually sick, not to decorate spiritual heroes."

Luther had walked to Heidelberg, carrying papers of identification from the Elector Frederick. Staupitz made sure he had a cart to travel in on the way back. Back in Wittenberg an observer said he looked *"habitior et corpulentior"*—fatter and fitter. It had been a good experience for him. Speaking for the first time to a gathering of his brethren outside Wittenberg he had gained recognition for his theology, which he believed so firmly was the true theology of the Word. His ascetic features had been admired, and his patience along with the sincerity, conviction and intellectually compelling nature of his exposition. Bucer, the future reformer, was among those won over. On his return in the cart Luther looked less tired and less worried. His sermons at Wittenberg became more forthright. One of these was a denunciation of "The Ban"—or excommunication, which Rome had used indiscriminately for centuries against anyone or any community or ruler, for instance, for failing to pay a debt. A whole region could end up without the sacraments if the local ruler was in disfavor at Rome.

Luther had never received a reply from the archbishop of Mainz, Elector Albert, to whom the theses were sent in the first place. The archbishop had taken advice and sent them on to Rome. Tetzel also got hold of them and boasted that this new "heretic" would be "in the flames within three weeks." He had some counter-theses written, full of low-grade abuse. The Dominicans rallied to defend their brother, Tetzel. Cardinal Cajetan, their cardinal protector, was living at the time with the Fuggers in Augsburg during the imperial Diet which was being held there. His first action was to try to get the Augustinians to discipline Luther. He suggested that the Heidelberg meeting would be an ideal opportunity. But, as we saw, the occasion turned out exactly otherwise, with Luther winning many over to his own way of thinking. During the summer some Dominicans drew up a set of forged theses based on Luther's sermon on the ban, following on an attempt to incriminate Luther in private conversation. The forged theses were sent to Rome. Luther began to realize that giant wheels were turning against him in the ecclesiastical machine. On July 10 a letter to a friend says: "There is only one thing left, my weak and broken body. If they take that away, they will make me the poorer by an hour of life, perhaps a couple. But my soul they cannot take. I know perfectly well that from the beginning of the world the word of Christ has been of such a kind that whoever wants to carry it into the world must necessarily, like the Apostles, renounce everything and expect death at any and every hour. If it were not so, it would not be the word of Christ. By death it was bought, by deaths spread abroad, by deaths safeguarded. It must also take many deaths to preserve it, or bring it back again. Christ is a bloody partnership for us."

There is some hysteria here which relates back perhaps to psychological factors. But, on this occasion, the emotions are matched by circumstance, which in fact merited well enough this somewhat "martyred" attitude. Rome had had many heretics burned within the last century, and indeed within the last few years. A month later Luther received confirmation of his fears, in a missive from Rome that reached him on August 7. This was the reply to his theses written by Fr. Sylvester Mazzolini Prierias, who had been made master of the sacred palace in 1515. He boasted that it was written in three days. It was a defense of the power of the Pope, and included a large amount of simple abuse. Luther was "a dog and the son of a bitch, born to bite and snap at the sky," having "a brain of brass and a nose of iron," and so forth. The theological arguments were similar to those in a later writing of his against Luther: "in the New Law the Pope's judgment is the oracle of God," and "the decretals of the Roman Church have to be added to scripture." Lortz describes Prierias' piece as "an exact expression of the irresponsible self-assurance of the curia."

Earlier on we noted the point at which the Protestant Reformation has its exact Lutheran source. It was Luther's psychological and religious experience—his personal solution, emotional, theological and practical, of a personal problem. We have now reached a point where Luther might have retracted partially, or somewhat modified his solution and his practical conclusions in both the pastoral and the academic spheres. But in the course of this year 1518 he had clearly begun to feel that there were matters of absolute principle involved. There were matters which were more important to him than his own life. And they involved a witness to something in the Christian tradition which the existing organization seemed to be betraying. Luther must live by this Christ in whom he believed, or die in the attempt if necessary. During this year numerous expressions of support came to Luther, and he must have begun to sense something already of the representative nature of his stand. Many others in various walks of life had sent him expressions of support. All this certainly came as a complete surprise to him at first. Now he began to realize that he was committed, not only on his own behalf but on that of others. The option was no longer honorably open for him to creep back into his *angulum,* his private corner, in Wittenberg. He must be prepared to brave the world and live out his convictions *ante foras* (a phrase mistaken by some of Luther's earlier and recent interpreters as a reference to the nailing up of the Ninety-Five Theses in the porch of the church).

Previous public critics of the Church's procedures and of the Pope himself had paid for their opinions with disapproval, sometimes death, sometimes, however, gaining approval and reverence, as in the case of St. Bernard. No previous critic had been able to reach society as Luther was able to, with the printers at his elbow glad to find something to print which people wanted to read. Luther replied to Prierias:

> You threaten me with maledictions, invectives, censures. What and whereto? Spare your threats, my father, Christ lives. He not only lives, he also reigns, not only in heaven but even in Rome, however much she may rage. If I am cursed for the truth, I shall bless the Lord. The censures of the Church will not separate me from the Church if the truth joins me to the Church. I would rather be cursed and excommunicated by you and your like than blessed with you. I have nothing to lose. I am the Lord's. If I perish, I perish to the Lord, that is I am found by him. Seek, therefore, somebody else whom you may terrify.

In the spring Luther had been engaged in talks with Spalatin and Karlstadt about the structure of the syllabus at the university and the introduction of a greater study of Greek and Hebrew— in the late summer they appointed Melanchthon professor of Greek. Luther fulfilled his normal round of lectures, sermons and other responsibilities. He is still bound by the words he had written in a letter to his archbishop the previous December: "People . . . believe that having bought a certificate of indulgence their eternal bliss is assured . . . But no man can be assured of his salvation by the action of any bishop, for he is not assured thereof even by the infused grace of God. The apostle demands that we work out our salvation in fear and trembling."

Judgments

Earlier we compared the examination of Hus by Gerson, D'Ailly and others at Constance to Luther's examination by Cajetan at Augsburg in October 1518. This is the event we now come to. The meeting between Luther and Cajetan is symbolical of the whole clash between papal authority and the reformers throughout the century, and later. It is also a crucial moment, along with events in the immediately following weeks, for Luther's personal survival.

In August Cajetan received the breve (*Postquam Aures*) from Rome to arrest Luther as a heretic. But Elector Frederick now became a key person in certain international developments. Emperor Maximilian was pressing at his Diet at Augsburg, then in session, for the crowning of his grandson Charles as his successor. But this was the last thing Rome wanted, because Charles would become the ruler of vast areas of Europe from the Atlantic coast of Spain to Bohemia, from Naples to the North Sea. Elector Frederick was standing out against the crowning of Charles; he himself was the most likely alternative choice, he would also be Reichsvikar in the interim. The Emperor Maximilian was keen to damage the reputation of Frederick. A process against the professor of theology in his upstart university would be ideal for this purpose. Equally, Cajetan could now see good reason for playing the matter down. Thus, when Luther asked for his case to be tried in Germany, and the elector put this to Cajetan, the latter said he would be glad to hear Luther himself and promised a fatherly hearing. Cajetan was seriously concerned about the possible heresy; but the operative forces behind the day-to-day decisions about how to deal with it were political and without relevance to the matters at stake.

Cajetan was not in any doubt about authority—his own and that of the Pope. He was almost alone in his day among theologians in taking a strong ultrapapalist line. But along with this went an acute awareness of contemporary abuses and the need for theological clarification. He had himself written about indulgences and certainly agreed with some of Luther's criticisms of current practice. But this was something for authority to deal with, as and when it thought fit. It was not the responsibility of an Augustinian friar in Germany. He had no intention of getting involved in the subject with the Wittenberg professor. He had, however, evidently studied Luther's writings with care. According to Bucer he said later that he regarded the Ninety-Five Theses as containing errors rather than heresies. Subsequent writings were a different matter; he had noticed Luther moving from hypothesis to assertion, as he said in correspondence with the elector after the Augsburg meeting with Luther.

At the meeting he decided to take two central issues on which he felt sure he could quickly show Luther that he was in error, and so demand recantation. He would do it as kindly as possible, and he would start by seeing whether Luther was not perhaps faint-hearted anyhow and willing to surrender. But of course all this was to reckon entirely without the man Luther. Cajetan was, however, perhaps not surprised when the preliminary visit of one of his Italian assistants cut no ice. One Serralonga called on Luther at his lodgings in Augsburg, deploring the whole sad business, and suggesting that "*revoco*" was a small word, and the best one for this occasion. He asked Luther what he would do if the hearing went against him, where he would go. "*Sub coelis*" was the strange reply—which one could take as one wished: under the open sky, to heaven, it's all in God's hands. Luther's mind had been saturated with Old Testament symbols in the past six years and his mind often reverted at this time, as we know from his letters, to the image of Abraham setting out, he knew not whither, but knowing only that he was setting out at God's command and to a place where God would lead him. *Sub coelis* sums up nearly a decade of study and of spiritual experience.

The meeting itself was delayed. Luther's friends insisted that he ask for a "safe conduct" from the emperor, to ensure that he could not be arrested once he arrived at Cajetan's house. Luther himself would hardly have bothered, although he knew what was at stake. Safe conducts, one may remark, had been of no use to Hus, once within the grasp of authority. However, an unlawful arrest in Germany in the sixteenth century was undoubtedly a more hazardous undertaking for Church authority than at Constance, in the fifteenth century. The implication of Luther's delay irritated Cajetan. Eventually the safe conduct came, and Luther went to the meeting in his usual sweat. He started off with an exaggerated obeisance and statement of obedience to the Pope. The chance of anything like a "meeting of minds" between them did not exist. Luther had hoped, somewhat as Hus had hoped, that he might be able to argue his theology. But Hus and Luther were both naïve in thinking that they were facing anything other than a process for heresy, however informally it may have been made to appear at first. Cajetan had not come to listen but to show Luther his error and persuade him to correct it, or else to put him in the position of a proven heretic, where the elector would be bound to hand him over quietly. But it was done kindly and Luther insisted afterwards that Cajetan had been very courteous and had kept his promise to act in a fatherly way.

Cajetan chose two points, one involving papal authority; the other, the sacraments. He cited the bull *Unigenitus* of Clement VI, which stated that Christ's death and suffering had acquired an infinite treasure in heaven, further added to by the Virgin Mary and the saints, and that these treasures were committed to Peter and his successors. Luther said this doctrine could not be found in Scripture but that he would subscribe to it if support could be found for it there. Then, as regards the sacrament of penance, Cajetan said Luther was wrong to insist on the faith of the penitent. The sacrament was always efficacious. If faith was insisted on, the penitent would always be in doubt as to whether he had really received the sacrament properly. But again Luther said that Scripture spoke of faith alone being our way to the grace of God. Cajetan said he was not prepared to argue but was drawn into a discussion nevertheless. This annoyed him. He said Luther must recant now that he had heard the correct doctrine. But Luther said he could not be convinced without scriptural proof, and asked to be allowed to submit a written statement.

Cajetan refused at first, then relented when Staupitz, who had

come with Luther, begged him to let Luther do this. Luther's
written statement insisted that Popes could make mistakes. This
statement also showed Luther beginning to make of his insights
something like a new orthodoxy. Penitents, he says, must believe
that they have been forgiven. They must know with all the power
of faith that they are forgiven. Luther is reacting to his own past,
when he was plagued with scruples, always wondering whether he
had confessed everything, and whether in the next few moments
after receiving the sacrament he had not sinned again. From his
general insight that the New Testament taught a doctrine of
justification by faith alone, he had now taken this further step and
insisted that true faith leads necessarily to a state of psychological
certainty. We have the origin of the Protestant doctrine of assurance, the evangelical's conviction that he is "saved." Along with
Luther's statement that Popes could err, the "subjective" nature of
his teaching on the working of the sacrament only confirmed Cajetan
in his belief that he was dealing with a heretic. He said that he
would send the statement on to Rome, along with his refutation of
it. Luther began to explain further, and this, the third and last
meeting, ended in shouting after Luther tripped Cajetan up over
a verbal inaccuracy. Cajetan dismissed Luther until he should
recant.

Luther appealed from "the pope ill informed to the pope better
informed," a conventional formula for appeals, and requested that
he be heard elsewhere than in Rome. Luther was now very conscious of the danger in which he stood. He had written to Spalatin
on October 14 from Augsburg: "If I am disposed of by force, the
door is open for an attack on Dr. Karlstadt and the whole
theological faculty—and as I fear the sudden ruin of our infant
university." Staupitz was very worried and freed Luther from his
vows to give him the greatest possible freedom of movement in the
awkward situation, before he, Staupitz, left Augsburg on other
business. He had an idea that Luther ought perhaps to flee to
Paris, where he guessed (wrongly, as it turned out later) that
Luther's theology might be more welcome and he might be safe.
Before Staupitz left, for Nuremberg, he said to Luther: "Remember
you have begun this affair in the name of our Lord Jesus Christ."
Luther waited to see if there would be any further communication
from the Fugger household, or if there would be any reply to a note
he had sent apologizing for speaking oversharply. The silence

eventually got on the nerves of his friends, and he was rushed from the city one evening, and rode half the night forty miles on a rather wild horse, without boots or breeches, a journey which left Luther prostrate, one never to be forgotten. Possibly they were right to get away, because Cajetan wrote soon after to Frederick, requesting him to surrender Luther as a common heretic so that he could be taken to Rome for trial.

Frederick was really in trouble now. He was not one who liked to take decisions—if you waited they usually got taken for you. It is only necessary to look at the portrait of this swarthy Saxon to have some idea about this. Frederick was pragmatic German phlegm at its best. No one ever knew which direction he would move in, and he often managed to move in none. He tried now to wait. Contingency arrangements were made for Luther to fly at a moment's notice if a formal ban of excommunication arrived. The matter was certainly one of major concern for Frederick. The atmosphere in Wittenberg was tense. Frederick received a round robin petition from the theology faculty, a request that he should support Luther. The first draft of this petition, sent to Frederick by the dean, Karlstadt, was actually drawn up by Luther himself, at the request of the faculty. But the cause was thought to be hopeless. Luther began to make his farewells. At the beginning of a supper party to mark his departure a letter seems to have come from Frederick expressing surprise that Luther had not yet gone. Towards the end of the party another letter came saying Luther was to stay. From that point on, Frederick never changed his position of support for Luther.

These years till 1521 contain several crucial events. This decision of Frederick's was perhaps the most striking. Just how and why he came to his decision is not known—a decision unlike him in its suddenness and certitude. When all the political and other extraneous motives have been accounted for, it seems impossible to rule out the influence of Frederick's own conscience. The past and future of the Luther case make it seem decisive. Frederick had had many opportunities in the previous six years for dispensing with Luther's services; and there were certainly occasions in the future when Luther's very radical and swiftly developing thought provided an opportunity for the elector to call a halt if he so wished. But this decision to protect Luther followed in the steps of a way already spelled out by Luther's close association with his chaplain Spalatin during the past five years. It was also consistent with a long-established policy of Frederick's. Since 1501 he had prevented Church revenues from going to Rome and used them instead to found the university at Wittenberg. The decision to protect Luther was persevered in till Frederick's death, in spite of the damage to his relic indulgence income which Luther openly perpetrated.

We are now at the time of the détente between Rome and Frederick, when Rome felt it was overwhelmingly important to keep Frederick happy. Attempts were therefore made to get hold of Luther without a lot of public trouble. We have the strange phenomenon of Cardinal Miltitz, a self-made German who managed to get himself onto the staff of the Roman Curia, and fancied his own diplomatic ability. He persuaded the Pope and Curia to allow him to go as special envoy to Germany, as he felt sure he could solve the whole Luther question. The Pope equipped him with the Golden Rose, an annual award from the Holy See for a European ruler. The rose itself was lodged with Cajetan. It was offered several times to the elector if he would help matters by surrendering Luther quietly. Maybe this had something to do with the elector's final decision to protect Luther, as a reaction against pressure from Rome. When he took this decision he wrote carefully to Cajetan, saying that Luther's case had still not been properly considered and that Luther's propositions had not been shown to be wrong on the basis of Scripture. This was significant. The elector was beginning to use the language of appeal to Scripture. The Miltitz incident throws a harsh light on bad diplomacy used on behalf of a failing cause. The crowning event of this particular aspect occurred the following summer, 1519. Miltitz informed Frederick on June 21 that the Pope would offer a cardinal's hat to any person he chose to name provided that the elector would help to elect the king of France as emperor. Historians are agreed that the "person" in mind was Luther; which provides us with a moment of hilarity.

One is often tempted to turn again to the three-day meeting between Cajetan and Luther. Here together were one of the ablest theologians of the papal Church, and the founder of the Reformation. Surely people of this caliber could manage to meet. Cajetan is still read today; he was an original thinker and no time server. But in fact the sands had run out decades, if not a century, ago. Every official of the established Church was bound, through a thousand precedents and conventions, to a theology which saw everything in terms of logical statements, raised to the status of law. Discipline and theology were, in the end, when disagreements threatened a crisis, a matter of black and white decisions by authority. One can point, of course, to men like Nicholas of Cusa in the previous century, of Erasmus in the sixteenth century, of Philip Neri in the second half of the century, and indeed of Contarini during the Reformation, who knew that the gospel could not properly be the subject, or object, of this kind of executive action. But they were unable to influence events within the community to which they remained loyal. They knew that many of its best minds had never subscribed to the cut-and-dried approach. They believed with reason that its theology at its most fundamental was truly expressive of the divine freedom and the human responsibility at the heart of the gospel. But the refusal had been made, century after century, as we have seen, by Church authority to depart from the legal and canonical way which Europe as a whole trod as it emerged from the Dark Ages. It was a tragedy and not potent of assessment in terms of a balance sheet of moral judgments. Men were caught up in a pattern. Even Francis, even Dante had failed to have any noticeable influence on the way the Church managed its affairs.

Cajetan, as he waited for Luther in the house of Fugger at Augsburg, had his books and his precedents with him, and a true charity. But he could never admit the Bible as the "authority." An "authority" for him was a man or a group of men capable of taking decisions, and having them put into effect. Rome had survived many previous appeals to Scripture. Cajetan was a man of middle age, forty-nine to Luther's thirty-five, an Italian, cultured, soaked in Aquinas, an intellectual, a diplomat, deeply committed to the view that the Pope enjoyed a special guidance and that his words and actions were spiritually privileged. He had had his own experiences of the personal nature of religion. He had joined the Dominican Order and submitted to its discipline. He had understood how all was well planned, arranged by God. For him it was a perversion of all this to think of some kind of special action of the Holy Spirit, operating for each man, even for the Church as a community, except through proper channels. God had founded an authoritative Church. The authority was plain for all to see. There was never any chance that Cajetan could really understand Luther's intersubjective approach to theology, using Scripture as a "dynamic" word which must lead to the truth and be the inspiration of the Church's life and actions, independently of all the past actions and precedents of Popes and councils. It was just these objective facts of Popes and councils that he dealt in, established over so many years as the best way of applying revelation to life. For him Luther's way was the way of so many previous heretics. It was not difficult to prove this. The Augustinian was sincere and must be treated as kindly as possible. But he must be refuted and disciplined, otherwise his perverted theology would begin to lead others astray.

Back behind Cajetan was the far less comprehending and far less serious attitude of the Pope and the Curia. Cajetan's report of the Augsburg meeting stirred no interest. It reached the Pope in October. The following consistories hardly mention the Luther case. Hunting and the theater were the order of the day.

The Roman Catholic historian Lortz comments: "In the Rome of the Medicis, with its many embassies, its law-suits against mutinous cardinals, its theatres, painters, sculptors, architects, where the masterpieces of Raphael and many others were everyday things, where there was daily excitement over the discovery of ancient treasures and priceless manuscripts, how could the complaints of a solitary monk in a distant land set off even the slightest reverberations?" Lortz, writing in 1939, feels strongly, and his moral judgment is worth quoting, since it indicates something of the tension in the original situation: "This difficulty, this very impossibility of Luther's breaking into the richly charged political and cultural atmosphere of the centre from which the curia ruled the whole earth *was* the evil, and proclaimed the guilt." In some ways it is a misjudgment. In 1522 a Pope was solemnly to admit the guilt. It was not so much that Luther's complaint could make no impression, as that his theological expression of it was an intolerable affront.

Twenty Months

The tension of the Augsburg encounter over, the extraordinary relief of knowing that not martyrdom but protection had come to him, Luther had now to face facts. His archbishop, Albert, had never replied to the letter Luther sent with the theses, twelve months previously. The Pope had never replied to the letter Luther had sent, except with threats of excommunication. And on his way back to Wittenberg Luther had received from Spalatin a copy of the letter Cajetan had had from the Pope, demanding Luther's arrest. At the same time numerous encouraging messages had reached him from his own bishop, and from a wide range of other priests and lay people. The contrast was striking and was already beginning to set up a new and terrifying tension in Luther's mind. He was teaching students, he was preaching to the people, according to the duties he had, and he was asking that some reforms be set in motion. Without being heard in any considerable way at all, he had been denounced as though he were a proven heretic. As yet, however, the tension had not become unbearable, and Luther was still declaring his loyalty to the Pope. For twenty months Rome remained silent, waiting first on the imperial election and then on a declaration of policy from the new emperor.

Soon after Augsburg, Luther issued a small tract in Latin, *Acta Augustina*, about the meeting, reaffirming his request to be judged by the norm of Scripture. He also said that Cajetan had treated him courteously. In the new year he wrote a Latin piece, intended to guide friends and enemies in the university world as to where he stood on controversial questions. *Saints* were mediators and might be prayed to. *Purgatory* existed and those in it should be prayed for. *The papacy* is of human not divine foundation (we shall see Thomas More warning the overmilitantly papal Henry VIII in three years' time that this might indeed be the case). *Indulgences* are to be tolerated but are not to be compared, in their value, with good works (the same judgment as Aquinas had made). *Fasting* and other Church discipline is less important than inward piety and helping one's neighbor. *Good works* come only from the regenerate man, who alone is pleasing to God.

Later he wrote his German treatise on marriage for general consumption. He reaffirmed a point he often made—that bringing up children is more important than going on pilgrimages! Luther was setting down in theologically sited form material which had been part of his sermons and lectures for some four years or so. He was still preaching in the parish church each Sunday and feast day, also speaking frequently to his brethren in the priory. It was a time of lull. Luther still accepted the existing Church structure. Though we can see how impossible it was going to be for official theologians of that time to accept his position, we can see now that what he said was not fundamentally contradictory of the gospel as the Catholic tradition sees it. This may be an unfair piece of hindsight, because the "Catholic" tradition, as we now see it, has been influenced both reactively and sympathetically by Luther's teaching. All the same, it is important to see that at this time, throughout 1519, Luther was not denounced as a heretic by those who heard him speak day by day. And it is clear to the historian that he was still sincerely trying to understand his own position in the traditional Church.

But the matter of authority had to be faced. Someone or some group has to take decisions, and see that they are put into effect, be it a single person, a small council or a large council. It was on the authority of the papacy that Luther had been challenged by Cajetan. And it was this that representatives of orthodoxy were determined to pursue. The next showdown on this matter was a public debate at the great university town of Leipzig (June 1519), where Luther was opposed by John Eck. Theses had been exchanged. The debate itself was built up in the usual theatrical fashion with a fool coming on between sessions mimicking the protagonists.

At this time Luther was very much in harness with Karlstadt, the dean of the faculty of theology. Since early in 1518 Karlstadt had been engaging in a pamphlet battle with Eck. The famous debate at Leipzig between Luther and Eck was originally to be a confrontation between Karlstadt and Eck, and in fact was such a confrontation, a long debate which went on both before and after Eck's debate with Luther. In one of his limbering-up pamphlets Karlstadt uses the word *Gelassenheit* for the first time. It means "resignation," and refers to the whole complex of mystical ideas, derived from the Rhineland mystics and from Dionysius, which recommend a spiritual passivity in the Christian, an abandonment of himself and his will to the being and will of God, though it has more of the sense of commitment than *Verlassenheit*, the word for abandonment. In practice this word signifies the little beginning of what became a great stream of Reformation spirituality, far to the left of Luther, and bitterly tiresome to him, a stream which comes close in its ideas to some modern ideas of "anarchism." It had a long pedigree and drew on a wide range of past experience. We shall see Müntzer, a man of outstanding intellectual ability, leading one group of peasants in such a cause. And soon the "Prophets" and the "Anabaptists," many of them in the medieval apocalyptic line, are actively opposing Luther for his conservatism. Even now Karlstadt is really a nuisance to Luther. He gets very worked up. He has a bad memory and cannot debate well. At one point in the debate Eck roared out: "This is a debate, not a homework display," as Karlstadt kept opening new books and reciting and dictating from them. The debate continued by post afterwards. Later Karlstadt got very angry with Eck. It gives us a remarkable insight into what was going on to find Luther writing to Spalatin about Karlstadt: "treat him gently, he has had a rough handling from Eck." Rupp states that Luther wrote to Spalatin "in some alarm that Karlstadt intended to call his reply 'Against that Silly Ass and self-assertive imitation doctor' and begged Spalatin to make him tone it down, but not to mention that he (Luther) had written, 'for the man is prone to suspicions.'"

Luther was not initiating the Reformation alone. The whole of Wittenberg University was with him. The student intake into Wittenberg in this year 1519 was going to reach the astonishing figure of 575, nearly three times the normal. At Leipzig many friends were present, and came to hear the crucial issues of the papacy debated. Karlstadt and Eck were throwing backwards and forwards the old arguments about grace and free will, roughly in the terms we used on page 102. It is always a matter of theological importance, but in this case Eck and Karlstadt were doing little more than trying to catch each other out, and in spite of his many debating gifts Eck was nearly caught, or was actually caught once or twice. But the really important matter at the time was the papacy, authority, councils. Cajetan had pushed Luther into making some reply on this issue. Eck was determined to raise it again. It was an issue for which men had burned. It was still a very live issue, particularly when men began to ponder at this time the practical conclusions of what they believed, in terms of daily life, in church, in society.

The preparation for it, and the debate itself, pushed Luther far on the road towards a hardening opposition to the papacy. By March he wrote to Spalatin: "I am looking through the papal decretals for my disputation at Leipzig and (I whisper it in your ear) I am in doubt whether the Pope is Antichrist or his Apostle, so miserably is Christ (this is the truth) corrupted and crucified by him in these decretals. I am terribly tormented by the thought that Christ's people is so fooled under this specious form of law in the name of Christianity." The debate itself enabled Eck to accuse Luther of being another Hus. Luther at first hotly denied it, but, reading through some of Hus's works, came to the conclusion that Hus indeed had been wrongly condemned and that he and Luther agreed on many points. Luther felt more sure than ever that Scripture was the only authority to be trusted and that neither Pope nor council should be taken as a final authority. When he said this publicly it drew a gasp of aggressive astonishment from Prince George, Duke of Saxony who was sponsoring the debate. It was just exactly what Eck had hoped he might get Luther to say. His goading of Luther with being a Hussite made Luther consult Hus's writings and led him to realize that some of his theology had indeed been held by Hus. He was beginning to recognize his pedigree. To the orthodox it was obvious—his denial of the Pope's authority made him a heretic. But for Luther, he must plumb the teaching to be found in the New Testament. To find that this teaching had been held by Hus in the same way as he understood it himself was at first perhaps alarming rather than anything else, just as it had been alarming a few months previously to read the historical decretals, which seemed to breathe so little of Christ. But Luther was set now on a journey to truth, a journey which he made in faith. He could not go back or turn it into any other kind of a journey. The disputation was to be judged by the University of Paris, who haggled over the proposed remuneration with Prince George, and only gave their verdict finally, in 1521, against Luther but without any particular pronouncements about papal authority.

The year after the Leipzig disputation is often jumped over quickly in books on the Reformation, in the author's desire to reach the famous "Reformation writings" of autumn 1520. But this gap of a year is important. Father Luther, district superior of the Augustinians, parish preacher, university lecturer, continued with his daily round at Wittenberg. No action was taken against him by Elector Frederick in the castle, nor by his bishop or archbishop, nor by his superior in the Augustinian Order. What Luther published is significant—some academic work, and some pious and popular work. The theology and exegesis of Scripture to which he has devoted his academic work is carefully presented in Latin. The pastoral implications of this theology, for everyday piety and daily life, are drawn out in other publications, often in German.

In this autumn after Leipzig Luther published his Commentary on Galatians. As we have seen, it fitted Luther's purposes very well. The legalistic approach, illustrated by indulgences, he wished to oppose, and to bring men back instead to something like an Augustinian "Love and do what you will." The introduction to it contains the core of his teaching, and we quoted from it on page 129. Luther returned to the epistle in commentaries twice again in his life. At this time Luther was also publishing the first section of his studies on the Psalms.

It is impossible to list everything that Luther wrote—there were twenty-five volumes piled up in the room when he was examined at Worms a year and a half later. But it is important to notice the pastoral works. He often wrote things specially for the elector. At this time the old man had been ill and Luther wrote a book of "fourteen consolations" for him—seven good things to think about and seven bad. The elector liked it and asked for a postil—a book of meditations on the Sunday readings on the gospel each Sunday (*Post illa verba*). Luther composed sermons on baptism, penance, the Eucharist, developing his new sacramental theology and its applications: "Anyone who neglects the duties of his calling will not be helped at all by fasting, making pilgrimages, telling beads, endowing Masses. First take care of your wife, your children and the poor." He wrote a piece which became famous on the Our Father.

A pamphlet he wrote in May next year is in the same vein. *On Good Works* may be seen as an epitome or a crown of the pastoral pamphlets he had been composing. In it he worked out something like a complete "spirituality" of daily life for ordinary people. Lortz said of it: "it was his most popular presentation of this theology of faith, of his spiritual concept of the Church as a spiritual fellowship of souls in one faith, recognised through baptism, the eucharist and the gospel, and of his theology of sin." Luther put into it a comparison which he liked and was typical of him: a married couple work for each other with confidence when they love each other—they do not keep fearing to lose each other's love if they fail to do this, or that. So in religion, with man and God. Fear is a bad counselor. Good works flow naturally from faith and love, which envelop the just man's life totally.

Leipzig had been decisive and divisive. Luther went on with his teaching at Wittenberg, but he had convinced himself that neither council nor Pope had any right to impose a doctrine on the faithful if it could not be shown clearly to be in Scripture. No longer the Church, but the Word of God speaking in a man's heart was to be the criterion. Of course these were not real alternatives. The Word of God would still need an organized Church. The New Testament clearly teaches that there is a community of the faithful Christians. So a whole new theology needed to be adumbrated—just as Marsilius had realized, and many others, including Hus. Luther was now in the hot seat; practical problems began to crowd in. Without meaning to he had been working the theology out for the last ten years. Now he must pour the thought into molds and let it jell. But Luther cannot be said to have rushed into it. It was not till the autumn of the following year, 1520, that the famous three "Reformation writings" were written, sparked off by Rome's final action against him.

Towards the end of 1519, once it was clear that Charles, now emperor, would remain normally Catholic and would not support Luther, thoughts were turned at Rome towards starting the Luther process again. The denials of Leipzig could not now be ignored. The heretic must be brought to heel. Cajetan remained his un-extreme self, and, while the process was being held in the early months of 1520, tried to persuade the other members of the committee that they should take the items of Luther's Ninety-Five Theses seriatim. He thought many of them could not really be judged heretical. The later writings were what mattered. But he was not listened to. As with Hus, all that mattered to Pope and Curia was the decision, the condemnation. The man had rebelled. Let him be destroyed. The theses were taken *en bloc*. To Cajetan's disgust Eck was brought in and helped to persuade the Curia to let the notably inadequate text of *Exsurge Domine* be issued in May 1520. Its perfunctory contradiction of Luther perpetrated among other things the statement that it is heretical to say that "to burn heretics is contrary to the will of the Holy Spirit."

The meeting between Cajetan and Luther had been in its way tragic. Two men believing in the strange idea that the Jew

Jesus was the image of God, the Son of God, sharing man's world and lifting it up for ever into God's life, were unable to face the real problems which were part of the position of each of them; problems, such as we outlined in the early part of Chapter 3, which can never be fully solved, about ecclesiastical authority on the one hand and the freedom of the inspired man on the other.

So, by the end of 1519, and during 1520, the tragedy continued to play itself out. Authority gathers up its robes and sets about a perfunctory and implacable condemnation of the man who will not bend to it. The inspired man becomes the prophet, turning to every subject within the range of his mind and experience, and uttering what can hardly be called anything else but prophesies —not forecasts of the future, but a speaking forth of the Christian truth, as he sees it and as he sees that it must affect the future; and he does this now, deliberately flouting and where necessary denouncing the authority which has refused to listen. Within twelve months or so a vast chasm opens up, and the distance between the two protagonists increases very swiftly.

We must now look at the three pieces Luther wrote. They became famous as the "Reformation writings." They have a unique historic importance. Written very swiftly on the spur of the moment, they exude all Luther's piety, and all his resentment; and his utter belief in God. They contain the complaints and hopes of centuries concentrated into the feelings, thoughts and words of one man driven by his own personal troubles, his conscience, thrust out *ante foras,* into the public arena, and knowing that he can no longer in conscience creep back into his *angulum,* his corner, even though he has no plan for the kind of revolution of which, he begins to realize, so many people are beginning to see him as the leader, peasants, priests, local rulers, knights, university men—both humanists and proto-Protestants, monks and friars, merchants, intellectuals and religious people at court. Among all these categories in Germany and other countries can already be found many people who were eager to know what this Wittenberg friar was saying. And so the spate of writings begun at the start of 1518 and, already far too numerous for this book to attempt anything like a complete enumeration, kept up its pace and included in these crucial months after the Luther process and its conclusion in the papal bull now being prepared at Rome:

(1) *Open Letter to the Christian Nobility*, (2) *The Babylonian Captivity*, (3) *The Freedom of the Christian Man.*

Prior to these three, in June 1520, Luther published *Concerning the Papacy in Rome,* written as a reply to a Franciscan Alveld, who had attacked his theology. It was a kind of overture to the three writings. He began firmly to sketch out the lineaments of the Church as he could see it should and really could develop. The Church is a visible community of believers, but its precise extent is known only to God. Rome's authority is not God-given. Celibacy for secular priests is to be abolished. Parish priests are to be elected.

In two and a half years Luther had begun to have a notable effect throughout Europe. Wittenberg was getting used to a regular stream of visitors from every country. Students poured in. No longer is it possible to say that there is no real sign of religious revolution.

Europe 1520

In October 1518, Erasmus' printer-publisher Froben published in Basel a volume of Luther's works, the first "collected works," less than twelve months from the day on which Luther dispatched the Ninety-Five Theses to his archbishop. Froben and his advisers were certainly no less on the watch than twentieth-century publishers for material which their readers might want. And they did not have to bother with copyright difficulties, or even, as a matter of courtesy, to ask permission of the author. Froben included an anonymous introduction, written, as we now know, by Wolfgang Capito. This introduction gives us an insight into the extent to which Luther was already changing the whole atmosphere, and into the likelihood that a general disruption would occur. Mixed in with its scholarly references is some abuse and an expression of hope that at last someone intends to restore doctrine: "Here you have the theological works of the Reverend Martin Luther, whom many consider a Daniel sent at length in mercy by Christ to correct abuses and restore the evangelic and Pauline divinity to theologians who have forgotten the ancient commentaries and occupy themselves with the merest logical and verbal trifles. And would that he might arouse all theologians from their lethargy, and get them to leave their somnolent summaries of divinity and choose the Gospel rather than Aristotle, Paul rather than Scotus, or even Jerome, Augustine, Ambrose, Cyprian, Athanasius, Hilary, Basil, Chrysostom, Theophylact, rather than Lyra, Aquinas, Scotus, and the rest of the schoolmen. May they no longer drag Christ to the earth, as Thomas Aquinas always does, but may they instruct the earth in the doctrine of Christ. May they cease saying one thing in their farcical universities, another at home, another before the people and something else to their friends; and may they cease calling good men who refuse to fool with them heretics as they do now for small cause or no cause at all. . . ."

During the following months this volume and copies of many others of Luther's writings, in German or Latin, were printed and circulated. Froben had issued three more editions by 1520. In France they were being studied, though in private, circulated often by merchants, at the Lyons fair particularly. Froben told Luther in 1519 that 600 books were en route for France and Spain.

At the Sorbonne from autumn 1519, the Leipzig debate was being examined. Bishop Briçonnet was going ahead with his reforms in the diocese of Meaux. He had given Lefèvre the task of administering the hospital in the cathedral town, which provided him with sufficient time to continue with his translation of the Gospels.

In eastern and northern Europe, students had increasingly been opting for Wittenberg for their studies. The Reformation in these countries was being prepared through the education of these students.

Switzerland, more remote than most parts of France and Germany from the control of king or emperor, continued to be the spearhead of the movement for moderate reform, which it had become when Erasmus elected to reside at Basel, and Froben to publish for him. One of the secondary figures, the German priest and humanist, Johannes Oecolampadius, helped with the editing of Erasmus' works. He had also gained a paid position in Augsburg—he preached a successful sample sermon there a few days after Luther's encounter with Cajetan.

But Zurich had been becoming the center of a more radical type of reform. Zwingli took up his appointment there on January 1, 1519, and began a new kind of preaching. He was living confidently now in what we might call the world of Erasmus and Colet. Not only were his listeners willing to respond, but they were also more free to do so than Englishmen or Frenchmen, or indeed Germans. The new type of preaching, though an innovation, was by no means in itself revolutionary. Zwingli went through the Gospel of St. Matthew and proceeded to expound it, instead of following the normal excerpts from Scripture. Colet had done this at St. Paul's in England in 1497 with Romans. In 1503 there had been published in Basel a *Manuale Curatorum Praedicandi Praebens Modum,* on which Zwingli probably drew considerably. What was new in the situation in 1519 was the new learning on which Zwingli could draw, the confidence with which he could now embark on this new approach, and above all the response of people generally. All this, together with the news from Wittenberg, enabled developments to be very swift. Already in 1520 Zwingli felt that he must surrender a regular payment he received from Rome. Zwingli asserted that at first he had taken his initiatives without any knowledge of Luther's activities. But Froben's edition of Luther had already been out for two and a half months when Zwingli took up his appointment in Zurich. And in the course of 1519 Zwingli made his first known reference to Luther, calling him "the Elias of our times."

Zwingli concerned himself with the everyday lives of his parishioners. Their individual misdemeanors were not excluded from his sermons. Zurich was a small town of 7000, where, as in other towns such as Geneva, Basel and Strasbourg, all the important people knew each other. Zwingli dreamed of a community which might be a "Christian Commonwealth," and tried to weld the town into a single community. Although he had a poor voice, it was his preaching which was the heart of his achievement. He was much influenced by Greek and Roman literature. Both his fervent patriotism and his generally socratic attitude of sifting everything, drew much from his classical reading. Zwingli's humanist approach led him to be less traditionalist than Luther. He wanted to weigh everything against the touchstone of reason. This was the last thing that Luther wished to do. For him Scripture was a dynamic Word. Theology, for Luther, had not only not lost the detachment given it by nominalism and the pre-eminence always due to it. It had rather gained in stature now that it was seen again directly as the science of understanding God's word in Scripture. And Luther was attached, with a certain

German sentiment or romanticism, to the old forms. He had no special wish to do away with every rite, or hymn, or gesture, and particularly not if many Christians found them useful for their inner life of faith. He had no wish to submit everything to a rational examination.

Zwingli also maintained a lively interest in foreign affairs—his patriotism led him eventually to take part in a battle, against the Catholic cantons, in which he was killed (1531). At Zurich he was at first busy denouncing the Pope, stirred on by his memories of Marignano, for siding with Francis I of France against the emperor. It was at this time that Wolsey in England was busy trying to organize a pan-European peace treaty, a kind of non-aggression pact, known at the time as the Treaty of London. He hitched it on to the Pope's wish, stemming from the Fifth Lateran Council, to launch a crusade against the Turks. Henry VIII was keen to make an honorable peace with France, if only as a breathing space while he got the new emperor and perhaps the Pope as well on his side.

It was towards this end that the great symbolical meeting of the king of England and the king of France was organized in 1520, near Calais, known as the Field of the Cloth of Gold. Just before this great occasion Henry had another triumph, in that the new nineteen-year-old emperor, Charles V, sailing for the Netherlands and thence for his first imperial Diet in Germany, the Diet of Worms, where Luther was to appear early in 1521, was persuaded to stop off at England. Three days were spent there, mostly in feasting and dancing, though the serious-minded young Charles did not join Henry at the latter. Henry persuaded Charles to come to England again in 1522. But these summit meetings were not repeated. Charles began to realize that Henry's troops were never going to be sent far enough into Europe to help him in his military arguments about territories with the Pope and the king of France. And later there was Henry's treatment of his queen, Catherine, aunt of Charles, to persuade him against working with Henry; and later again, Henry's rejection of the papacy.

When landing at Sandwich, Charles's entourage found itself encountering the vast assembly of people and things which were preparing to make the crossing for France. This was the time perhaps of Wolsey's greatest triumph. Scarisbrick (in *Henry VIII*) gives us a wonderful picture of it all. Five thousand people finally went across in Henry's entourage, with hundreds of pounds worth of velvet, sarcenet, satin, cloth of gold, doublets, bonnets, shirts and boots; tents, pavilions, plate, cutlery, glass. Wolsey "dealt with all the queries concerning the buildings, worried whether it would be cheaper to buy the flour in England or at Calais, whether there would be enough beer and wine, green geese, rabbits, storks, quails and cheese, enough fuel for the kitchens."

Wolsey was not indifferent to the new learning. He had read Thomas More and Erasmus on the need for peace. There was certainly some of this behind the peace he tried to bring about. There was a conscious theory that it was better to get the nobles of the two countries to go jousting, tilting and wrestling together instead of fighting. And not only the nobles, for the two young kings took their fair share of the sport, including the wrestling, Henry being, to his surprise, thrown by Francis in one bout.

For twenty-seven years, Francis, Henry and Charles remained on their respective thrones of France, England, the empire, until the deaths of Henry and Francis in 1547. The emperor did not much like fighting against the Pope's armies, nor did he much like compromising with Protestant armies, but when *raison d'état* or the survival of his own armies seemed to dictate it he never hesitated to act according to the practical desiderata, and not on any other principle. So also, King Francis I, when necessary, made secret or even open arrangements with the Turks on the emperor's eastern borders. Equally the Pope on occasion acted pragmatically in matters of foreign affairs, making agreements with Protestant princes. The history of the wars they fought is inextricably woven into the history of the gradual emergence of Protestantism. Often enough the wars and treaties and other "foreign affairs" provided an occasion for some development in the religious sphere. But hardly ever were they decisive. The following year, after the Field of the Cloth of Gold, wars began again. In no time Henry's soldiers were trudging across the few miles of northern France they ever managed to cover. In Eastern Europe the Turks drew nearer.

In England Henry had been consolidating his position as monarch. He had reacted very severely in 1517 to the May-day riots, when apprentices rioted in the belief that foreigners were the cause of their poor pay and conditions. Hundreds went to prison and many were hanged, drawn and quartered. Four hundred were pardoned after a ritual appeal. Henry's wife, Queen Catherine, six years his senior, knelt before the king to beg pardon for the young men. Cardinal Wolsey made a speech supporting the appeal. Civil peace was valued very highly by a king and ministers who remembered, or whose fathers remembered, the civil wars.

At this time young Thomas Cromwell was a lawyer in London, working for Wolsey, but as yet unknown. He had acquired a knowledge of foreign banking in Italy, and of business in Antwerp during a teen-age trip. Now he was married and working very hard, and reading much.

Lollards were still active. Within a few years the conservative bishop of London, Tunstall, successor to Fitzjames, would say in a letter to Erasmus about the Continental reformers: "It is no question of pernicious novelty; it is only that new arms are being addd to the great crowd of Wycliffite heresies." There is much evidence of continuing Lollard activity in London and elsewhere, though mostly confined to weavers, wheelwrights, smiths, carpenters, shoemakers, tailors, together with a few secular priests, schoolmasters, and merchants. Thomas Grove, a well-off butcher, gave £20 to Dr. Wilcocks, vicar general of the diocese of London, to avoid doing open penance. In 1511–12, seventy-four heretics (a third of them women) appeared before the court of the bishop of Lichfield.

In 1520 it was necessary to keep the reading of doctrinal novelties or even of Scripture in English strictly as a private affair. But there is no doubt that the influence of Luther was already being registered. In 1519 agents of Wolsey had discovered a book of Luther's in a bale of imported cloth. The Oxford bookseller John Dorne sold some dozen books by Luther between January 29 and late December 1520. Luther was told that his books were going into England—to some *maximi* there who admired his writings, so Erasmus told him. In Cambridge the famous group which met at the White Horse pub was coming together to discuss theology and read Luther and others. Chief among them was the prior of the Augustinian house, Robert Barnes; Miles Coverdale was also resident there and attended the group meetings. The following year the university burned Luther's writings in a public burning. Young Father Tyndale, secular priest, an Oxford graduate, was at Cambridge probably 1519–21. In 1528 Tyndale wrote of his time at the universities: "They nosel in sophistry. . . . corrupt their judgments with apparent arguments, and with alleging unto them texts of logic, of natural philautia, of metaphysic. . . . one is Real, and another is Nominal. . . . When they have in this wise brawled eight, ten or twelve years, and after that their judgments are utterly corrupt, they then begin their divinity; not at the Scriptures, but every man taketh a sundry doctor; which doctors are as sundry and as divers, the one contrary unto the other, as there are divers fashions and monstrous shapes, none like another, among our sects of religion. Every religion, every university, and almost every man hath a sundry divinity."

Cranmer was university preacher in 1520. Neither he nor Latimer, apparently, took part in the White Horse meetings, but did their reading privately. Jasper Ridley, Cranmer's most recent biographer, is wrong to say that Cranmer was already a heretic in his heart on account of his reading Luther after he had been excommunicated and his writings forbidden, as was shortly to occur. Things were never as black and white as that. A man of great integrity and a lawyer, Thomas More asked permission before reading Tyndale to confute him. And More was always aware of the danger in which every man who became a government servant stood. But many a man read his Eckhart or Lull or Averoës— or Luther—without any kind of hidden heresy in the heart. The mind of the Church was made up precisely as a result of the conclusions to which such scholars and theologians came. Canon law was severe, but widely got round by the educated without any sense of guilt. Which is of course just the trouble with legalism, and just what Luther was fighting—laws which bound some people purposelessly (for spiritual purposes), laws which were themselves further devalued by those who ignored them. Any cleric in a teaching post in a university could feel himself to be part of that general magisterium of Church, state and university which needed to have an understanding of what was going on. Everywhere, in fact, men were reading Luther.

1520; Excommunication and Blueprint for Reformation

In May 1520 Rome issued the bull giving Luther and his followers sixty days in which to recant. On July 17 Eck and Aleander were appointed papal nuncios for the execution of the bull in Germany. In August Luther published his *Open Letter to the*

Christian Nobility of the German Nation, Concerning the Reform of the Christian Estate. He has now despaired of the Pope, council or bishop as authorities which might bring in the reforms that he has seen to be necessary at every level. So he turns to the only other authority available, that of human society itself. This was not a counsel of despair but an integral part of a secularist theology. God made the world and man. Society springs from man's God-given nature. Whatever authority emerges within society is to be respected—the advice St. Paul had given to his converts in the Roman Empire. In Luther's time it meant that a pan-Christian society could call on its rulers to make sure that state and society followed the faith which they held. Thinkers were beginning to ponder the question of what should be done in non-Christian societies. Thomas More tackled this in *Utopia*. The Turk, the Mohammedan and the Jew had always posed the problem for the theologians.

Luther was not concerned with such theories but with the case in front of him, with urgent needs—of himself, his immediate acquaintances and society generally. For he is now aware that not only can he not retire to his *angulum*, but that he must face a worldwide encounter. His solution is coterminous, as it were, with the society in which he has been brought up. He does provide a full theological orchestration, but the point here is that his solution is the kind of thing which was immediately practical in a way that *Utopia* was not and did not pretend to be. Luther's turning to secular authority was in the medieval tradition. The Church had always relied on the secular arm. From Marsilius onwards there had been full-blown theoretical attempts to foresee a society entirely controlled by the secular arm, instead of a balance of power between Church and state, which was the usual recipe. The problem is clearly not patient of any permanent solution in practice or in theory. There will always be tension and opposition. To put it in terms relevant to the twentieth century, in any polity, authority will want to try to exclude activities by groups which might threaten the integrity or the prosperity of the state. But in every polity groups who are concerned for the ultimate good of man and are convinced about the purposes of his life are sure to try to alter society, by persuasion or by force, to enable their ideals to be realized. The outcome of such tension will be various. In the sixteenth century it seemed obvious to Luther, and to many

others, that ecclesiastical authority which in their view failed to
live up to the ideals of its Church should be denuded of power
and reformed by the secular power. As we have seen, the theory
of this had been written down, long before there was much sign
of it being a really practical proposition—though we must not forget
the early experiment of the short-lived Roman republic under
Arnold of Brescia.

Luther's purpose in turning to the secular arm was religious and
ostentatiously "non-political"—he had recently declined offers of
help from the knights Ulrich von Hutten and Franz von Sickingen.
The fact remains that in Germany, as in many other places in
Europe, the state had already been bringing the Church well under
its power. What was to emerge, in embryo, in 1526 at the Diet of
Speyer as the regional religious principal of *cuius regio, eius religio*
(a man's religion is that of his country or district), had been
to some extent foreshadowed in the *Eigenkirche* of the German
princes. Luther was concerned for the reformation of society as
part and parcel of a reformed Church. In spite of himself he was
becoming a kind of revolutionary. His *Open Letter to the Christian
Nobility* proposed various educational, legal and social reforms—
excessive eating and drinking, overrich clothing, brothels are denounced. University faculties of theology and philosophy are to
be reformed. Clerical celibacy is to be abolished—and with it
the concubinage which provided an income for the Church bureaucracy in the form of fines or bribes. The Hussites are to be
tolerated, the mendicant orders reduced. Parish priests are to be
elected in future.

It is the duty of laymen to intervene to achieve these purposes,
for they are baptized Christians. As such they even have the
authority to call a council—a hint to the emperor. For the first
time Luther coins the phrase the "priesthood of all believers."
The detail of a reformed theology is not given in this popular
pamphlet in German, but the basis is there in all its shocking
simplicity. The ordained priesthood is only a way of ordering the
universal priesthood of all baptized Christians. Then there was the
usual list of things to be reformed, the luxurious living of the
clergy and the large income Rome took in the various taxes it
managed to impose on the faithful.

Within a few days four thousand copies were sold, and thereafter edition after edition was sold. Virtually every literate person

in Germany must have had the opportunity of sight of a copy at some time. And many who could not read listened to it. And the message went through them like a shock: "All Christians possess a truly spiritual status and among them there is no distinction save that of function. This arises because we possess one baptism, one faith, one gospel, and are equal as Christians. Anyone who has emerged from the waters of baptism may pride himself on already being ordained priest, bishop or pope, although not everyone may be suited to exercise such an office. Therefore let every congregation elect a devout citizen to be their priest." Here is the authentic Waldensian reaction, now proposed in clear formulations, applied in detailed practical terms to all people and to the existing communities. This booklet of Luther's sums up the reaction to hundreds of years of history and voices the feeling which lay behind the repeated presentation of lists of gravamina to the imperial Diets. The Roman Catholic historian sees it in its long historical context. Lortz writes (in *The Reformation in Germany*):

> Here at last was a radical solution to the problem of the coming of age, the declaring responsible, of the members of the Church. The air was filled with a host of demands for independence in all spheres of life—social, intellectual (humanist) and religious. Luther's call was like the conceding at last of a long-deprived right.
>
> This book shows how fatal had been the effect of the onesided administration of the Church in favour of the clergy. And it had not even been done lawfully. Seen from the angle of the innovators, the whole Reformation can appropriately be described as a protest against this clericalism—a protest of the ordinary Christian against clerical exploitation. This exploitation extended beyond the fiscal sphere. Luther, the shaker of foundations, was much more deeply gripped by the the idea that the ordinary Christian had been defrauded of his rights as a Christian. Since the thirteenth century at least, the active enlistment of the laity in the work of the hierarchical apostolate as a fruit of the Church's educational programme, had been overdue amongst the now autonomous nations. But Avignon and the Renaissance, i.e., the mighty secularisation of the papal secular power, had interrupted the line of development providentially set in motion by Francis of Assisi, himself a layman, with his third order.

Two months later Luther published in Latin some of the detailed theological implications in *Prelude on the Babylonian Captivity of the Church.* It spelled out Luther's understanding of the
nature of Christian sacraments, those religious acts which express
and symbolize a Christian's faith. The denunciations contained
in this and in the *Open Letter* were to lead directly to the religious revolution. There was no longer any attempt at gradual
change. Rome was Antichrist, its system evil. Radical changes
in the practice of religion were demanded. This involved, for the
popular mind, and indeed for most theologians, as its rationale, the
assumption of two sets of doctrines diametrically opposed to each
other, a black and white picture. Most historians and most theologians, both Protestant and Roman Catholic, still tended, until very
recently, to accept this, and then make some subsequent qualifications if the actual historical details did not fit Luther's black
and white picture. The facts are indeed more subtle. The eventual
emergence of reformed churches whose doctrines and whose practice of the sacraments were not simple contradictories of traditional practice and theology illustrates this fact.

Precision at this point is of great importance. Without it, history
is traduced and religion is made to appear in itself as foolish
as a few extremists of both sides sometimes make it appear. On
the one side is an extreme Catholic view that a sacrament works
automatically. The priestly action performed (*opus operatum*),
the effect is obtained regardless of the faith of the subject. At
the other, Protestant extreme, the Christian is directly inspired
by the Holy Spirit as an individual; the two sacraments which
such Protestants may recognize, baptism and holy communion,
fit uneasily as formal church occasions into this latter theory,
which logically requires no organization or any particular rites to
sustain the inspired lives of Christians. Neither of these extremes does justice to the Christian theologians of the Catholic
and the Reformed traditions who have worked out sacramental
theologies. Luther did denounce the Catholic system in terms of
a magical system, because it had been reduced to something very
like it in practice, though not entirely so. But his affirmations
were closer to the theology, for instance, of Thomas Aquinas than
to that of the extreme "spiritualists."

The point is that no adequate definition of a sacrament can
make of it something independent of the intentions of those taking

part—the Catholic theory assumes a "believer." A man who does not believe is not capable of receiving a sacrament. However extreme an "objective" theory may be in insisting that a priest-operated sacrament is a channel of grace, it cannot dispense with an assenting believer. Contrariwise, however extreme the spiritualist may be in insisting on the inspiration of the individual by the Holy Spirit, no sacrament even of the simplest and most inward kind can take place without the presence and assent of at least two Christians, one who administers it, and one who receives. Christianity concerns itself in the sacraments with the nature of human encounters of a kind which it takes to be of a special and symbolical sort, giving an almost divine power, at one end of the thesis, and some human comfort at the other end. The occasions concerned have the character of being just such encounters as all human experience witnesses to. Men are received into communities, and they have commemorative meals: to refer to the two sacraments of baptism and the Last Supper to which the Protestants eventually confined the sacramental system. Men marry; they also order people to special offices and purposes; they are sorry and forgive; they fall ill and are cured or die: to refer to the sacraments of matrimony, the priesthood, penance (reconciliation as it is being called, more properly, today) and unction.

Clearly sacramental life and theory is a sphere which allows of great latitude of approach with enormous scope for argument, for disagreements or synthesis. In the end, of course, very often it is the practice, the conventions, the style, the culture-orientated characteristics which impress and which count. In the twentieth-century world these count perhaps a little less than before; and people more easily perceive the area of Christian faith which is held in common by all Christians. But in the sixteenth century the situation was fraught with antagonisms. In 1520 a stage had been reached where a clean break, a revolution was almost certainly inevitable. What many reformers in the Church and many who had been declared heretics had looked for during four hundred years, was coming true—Christian communities were opting for simple ceremonies based on the best reconstructions they could make from the Bible and early Church practice. And they would do this with a full consciousness of throwing over an existing canonical system. There was all the attraction of release from a system, which in practice was obviously rather corrupt, all the attraction of creating something quite new which one might hope would be free of such corruption.

It is in this context that we need to see Luther's outright and methodical rejection of the contemporary Catholic system in *The Babylonian Captivity*. It was written in Latin for all the educated world to read; as distinct from books in German, which Germans of all classes, but not many others, could read. The Mass was not to be a "sacrifice" any more, but a rite of thanksgiving and commemoration in which Christ was truly present in bread and wine—but not in a way to be defined as transubstantiation. Above all it was no longer "meritorious," a "good work." It could be celebrated by any baptized person designated or licensed by the community to do so. The laity were to receive the chalice. The sacraments or sacramental signs were to be confined to baptism and the Eucharist, and perhaps penance, which Luther himself continued to use till the end of his life. The primary sacrament was the word of God in Scripture. Luther's comparison of the Church under the papacy to the Jews in captivity was a typical medieval comparison and typical of Luther, steeped as he was in the Old Testament.

Thirdly and finally Luther wrote *The Freedom of the Christian Man*. He was writing just now to Spalatin that he was feeling so free these days. He knew that the excommunication would be formally pronounced soon and that the emperor would want to proscribe him. As two years ago he had said to Cajetan's messenger that if necessary he was not unhappy to be committed *"sub coelis,"* so now even more he felt all was in God's hand. But he continued with his pastoral writings, following on the publication of this, the third of the three "Reformation" works.

The last pamphlet was, like all Luther's other writings, no considered set piece. Miltitz was still about, and still convinced that things could be patched up if Luther would only write in the correct way to the Pope. Invited, Luther said he would write and in twelve days completed *The Freedom of the Christian Man*. It both expressed a sincere solicitude for the Pope himself and a sad harsh conviction that Christ had abandoned Rome long ago. It enabled Luther to give expression to the noble sense of spiritual freedom that lies at the heart of all true religion. The religious man

is free to live for God, to follow his conscience, free from the re-
straints of the world, free to do good works, free to be the servant
of all men. Luther expresses the theme which Karlstadt had at
heart, that man should empty himself and serve his neighbor.
A Christian lives in Christ and in his neighbor, in Christ by faith
and in his neighbor by love. We can find this teaching in *Piers
Plowman,* in eastern orthodox mystics, in St. Peter, and St. John.
The medieval Church had not forgotten it, in spite of its failures.
St. Francis was stirred by it. The papacy itself always styled
itself the servant of the Church.

Lortz writes of *The Freedom of the Christian Man:*

It affected the whole of Christendom, even his opponents,
by its sensitive simplicity and warm piety. It is here that
Luther is closest to the Catholic atmosphere. The pamphlet
became a Reformation pamphlet only in virtue of the one-
sided views which had been expressed in its two precursors.
One of its basic views is that of the priesthood of all believers,
already expressed in the letter to the nobility. With extraordinary evangelical depth and a fervour that came close to the
people, Luther preached free surrender to the heavenly Father
and the free Christian service of our brother that arises from
that surrender.

There is a new element, too. With a tremendous feeling for
the world and language of the synoptists he presents the
gospel of Christ and forgiveness through faith in him. Frequently justification is portrayed in a thoroughly Catholic manner as something actual, just as the doctrine of the necessity
of good works for the disciplining of one's own body and the
advancement of Christian corporate life is affirmed.

Christian freedom, as Luther had already taught in *The
Babylonian Captivity,* is not some precious extra but the quin-
tessence of the redeemed man. "Christians" is but another
name for the people who enjoy Christian freedom, who stand
in contrast to the people who are slaves of the law. It is true
that it is only when we come to polemics against the multitude of Roman regulations and the resultant multiplication of
possibilities of sin and the danger of legalistic piety, that this
concept becomes so sharply accentuated. We must be on our
guard, however, against understanding it only in the light

of this polemic. It is essentially positive in its application and a consequence of the dogma of justification: by faith alone man is completely freed.

The *Prelude on the Babylonian Captivity* may be reckoned to be that writing which brought an understanding of the schismatic, revolutionary nature of Luther's initiatives most swiftly and emphatically to Europe. Its Latin text could be understood by all. In several notable respects it was unequivocally opposed to Christian teaching in the form that the Catholic Church had propounded it. Young King Henry VIII, with his troubadour-like spirit, decided that this bumptious German monk must be answered; he launched out into the theological arena, with a brash and rough and inadequate defense of the seven sacraments, and gained the famous title Defensor Fidei from the Pope. Erasmus was appalled by the *Prelude*. He saw now that his hopes for some kind of a reform of the Church were unlikely to be realized. For to him this was destruction, not reformation. And so too, many others. Among them was Cochlaeus, parish priest of Frankfurt, until then humanist and supporter of Luther, and from now on a bitter enemy and later calumniator. A catalyst was now at work, and sides were rapidly taken up by many from this time on. Erasmus tried precisely to avoid doing this; the first victim of all warfare, whether violent or verbal, is truth, and truth was his greatest love. But even he only survived another three or four years before finding he could not continue with his own work unless he made his own position clear. This position was one of loyalty to and trust in the traditional structure and doctrines, however badly in need of reform.

Eck and Aleander were having some difficulty in the autumn of 1520 in publishing the bull of excommunication. Eck had increased his own unpopularity, and helped the cause of reform to see itself as that of a community of peoples by adding the names of Karlstadt and others to the bull of excommunication as Luther's fellow conspirators. Both Eck and Aleander had to go carefully, for fear of their own lives. Aleander tried to have bonfires of Luther's writings; but at both Cologne and Mainz students interrupted this and rescued Luther's works. At other places they added anti-Lutheran works to the fires. Violence was supervening. It had hung over Luther's head in a personal way for two years. Now it threatened him again. But the whole cause of reform, of opposition to the papal Church, was also attracting violence in defense of itself, as well. Luther was driven on to delineating that black and white picture which is always painted when men want to justify extremes, and to see life in something other than the varying shades of gray, the varying shades which are those of truth. Luther wrote his solemn reply to the bull, *Against the Bull of Antichrist*. The Latin version included a solemn rejection of Roman authority and his solemn condemnation of the see of Rome to Satan. In a vernacular version he included the words "I know well where my consolation and my courage abide, and who makes me safe before men as well as devils. I will do what I believe to be right. Everyone will have to stand up and answer for himself at his death and on the Last Day; then perhaps my faithful warning will be remembered."

When it was clear to Luther that he was excommunicated, he decided to make the break quite clean by a symbolic gesture. On December 10, he burned a copy of the book of canon law. He made it a formal occasion. Melanchthon put up a notice saying that there would be a burning outside the gates at the place used for burning the clothes of people infected with plague. Canon law was at the center of what Luther considered to be wrong with the papal Church. As we have seen, the Church's method of administering its affairs was indeed firmly based on a system of law, centered on Rome. To burn the book of canon law was a sign of absolute rejection of the sovereignty of Rome, and of the legal system by which the Church ran its affairs. Luther threw in the bull of excommunication recently delivered to him, for good measure. No doubt most of the students did not fully realize the significance of it all. It was a great occasion to knock all authority. Some dressed up as cardinals and Pope. There was a general rowdiness in the town, which had to be brought to an end by the town council.

It was not only the students who were nearly everywhere backing Luther. In another part of the social spectrum stood the knights, particularly Ulrich von Hutten and Franz von Sickingen. The former was a poet, a literary connoisseur and a decadent. He had contributed to *Letters of Obscure Men* in the campaign on behalf of Reuchlin (see pages 143–44). Now, in the autumn of 1520, just as Luther was publishing his Reformation writings, Hutten decided to leave the court of the cardinal of Mainz, and to join Sickingen at his castle at Ehrenburg. The following year he published *Conversa-*

tion Piece. On the opening page he wrote: "I hate the church of the evildoers." The text as a whole implies the need for support for Luther, and virtually threatens violent revolution. This initiative was not welcome to Luther. It was in fact no more than the dying jerk of an effete and moribund social tradition. In 1523 Sickingen was defeated and killed in an attack he had launched on Trier. Hutten died the following year. But there is no doubt that it was the phenomenon of Luther which set the knights off on their last attempt at asserting themselves. It is also true that the pamphlets Hutten published, with their lively woodcuts, and their threatening language, were typical of much other printed material that was going the rounds, up and down Germany. They were to be found everywhere and led Aleander to report to Rome in 1520 that the whole of Germany was anti-Roman. Luther himself began to take an unhappy lead in violent denunciation, with its no doubt psychopathological significance. He wrote at this time, dangerously and in a way which owed more to medieval apocalyptic heresy than to the Gospels: "Emperor and princes must take up arms against the Roman Antichrist and the Roman Sodom. We must wash our hands in their blood."

The Break—and First Steps

Luther had reached that point reached by so many previous reformers where the logic of the situation required them either to change their minds and recant or else to regard those in authority at Rome, or the papal authority itself and all in communion with it, as the enemies of Christ. If the civil authority had complied in traditional fashion with the ecclesiastical demand, Luther, a proscribed person, would have been arrested and handed over to ecclesiastical authority, who would have then tried him and returned him to the secular arm for punishment. But the movement of support for Luther in Germany was such that the edict of excommunication could only be posted in a few towns. The emperor, young Charles, fresh from Spain, with little Latin and no German in his head, a French-speaking Burgundian, had to rely on advice. This was not consistent. Luther suffered first commands than countermands, to attend and not to attend the coming Diet at Worms. Finally it was clear that he was ordered to attend it. This in itself was a sign of weakness, for the excommunication was supposed to be sufficient for the civil authority to act on. No further examination was in order.

Luther's journey to Worms was something like a triumphal procession at times. He preached at several places. The climax of the journey was at Erfurt, where the excitement was very great. He was returning to this town of his university days, novitiate, and ordination in a very different style from that in which he left—in a minority of two. On this occasion he was treated with great honor. He preached to a large crowd.

At Worms news of Luther's imminent arrival was conveyed to the town by trumpet. A party of horsemen went out to meet him. Luther had been accompanied the whole way by the emperor's official, ensuring his safe conduct; this was legally necessary since Luther was excommunicate. Several attempts were made to stop him from reaching Worms, by messages of various kinds reaching him en route. But once he had set out Luther was determined to go on. In Worms he was brought to his lodgings by a great crowd. Aleander reported that he turned and looked at the crowd once "with his demoniac eyes" and then went into the house.

If communication between the twenty-one-year-old emperor and thirty-seven-year-old Father Martin Luther was nil, the encounter itself was even more prophetic than that between Luther and Cajetan had been. In public Luther made his position clear and simple—he took his stand on Scripture. Neither Pope nor councils had the right to override Scripture. The emperor took his stand on authority and tradition. To him the issue seemed very clear: "A single friar who goes counter to all Christianity for a thousand years must be wrong." Charles appealed to those thousand years in a personal sense: "I am descended from a long line of christian Emperors of this noble German nation, and of the Catholic kings of Spain, the Archdukes of Austria, and the Dukes of Burgundy. They were all faithful to the death to the church of Rome, and they defended the Catholic faith and the honour of God. I have resolved to follow in their steps." It is a powerful plea, just as Luther's is. But neither party argued their case fully. Luther did not face the practical consequences of his position. He was not asked to. Did Scripture set up an organized Church? What authority does the Church have? Who is to interpret Scripture? On his side the emperor did not consider the fact that something is not necessarily right by surviving for hundreds of years and that the general condition of men, so frequently at violence with one another, does not allow one to assume that a wrong could not go unrighted for so long.

The split between Luther and all who would follow him on the one hand and the Pope and bishops and those in communion with them on the other was made at the point of excommunication a few months earlier. Now at this public council of Europe's principal ruler, the split is made explicit. The lack of communication between the two sides is total. That which has happened on a lesser scale so many times between canonical ecclesiastical authority and incipient heretic in the past, is now raised up as a catalyst for the whole of Europe.

The whole affair was less unpleasant and sinister than the meeting with Cajetan, when Luther and his friends feared to be kidnaped. The two brief meetings before the emperor seem not to have been unfair to Luther, although the tense atmosphere weighed hard on him. His own life was once again in the balance, and much else that he held dear. At the first meeting there was a simple identification of twenty-five of his works and an adjournment at Luther's request. At the second Luther suggested that a distinction be made between his pastoral works and his theology, and apologized if at times he had been too vehement. The emperor understood no Latin and little German, interrupted Luther and retired for consultation with Eck (a new Eck), chancellor of the local archdiocese of Trier. They came back and went straight to the point. Luther had denied the authority of councils of the Church and defended Hus. Would he recant? Luther repeated what he had said before, that he must be convinced by Scripture. Otherwise he must keep to his previously stated position. He spoke clearly and emphatically and made a great impression. It was clear that the magisterium, the authority of Pope and emperor, indeed, *tout court*, "authority," understood as a legal entity, was being withstood. Whether he said it or not, the sense of his words was, "*Hier stand ich, ich kann nicht anders* [Here I stand, I can do no other]." He left the meeting amidst some confusion—some treating it as a victory for Luther, some for the emperor. Luther seems to have made the gesture as of confidence, or even victory, of a knight. His local lord, Elector Frederick, referred in his usual enigmatic way to the scene: "Doctor Martin has spoken right well in both Latin and German in the presence of the Emperor, the

Princes and the Estates. He is far too bold for me." But it was Frederick who had assured Luther of this hearing and refused to accept the normal implications of the excommunication.

Unlike the meetings at Augsburg with Cajetan there was no sinister ending. On the contrary, a few very civilized days followed. Attempts were made to patch things up—the usual bribes were offered in the form of an offer of a good rich priory to Luther. The archbishop of Trier had Luther to lunch one day, and ended by asking him what more could be done, since all avenues seem to have been explored, and Luther replied, as so often, with a very apt quotation from Scripture, which while hardly patient of the charge of arrogance, displayed his confidence, a confidence clearly in God, not himself. He quoted Gamaliel's words to the Jewish authority when they were wondering what to do about the preaching of the disciples in Jerusalem: "If this counsel or this work be of men, it will come to nought. But if it be of God, you cannot overthrow it, unless you may be found fighting against God." The day before he left Worms Luther sent the emperor a note assuring him of his loyalty and saying he wished only to reform the Church (a respectable wish) and to bear witness to the Word.

The emperor sent Luther back to Wittenberg with an escort, under the safe conduct which had brought him to Worms, but said he would then be proceeded against as a notorious heretic. However, he was not certain that the Diet would vote in this way. He waited till most of the electors and princes had gone home, including Elector Frederick, and only then issued the edict. After twenty-one days Luther was proscribed, no one was to harbor him, his books were to be destroyed. He was ready. The previous September Luther had written to Conrad Saum, a Wittenberg disciple: "What will happen, I know not, nor am I anxious to know. Certain I am that he who sits in heaven governing all things has foreseen from eternity the beginning, the progress, and the end of this enterprise, which I await. However the lot may fall, it will not move me, because it will not fall except in accordance with the best will. Be not anxious therefore; your Father knows what things you have need of even before you ask him."

The eleven months which followed Luther's appearance before the Diet at Worms represent the final "crucial moment" for him and the Reformation. Luther was an excommunicate, under the imperial ban, a man whom everyone owing loyalty to the secular

ruler or honoring Christian authority was bound to shun or apprehend.

It was clear to Elector Frederick that emotions had been raised
to breaking pitch. Anti-Roman feeling spread right across the population. In spite of the ban on him, Luther was invited to preach
several times on the way back. Somehow the heat must be taken
out of the situation. Luther, whether arrested by the emperor or
preaching in Wittenberg, was going to create tension which could
erupt into widespread violence. It was the elector's idea, then, to
remove Luther from the situation, without, however, doing him
any harm. This he did. Luther was warned that during the journey
back to Wittenberg the party would be attacked by friends mas-
querading as enemies and he would be apprehended. They should
put up a show of resisting but give in before superior strength.
The party was duly attacked. Luther spoke quietly to his friend
Amsdorf, riding by his side, telling him not to resist—and Luther
was taken off to the Wartburg, the great castle in the town of his
secondary school, Eisenach. He was guarded closely for two weeks
or so, while he grew a beard. He was told that he must call himself
Junker Georg while staying in the Wartburg for a few months.

Luther was removed from the situation, but it was not a total
absence, for he sent communications to his friends at Wittenberg,
and they sent queries up to him. Luther asked for writing materials, and proceeded with the writing which had been broken
off when he left Wittenberg for Worms, a translation of the Mag-
nificat, the song of praise put by St. Luke into the mouth of Mary.
He also started on a reply to the verdict of Paris University
condemning his writings, and later to Latomus, one of the professors of Louvain.

In Wittenberg things did not stand still. Karlstadt raised the
matter of celibacy on June 21, proposing that marriage was obligatory on secular priests and optional for monks. Luther's opinion
was sought. He confessed to being surprised by the suggestion that
monks should be free to marry. Secular priests he had already
agreed in principle need not be tied to celibacy, but he had not
thought about the whole matter in detail, and had not envisaged
the release of religious from their vows. Thought, and a search of
the Bible, compelled him to admit that, on the principles he had
been enunciating, to make a permanent vow of celibacy might be
to surrender the freedom which God had intended that man

should have. Furthermore such a vow was treated by the Church as a meritorious act, which again was unacceptable. So eventually Luther sent down to Wittenberg his Latin essay *On Monastic Vows*.

This piece has sometimes been called one of the dissolvents of the medieval Church. But this is to give too much emphasis to one event. It could not have done this dissolving work if the whole complex of vowed religious life had not itself been weak almost to the point of collapse. The truth is that religious were already leaving their houses in Wittenberg and elsewhere, even while Luther was writing. This has sometimes seemed to Catholics one of the saddest moments of the Reformation. The "contemplative life" was disappearing; within a few years over large parts of Europe the community houses of men and women vowed to many hours of prayer a day had completely disappeared. A distinction has to be made here. The majority of monasteries and convents were not houses of the strict contemplative orders. They were rather houses of friars and others devoted to various works, such as preaching and teaching. All the same, it is true that members of these houses were bound to many hours of prayer, though not in the rigorously ascetic and cloistered atmosphere of the Carthusians or the strict Cistercian houses. In a broad sense, then, houses of prayer, houses specially committed to religion, did close down in large numbers. Yet this happened often by the wish of the members of these houses themselves; or with only a small protest from a small proportion of the members in each case. Mediocrity seems to be the best word to describe the state of these houses. It is not easy to establish just what had led to the leaking away of the idealism of the original foundations. Somehow the absolute commitment and devotion had got watered down. We have some idea today of the great complexity of all human motivation. The privileged status of religious must have played a big part in the corruption of the religious ideal. The religious life had been invaded by a whole complex of other considerations. It became part of the social structure; the essentially independent religious raison d'être had been lost. Only a hollow shell remained.

Religious fervor was found elsewhere. Something of the religious fire which had inspired the lives of St. Francis and St. Bernard was now found among some who were trying to set the standards for a Christianity lived fully by married lay people, for a Christianity which thought of the life of Everyman not as a second best or third best, a mere "do well" as against Langland's "do better" (monks) and "do best" (bishops), but as a life lived entirely for God in the world created by him.

It was maybe a realization that they never had tried to, or perhaps even wanted to, live up to the original ideals of the rule of the houses they belonged to which led so many religious to leave their communities and abandon their vows. But for Luther it was not just a question, or a question at all, of a failure to live up to an ideal—he had discounted and recovered from his guilt on this count some years ago. It was the whole question of the religious life itself, whether a man or woman had a right to sign his life up in this sense. It was only when Karlstadt sent up his straight question whether monks might marry, that Luther began to think the matter through from the beginning. He was faced now with the first of very many questions which were to be put to him. He must answer on his own authority. He turned to the Bible. But in the end he had to give the answer, and give it simply on his own authority, after prayer and the reading of Scripture, and taking account of the Church's present and past practice. He came to the conclusion that lifelong vows of celibacy, poverty and obedience, canonically binding like a marriage vow, were not envisaged by the Bible. The Church considered such vows to be binding under pain of grave sin; they were also seen as meritorious, good works in themselves. Both these approaches were rejected by Luther on the basis of Scripture.

This is not a merely medieval question. Throughout the Roman Catholic Church, people are asking similar questions today. Specifically, many are saying that there should be the possibility of temporary vows, temporarily renewed if the man or the woman so wishes. In effect, they are asking the same question as Luther, whether the Church has the right to enable Christians to impose on themselves a canonical obligation, binding under sin, in this matter of celibacy, poverty and obedience, for life.

For Luther the conclusion to which the biblical text drove him was a shock. He hastened to say it would make no difference to himself—he certainly did not wish to marry. But the shock was psychologically complex. Luther dedicated the essay to his old father and wrote to him that he was no longer obliged to keep his vows. He knew that would please the old man, who had never expressed a full acceptance of Martin's career as an Augustinian.

The falling of this, one of the great secure walls of the medieval structure, first in Germany, and Switzerland, then fifteen years later in England, left Luther and everyone, at the same time more free and more vulnerable. There was loss and gain.

During his first weeks at the Wartburg, Luther found the change from the hurly-burly to solitude very trying. At first he saw little of anyone except the man who waited on him. The castle made him jumpy. He was lonely, became depressed and brooding—a severe attack, *Anfechtung,* came on. Had he done right? Ought he not to have answered up more forthrightly at Worms? Perhaps in any case he was simply wrong. He couldn't sleep. Constipation was bad. Later, writing to friends, he gave his address as "Patmos," "The Desert" or "The Land of the Birds." As Junker Georg he was allowed out with the hunt. But he found this unpleasant. They were hunting rabbits or hares; he thought it cruel. One ran into his arms and the dogs came after it. It reminded him, he said, of the hunting of souls by prelates. This *Anfechtung,* this attack, meant a realization of God's wrath, of the devil's attacks, of his own subjective uselessness. It meant a test for his faith, but also a strengthening of it as he came through the dark night.

One matter on which Luther was able to begin to exercise his authority in a new direction concerned the celebration of Mass in the Wartburg. He requested that the chaplain should not celebrate Mass there when there was no congregation. Private Masses had been a subject of discussion among theologians for a long time. Many priests lived on the small stipend they received for saying Mass each day, often for the soul of a deceased person. Luther rejected this practice as "a degradation of the mass to the status of a mere work," something "to be done" which "gained merit." Theologians had disapproved of abuses connected with the practice of private Masses but had not tried entirely to abolish them, for the theological reason of the nature of the Mass itself as a representation of the sacrifice of Christ. It was thus a good thing to do in principle. This was what theologians today might call an "essentialist" position. Luther turned rather to the nature of the Mass, in an existential and scriptural sense. What function did it have? What really is it as part of our life and worship? His answer is indicated by his words that the Mass should not be "said" but "preached." In his important piece on private masses, *Dunkelmesse,* written in 1533, he wrote: "For Christ's ordinance and intention

are to have the sacrament dispensed and to have himself preached
in order to strengthen faith. This ordinance they [the papalists]
suspend, and they invert everything. They keep the sacrament for
themselves alone and distribute it to no one; they remain silent
and preach to no one; they strengthen the faith of no Christian
but lead him from faith to the sacrifice and work of the Mass
which they apply or sell for money."

The Reformation writings of 1520 demolished in theory a great
deal of the existing structure of the Church. If it was to be demolished in practice, something would be put in place of some of
it. In fact the demolition would really be part of, or the corollary
of, a change to some new practice. After the Diet of Worms, the
Pope and emperor failed to put into effect the ecclesiastical and
civil ban on Luther and his named followers, Pirkheimer, Adelmann
and Karlstadt. There was an organizational breakdown. Into the
vacuum the theories of Marsilius, or of Ockham, or of Wycliffe, or
of Hus, or of many others might have been pushed. However,
Luther himself had not built up any complete alternative theoretical
structure, nor was anyone else thinking of working on such lines.
Only the millenarians, or followers of the apocalyptic tradition,
thought in terms of a total alternative, and this in any case was
entirely non-structural, or anarchist. The reformers were faced with
practical problems and proceeded with whatever question seemed
most urgent. The practical result was, inevitably, different in each
place. Reform soon had a hundrel different faces. There was no
universally recognized Napoleon to impose a grand scheme. Part
of the drive behind the Reformation was precisely a rejection of
any all-over man-made scheme. The New Testament seemed to
encourage a large measure of freedom in Christ, relying on the
Spirit of himself and the Father, the Holy Spirit. Where the reformers rejected all existing convention and practice, this existential
theology played into the hands of a totally subjective and apocalyptic approach.

Everywhere, however, the same driving inspiration can be clearly
identified. It was never in any sense a movement against religion.
Some such anti-religious movement could conceivably have come
from the humanist scholars. But it did not. The reformers themselves, and the popular support which enabled them to achieve so
much, were all intensely religious. Their basic inspiration was
simply a wish to uncover and to practice the Christianity of the

Gospels. Everywhere the Bible in the people's own language played a major part in the reforms. Along with it was a demand for a religion which was not primarily something imposed, organized and everywhere the property of "churchmen," but was a religion for everyone equally. It must therefore be in forms intelligible to them. Involved in all this was the strong universal anti-clericalism, and in particular an animus against monks and nuns. In Christianity according to St. Paul there is neither Greek nor Roman, slave nor freeman. All are equal. There was animus against anything which seemed to be some sort of mystification. And on the other hand the opportunity occurred naturally for a fresh grasp of the universality of Christianity, its relevance to every person, every kind of life, all actions. There was nothing "unclean."

There was an identity of general inspiration, of primary powerful motivation. But the lack of any executive authority, together with the emphasis on freedom in the Spirit, made it certain that conflict would break out immediately within the ranks of the reformers. However, the sense of religious community ingrained over the centuries, a love of the Church and of many of its ancient rituals and traditions (not everything was corrupt, or an abuse) remained among many reformers. And the sheer practical needs of the situation demanded some general agreement. So what we see in the end is the gradual coalescing of several large groups, each with variant versions of a newly defined Christianity. But they became mutually intolerant. Virtually nowhere did any group manage to make tolerance of other groups and other interpretations part of their own profession. The sense of need for uniformity, previously emphasized by civil and ecclesiastical law as European civilization emerged (and particularly as it needed to control crippling intercity, and interregional wars), was switched from Christendom to each new individual orthodoxy. Only a few uncommitted humanist skeptics were able to envisage any kind of universal religious tolerance. They were not the stuff of which leaders are made. New orthodoxies arose as year succeeded to year. At first Luther and other reformers counseled tolerance, and a careful gradualism. As time went on, sitting as they were in the hot seat where Everyman learns that politics is the art of the possible, they increasingly bowed to the brutal facts of human society and become part, eventually condoning violence, of a new conforming and compelling group. New structures were built up, against which further revolutionaries would rebel, whose own organizations would need to be reformed once again in the name of true religion. And again the process would start anew, a process which can only come to an end perhaps through the emergence of fewer and more flexible structures in Christian religious communities.

There had been a lull at Wittenberg in the first few months, during spring and early summer 1521, after Worms. Karlstadt was in Copenhagen, having been lent by Wittenberg University to help King Christian II in his attempts at reform there. But soon after his return, he, Melanchthon, Justus Jonas and others, including Bugenhagen, who had arrived from the Baltic region as postgraduate student and lecturer, began to feel the responsibility which rested on their shoulders. They were temporary heirs to the program outlined in Luther's writings of twelve months previous. They must do something about it. Melanchthon's contribution was to reply to the condemnation of Luther's writings by the University of Paris, and to write the first of his own many attempts to express Luther's teaching, unprovocatively. The first *Loci Communes* was published.

But action was demanded too. They began with the issue of celibacy, as we have seen. Then, evidently with considerable general, though by no means universal, support from the other academies, and from the town, they set about reforming the liturgy. The laity were to receive communion in both kinds, the wine and the bread. The words of consecration were spoken in German. Statues were smashed, in a campaign against idolatry led by ex-friar Gabriel Zwilling. On Christmas Day 1521, Karlstadt, wearing lay clothes, celebrated a new Mass, largely omitting the central prayer of consecration, with its references to sacrifice. The elector, worried and confused, had retired from Wittenberg and dealt with the reformers through a third party, and kept trying to restrain them, all to little effect.

Just before Christmas, Luther, disturbed by all he had heard, made a dash to Wittenberg in disguise, for a couple of days. He was angry to find that Spalatin had not had his piece on monastic vows printed—Spalatin was acting on the "go slow" orders of the elector and supposed Luther to be safely locked away in the Wartburg. Back in his castle Luther decided that above all what was needed was that primary sacrament—the Word of God. He proceeded swiftly forward with the translation of the New Testament, on which he had already started.

On St. Stephen's Day, Boxing Day, Karlstadt went to a local village with Melanchthon and Jonas and had himself formally betrothed to a girl of about sixteen, Ann von Mochau. They were married in January, and Karlstadt spent a good deal on the celebration of the event. Before the first day of the new year, three "preachers" arrived from Zwickau, the leader being a weaver, Nicholas Storch. They told of visions they had had. They lived, they said, solely under the authority of the Word of God, waiting for the inspiration of the Spirit. At Zwickau they had been friends, probably disciples, of Müntzer, and had been driven out of the town after Müntzer himself had left earlier, in a hurry because violence had broken out, going to Prague, capital of the Hussite country. These preachers had taken Luther's teaching to a final conclusion in the sense of relying solely on the Word. They were in the common medieval apocalyptic tradition. Müntzer had soaked himself in Tauler, carrying his sermons about with him always. He used a description of his true Christians which we have met before, "The Friends of God," but adding to "Friends" the adjective "elect." The usual influence of Joachim was there: "With me the witness of Abbot Joachim has counted for much," Müntzer declared. And, as in the past, there was a demand for violent revolution in the cause of social justice.

Melanchthon was confused by these "spirituals," who knew the Bible very well, and he found it difficult to counter their arguments. His colleagues too. Reports were sent to the elector and Luther. Karlstadt was probably in sympathy with these spirituals. His writing had shown an increasing tendency towards a simplified mysticism, and a kind of secularized religion based on a universal priesthood. In 1520 he had made a tour of the mining area of Joachimsthal. Some of his income came from the parish of Orlamünde; the vicar who acted for him there had been in contact with Müntzer. The latter had been preaching that the poor and suffering were the elect. Luther's preaching of complete abandonment of oneself to the Word had been lifted out of its actual context of the daily life of Church and society, and placed in an apocalyptic setting in which the sole authority was the Word of Scripture and the inspiration of a prophet. The millennial impulse of many centuries had found a fresh outlet. Speaking of Müntzer's language, Rupp says: "We know that a common mystical jargon circulated among Müntzer, Karlstadt and the Zwickau prophets. . . . It might even be that this was a kind of evangelical language which was current as oral tradition among associations of 'Friends of God,' or those heretical conventicles very loosely labelled in Germany 'Waldensian' or 'Hussite,' as in England 'Lollard.'"

As in the case of the Waldensian influence in the thirteenth and fourteenth centuries evidence is naturally not easy to come by of these illegal groups. But there are some known elements of continuity here. It is unhistorical to look on any of the peasant- and craftsmen-supported movements at the Reformation as simply movements of the sixteenth-century Reformation. They were the continuation of a perennial religious movement which was partly Christian and scriptural, partly apocalyptic and millennial, and may reasonably be called also partly superstitious and pagan. The mystical aspect lay deep in German culture. Karlstadt had been developing his understanding of *Gelassenheit*, resignation-abandon-ment, and wrote in his *Open Letter about the Very Highest Virtue of Resignation:* "I know there is no higher virtue on earth or heaven than resignation. A man must renounce all his goods, honour, friends, body and soul. . . . I must sink my will com-pletely in the divine will and submerge my own will in all things." Karlstadt had of course been working along this line for several years, and he owed it to Luther himself. Soon after Luther had converted him to Augustine, he had started to lecture in the uni-versity *On the Spirit and the Letter* (1517–18). These lectures he had eventually published in 1519. In his dedication of them to Staupitz he wrote of his conversion to the Augustinian approach: "*obstupui, obmutui, succensui.*" Rupp censures Karlstadt for a fun-damentally medieval and rather melancholy approach to religion, citing his *Of the Sabbath and of Commanded Holy Days*, written about this time: "in its absence of reference to the Lord's Day and to resurrection is defect of a western theology of the Cross which did in fact give insufficient room for Easter and its joys. For Karlstadt, as for so much later Sabbatarianism, Sunday is 'a day of Rest—and sadness' . . . preoccupied with states of soul and set throughout in the doleful minor key. In the end Karlstadt's sabbath is under the sign of the Law rather than of the Gospel."

On January 1522 the town council at Wittenberg took a hand

in developments. It proclaimed the "Statutes of the Town of Wittenberg." These included the following items: Communion was to be in both kinds; the Mass was to be celebrated in the way Karlstadt had been doing; no church was to have more than three altars; funds from closed religious houses were to be put in a common chest for poor people and students. This intervention, generally speaking, inspired by Luther's writings and possibly specifically due to the intervention of Karlstadt, is of great importance to the historian as the first, a kind of prototype, of many future civil interventions. It can be called "political," an intervention by civil authority in support of reform. But this intervention, like many others, seems to have had no spurious motives, and to have expressed the wishes of the local community.

A further fateful development just now was the decision by the general chapter of the Augustinians to endorse the actions of the monks, a majority, who had left and married, and to close their houses in a number of other towns. So swiftly did this major medieval institution begin to disappear! The rowdiness and incipient violence at Wittenberg no doubt assisted the decision. And at Erfurt there had been another of those riots of which Luther had had experience in his early monastic life there. But neither this anti-clericalism nor the formal acts of town councils can really be identified as the primary cause of the closing of these houses. In these early days of the Reformation religious houses closed of their own volition. Their members seemed to have had a general recognition that for many of them the original purposes had almost vanished. Even the large minority of fervent members who did not wish to disband lacked the will power for the most part to set themselves up as best they could as a continuing community.

The town council took a further initiative. It invited Luther to return. The elector was horrified and begged Luther not to come back. He then received the most famous of the missives sent him by Luther. If anything could have persuaded him that he had better change direction, bring Luther to heel and come into line with the other fully papal supporters of the emperor, this letter was surely it. For Luther simply brushed Frederick's fears aside in the most imperious manner: "I would have you know that I come to Wittenberg with a higher protection than that of your Grace. I do not ask you to protect me. I will protect you more than you will protect me. . . ." Luther then went on to develop the

moral-political requirements of the moment, treading a very deli-
cately balanced path between the elector's various duties to God,
the emperor, and his Wittenberg professor and prophet. "As a
prince you should obey the Emperor and offer no resistance. No
one should use force except the one who is ordained to use it.
Otherwise there is rebellion against God. But I hope you will not
act as my accuser. If you leave the door open, that is enough. If
they try to make you do more than that, I shall then tell you
what to do. If your Grace had eyes, you should see the glory of
God." In a previous letter, in which Luther said he was thinking
of coming back and to which the elector had replied, almost
distraught, begging him not to, Luther congratulated the elector
on getting hold of a bit of the real cross of Christ, instead of one
of those bogus relics. Was there the slightest glimmer of a smile on
the elector's face? Whatever the answer to that, publicly the elector
remained unmoved. The return of Luther to Wittenberg did not
really require any action from him and he never took action unless
it was required on account of some violent threat to the security
and peace of the region for which he was responsible. Luther's
return was not immediately any such violent threat.

Early in the new year however, there had been such a threat.
The destruction of altars, statues and side chapels had taken place
in an atmosphere of violence. Furthermore, the imperial council
had issued an edict from Nuremberg, where it was sitting, which
insisted that all such activities were illegal and that the churches
should be restored to their previous condition. The elector had
issued stern instructions and warnings to the town council, and
then protested when only a compromise was reached between his
representative and the council. But he was a man of great political
prescience, and desisted when his protests received no further reply.

Luther was no Napoleon of the Reformation, but he was the
next best thing. He lacked any allover engineering or military plan
of reform. But he did have a thorough theology on which to base
reform; and he was thinking out many details of what ought to be
done. His personality was sufficiently attractive to bind many people to him. His sincerity, determination and practical ability ensured that things got done. From now on there resided at Wittenberg an authority, to whom all who wished to reform the Church,
and all who wished to break with Rome, could turn for advice.

He remained under the ban of emperor and Pope. But the ban was not effective, except only in excluding him from appearing at imperial councils. Civilly and ecclesiastically it was a time of interim. The perceptive saw that a new era had begun. Never before had the ban been so ineffective. Never before had a single man, with only the authority of his lectureship in the university and of his post of parish preacher, had so much power over the affairs of the region, of all Germany and further afield. The imperceptive were aware only that the local man had made good and that for once the papal money collectors and the other agents of faraway central authority were getting much the worst of it.

Reform

Luther took charge in an impressive way immediately on his return. He arrived as a knight with several others. But once at Wittenberg he changed back to his Augustinian habit. Having arrived on Friday, March 6, on Sunday the eighth he was in the pulpit of the parish church, and on the seven succeeding days he preached. These sermons transformed the situation. Their tenor was conservative, tolerant and opposed to the violent attempts to impose reforms on others: "dear friends, a man must not insist on his rights, but must see what is useful and helpful to his brother. . . . I would not have gone as far as you have done if I had been there. What you did was good, but you have gone too fast, for there are brothers and sisters on the other side who belong to us, and must still be won. . . . Faith never yields, but love is guided according to how our neighbours can grasp or follow it. There are some who can run, others must walk, but still others who can hardly creep. Therefore we must not look on our own, but on our brother's powers, so that he that is weak in faith . . . may not be destroyed. . . . Let us therefore throw ourselves at one another's feet, join hands and help one another. . . . I will do my part, for I love you even as I love my own soul. . . . We must first win the hearts of the people. And that is done when I teach only the Word of God, preach only the Word of God, for if you win the heart, you win the whole man."

He chided them for their lack of love: "Without love, faith is nothing . . . and here, dear friends, have you not grievously failed? I see no signs of love among you. . . . I have opposed indulgences and all the papists, but never by force. I simply taught, preached, wrote God's Word; otherwise I did nothing . . . the Word did it all. Had I desired to foment trouble, I could have brought great bloodshed upon Germany." Luther was well aware of the dangerous state of affairs in the country at large, that revolution could easily be set off. Within a year or two, his own impatience, and failure to act on his own advice was indeed going to help to set it off. But meanwhile his influence at Wittenberg was more or less absolute, and it was entirely on the side of going quietly step by step. So much so that although the social measures taken by the town council, which involved the setting up of a fund for economic assistance from the funds of the Augustinian house, were to remain, Luther had the liturgical innovations reversed. He propounded his theory of the things which are to be called *adiaphora*, concerning which man is allowed a free choice. Marriage, burial, monastic vows, liturgical forms, statues, language were all in this category. Luther pointed out that the destruction of statues achieves nothing. He fell back onto the gospel and the theology built on it, waiting on the Spirit and on practical needs to see how best it could be put into practice.

Albert Burer, a student at Wittenberg, listened to these sermons and wrote to his friend Beatus Rheanus in Switzerland: "On March 6 Martin Luther returned to Wittenberg in equestrian habit, accompanied by several horsemen. He came to settle the trouble stirred up by the extremely violent sermons of Karlstadt and Zwilling. For they had no regard for weak consciences, whom Luther, no less than Paul, would feed on milk until they grew strong. He preaches daily on the Ten Commandments. As far as one can tell from his face the man is kind, gentle and cheerful. His voice is sweet and sonorous, so that I wonder at the sweet speaking of the man. Whatever he does, teaches and says is most pious, even though his impious enemies say the opposite. Everyone, even though not Saxon, who hears him once, desires to hear him again and again, such tenacious hooks does he fix in the minds of his auditors." This is a useful witness, from a young student, to Luther's charisma, to the great attraction which he continued to exert. Of the same sermons one of the senior dons, Jerome Schurff of the law faculty, wrote to the elector: "There is great gladness and rejoicing here, both among the learned and the unlearned, over Dr. Martin's return and over the sermons with which, by God's grace, he is daily pointing us poor deluded men back again to the way of truth, showing us incontrovertibly the pitiful errors into which we have been led by the preachers who forced their way among us. . . . Even Gabriel Zwilling has confessed that he has erred and gone too far."

Luther was master in Wittenberg. It meant the end of his association with Karlstadt, who took his own line even more seriously and retired to the parish of Orlamünde, and began to live the life of a peasant farmer in between his parish services and work. Corresponding with Müntzer, who was soon in trouble in Prague, Karlstadt invited him to come and dig, like any twentieth-century back-to-the-lander.

So entirely pro-reform was Saxony that Luther was now able to go on a preaching tour, with the purpose of directing the reforms. Before the end of the year he had been to Borna, Altenburg, Zwickau, Eilenburg, Torgau and Erfurt. Zwilling expressed himself converted to a quieter way and Luther wished to appoint him as preacher at Altenburg. But the elector objected. Luther and he agreed as a compromise to appoint Link, the one-time superior of the Augustinians in Germany.

Soon after his return to Wittenberg Luther showed Melanchthon his translation of the New Testament. It was published in the summer of 1522. He then began on the Old Testament, with the assistance of colleagues whom Luther grouped into a regular Old Testament translation committee. Their work took twelve years. Luther continued with his own writing, most of it concerned with pastoral concerns, or reforms of worship, though interspersed with his academic lectures. His life was now, as before, a mixture of pastoral responsibilities and university work. In 1523 he published an authorative work, in Latin, for the guidance of ministers responsible for worship, *Formula Missae et Communionis*. It followed the same lines as his sermons on his return from the Wartburg: "We assert that neither now nor in the past has it been our intention to abolish entirely the whole formal *cultus* of God, but to cleanse that which is in use, which had been vitiated by most abominable additions." His work *On the Order of Divine Worship* in the same year declared that the Bible should be read and expounded every day, followed by prayers and thanksgiving. Two years later, when things were running faster and wider, he wrote the *Deutsche Messe*, a Mass in German, a folk Mass embodying what he thought was the best way of celebrating for an ordinary uneducated parish community, on a weekday, as distinct from the Sunday Mass, which he still thought was best celebrated in Latin. It enabled the people to take part in the service. Communion was in both kinds. The Epistles and Gospel were of course in German, and audible. The sermon was a central feature. But much of the traditional Roman Mass remained, the vestments, incense, the elevation of the host and chalice. Only the elements which spoke of the service as a "sacrifice" were always firmly removed. Luther went back to the Last Supper as found in the New Testament, but declared that the development of it into the Mass or Eucharist was in principle legitimate. Luther was proud of the traditional, formal and correct nature of the liturgy in the churches where he had influence: "our enemies accuse us of abolishing good ordinances and Church discipline. We can truthfully claim that in our churches the public liturgy is more decent than in theirs, and if you look at it correctly we are more faithful to the canons than our opponents are."

Luther's objection was primarily to the "priesthood" understood as an order of men in the Church who by virtue of the ordination ceremony had the power to offer Mass, a sacramental power operating in an automatic fashion, purely by virtue of the ordination service, a kind of white magic; and this objection then extended to the use of this power for gaining a financial income; and thus to all the minor doctrinal developments and ceremonies which occurred to harmonize with this conception. Luther's conception, in common with that of so many of the reformers in the previous centuries, was of a common priesthood of the baptized, from whom particular men were selected and licensed to preside and celebrate, normally for specific communities. As well as the formal celebrations for the eucharistic assembly on a Sunday, and for the less formal weekday parochial assembly, Luther envisaged a third type, a celebration for a smaller *Gemeinde*, or community. This was the house congregation, in some ways the most important of all; the small group of "committed Christians," as we might say today, who met together in a private house, to read the Bible, to celebrate a Communion service, and to talk and take decisions about the needs of the district. It looks like an ancestor of the Methodist class meetings. Today, groups such as those of the Young Christian Workers, of the Family and Social Action, of The Grail and many types of Christian ecumenical groups do just these things. To be bracketed with his suggestions for the house congregation perhaps is Luther's *Small Catechism*. The ordinary person needed a short and clear guide for himself and his family. The *Small Catechism* was one of his few publications that Luther himself rated very highly.

Following on from a pastoral visitation of parishes which had greatly depressed him, Luther set about providing reformed texts for other occasions. He revised the baptismal service, wrote an Ordinal, a litany and hymns, together with books of advice for the pastors on the practice of confession, marriage and baptism. The practice of private confession and absolution is often thought of as a particularly Catholic practice. But it was not something that Luther rejected. He doubted whether it should actually be called a sacrament. But he wrote instructions to pastors as to how it should be conducted. He went to confession himself throughout his life.

Integral with these pastoral concerns was Luther's work in the educational sphere. Soon after he got back to Wittenberg he began to reorganize the schools there. This work is characterized by his publication in 1524 of *Weckruf—A Call to the Councillors of All the Towns in Germany, That They Should Establish Christian Schools*. Luther points out that education lies at the heart of a society's nature, and that it is pointless to spend money in defense of society, if the thing itself is left to rot. He said that if a town gave a guilder to defend the empire against the Turk, it would do well to spend as many as a hundred on the education of one of its citizens. Luther ranges over primary, secondary and higher education. Girls should be educated as well as boys. And like educationists through the ages he sees himself as a prophet when calling for the abolition of corporal punishment and learning by rote. He wanted the elector to insist that every village must provide a school just as it must maintain its bridges.

The historian is sometimes tempted to say that Luther seemed hardly to be touched by the general movement of the Renaissance. At times he was certainly strongly opposed to its dilettante aspect, and the skepticism which tended to manifest itself in Erasmus. But the good heart of it, respect for scholarship and the recognition of the fundamental importance of a thorough and rigorous intellectual education and respect for education in the ancient languages, was never disowned by Luther, and indeed was something he imbibed first at his secondary school at Eisenach, then for a year or two at Erfurt University and finally during his later formative years at Wittenberg. He remained entirely convinced of the necessity of education, and of scholarship and higher education for ministers. In 1523 he wrote to a friend at Erfurt ". . . without an expert training in literary studies, no true theology can establish and maintain itself. . . . there has never been a clear revelation of divine truth unless the way has been prepared . . . through the revival and practice of the study of languages and literature. Surely, there is nothing I should less desire to happen than that our young men should neglect poetry and rhetoric. . . ."

For Luther's personal life, this first short post-Worms period ends with his marriage. One could say that the event has been more important for many historians and religious controversialists than it was for Luther. It changed his life very little as regards his purposes and his daily work. The almost casual way in which the marriage occurred is characteristic of it. Luther had been celibate for his adult life to the age of forty-one, and for the last three years there had been nothing to stop him getting married, as many of his friends and colleagues from the Augustinian priory had done. Luther himself was helping a party of ex-nuns to find husbands in 1525, when one of them, Katie von Bora, refused first one suggested husband and then another, and said she would marry Amsdorf or Luther. She and Martin were married at the end of June, 1525. The elector gave them the old cloister for their home. Luther's old antagonist, and one-time superior, Archbishop Albert, sent along a handsome present of twenty golden guilders. On the very evening of their wedding Karlstadt arrived as a refugee from the Peasants' War, with his family. The Luthers took them in.

By now all over Germany Lutheran ministers were preaching Christianity from the Bible, using Luther's books. To the north and east religious revolt was stirring. Also in Switzerland and parts of France. The speed with which the movement for reform began to spread was due to the popular unrest and discontent in religious matters. Great scope was now given for the development of the "spirituals," of all like the "prophets of Zwickau," of Karlstadt in his new guise, of Müntzer, of all whom Luther eventually referred to as *Schwärmerei*. The endemic millennial and apocalyptic movements suddenly had a new freedom. The reaction to the canonical and formal face of the Church was running as strongly

as ever it did when three or four centuries previously the merchant
Waldo turned to poverty and Scripture in Lyons, and the merchant's son Francis turned to Sister Poverty in the little town of
Assisi. But now there was a peasantry in Germany with some
greater prosperity in sight. There were members of it who could
read. There were vernacular versions of the Bible circulating
widely, and a whole literature of mysticism and social justice.
There was general assent to a conviction that some sort of change
must come to modify the feudal, imperial and papal, structure.
The roots of society lay deep in religious conviction. Once the
religious structure was challenged successfully, all the rest began
to shift as in a great earthquake. Peasant uprisings which might
have been put down easily in the past began to assume a greater
importance. The crack in the religious face was their opportunity.

At no time did Luther wish to foment social unrest. It was a
threat to his own reform of Church and society. He did not want
a destruction of the old Church and the founding of a new. But
the need he felt to denounce what he saw to be wrong was psychologically and socially inappropriate for a merely gradual and
moderate reform. Denunication of the system of the papacy as
that of Antichrist, denunciations of the theology of "merit" and
the sacrificial theology of the Mass as blasphemous stirred up
emotions in others which he was not able to channel as he channeled his own into moderate reforms, gradual changes in the forms
of worship, into improvements of local education, Christian pastoral
work generally. His disclaimers and criticisms of violent revolution
were ignored.

Over a great range of activity Luther was not at all a revolutionary but ran a middle-of-the-road course. There is nothing in
Luther of the proud prophet turning over every traditional practice
associated with the old Church. In this sense the specifically Lutheran reformation was not a cataclysm, but a careful and quite
relatively slow purging of the old body, retaining strong continuity
with the Church of the past centuries. It became a cataclysm
partly because the old Church refused to have anything to do
with it and made as sharp a break as was possible between it, the
papal Church, and Luther, and partly because people of all classes
all over Europe found themselves generally in agreement with
Luther, but were either impatient or considered thorough religious
revolution desirable and brought into the religious movement every

other conceivable concern; and partly because the perennial apocalyptic movement found an opportunity for enlarging its influence
and set other radical revolutions going. In the aggregate, then, we
have the thing which historians call the Reformation. It comprised
quite disparate elements, though everywhere retaining the character of religious revolution.

At the same time it was Luther's charisma, his combination of
courage, conviction, intelligence and practical ability, which started
it all off, kept it running in German-speaking regions and strongly
influenced it everywhere else. Every time he denounced the papacy, or merit theology, or the Mass as a sacrifice, the extremists
were stirred on. And there is a sense in which Luther, so swiftly
famous, within five years having to live with his own reputation,
his name known to every educated person, became a caricature of
himself. As time went on the denunciations became obsessive and
more violent and at the same time almost routine. The doctrine of
justification by faith became an all-embracing key to his interpretation of the Bible, and at times pretty well inevitably has the
appearance of a routine rant. The caricature aspect is illustrated
by the quotation from his own conversation: "While I drank beer,
the Word reformed the church." It is the kind of epigram which any
Christian might compose at any time, convinced of God's overriding
grace and power in all matters. But in Luther's mouth it becomes
almost normative; it provided an enabling atmosphere for the
"spiritualists," even though Luther reserved his most violent denunciations precisely for them. And he was easily mimicked and
ridiculed by both conservatives and near-anarchists. For the latter
he became Mr. Pussyfoot and Dr. Easychair. Luther retorted with
Herr Omnes for those he regarded as demagogues.

The four years and a few months from his return in 1522 to the
defeat of the peasants' revolt in 1526 constituted a considerable
disillusion for Luther. He began with an expression of great tolerance. But tolerance for fairly quiet and law-abiding conservatives
was one thing. Tolerance for the wild millenarians on the left was
another. They attracted some intelligent men of great ability, outstanding among whom was Müntzer. He had less direct influence
on the social revolution than on religion. But in the religious sphere
he had great influence, and such influence always had a further
secondary influence on society. Certainly in the places where he
preached his influence coincided with violent movements for social

justice. He became preacher at Allstedt in 1523, invited there by the council. He introduced new liturgical arrangements, forthwith, intelligent and subsequently quite influential arrangements. And he began to preach social revolution. He quickly gained much support, both from poorer people in the town itself, and from the surrounding district, people coming specially to Allstedt to hear him, in spite of the count of Mansfeld, who forbade his subjects to go to Müntzer's liturgy and demanded his arrest. Luther accused Müntzer of taking advantage of his own victory over authority, which was true enough. Müntzer retorted with "Brother Porky-boy" and "Brother Soft-life." Müntzer was fully convinced of the intellectual validity of his apocalyptic approach: "Yes, it is a truly apostolic, patriarchal and prophetic Spirit which attends to visions. . . . If Christianity is not still apostolic what on earth are we preaching about?" All this was easy to speak against. Luther referred contemptuously to *"Geist hin"* and *"Geist her"* [Hither Spirit, thither Spirit].

In this early period after Worms Luther proclaimed the right of parishes to elect their own preachers. He had also proclaimed the ineligibility of civil government to act directly in the affairs of the Church. But both these more or less idealistic, theoretical positions were to be abandoned as a result of the twin experiences of the wild reformation of the spirituals and of the Peasants' War, with which it was connected. The spirituals coalesced in many places into groups called "Anabaptists." In their determination to have a community of completely committed Christians, they rejected infant baptism and baptized only fully committed and believing adults. It is true that infant baptism remains something of a logical absurdity in Luther's system; it is not too easily included in any Christian system and there continues to be serious questioning of it among Christians, including those in the Catholic tradition today.

These Anabaptists were to raise the anger of the reformers. Before the decade was out Luther was to find himself approving of the widespread burning or drowning (a watery death for a watery sin) of these "heretics." The assumptions of the Roman Church that there was a "right" and a "wrong" in Church beliefs, and norms of behavior so absolute and important that death was the only suitable penalty for those opting for the "wrong," were taken over by the reformers. A whole series of new orthodoxies grew up, ever rebelled against, and ever issuing in smaller and smaller new groups of "true" Christians.

This is to look ahead. But the future is important. For it is already to be found in embryo in the angry denunciations which Luther began to issue when the extent of Müntzer's and Karlstadt's defection was clear, and when the various outbreaks of peasant insurrection were coming to look like a single Peasants' War.

Luther had foreseen the troubles and thought of them as God's vengeance on the unjust rulers. In January 1522, still in the Wartburg, Luther published this warning: "The people are everywhere restless and their eyes are open. They can and will no longer submit to oppression by force. It is the Lord who is directing all this and who is concealing this threat and imminent peril from the princes. It is he who will bring it all to pass through their blindness and their violence; it looks to me as though Germany will be drenched with blood." But as a public statement this amounts to an encouragement of those who rebel. It is one thing to perceive what is happening and to understand the judgments of history or of God. It is another to speak publicly of them. When the revolt was on, Luther issued his famous encouragement to the princes to put it down ruthlessly. Without having any idea that he was becoming to some extent what we might today call a pragmatist, it was the art of the possible which Luther was now having to follow if he was to remain in charge. Society has to continue with some economic and political structure. Luther had no consistent special theory of society on which to set up a new policy. He worked with what there was and adapted his theory, itself always, however, in tune with traditional Christian respect for the de facto civil authority.

In effect the religious revolt against the emperor, against the Pope and against the local bishops left the regional authorities, the electors, the princes and the big city councils, as the inheritors of authority, in both Church and state. And this is how it was to work out. That is the story of the decades after 1525. Yet even in these first four years it is clear what will happen. The revolution is already quasi-universal, and it is possible to compile a long list of regions, cities and leaders who set practical reforms on foot, which were essentially part of the Reformation. Luther neither could, nor wanted to, control them. Among these, apart from towns in Switzerland, we can include: Augsburg, Memmingen, Ulm,

Nuremberg, Magdeburg, Breslau, Regensburg, Frankfurt-am-Main, Stettin, Altenburg, Schwäbisch Hall and of course the towns previously listed which Luther visited on his first circuit. Of people there are: Albert of Prussia, the last grand master of the Teutonic Order, Ambrosius Blarer, the monk converted by Melanchthon, future reformer of Constance, Hans Sachs, the Meistersinger, Georg Polenz, who was bishop of Samland, and many others too numerous to list in Switzerland, France, England and Scandinavia, some of whose names have already occurred or will occur in the next section.

No one yet thought in terms of new and separate churches but only of a thoroughly reformed Church which would be independent of Rome. The local initiatives were taken against a background of centuries of rivalry between Church and state authorities. The civil authority became convinced of its own duty to reform what seemed to be a degenerate ecclesiastical life and structure. In 1524 at Nuremberg, home of Albrecht Dürer, the provost reformed the liturgy and was then excommunicated by the bishop. The city council refused to let the bishop have a new provost elected. It dissolved the religious houses and had a visitation of the parishes made. The historian knows that this, like the action of the Wittenberg town council in 1522, was an early example of very many similar actions all of which together comprise the Reformation. But as yet those who took part only saw themselves as doing something not so very dissimilar from what many previous protagonists had done, only this time, instead of the ecclesiastical authority achieving victory by means of excommunication, the local civil authority triumphed. This they could not have done without substantial support from large numbers of the town community as a whole, and acquiescence from many more. With the imperial authority opposed to change, revolutionary initiatives could not have survived general opposition from the community as a whole.

The whole scene is brought beautifully into focus by Lortz. He has been speaking of the way in which a facade has been maintained, behind which was a spiritually rotten interior. He goes on: "One day the great patrician families of Nuremberg were calmly donating new, wonderful, costly altars and numerous splendid statues in honour of the saints; next day they were dragging out of the cloister the child whom they had dedicated to the life of perfection as a nun under the seal of the threefold

vows of the Church—rescuing her from the net of the godless
human ordinances, from the sacrilege of papistical idolatry."

Europe 1525

News of the success of the new Hus had spread to every
country. His writings were being devoured by many people, and
studied carefully by many, to see what sense they made. They
even reached Spain by 1520. There, however, the Inquisition
was still active. Adrian of Utrecht, one-time tutor of Charles V,
to be elected Pope shortly, now in Spain as bishop of Tortosa, and
regent when Charles left for England en route for Germany,
insisted that Luther's writings be kept out. Previously a professor
at Louvain, he had recently sent his assent to the condemnation
of Luther's writings by Louvain University. In Spain government
was strong. Vernacular versions of the Bible had been suppressed
more thoroughly than in any other part of Europe. It is a cliché
to say that the Spanish temperament thrives under severe rule.
There have been many minority movements there, religious and
political, as vigorous and violent as anywhere in Europe. But they
have been suppressed or kept under control most of the time.
Luther's books only reached a small number of people, and generally
speaking Spain has legislated to exclude all Protestant writing
ever since, with a large measure of success.

In parts of Italy, the other Latin country where eventually the
Reformation had no more than minimal success, something like
an almost diametrically opposite picture is to be found. Vernacular
versions of the Bible, although not as widespread as in Germany,
were read with less danger in Florence than anywhere else in
Europe. The Italian character, then as now, was flexible. At one
extreme it could provide the highest acme of fastidious scholarship and precision. These Renaissance scholars were mostly not
impressed by existentialist theology. At the other end was mere
slackness and indifference. Renaissance dilettanti were not attracted by the theology of the cross—unless they were converted,
and even then they preferred their native Italian ascetic traditions.
To the Italians belonged the great organized structure of the
established Church; or at least its sovereign, and its bureaucracy
resident in Rome. One reason why Italians did not fly from the
Church's manifold abuses to Protestantism was perhaps that they

were already well inoculated against all sorts of heretical movements. The Joachists, the Flagellati, the Fraticelli and a hundred
other smaller heretical movements had passed their intense
emotional distraught way through the countryside and towns of
Italy. The Italians have a métier and a passion also for the family
group, the *famiglia*. Under the Italian sun Protestantism was turned
into another such intense religious group, evangelical, one among
several inheritors of a long medieval dissenting tradition. The
emphasis and influence of the papal Church organization was so
pervasive of every part of life that it was perfectly possible for
these small heretical groups to exist without being any threat to
the Church itself, still the political, as well as the ecclesiastical
authority, in that large area of Italian-speaking land which was
governed by the Pope.

Then there were still in Italy some remaining strands of the
everyday cultural complex of the ancient Roman world. The
Church structure was respected in the same way that the ancient
Roman authority had been respected, and it exercised its rule in
a similar way. This rule of law was reinforced further in those
areas controlled by Spain and in these areas the Lutheran influence
was strongly opposed. In addition there remained also a streak of
paganism, parallel to the "spooky" belief in spirits of all kinds which
was still to be found widely in northern Europe, having an outlet
in witch hunting. Italian paganism did not mix easily with "spiritual," anti-ritualistic Protestantism.

Finally the medium does greatly affect the message. Protestantism was clothed in northern, often in Anglo-Saxon, semi-democratic
clothes, with a strong emphasis on the importance of mutual
consultation and of the quality we know as "equity" in law. These
qualities proved difficult to export in the sixteenth century, and
only very slowly have they come to find people and movements to
champion them in the Mediterranean lands.

In 1521 Pope Leo X died unexpectedly. The cardinals considered
that they must have a Pope who was acceptable to the new young
emperor. If Charles had agreed, it is quite possible that the
English cardinal, Wolsey, might have been elected. As it was, the
college of cardinals opted for Charles's old tutor, Adrian of
Utrecht, who, as we saw, was acting as regent in Spain during
Charles's absence in Europe. Some of the Italian cardinals were
very dissatisfied, and something like a looting of Vatican treasure

occurred before the man from the Netherlands arrived. An ascetic, a scholar, a man determined to reform, but strongly opposed to Luther, he was not made welcome. He died, disappointed of virtually all his hopes, in 1523. As far as power is concerned, he left the papacy weaker. The Curia had frustrated his policy. And Adrian was no politician. He is remembered by historians for the speech made at the Imperial Diet of Nuremberg in 1522 by his legate, publicly admitting that the sins of the Curia and the clergy were largely responsible for the present troubles in the Church and promising to grapple with the disease. But it was a matter of crying "Wolf, wolf," because promises of reform had been made so often before. No one any longer believed them. Adrian died, a failure. His successor was elected after the emperor and the monarchs of England and France had exercised their due measure of influence. It was back to the Medicis. Clement VII, cousin of Leo X, illegitimate son of another Medici, was brought up by his uncle, Lorenzo the Magnificent. A weak but not a bad man, his most important characteristic was inability to make decisions. He steadfastly refused to call a new council, which it was increasingly obvious was necessary if the papal Church was to cope with the deteriorating ecclesiastical situation. The Germans continued to demand a "free council held on German soil."

The eastern and northeastern countries were closer than others to Wittenberg, both geographically and linguistically. Luther's writings had not been long in reaching Hungary, Bohemia and Poland. The Hussite Church was still in control in Bohemia, though retaining a loose connection with Rome through the ordination of priests by bishops in communion with the Pope. They retained many Catholic practices and virtually all Catholic doctrine, only excepting the authority of the Pope. The principal distinguishing characteristics were insistence on use of the vernacular, and Communion in both kinds for the laity. They had infiltrated into a small part of Poland, and into northern Germany, and had helped perhaps in a small way to prepare for the Reformation there. The crowns of Hungary and Bohemia were united in the person of King Lewis II, who kept his court at Buda. Trade routes provided a network for intellectual influences from Italy, and from the West. The result was a cultural life in the Bohemian and Polish universities of Prague and Cracow stronger, for instance, than that in England—many more books were being published in Poland than in England. The influence of Erasmus was strong. And there were the usual factors of anti-clericalism, abuses, nationalism, a desire to read the Bible, predisposing people to welcome religious change. At this stage there was even less sense of "heresy" in the new influences than there was in Germany. Erasmian and Lutheran reformers preached without causing any ecclesiastical ruptures. An exception perhaps is the German part of Poland. Here craftsmen, journeymen and the proletariat generally were encouraged by the friars Jakub Knade, Alexander Svenicken and Matthias Binewald to revolt against patricians and merchants—a revolt put down in 1526 by King Sigismund. In Prussia the Teutonic Knights were a further embarrassment to authority. Their loyalty to the Pope led them to refuse to swear loyalty to the king of Poland, one of the Jagellon dynasty, as was Lewis of Bohemia and Hungary. Poland tended to be "progressive," as we might say today. Inclined to support conciliar rather than papal authority, the Poles had been supporters of the Council of Basel in its early stages. They were conscious of their cultural life, and regarded the papacy with some detachment. The same detachment can also be seen in their attitude to reformers, but at first Lutheran preachers were not unwelcome.

In the Baltic again, Erasmus' influence was to be found. He had corresponded with Andreas Knopken, who also studied at Treptow under Bugenhagen before the latter went in 1521 to Wittenberg. Knopken went to Riga and began to lecture on Romans there and to speak against present ecclesiastical authority. In Finland, Norway and Iceland there is nothing to record yet. But in Sweden the process had begun. Father Olavus Petri studied in Wittenberg 1516–18. He began preaching Lutheran doctrine in Stockholm in 1524. The year before there began a revolt of the Swedes against the occupying Danes and their King, Christian II. Gustavus Vasa was declared king of Sweden. National independence and the Reformation went hand in hand. They helped one another, and the political change came first. But it is misleading to speak simply of the Reformation in Sweden being "political." Religious affairs had their own dimension there as everywhere. In Denmark, 1523, the year of the Swedish revolt, was also the year of King Christian II's deposition. But the king was no traditionalist. He chose Wittenberg for one of his first places of exile, and subsequently, while living in the Netherlands, had the New Testament translated into Danish and sent copies into Denmark. Lutheran doctrine had first been preached there in 1522 by Herman Tast. The Carmelite friar Paulus Helie had been lecturing on the Bible in the university at Copenhagen and helped to make the Reformation possible, though he himself remained a Catholic. From 1525 the monk Hans Tausen, having studied at Wittenberg, was preaching Lutheran doctrine.

In 1525 the grand master of the Teutonic Knights, Albert of Hohenzollern, put off his ecclesiastical office, declared himself duke of Prussia and put through Lutheran reforms. Through his Danish wife he had contacts with Denmark and assisted the reforms there. Another Hohenzollern convert was Prince Casimir of Ansbach, living near Nuremberg and supporting the reforms there.

In England the tension between Church and state continued, with Henry keeping an uneasy peace between them. Polydore Vergil, London agent of the papal collector, wrote that the people were "raging against the clergy, or would be if the King's majesty were not curbing their fury." Henry fancied himself as a theologian and leaped to the defense of the Church with his *Assertio Septem Sacramentorum* (1521) as a reply to Luther's *Babylonian Captivity*—the writing of which earned for English sovereigns the title Fidei Defensor, given to Henry VIII by the Pope and retained ever since in a modified sense. In the middle twenties Thomas Cromwell began to assist Cardinal Wolsey in the closing of a number of small and seemingly redundant religious houses, with the agreement of papal authority, in order to provide funds for new educational buildings and endowments at Oxford and Ipswich. He arranged the closure of twenty-nine between 1524 and 1529.

Henry's private life was not yet of any importance for religion. He was bitterly disappointed that Queen Catherine had not provided him with an heir to the throne, suffering a series of miscarriages and stillbirths apart from one girl, the future Queen Mary. Henry had mistresses, like so many other rulers, and at least one illegitimate son. It is probable that the possibility of a divorce had been considered, since the matter of the succession was of such importance for the country's prosperity. But as yet there was no more to it than that. In the autumn of 1525 Henry and Catherine read a book together and appeared very friendly—

the last time such happiness is recorded. Henry was then thirty-four and Catherine forty.

Meanwhile the yeast of Luther's writings was working. At Cambridge the meetings at the White Horse Inn were producing results. Miles Coverdale, George Joye, William Roy, Robert Barnes, Thomas Bilney, Hugh Latimer, John Frith, John Lambert, Nicholas Ridley, John Taylor—all had been pondering Luther's theology there and coming to be convinced of its rightness. Cranmer too, in his room at Jesus College. It is just possible that Tyndale was at some meetings. Certainly he must have read Luther while at Cambridge. Leaving in 1521, the year in which Luther's writings were publicly burned in Cambridge, he became schoolmaster and chaplain to a family at Chipping Sodbury. He became convinced that translation of the New Testament was the one thing necessary for true religion, which he found notably absent among the abbots and middle-level clergy who used to visit his employer and enjoy the hospitality there. The rest of his story has been told in Chapter 2.

Tyndale relied very largely on Erasmus' Greek New Testament. His English rendering was a work simply of outstanding genius, which has survived four centuries and more, much of it still discernible in the Revised Standard Version, and occasional phrases still in the twentieth-century translations. Some of its translations of key words seemed grossly heretical and tendentious to orthodox contemporaries. Instead of "church," *ekklesia* became "congregation." Instead of "priest," *presbyteros* became "elder." Tyndale's intentions were undoubtedly subversive towards the existing structure of priesthood, organized Church and canon law. On the other hand, today one might judge that his translation could be strongly defended. Tyndale was entirely fearless, entirely frank, extremely reliable as a scholar, and, quite astonishingly for a man who seems hardly to have had any friendships and whose portrait indicates something sad, even bitter, greatly gifted in imaginative, expressive and lyrical use of words. An artist manqué in some sense perhaps, the whole of his emotive life seems to have been poured into this great text.

It must have been sometime about 1525 that a famous conversation occurred between Thomas More and his son-in-law William Roper, as recorded in the latter's biography of More. It was sometime after Roper had turned back to Catholicism after flirting

with Lutheranism, but before the question of the king's divorce
was being mooted. Roper says he was speaking to his father-in-
law about the happy state of religion in England, which "had so
Catholic a Prince that no heretic durst shew his face." After
they had both congratulated themselves on the good situation
More said, "And yet, son Roper, I pray God, that some of us,
as high as we seem to sit upon mountains, treading heretics
under our feet like ants, live not the day that we gladly would
wish to be at league and composition with them, to let them
have their churches quietly to themselves, so that they would be
content to let us have ours quietly to ourselves." Roper says he
was annoyed with his father-in-law, got into a "fume" and accused
More of despair. He goes on: "Who by these words, perceiving
me in a fume, said merrily unto me: 'Well, well, son Roper, it
shall not be, it shall not be so.' Whom in sixteen years and more
being in house conversant with him, I could never perceive as
much as once in a fume."

The Reformation was programed in England. From 1526 the
New Testament was widely available. Luther's theology was
being widely read by the academic theologians and by educated
laity interested in their religion. Among the merchants, lawyers
and politicians was an increasing number of perceptive and
determined men who saw unworthy, inefficient, unreasonable characteristics and procedures in contemporary religious practice. These
forces were certain, whether slowly or swiftly, to convince substantial numbers in the country as a whole that radical changes
must be made. Given the more or less acquiescent attitude of
large numbers of people, these changes were almost certain eventually to be made. It was only a question of how political authority
would put the changes into execution, or allow them so to be
put. Parliaments were strongly anti-clerical and would easily decide to take radical measures, once the arguments were deployed.
But for the moment, although more of a cavalier figure than the
emperor, the king remained like him a loyal Catholic and papist,
and conscious of his position of mediation between the Church
and the community generally.

It is significant here, however, that in spite of the implacable
religious traditionalism of the young emperor, he had no scruples
about attacking the Pope's army, if that army was lined up with
the French army. And he did not worry overmuch if many

of his army were inclined towards Luther's teaching, or perhaps he rather accepted that he could do little about it. At Pavia in 1525 his army defeated the French armies, captured the French king, and took him prisoner into Spain. Two years later these imperial troops, out of control, submitted Rome to a terrible sacking, the Pope safe behind the great defenses of the Castel Sant' Angelo, still today such a prominent landmark in Rome.

The disappearance of King Francis from France for a year while a ransom was negotiated provided the occasion for those opposed to reform in France to intensify a campaign against the more or less Erasmian reform which had been proceeding. Lefèvre had been proceeding with his translation of the Bible. His commentaries on the four Gospels came out in 1522. The Sorbonne, headed by its rector Nicholas Beda, condemned him for saying that the "three Marys" were different persons. The king had quashed this. Lefèvre read *The Babylonian Captivity* with approval, but kept his own support for moderate reform only. He wrote: "Let this be in all things the only zeal, comfort and desire: to know the Gospel, to follow the Gospel, to promote the Gospel everywhere. Let all firmly hold to what our Fathers and the primitive church, red with the blood of the martyrs, felt: to know nothing but the gospel, since to know that is to know everything." Meanwhile Briçonnet, the reforming bishop of Meaux, had been persuaded to retreat somewhat and to take measures to forbid people to have or to read Luther's books. Search was made for them in houses where they were thought to be. Leading French reformers began a stream, that continued throughout the century, of departures for towns in the southern Rhineland, and Switzerland, which were opting clearly for reform. Farel went to Basel, Lefèvre and Roussel to Strasbourg. Young Calvin, catholic son of a Catholic official in the town of Nozon arrived in Paris in 1523 to study. August 8 of that same year Jean Vallière, Augustinian friar, was burned in Paris as a heretic. Luther's books were everywhere, in spite of the Sorbonne's condemnation of April 1521, and it is certain that Calvin must have had sight of some of them.

Strasbourg had for long had a non-resident bishop, but also a tradition of religious fervor. The Reformation began there perhaps more easily than anywhere else. Luther's books were published by its printers. Vernacular versions of the Bible had been available in the district to a greater or less extent for a long time. The first two printed vernacular Bibles were published in Strasbourg 1466 and 1470. Soon Luther's German New Testament would be available. In 1521 Matthew Zell began to preach reformed doctrine, was refused permission to go into the pulpit, but found himself with another pulpit when the guild of carpenters built him a wooden one. In 1523 arrived Wolfgang Capito, the man who had written the introduction for Froben's first edition of Luther's collected works, a Hebraist, previously professor at Basel, but also a fervent preacher. Then came Martin Bucer, first captivated by Luther at Heidelberg in 1518. As at Zurich the town was small enough to enable it to have a single community of educated people, all acquainted with each other. Marriage of the clergy, vernacular worship, removal of statues, educational reforms, reorganization of parishes, proceeded from 1523 onwards.

At Zurich Zwingli had been making for himself the name of the second great Reformation leader, yet so entirely different from Luther. On Ash Wednesday 1522 he sat down with fellow reformers, who deliberately broke the solemn fast enjoined for that day by canon law by eating smoked sausage. Zwingli did not eat but defended the action of his companions in a sermon "On the Choice and Free Use of Foods." A petition was sent to the bishop to permit the marriage of priests, and Zwingli himself married secretly (it was made public in 1524). In November Zwingli formally "put off" his priestly character and accepted the city council's appointment as official preacher. Disputations were held, and the reforms defended on the basis of Scripture. In 1523 Zwingli preached on the Mass, going through it sentence by sentence, showing where it was "blasphemous" and disagreed with Scripture. The town council ordered the reform of the Great Minster, the reduction in number of its fifty-four clergy and the use of the money thus saved for other "Christian and useful purposes." There were to be daily lectures in Hebrew, Greek and Latin.

Anti-clericalism was less widespread than in Germany or France. The countryfolk, as in the similar country of Bavaria, tended to be conservative and to resist change firmly. The Swiss region has always tended to stand apart from European movements on account of its geographical isolation. Its towns had agreed on their Confederation in the first years of the century—perhaps the first real "federation," or "united states" of modern times. There was strong popular opposition to the reforms, similar perhaps to the opposition which would come in the following decade in England from the country areas far from London. The council at Zurich sent invitations out for one of the disputations to be held there. From the district of Obwalden they received the following reply (October 25, 1523): "We are always glad to be at your service, but we have no specially well-learned people, only pious and reverend priests who expound to us the holy Gospels and other holy Scriptures, such as were expounded to our forefathers and as the holy Popes and the Council have commanded us. This will we follow and believe to our lives' end, and sooner suffer death therefore, until Pope and Council command us the contrary. Further, we have no intention, so far as it rests with us, of changing what of old time has been so regularly resolved, in common with the whole of Christendom, by consent of Spirituality and Temporality. Moreover, we are not disposed to believe that our Lord God has bestowed so much grace on Zwingli, more than on the dear Saints and Doctors, all of whom suffered death and martyrdom for the Faith's sake: and we have not been specially informed that he leads a spiritual life above all others, but rather that he is more given to disturbance than to peace and quiet. Wherefore we will not send any one to him, nor to the likes of him. For we do not believe in him: and [in proof] that this is so, our mind is that if we had hold of him and could contrive to make our own reckoning with him, we should so reward him that he would never do any more. No more, save to commend you to God."

This is one with the emphasis of the emperor himself when writing his memorandum about Luther at Worms. We shall hear the same tones a decade later from Thomas More at his trial.

But in the end these replies were partially ineffective if the questions raised by Scripture and theology were not answered, and the Church meanwhile continued to seek privilege, and to condone practices which did not fit with New Testament teaching, however moving and sincere they were. Meanwhile in 1525 the Mass was formally abolished in Zurich, four years before that step was taken in tolerant Strasbourg. The new rite is described by Zwingli: "As soon as the sermon is over, unleavened bread and wine shall first be placed upon a table on the floor of the nave, and then the ordinance and action of Christ, in accordance with His institution of this memorial, shall be recited openly and intelligibly, in German, as hereafter follows. Then the bread shall be carried round by the appointed ministers on large wooden trenchers from one seat to the next, and each shall break off a bit or a mouthful with his hand and eat it. Then they shall go round with the wine likewise; and no one shall move from his place. When that is done, in open and clear words praise and thanksgiving shall be offered to God in an audible and distinct voice: and then the whole multitude of the congregation shall say 'Amen' at the end."

In the account given to Charles V at Augsburg we are told, "While the sacrament of the Lord's body and blood is eaten and drunk another of the ministers reads from the pulpit from the gospel of St. John, beginning at the 13th chapter. . . . For we eat and drink the sacrament of the Supper sitting down and silently listening to the word of the Lord."

This of course goes far beyond anything Luther was doing now or would do later. Zwingli, along with other more or less "rationalist" reformers, was attempting to reconstruct a "Last Supper," using the biblical text. Luther believed, on the other hand, in the at least partial or possible validity of all past Christian procedures, and respected the ritual at present in use sufficiently to wish only to modify it slowly, and only to omit really false material.

Zwingli's action is close to that of previous reformers, declared heretical, who had wished to simplify the whole of ecclesiastical ritual. But once the authority of the papal Church was disowned, it was certain that a vast number of different interpretations of Scripture would arise. In the absence of leadership from emperor or Pope the local civil authority speaks up: "We ourselves must take care of our subjects and put an end to the disputes which divide them . . . It is our wish that every man should be free to specify publicly the opinions he deems heretical and to fight them gospel in hand. We shall be present at this conference and shall listen carefully to what is said on the one side and on the other; after which, enlightened by the insight of our principal theologians and preachers, we shall introduce measures calculated to end this scandal [various abuses already referred to in this document]." This comes from the proclamation issued by the

Council of the State at Zurich, convening a disputation for January 23, 1523. Zwingli submitted sixty-seven theses to the disputation and these were adopted. They were all points covered by Luther. But the interest of Zwingli and Zurich is that while there was less theology behind their reforms, the practical reforms themselves were more radical and swifter than Luther's.

Things were going slower at Basel, where Erasmus was working at his books, helped by Oecolampadius. The latter had joined a religious order in 1521 in order to try to get some peace and quiet for his studies and writing, but found he could not get on with the brethren. He left and ended up reading proofs for Froben at Basel, also lecturing on Bible and theology in the university. His lectures attracted many citizens as well as students. Basel's community of wealthy merchants boasted many sufficiently well educated to want to hear the detail of how Bible and theology worked out, and what the new men were saying. Hundreds of them came to Oecolampadius' lectures.

In 1524 Erasmus felt the need to come out on one side or the other. He had strong reservations about Luther from the time of the publication of *The Babylonian Captivity*. He had had a vision of a more simple religion, inspired by the traditions of the Brothers of the Common Life, and by his own study of the New Testament. He would have liked to have refined the whole operation of religion. He wrote his *Colloquies*, little conversational vignettes, to try to put the idea across. They breathe the very essence of idealistic Christian humanism. But Luther now appeared to be working for a kind of revolution, and furthermore to be basing it all on yet more theology—and theology was one of Erasmus' most black of bêtes noires. Even so he was reluctant to attack Luther. He told Elector Frederick shortly before Worms that Luther was sure to be unpopular, because he had attacked the monks in their stomachs and the Pope in his crown. But the condemnations of Luther by emperor and the Pope were catalysts which, sooner or later, obliged all public figures to speak up pro or con, however much hedged around. In Erasmus' case he needed sufficient peace and quiet to go on with his work of editing the works of the early Fathers. In Luther's developed theology he found just what he felt he really could attack sincerely. He found Luther's key theme as ridiculous as he found most theology. How could man be said to have his will entirely in bondage to the divine will? In attacking Luther's full-blooded Augustinian thesis of the total inability of man to initiate anything relating to his salvation, Erasmus was, probably without being fully aware of it, or perhaps aware of it at all, following in the fifteenth-century tradition of semi-Pelagianism. In parts of *The Diatribe on Free Will*, Erasmus is doing little more than say that man's every action is not predetermined. When he gets into the truly theological question he finds it less easy to be forthright and shows his own skeptical approach falling back on a "probable" view at times. Luther's reply, written at Wittenberg in the midst of the troubles of the Peasants' War and just after his own marriage, really sweeps Erasmus' arguments away. He had never been concerned, he said, to deny man's freedom to choose between two courses of action, and this applies of course to his religious actions. But he is concerned with the crucial matter of his relationship with God. Luther thanked Erasmus for going to the subject which was really at the core of his thought, to his key theological principle. The situation is ironical, because Erasmus certainly did not think of Luther's theology as the chief part of his work. Rather he had been delighted to see someone challenging the scandalous practice of indulgence farming, and to see this followed up by a defense of Scripture as the norm against which the Church should measure all her life. It was only in 1520 that Erasmus was sad to find the same man challenging much of the sacramental framework of the Church, calling for revolution in religion, and expounding theology in support of it.

This subject of free will, of semi-Pelagianism, and of the nature of God's grace is that which was debated between Eck and Karlstadt. It was a core subject of professional theology and that is how Erasmus saw it. But with Luther it was also at the heart of his own personal experience. Luther's *"sola gratia, sola scriptura, sola fides"* are the inner vital energizing flame of his inspiration. They are the expression of the total reliance on God which he had come to see as the central doctrine of Christianity, an absolute reliance and trust in the Word of God, the same abandonment of one's own will to God's as that to which Jesus had referred in speaking of doing the will of the Father—"I come to do the will of him who sent me"; "Not my will but yours." Faith justifies. Luther was speaking from the depths of his own experience. For Luther his theology led straight on through to all the practical positions he took up. And within a year or two these practical positions had come to differentiate his theology from that of the papal Church. Looking back we can see that in many ways, if not in practically every way, this theology of justification, grace and faith was not out of harmony with the theology which down the ages the Church's great theologians found in the Scriptures, or with the work of reason in formulating natural theology and philosophy. It was out of harmony, however, with much of the current practice of the Church and out of harmony, therefore, with its theological rationale, the particular doctrines selected to justify current procedures. Indulgences, legalistic sacramental administration, relics, pilgrimages, privilege of clergy, the legal approach to all things spiritual, the doctrine of the merits of Christ and the saints, of personal merit to be accumulated, of mortal sin, of the "better" life of the three religious vows, of the absolute jurisdiction of the Pope. Such practices and doctrines were what sometimes seemed unchristian to Erasmus as a biblical scholar and to many people in other walks of life when the matter was put to them. It was the love for religion and the seriousness of their concern to do God's will, of all these people, which provided a general drive against the sum of all these current practices and doctrines and made the Reformation viable.

The theology of all this had energized Luther. And it energized some of the other great Reformation leaders. Also, among the general run of people, clerical and lay, in addition to those factors referred to in the above paragraph, this theology was an energizer. It picked up the note of mysticism and of spiritual commitment we have found so often in the religious initiatives heretical or not, of the previous centuries. In looking then at the detail of this controversy of Luther with Erasmus we need to bear in mind its importance for Luther, its rather tiresome and secondary importance for Erasmus, and its importance for other people generally.

It is worthwhile to quote from Luther's reply. Although in itself it was part of a personal theological debate, Luther's piece does express some of that forthright single-mindedness and something of the doctrine of faith alone, grace alone, Scripture alone, which was preached from many parish pulpits and played an important part in persuading people already predisposed towards expecting some change in religion. It also illustrates the animus, conviction and emphasis which are commonly found in these debates. They meant everything to some of those who took part in them. Luther wrote:

> Erasmus informs us, then, that free-will is a power of the human will which can of itself will and not will the word and the work of God. . . . Yes, it can will all things when it can will the contents of the word and work of God! What can be anywhere below, above, within or without the word and work of God, except God himself? But what is here left to grace and the Holy Ghost? This is plainly to ascribe divinity to "free-will"! For to will the law and the Gospel, not to will sin, and to will death, is possible to divine power alone, as Paul says in more places than one.
>
> Which means that nobody since the Pelagians has written of "free-will" more correctly than Erasmus! For I said above that "free-will" is a divine term, and signifies a divine power. But no one to date, except the Pelagians, has ever assigned to it such power.
>
> You grant that without special grace man cannot will good . . . and this is just to grant that it cannot apply itself to what bears on eternal salvation—which was the burden of your definition! Further more: a little earlier, you say that the human will after sin is so depraved that it has lost its freedom and is forced to serve sin, and cannot recall itself to a better state! . . . Now here, I think, no way of escape is open to Proteus; he is caught and held fast by his own plain words, namely that the will has lost its liberty and is tied and bound in slavery to sin! Yet when Luther said the same, "nothing so absurd was ever heard of!", "nothing could be more useless than that this paradox should be broadcast!"
>
> Perhaps nobody will believe me when I say that Erasmus says these things. Let doubters read the Diatribe at this point; they will be surprised! Not that I am particularly surprised. A man who does not treat the question seriously and has no interest in the issue, whose mind is not on it and who finds it a boring and a chilling and a distasteful business, cannot help uttering absurdities and follies and contradictions all along

the line; he argues his case like a man drunk or asleep, blurting out between snores "Yes!", "No!" as different voices sound upon his ears!

Luther is strongest when dealing with first principles and fundamentals. Technically his philosophy as well as his theology is more rigorous than that of Erasmus. Luther takes his stand on God as the only free agent. But when he came to working out the detail there were logical difficulties, and here Luther is sometimes vigorous rather than rigorous. He swept difficulties aside imperiously. There are many passages in Scripture, Erasmus had pointed out, in which Scripture speaks of "reward." There is no real way round them. Luther doesn't like them because they might seem to militate against the idea of complete gratuity in God's grace. If there is reward, then grace may seem to be given in return for something man has done. In fact these passages about rewards could be treated as part of the psychological mechanism without damaging Luther's thesis. Once it is established that man is working under grace and that the initiative is God's, there is no need for a "reward" to be treated as part of a theology of the merit of man's action.

The exchange between Luther and Erasmus had its lighter moments. Even Luther managed to be mildly amusing when playing down his literary efforts as those of a mere barbarian, "*barbarus in barbarie versatus.*" And he turns the argument round rather deftly in expressing sadness that Erasmus' beautiful style is lost on such poor material. The shaft goes home. Erasmus' style is perfect in his *Colloquies*, classical, pious, human, witty, economic, nicely chiseled. He is really not suited to theological polemic. Luther is right: "My heart went out to you as having defiled your lovely brilliant flow of language with such vile stuff. I thought it outrageous to convey material of so low a quality in the trappings of such rare eloquence."

Luther ends his reply with a sentence which takes us back to a fundamental consideration of Christian theology: "Finally if we believe that Christ redeemed men by his blood, we are forced to confess that all of man was lost; otherwise, we make Christ either wholly superfluous, or else the redeemer of the least valuable part of man only, which is blasphemy and sacrilege." Here was medieval theology speaking with all its faith and all its logical rigor—a systematic approach which Erasmus and many other humanists, including Thomas More, wished to leave aside in favor of a more pastoral attention to the text of the Bible. In the end the two approaches were not really in direct contradiction one with another, but were approaches at different levels. And in any case, within the systematic approach it was possible to have what could become a direct opposition between the essentialist and the existentialist. And again the existentialist approach of Luther had obvious affinities at some points with the pastoral approach of the humanists. What bedeviled the whole argument was the actual institution, the hard realities of canon law and the theology which they required, a theology of formulae which both Luther and Erasmus were right, in their own ways, to wish respectively to reform or to abolish. But these evaluative remarks need to add that the institutions and laws were the framework which had made possible the Christian life, the theology and the scholarship of the Reformation. Luther had to re-erect institutions not always very dissimilar to those he discarded. It was not so much the institutions themselves as their almost entirely inflexible nature that had caused the damage, an inflexibility which at times was mistaken for or equated with the spiritual inflexibility of Christian revelation, the inflexibility of truth itself.

Church and State in Germany, 1524–32: Luther's Reformation Established

Increasingly from 1522 the religious issue became mixed with the political issue. Inevitably. Europe had been governed in effect by a "magisterium" of Church and state, in a variety of guises. Once the structure of the Church was challenged, and new Church authorities began to emerge, the political authority had eventually to decide whether to back the old or the new, together with the whole accompanying ideology which increasingly went with each. The historian today can see how complex the issues all were and how little the theological gap need have been between papalist and reformer. But once the Pope and the bishops in communion with him had formally rejected Luther and his supporters, and once the latter in their turn had accepted the rejection, inevitably two opposing parties emerged. Their expression in political terms was only a matter of time.

At the Diet of Nuremberg of 1524, the estates of the empire promised to put the Edict of Worms into effect "so far as they were able," a qualification which nullified the promise. And they demanded a general assembly of the German nation, in order to review both the religious problem and the demands of the cities for a general council of the Church in German lands. Clearly the emperor and the Pope no longer commanded a ready loyalty. Things went further at the next Diet, or Reichstag, at Speyer in June 1526. By this time two notable victories had been achieved by civil authority. The peasants' revolt had been put down just a month previously. Müntzer, one of its religious leaders, had been beheaded outside Mülhausen. Thousands of peasants had been slaughtered. Luther had disowned the rising from the start. On the international front, in the previous year, the imperial troops had defeated the French and papal troops at Pavia. Speyer was surely an occasion where the established authority, the emperor, with his majority of Catholic electors and a strong army, could have turned the tide. In the end the only explanation of their failure to reverse the tide of religious revolution, a revolution which had little in the way of real force to support it, was the combination of fundamental lack of conviction among most Catholics, and fundamental wealth of conviction among many reformers. In the past five years Frederick the Wise, the elector of Saxony, had been a key figure. His conversion, slow but sincere and immovable as regards its practical effects, was perhaps the most notable ecclesio-political event. The other electors remained lukewarm. Frederick himself was always profoundly prudent, but in the end he always protected Luther—against the emperor's wish, against the Pope's excommunication, against the decision of the rump at Worms, and against canon law. His brother John, who succeeded him in 1525, continued this support.

The Diet at Speyer was intended by imperial authority as an occasion among other things for trying to put the Edict of Worms into real effect, and to take measures against religious revolutionaries and heretics of all kind. But this had no priority and there was no overwhelming feeling of urgency about it. The threat of the Turks took the attention of the imperial authorities. The matter of the religious controversies was put in the pending tray with one of those phrases which all could accept, and everyone could interpret as he wanted. Quite against the emperor's intentions it became the origin of a new and famous policy. Until a general council of the Church should settle the religious question "every state shall so live, rule and believe as it may hope and trust to answer before God and his imperial majesty." For the ministers of the emperor this was just a holding operation. But for the Protestant princes and rulers it was the origin of *cujus regio, ejus religio*—one's religion is that of one's state. Every state has its own religion. Charles would never have countenanced any such arrangement. But he was busy in Spain and his ministers were in a hurry and wanted to ensure that the Turks should be stopped before they got too close to the imperial frontiers. In fact, two days after the end of the Diet the Turks won their great victory at Mohacs.

This was something of a climactic year. The historian can see it as one in which the reforming movement became virtually accepted as part of the scene, as a result of the compromise at the Diet of Speyer. But things looked different in Wittenberg, where the enrollment of students dropped to its lowest level for a very long time, a mere seventy or so, due to the Peasants' War, also to the now definite decisions of Catholics not to send students there. Luther could not know that the recovery would be rapid, substantial and permanent. During this and the next year he became very depressed about the state of parishes he visited. He was ill himself from time to time. His first child, Hans, was ill in 1527. It was a period of perhaps the worst of his *Anfechtungen*, trials of depression and temptation against faith. He came through it and wrote *Ein' feste Burg ist unser Gott*. Perhaps it was all part of settling down to marriage. At any rate he and Katie seem to have been happy enough, and Luther was now looked after and led a more regular life. He kept up long regular times of prayer each day.

One of the results of this period of *Anfechtungen* was an emphatic change of front by Luther, to approval of greater administrative involvement by the civil authority in Church affairs, and to the consequent eventual use of force from time to time in the national and international sphere in religious matters, though this corollary was not greatly in evidence at first. The change of front was virtually inevitable. The medieval system was an ecclesio-political system. As we have often said, in general, authority in Christendom was a combined political and religious matter although the two were also always in competition. In the practical local detail the state had been steadily winning back the influence and decisions in Church affairs taken from it for the Church by Hildebrand, Pope Gregory VII, 450 years previously. In Germany parishes had been formally visited by representatives of the local elector for many years. The Church was not independent of the local political structure in Germany.

Luther had at first looked for a reform of the Church which would have led to its independence from central papal authority, and a substantially autonomous life locally, stemming from the right of every local Christian community (*Gemeinde*) to manage its affairs in the light of God's Word in Scripture and relying on the Holy Spirit. Both priest and bishop he saw as officers who were licensed by the community, but must then be obeyed. He had a strong theory of the strict obligation of the citizen to obey all established authority, and to this he always kept. The crucial question was how that authority was chosen, and what was the rationale behind it. From 1527 onwards Luther increasingly accepted the local civil authority as having the right to manage Church affairs. It was not an absolute right by any means. The University of Wittenberg was represented when theological and educational matters were concerned, and the Church itself must advise on all doctrinal matters. But the civil authority had the executive task; 1527 was the year of the first organized electoral visitation of churches in Saxony on Lutheran lines. Melanchthon sent instructions for the visitors, on pastoral, moral and pedagogic matters. A multitude of problems relating to endowments, benefices, stipends, education, appointment of clergy, administration of the sacraments and public worship were dealt with. Wittenberg was the source of the decisions in principle, the elector the source of the execution of them and of the execution of the detail, particularly on the legal side. Luther's own interest was theological, pastoral, educational—beyond that he left matters to the elector, and Melanchthon. For him the Word, and the relation of the Word to each individual soul remained the one matter of overriding concern.

Philip, Prince of Hesse, was the first prince to take a strong political lead to promote the Lutheran cause effectively and generally. In 1528 he began to try to form a political alliance to be capable of waging war. Next year he emerged as the leader of the reformers' cause in more than one way. At Speyer, Ferdinand, the emperor's brother, held another Reichstag in this year 1528 and a motion was carried by a majority that the decisions of the previous Diet of Speyer (1526) should be annulled. Religious changes, it was decreed, must cease. The bishops must have authority restored to them. But the Catholic authorities were simply not strong enough to make it illegal, as they wished to do, to spread reforms further and to make it illegal to prevent Mass from being celebrated anywhere. Their proposals led Prince Philip of Hesse to try to raise violent opposition to them. The reformers, however, would not agree to resort to force and were content with a "Protest" which became famous since it was at the origin of the word "Protestant." The Protest was signed by the elector of Saxony, Philip of Hesse, Margrave George of Ansbach, Prince Wolfgang of Anhalt and representatives of fourteen cities.

Philip's second initiative was to try to bring the reformers themselves together with the purpose of unifying the whole reform movement. In particular he wanted to try to compose the differences between Luther along with his followers on the one hand, and the reformers in the Rhineland and in Switzerland, notably Zwingli, on the other. Luther regarded the latter as too close to the *Schwärmerei*, the apocalyptic and millenarian left wing, and had spoken bitterly against him. Zwingli had dispensed with Catholic traditions and theology much more fully and easily than Luther had, even though, like Luther, he had had to agree to and eventually entirely to approve measures, including the death penalty, against the Anabaptists and other left-wing sectaries. It was a wise and quite practical move politically of Philip's to try to bring Zwingli and Luther together. In the event it was more successful than had been expected. Luther tended to be more provocative on paper than in person. He started the first of the main sessions at Marburg indeed provocatively by his famous gesture of writing *"Hoc est corpus meum"* in large chalk letters on the table—in a way a not very satisfactory or appropriate gesture, for Luther's most obvious approach would have been to look to the Greek words of the New Testament and thence to the Hebrew or Aramaic words which lay behind them, rather than to the Vulgate text and by implication to the Catholic doctrine associated with them. However, Philip had managed to take some of the heat out of the situation by an arrangement of two dialogues, one between

Luther and Oecolampadius, and one between Melanchthon and Zwingli, in the first hours of the meeting. At the end Luther asked pardon for harsh words he had spoken against Zwingli, "for after all I am only flesh and blood." The reformers were at least able to agree on fourteen out of fifteen points drawn up by the Wittenberg theologians. The failure, however, to agree on the fifteenth, a definition of the Eucharist, kept the two sides apart and was one principal cause for the subsequent separate developments of the two traditions. The Swiss and Rhineland tradition eventually became Calvinist and exercised a greater influence on Christianity throughout the world than the Lutheran tradition.

After an absence from Germany of nine years the emperor came to the Diet of Augsburg in 1530, fresh from the triumph of reconciliation with the Pope, who had crowned him at Bologna, the last of the Holy Roman emperors to be thus crowned. Augsburg had once again on its agenda the Turks, and the religious question. For the emperor the Turks were the urgent matter. As far as religion was concerned, he would act as ever *d'haut en bas*, would cope with the warring theologians, and would act as a good Catholic. He had not yet understood that this was now a matter of major concern. In Spain reformers were not allowed to make their opinions known.

In spite of their wide popular support, the Protestants, as we may now call them, were still not in a strong position. The most recent Diet at Speyer had voted a "no more changes" policy and a return to Catholic practice where a majority demanded it. The emperor was now reconciled with the Pope in the political sphere. Theoretically Augsburg might have put a more definite stop on Protestantism. Although the movement had spread into many places in Europe there was not as yet so coherent and marked a change from Catholic practice for it to be possible to speak of a single European Protestant movement, but only of numerous reform movements with a common inspiration. Philip of Hesse had failed to unite the reformers or to raise a Reformation army. But Augsburg was one more of those decisive occasions which proved the power of the new religious movement, and showed the force of the purely religious dimension.

While the Diet of Augsburg was being planned the emperor was strong enough to insist that the legal realities of the situation be respected and that Luther be not admitted to the Diet, since he was still under the imperial ban and an excommunicate. On the other hand he was not strong enough to prevent the Saxon elector, John, brother of Frederick the Wise, from bringing Luther near enough to Augsburg to be able to give advice and to influence it. The compromise was for Luther to live in the castle at Coburg. Here he stayed for the duration of the Diet. His time there was not unlike his time at the Wartburg. His books were brought to him and he continued his translation of the Old Testament, and other writings. As at the Wartburg it was a time of suffering. While there he had news of the death of his father. Unable to go to him when he was dying Luther felt the anguish he always had when his father was involved. It was a time of worry, of illness, sometimes severe.

At the Diet Luther's followers insisted that the religious question be taken first, prior to the Turkish question. Melanchthon and others had composed a statement at the invitation of the emperor. The result of this was a notable victory. The statement took two hours to read (sending the emperor to sleep—his nine years in Spain since Worms had not helped him to learn any more German), but was greeted with astonished admiration by many of the Catholics present. The bishop of Augsburg called it "the pure truth." The statement was signed by seven German princes, and it was immediately clear that the Protestants were stronger than had been supposed. The approach by the emperor almost inevitably strengthened them, for he assumed the necessity of some kind of dialogue. At one point there had been a hope that he might persuade Erasmus, an elderly (sixty-four) and now revered figure in the eyes of most people, to come and lead a discussion with Melanchthon. The emperor ordered a confutation of this "Confession of Augsburg." When it came he judged it to be too sharp. After five revisions he accepted it. But it is generally allowed to be a much less capable document than the Confession, which had been in the making for some weeks. In reply again to the confutation came another text from Melanchthon, *The Apology,* which was to have a classic status in Protestantism. The systematic Confession and the discursive *Apology* together may be said to form the first reference documents of Protestantism. They have some continuity with the programs of reformers in the previous four hundred years. Among the abuses to be reformed are: (22) The refusal of the chalice to the laity. (23) The celibacy of the clergy. (24) The theory of the sacrifice of the Mass. (25) Compulsory confession. (26) Fasts and feasts. (27) Monastic vows. (28) The secular power of bishops. But the Confession had been drawn up by Melanchthon as an irenic document, and much was omitted from it that Luther would have put in it. Nevertheless Luther, in the Coburg castle, agreed that Melanchthon should present it. Its opening sequence of items indicates clearly that this is an attempt at a complete Christian statement: (1) God: the Nicene doctrine. (2) Original Sin. (3) Christ's divine-human personality. (4) Justification by faith—here the word "alone" was omitted. There was good sense in this. Luther would have left it in; and it is generally agreed that the sense of the passage in St. Paul is in fact that which would be given by inclusion of "alone." It is also true that Thomas Aquinas adds the word "alone" in his exegesis of this passage. But Melanchthon was determined to avoid unnecessary provocation. The statement retained both the practice of confession and the ordination of priests.

The Confession was a very moderate statement of the reformers' position, not compromising it, but omitting the thunder that Luther always brought to such a statement, and presenting it all in the humanist tones of a sixteenth-century biblical scholar. It retains the essential objection to legalism, to spurious authoritarianism and "priesthood," to the demotion of the laity, to the elevation of monastic vows, which had formed the heart of previous reforms. The reformers were no longer frightened by the threat of summary condemnation and death. And with this new assurance goes a complete absence of the apocalyptic and millennial element. This statement was something like a calm middle-of-the-road statement, clearly accepting many traditions which led back historically through the whole experience of the Christian Church. It was the approach which was to enable Lutheranism, and the Church of England later, to develop distinctive yet conservative traditions. This irenical approach by Melanchthon to the Catholics at Augsburg led to a split from those further to the left. The seven princes and two cities who signed the Confession would not allow Strasbourg, Lindau, Constance and Memmingen to sign, on the grounds of their being Zwinglian or near-Zwinglian. The Diet had a statement from these four cities which was non-official and received no regular cognizance. This Tetrapolitan Confession laid a greater emphasis on the authority of Scripture. Bucer, who had

had a major part in composing it, hoped that it would be possible to show that the Lutheran and Zwinglian views of the Eucharist were not entirely incompatible. But his statement and another one, from the city of Augsburg itself, were given no official consideration.

The Diet was one more step forward for the reformers. As the emperor wrote in a letter to the Pope: "The Protestants are more unyielding and more obstinate than ever—while the Catholics are generally lukewarm and but little inclined to lend a hand in the forcible conversion of those who have fallen away." The emperor was also feeling himself basically unable to cope with all his problems. He asked his brother Ferdinand to assist him in the German empire. In his diary during this year 1530 he wrote: "At this time there was much disagreement with the princes. Because the emperor realised that by reason of the vast kingdom and territories entrusted to him by God it was impossible for him to reside so much in the empire as he would have liked, and as he ought, he resolved to have his brother elected as king of the Romans." The following two years saw further advances. In 1532 Philip of Hesse's plans for a league of Protestant states came to maturity. Led jointly by Saxony and Hesse, the Schmalkaldic League was able to negotiate formally with the emperor. The threat from the Turks had become even more worrying to the emperor's advisers than before. Negotiations with the Schmalkaldic League were unavoidable. At the Peace of Nuremberg in 1532, it was understood that in return for peace between the league and the emperor the league would make common cause with the emperor against the Turks. The result was a vast army of 80,000, which, after essential assistance from Hungary, led to the defeat of the Turks.

Zwingli died in a battle against the Catholic cantons, in 1531. From about 1531-32 we can say that the work of the first generation of Protestantism is over. The existence of "reformed" Christian churches is not only widespread. It is now supported, whether they wished it or not, by political forces. Zwingli has gone. Luther ceases to be the figure towering over every Reformation event. Already for more than ten years there have been numerous reforms which occurred without his immediate directing influence, and a few which had little or nothing at all to do with him. Yet he has remained incomparably the most important influence. However, in the 1530's great new steps forward were taken; although indirectly influenced by Luther they were quite independent of him. In Switzerland and the Rhineland on the one hand, under Calvin and others, and in England on the other, Reformation events occurred which ensured that the Reformation was to have many legatees, with many different characteristics. They also ensured the survival of the Reformation for the next thirty years or so, until in about 1559 a complete reversal became entirely inconceivable.

CHAPTER 5

England under Henry VIII

In the lives of Luther, of Zwingli, of Calvin it is possible to trace definite stages in their growing conviction that changes needed to be made in Christian teaching, in worship, and in organization. These changes can be shown to have had swift far-reaching effects on a great aggregate of Christian communities and individuals. In England there is nothing so simple. Instead of one dominating figure there are a number of people, lay and clerical. Instead of clear-cut decisions, they become convinced only in a gradual way. For many indeed there are moments of conviction as they first grasp Luther's simple proposition of justification by faith alone. But there are no leaders of the first line for whom we can find great climactic moments. On the contrary, all proceeds in a pattern of complexity, not to say confusion.

William Tyndale, perhaps the most retiring and lonely of all the Reformation figures, is a major influence on the start of the Reformation in England. We have seen that his New Testament was circulating from 1526 onwards. But in 1528 he wrote another book. He was no exception to the rule that in those days everyone was deeply concerned with the organization of human communities. Religion led directly into a concern about how society should organize itself. Tyndale felt obliged to write and publish his opinions. His book *The Obedience of a Christian Man* came out in 1528. We have already seen how the traditional Christian conviction about the validity of the de facto political authority, an essential part of the organization of medieval Europe, was held even more emphatically by the reformers. It became increasingly a matter of political necessity to accept the protection of the local civil authority. Yet the origins of the reformers' theological convictions on this matter are demonstrably free of any opportunism. The strength of their conviction ties back both to the Bible and to their theology. This is true above all with Tyndale. He had no love of Henry VIII. In spite of his emphatic statements about the necessity of obeying one's sovereign, like Thomas More, with whom he carried on a literary duel, he had a conscience that said a line must be drawn somewhere. He declined invitations to write something to help Henry in his campaign to persuade the Pope, and everyone in Europe, that he had never been legally married to his first wife, Catherine, and that he must have an annulment. He and More were at one on this. Tyndale received the invitation after Henry had read Tyndale's book on obedience. The book came into Henry's hands through Anne Boleyn. Its thesis was thoroughgoing caesaro-papism. The unitary religious and political authority found in the Old Testament; the recommendations to obey Caesar in the New Testament; finally, a theology of the secular as part of the Reformation revolt against ecclesiastical legalism; all these provided inescapable pointers to the acceptance of the de facto authority as divinely intended, for reformers throughout Europe. "This is a book for me, and for all kings," said Henry!

The ironical nature of the encounter of Henry VIII with Tyndale's book is that just at this time Henry was encouraging the campaign to have copies of Tyndale's New Testament collected and burned, and those who possessed copies prosecuted. In May 1530 Henry called a special meeting of the two archbishops and others to mount special measures. A sermon was ordered to be preached against Tyndale's New Testament on account of its tendentious nature. This sermon was to include a promise that, if suitably peaceful conditions could be assured, a new accurate translation would be made and provided for the use of people generally. Irony is added to irony when it is realized that the "Great Bible," eventually distributed in 1539 under the aegis of Thomas Cromwell, was virtually Tyndale's. Coverdale had followed Tyndale very closely in the New Testament and the Pentateuch. The translation was destined to influence the English language and culture no less than Luther's translation to influence German. Confusion is added to the irony when it is realized that we cannot be at all sure whose idea lay behind the promise of 1530 to translate the Bible. It may have been Henry's own. The decision may have had some elements of an anti-papal nationalistic attitude behind it. It had no doubt some element of ordinary common sense in relation to religious needs. It could hardly have had any element of sympathy with the Lollards, although they alone for the previous century and a half had been responsible for circulating translations, and were at this time still continuing to prepare the way, unconsciously, in a widespread underground movement, for rapid assimilation of Reformation teachings. The continuing strength of Lollardy was worrying the authorities.

The Lollard Underground

Tyndale's translation linked up with Lollard concerns. The use of the words "congregation" and of "elder" was directly in line with the more or less inarticulate Lollard belief in a non-hierarchical lay-dominated and non-sacramental religion. Like so many other reformers in the past, they continued inevitably not only to be labeled heretic but to be considered a real threat to the state. Their widespread underground influence is no longer in doubt. It continued far into the time when the teaching of the Continental Reformation was widespread in England. Although the great majority of known fifteenth-century trials occur in the southern half of the country, it is impossible to ignore, for instance, the accusation of thirty Lollards in North Ayrshire in 1494, in the diocese of Glasgow. The diocese of York had a network of Lollards in it.

Dickens points out that the strong survival of the Lollards led to a strong continuing reaction by the bishops, so that new theology coming in from abroad was treated with all the greater suspicion. Also there was a real fear of the possibility of anti-clericalism breaking into violence. Fitzjames, Bishop of London, had admitted that he dare not trust the case of Hunne to an ordinary jury. People were so anti-clerical generally that he could not expect a fair hearing. The bishops were committed to defending the existing situation in a more or less sterile fashion, and at the same time were thrown more and more into the hands of the king. The continuing Lollardy provided a springboard for Protestantism as it began to arrive from the Continent.

The first intellectual converts to Lutheranism were treated with all the blunt severity of the Lollard persecution. Thomas Bilney, ordained by the bishop of Ely in 1519, read Erasmus' New Testament, studied Luther and became convinced of Luther's theology of justification by faith. He converted Latimer to his way of thinking in 1524. Bilney remained orthodox in many ways but liked to cut down on "external observances" and rejected belief in the intercession of the saints and of purgatory. Licensed to preach in the diocese of Ely from 1525, he was brought to trial for preaching heresy in 1527. Although he agreed at his trial that Luther was a "wicked and detestable heretic" he was finally burned at the stake in 1531.

An interesting example of an everyday type of contact of quite ordinary people with Luther's teaching occurs in the case of some Hull sailors. They fell under suspicion after being in Bremen, and some Netherlands ports in 1527. They had been to church at Bremen and found that "The people did follow Luther's works, and no masses were said there, but on the Sunday the priest would revest himself and go to the altar, and proceed till nigh the sacring time, and then the priest and all that were in the church, old and young, would sing after their mother tongue, and there was no sacring." One, when examined, said he had not visited Germany in order to learn Luther's opinions. One of the party had a copy of Tyndale's New Testament.

In 1528 prosecutions for distributing the New Testament, and some of Luther's works, included such people as Jeffry Lome, a former porter of St. Anthony's School, Sygar Nicholson, a stationer of Cambridge, and John Raimund, a "Dutchman" who had brought 500 copies into England. Three others died in the prison of Cardinal Wolsey's college (Christ Church), Oxford, which was also a storehouse for salt fish. John Frith, another of the Cambridge group, who had also been at Oxford with those who were caught, managed to escape to the Continent, to the town of Marburg and then to Tyndale. He wrote an answer to More's answer to Tyndale on purgatory. He returned to England, was caught and burned for heresy in 1533. More said of his work that "it teacheth in a few leaves all the poison that Wyclif, Oecolampadius, Huss, Tyndale and Zwinglius have taught in all their books before." Frith himself wrote rather precisely and coolly, standing out as one of the few men on either side able to show tolerance. Of his own approaching death, he wrote, "The cause of my death is this because I cannot in conscience abjure and swear that our prelates' opinion of the sacrament (that is, that the substance of bread and wine is verily changed into the flesh and blood of our saviour Jesus Christ) is an undoubted article of faith, necessary to be believed under pain of sin." The Lollard influence continues alongside and mixed up inextricably with the new doctrines. Between 1530 and the death of Henry VIII in 1547 nine separate Wycliffite treatises were printed in England. In 1536 the convocation alleged a list of *mala dogmata* "commonly preached to the slander of this noble realm, disquietness of the people, damage of christian souls," and these were all well-established Lollard doctrines, mostly described in the old crude terms. Dickens says it is possible that one or two of the headings could refer to teachings held by immigrant Anabaptists, but for the rest, what was worrying the English authorities at the popular level in town and country was not Continental Protestantism, but Lollardy. Protestantism was still confined to a few individual intellectuals, although already potentially very powerful in the persons of Cromwell and Cranmer.

A Protestant in the Diocese of York, in Mary's reign, could still be accused of "*crimen Lollardiae.*" Earlier an English merchant told Bullinger, the English reformer in Switzerland, that a man who had been condemned and burned as a Protestant had actually held the doctrines of "our Wycliffe." Lollardy was strong enough to avoid complete submergence either in the Anglican Church or in Continental Protestantism and finally to evolve into "congregational" dissent.

Henry VIII

The process of events in England even in its complexity bears out the general assessment of the Reformation as primarily a religious event, something which happened because large numbers of men entertained or did not entertain particular religious beliefs. It is clear that the king's need of an heir by itself need never have caused anything like a doctrinal reformation. Rupture between Pope and king, excommunications and suchlike had occurred before. The need for an heir became one of the occasions of the Reformation for other reasons. It became so because Cranmer had for twenty years been reading theology, and studying Lutheran writings. Again the king's need for money would hardly have led on to the dissolution of all the monasteries had not his chief minister Cromwell become convinced long before that many things in the Church needed reform and that Christian truth itself was being well served by the writings of Luther and other reformers. Again the widespread desire to read the Bible need not have led to any very remarkable results, as indeed it had not done for the past 130 years or so, had not Tyndale, then Coverdale and others, taken the risk of translating it and of sending their versions into the country from abroad.

In England as elsewhere, religion still lay at the heart of life. There were plenty of people to defend the existing way of life, from the king downward. But the king himself never kept a consistent line. Claims have been made that he laid down the *via media* which the Anglican Church was destined to tread for the future. But this idea can hardly survive the most recent study of him by Scarisbrick. The truth is that the king veered about, ever influenced by the latest person he had been with. He always retained a basic conservative attachment to that with which he had been brought up. But he came to agree that the Scriptures should be made available to the people. He came also to agree that Rome deserved to be criticized, and could not command loyalty on theological grounds. He found Cranmer's mild Protestantism to his liking—even more, no doubt, his flexibility, a function of his determination to obey his sovereign and always to do his will in the service of national and ecclesiastical unity.

A comparison with Germany is interesting. Luther's Reformation was enabled by the extraordinary passivity of the elector of Saxony, a passivity always directed, however, from the late autumn of 1518 onwards, on the assumption that Luther must be shown to be wrong in theology, wrong in his reliance on Scripture, wrong in his criticism of Rome if he, Frederick, was to co-operate in any move against him. Proof of his wrongness was never made to Frederick's satisfaction. On the contrary, Luther's writing found an increasingly sympathetic ear, and not least in matters of piety and of pastoral concern.

In England we have a directly opposite picture. The monarch was never passive, and had no consistent religious attitude. Immensely ambitious, highly emotional, rather intelligent, he liked to take the lead in all things. The whole trend of political and social thought and experience was towards the strengthening of the national unit. This is the one stable factor to be found through Henry's reign. Never passive, he reacted to every event as preserver of the state.

More had seen quite early how things were and had told his son-in-law, Roper, that in spite of the great affection the sovereign had or seemed to have for him, his arm on More's shoulder as they walked in the garden, yet if he were able to gain a single castle in France by removing More's head from his shoulders he would not hesitate to do just that. There was perhaps an element of fatalism here, the fatalism of the man of total integrity, yet More can never be accused of asking for martyrdom. It was in truth a calm statement of Henry's character.

Henry's strongly religious nature expressed itself within the bounds of policies continually being redrawn by considerations of state. This strongly religious nature was part of a nature which was also strongly sporting, literary, sexual and many other things. It is of interest to see how two entirely different types of sovereign enabled the rapid success of the Reformation. Henry and Frederick could hardly have been more different. Each in his way enabled the Reformation to happen. In the end, however, it only happened because this "enablement" found a section of the population who wished it to happen and another large section which was indifferent. One might paraphrase Luther and say that while Henry married, divorced and killed or disowned his wives, God reformed the Church in England. The Reformation sped forward whatever the surrounding events, feeding on them as it might. This is not to deny that the events were accompanied by brutality and perfidy, a whole procession of deplorable events so that eventually Henry becomes a figure almost impossible to descry, so strangely macabre. Wolsey hounded out, and to his death. More executed on perjured witness. A solemn Mass of rejoicing ordered by Henry on hearing of the natural death of his first wife, Catherine—he appearing fully dressed in festive yellow for the occasion. His second wife executed. Cromwell hounded to death. Henry's fifth wife executed. And so on. It began with the very reasonable belief that England's internal security depended on there being an heir to the throne and with Henry's resentment at Queen Catherine's sad succession of miscarriages, interrupted only by the birth of a girl. It continued with the possibility that Henry's marriage might be annulled, since both it and Catherine's previous marriage to Henry's ailing elder brother Arthur had depended on papal dispensations from laws against marriages of the particular kind involved. When the Pope proved unwilling to grant an annulment, Henry's prestige began to be involved. And this involvement escalated into resentment against his first minister, Cardinal Wolsey, a papal legate, who had failed to obtain the annulment, and against the Pope himself.

The State and the Church

The nature of the Pope's authority was a controverted matter theologically. But the precise provenance of the controversy is important. If the authority was controverted by Lollards, their activity was seen as part of a criminal attack on the established structure of state. In the early twenties, any suggestion that the papacy was Antichrist, as Luther and the Lollards agreed in saying, led to a strong reaction from Henry VIII, in particular to his literary intervention against Luther. Thomas More cautioned him against ascribing the Pope's virtually absolute authority to divine initiative, the specific intention of Jesus Christ. More thought it might well be a simply "human" institution. This approach harmonized with the political view that led every state to make laws limiting the powers of intervention of the Pope. As soon as Henry's purposes, personal and national, began to be touched, his theological attitude began to suffer a rapid change and to veer into tune with the political. And at this point he began to be influenced by popular writers whom otherwise he would have condemned as heretical, Lollard or treasonous. We have already seen his gleeful reaction to Tyndale's book in 1528. Two other more popular writers need to be noticed.

Christopher St. German was a typical pragmatic English lawyer. He wrote against ecclesiastical abuse and although very up-to-date in some ways, in others his writings had a long pedigree. He takes Gerson as his reference point when asserting that canon law is far from being identical with divine law and that jurisdiction over all temporal things belongs to the secular state. And he is clearly indebted to Marsilius of Padua when he makes the statement that the clergy "undoubtedly make not the church, for the whole congregation of Christian people maketh the Church." St. German's democratic approach, based on Sir John Fortescue's *"jus politicum et regale,"* comprising the notion that legislation by the sovereign depends on the consent of his subjects, was not welcome to Henry. But when his emphasis came increasingly to be on the independence of the state as against the Church, his writing became more welcome. In 1532 he published *Division between the*

Spirituality and the Temporality. In it St. German gave Parliament the power to redistribute all temporal things between subjects whether laymen or clergy, and would not allow Church courts the right to make a heretic's property forfeit.

Another lawyer, but of a more demagogic nature, was Simon Fish. His famous *Supplication of Beggars* was circulating in London in 1529. Fish says there is no money for the poor because of the riches which the Church takes. The beggars speak: "What remedy is there for us, the poor and the sick? Should men found more hospitals? No, the more the worse, for always the fat of the whole foundation hangs on the priests' beards. If your Grace will build us a sure hospital, take from these oppressors all their ill-gotten gains. Set these sturdy lubbers to work, to get them wives of their own, to earn their livings by the sweat of their faces." This and more violent material was typical. Dickens comments: "These were cruel, unjust and wildly exaggerated attacks, yet since clerical avarice and immorality were far from totally fictitious, the *Supplication* retained just that substratum of truth that made it dangerous. Tavern talk had now found open and eloquent expression." There was a story that the king carried a copy of the pamphlet about with him for four days.

The principal law in England limiting the powers of the Pope, and of the Church generally, was the Statute of Praemunire, passed as long ago as 1396, the law Hume wished to use. This made it an offense for anyone to introduce some foreign power in the land, creating *imperium in imperio,* thus "paying obedience to alien process which constitutionally belonged to the king alone," Blackstone's definition. It was this act to which Henry turned in 1529, when he was persuaded to turn against his first minister, Cardinal Wolsey. The truth about the brutalities of this kind of practical politics is not properly presented solely in terms of great generalities. The reasons why Henry turned against Wolsey, and the reasons why he used the Statute of Praemunire are complicated, and range all the way from the facts of Henry's temperament through the detail of contemporary politics to the trend towards a fiercer popular anti-clericalism. We need to look at these in detail. This first use by Henry of the long-established act of Parliament intended to restrain the Church is the beginning of the English Reformation.

All politicians have enemies. The majority of them have fierce enemies who wish to take their place. Wolsey's enemies included aristocrats jealous of his humble origins; and these aristocrats were also laymen increasingly riled by his ecclesiastical status and the privileges that went with it. They helped to persuade Henry to dismiss him. Wolsey had failed to fulfill Henry's wish that he should obtain a divorce for him from the Pope. This failure, and her consequent discomfiture, led Anne Boleyn to be a great enemy of Wolsey. She certainly helped to persuade Henry to get rid of him. Wolsey's foreign policy was also in a state of disarray. And this again touched Henry very closely. He was a proud sovereign and had set much store on the idea of being a great influence in European politics, of subordinating French policy to his and enlarging England's possession across the Channel from French-held land—indeed to make good that part of his traditional title which called him king of France. In 1529 the emperor and the king of France were making peace with each other at Cambrai, a peace which could obviously lead on to reconciliation between the emperor and the Pope, reconciliation which would make even more problematical the possibility of the English sovereign obtaining a divorce from his wife Catherine, aunt of the emperor.

The character of all these three great trends against Wolsey, in home politics, in the matter of the divorce, and in foreign affairs, all would be further fed by using against him a statute which was essentially a statute for restraining the Church. The statute was highly appropriate in respect of Wolsey himself, in that his entire authority in the country stemmed from his ecclesiastical status, *Legatus a latere* of the Pope, papal legate, cardinal and archbishop.

What of Henry's own mind? He had no single mind on the subject. Decisions went to and fro inconsistently. One moment Henry seemed to be talking to Wolsey in the old way, the next there was no place for him and he had to rely on friends to find him somewhere to sleep. Soon after he had surrendered the great seal, he was riding away after an apparently final dismissal, when a messenger from the king brought Wolsey an old talisman, known only to the two of them as a private sign. For a moment Wolsey thought he was back in Henry's favor. He knelt on the road, tore the hood from his head to receive this symbol of his king. Scarisbrick tells us we cannot know what was the purport. Was Henry being excessively cruel, even for him? Was he just being sentimental? Was something else going on of which we have no record? In any event the persuaders proved too strong. Wolsey went north to enter for the first time in his life his own archdiocese of York, before being summoned south twelve months later to answer charges of offenses against Praemunire.

Praemunire had been part of the written law of the country for the past one hundred and thirty-three years, intended to enable a king to protect his essential sovereignty, as need might be, against interference from the chief bishop of the Church. Henry's use of it stemmed not so much from a need to protect his threatened sovereignty as to establish that sovereignty more clearly as absolute. Until now the king's sovereignty had always been qualified in practice by the privileges which the Church had had over a very wide range of affairs for hundreds of years. The use of Praemunire to demean churchmen in England, and to abolish the possibility of any effective influence of the Pope there, was now in tune with the very widespread popular anti-clericalism. As in Germany, the rebuff to a personal representative of the Pope was not in itself foreboding. However, the change in the degree of rebuff, in the popular support for it and in the weakness of the Church's response eventually progressed so far that from being a merely quantitative, it became a qualitative change. The impulse towards asserting national independence and power had become very strong. In England this impulse was perhaps stronger than anywhere else in Europe. The long civil strife of the Wars of the Roses seems to have left something like an obsession with the need for a strong sovereign. The characteristic English respect for law also fed the same obsession. Thomas More was making no mere figure of speech when he spoke, a minute of two before his death, of having been "the king's good servant, but God's first." He had an intense respect for the sovereign, stemming from his under-standing of the irreplaceable benefits of the law, "a causeway down which a man may walk in safety." As we have seen, Tyndale's *The Obedience of a Christian Man* fed the same stream. Cromwell, still not widely known, a lawyer and linguist, though already a main figure in the background, was reading and thinking of these matters. Ten years later he was to assist in the publication of the first translation into English of Marsilius' *Defensor Pacis*. Almost certainly his mind was already running fast in this same secularist, absolutist, direction. Although a close friend of More's he was also reading the new Continental theology.

Cranmer, Cromwell, Parliament and Anne

The dismissal of Wolsey in 1529 prepared the way for the two new men, for Cromwell, and for Cranmer. In April 1533 Cromwell, well into middle age, will become the king's chief minister. Cranmer we have watched as an obscure Cambridge don. His sudden emergence after half a lifetime of not specially remarkable university life is unusual but not really difficult to explain. He evidently combined characteristics of reliability, sufficient intellect, and some ability to administer and in a quiet way to lead, mostly perhaps from behind, but on occasion well out in front, with a courage which makes cowardice an insufficient explanation of some apparent betrayals.

In 1525 Father Cranmer had been selected as one of those to go to Oxford as part of the first nucleus of Wolsey's college. Actually on his way there he met a friend who said emphatically to him that he would do much better to remain humbly at Cambridge. He returned to Trinity College—and was promoted to the readership in divinity. The indecisiveness and the mild success are typical of his life, lending an air of absence of principle to it from time to time, probably unwarranted. He is apparently shifty, and engineers vast shifts of government and influence. It is impossible to enter in detail here into the fascinating topic of Cranmer's motivation. But it is relevant to our purposes to remark that this characteristic of indecisiveness can be due to a very sensitive conscience as well as the opposite—or merely to an excessive ability to see all sides of a question.

The occasion of Cranmer's emergence from the obscurity of academe was described, probably correctly, in Foxe's *Book of Martyrs*. Cranmer was staying as tutor at Waltham Abbey when the king came there on circuit in the summer of 1529. The search for a successful way of prosecuting the campaign for a divorce or annulment of the king's marriage to enable him to marry Anne Boleyn was in full spate. It was clear that Henry would be very unlikely to have an heir by his wife Catherine. He had set his heart on marrying Anne Boleyn. Opinions differ as to when Anne finally admitted Henry to her bed. He did not need to marry her.

Her sister had been one of his mistresses. But Anne kept him at bay for many months, probably some years. She wished to be queen. Henry wanted her as queen. The search for a fully legal divorce and remarriage, at first a campaign in search of an heir, became a campaign both for a new *amour,* and one which involved Henry's *amour propre.* Sex and pride poured fierce fuel into a campaign which in itself was not really anything very unusual for the time. Everyone in the service of the king was discussing how it might be done. The law books were endlessly scanned. Cranmer came up with the suggestion that not law but theology would provide the right way of looking for an answer, and that the universities could help. The crucial matter was whether the Pope really had the power to dispense from the law as stated in Leviticus that a man may not marry his deceased brother's wife.

The whole of the divorce issue is argued in terms of law, of a highly legalistic theology, and of politics. These were just the things which reformers implicitly denied to be the proper criteria. The law of love, the ethical ideals of the New Testament are virtually ignored. The whole argument proceeds virtually to the total exclusion of the facts of Henry's twenty years of married life with Catherine, and the obligations incurred by it. The argument is a prime example of medieval legalism at its worst. It veered about from the highly sophisticated and abstract manipulation of scriptural texts to the influence of pure opportunism and the politics of *force majeure.* The real concerns of Christianity, the religion of the New Testament, were apparently irrelevant. The whole episode, involving perjury, judicial murder and other villainies had little to do with religion in its proper sense and added fuel perhaps to the fire of anti-clericalism and increased the drive towards extreme radical religious reformation.

Cranmer was asked to write his opinion out in length. He was brought from Cambridge to London and lodged at Durham House in the Strand, the house of the earl of Wiltshire, father of Anne Boleyn, there to write his "book." Cranmer maintained that the Pope might not dispense anyone from the Law of God, as written in Leviticus, that a man might not marry his deceased brother's wife. This was a legalistic application of the principle that Scripture was to provide moral criteria, and out of harmony with the essential purpose of the reformers. Virtually none of them, from Tyndale to Zwingli and Luther, were convinced. But meanwhile the king was following Cranmer's advice and a campaign was set on foot to get the universities of Europe to express an opinion. A few years later another sovereign, Philip of Hesse, wanted a second wife. This became a famous case in that Luther counseled bigamy rather than insisting on monogamy which would only mean that Philip took one more mistress. A weakness of the reformed position was that it tended to be an ideal religion for the totally committed, to be short on structures to help the lukewarm and on rules and authority when it came to the minimal Christian.

Wolsey had surrendered the great seal in September 1529. Thomas More had been appointed as his successor and the Parliament which was to be known as the "Reformation" Parliament met for the first time in November 1529. Nothing like its final achievement was envisaged in 1529. All we can say is that Henry was now in full pursuit of divorce and legal remarriage to Anne, that in the course of this he was, though only quite slowly, in fits and starts, tending to turn against ecclesiastical authority. But as yet the arguments and threats put to the Pope, the dismissal of Wolsey, and the other current events of the divorce campaign were no more than normal stock in trade of late medieval international politics. Parliament was sure to be anti-clerical. Henry was increasingly in need of money to pay for the divorce campaign. And there were the first ominous signs of Henry's concern about his real sovereignty having been aroused. These three facts combined easily into an attack on the ecclesiastical establishment.

There is a question about the degree to which the Commons were all king's men, bribed, or elected by his order. This is not easy to settle. It is a question of comparison of this Parliament with previous Parliaments. And it seems highly unlikely that in terms of anti-clericalism the results, the activities of the Parliament, would have been greatly different if its members had been nominated and elected on a freer basis. It is certainly true that the Reformation Parliament did show some independence of and opposition to the king when it had a mind to do so. It was not simply a creature of the king.

Sometimes, during its early months, the king occupied his characteristic stance of mediation between Commons and clerics. But there is no doubt that he encouraged Parliament to start with an attack on clerical abuse. Sir Thomas More said that this

was what the king was minded to do in his opening speech on
November 9.

At first the Commons requested the king to demand from the
clergy an answer to accusations about the misdemeanors of their
estate. These complaints were then turned into formal bills for
reforming abuses. At this Bishop Fisher complained in the House
of Lords criticizing the bills and likening their begetters by implication to heretical Bohemians: "My Lord, you see daily what
bills come here from the common house . . . For God's sake
see what a realm the kingdom of Bohemia was, and when the
church went down, then fell the glory of the kingdom." It is
remarkable how much of a psychological running sore Bohemia
had remained. And the allusion was considered grossly scandalous
by the Commons, who requested the king to demand an explanation from the bishop. This led nowhere. Eventually three bills
became acts. Clerics guilty of non-residence, of holding land in
farm and of engaging in commerce were henceforth to be brought
not before a Church court but before the Chancellor. To Thomas
More it may perhaps have looked like a very reasonable start
on the reform of ecclesiastical abuse. Bishop Fisher and others
were deeply concerned that the reform should have been imposed
on them by the Commons. However, there had been many
decades for the clerics to look after their own house. At the beginning of the reign Colet had warned them that if they wished
to keep their liberty they must look to their responsibilities. Time
had run out. The reforms were to be pressed on them now.
Caught up in the king's "great matter," as the divorce was called,
and thence faced with a great whirlwind of a monsoon blowing
all towards absolute national sovereignty on the one hand, and
to a more scriptural and less legalistic religion on the other,
much of the ancient structure was to be found rotten, on the
point of collapse, easily disposed of, just as we have seen it in
Germany.

For the moment the pieces are moving all unconsciously into
their appointed places. Cranmer is now part of the diplomatic
world. On January 31, 1530, he was whisked off to Rome and
Bologna, accompanying the earl of Wiltshire, Anne Boleyn's father, to be present at the crowning of the emperor by the Pope
and to help in the rescue of what might be rescued from the total
failure of Wolsey's policy—or partial success, if one simply takes

international peace as the desideratum. But it was total failure
in the sense that it left England with little or no influence on
the international scene. And it was just now that in the matter of
his divorce the king needed desperately to be able to bring some
pressure on Pope and emperor. He told Wiltshire to tell the
emperor about Cranmer's argument, and to say that Henry now
had a "wonderful and grave wise man" to advise him.

Cranmer's appointments began to mount. In April he was made
grand penitentiary for England—the local official in charge of
granting dispensations. This was on Henry's recommendation.
Cranmer had been instructed, while abroad, to try to get opinions
about the divorce, in Henry's favor, from as many universities
as possible. Cranmer's own University of Cambridge pronounced,
in his absence, in Henry's favor, during March.

It was at this time, in May 1530, that Henry called the meeting
of the archbishops and others we referred to it the beginning
of this chapter to consult with him about heretical literature and
translations of the Scripture coming into the country. The sermon
to be preached throughout the kingdom was to include the promise
of a translation to be made available if peaceful conditions favored
it. The ancient policy had been breached. Henry's hand was
sufficiently on the pulse of England either to have made this
suggestion himself or at least apparently to have been well disposed to it. However, the qualification is important, and gives
the key to the whole of the remainder of his reign. Only if the
country was peaceable would this new translation be forthcom-
ing.

The campaign for the divorce went on. In June Henry assembled
many of the great people of state to sign a letter to the Pope
pressing him very hard to come quickly to a conclusion in the
matter of Henry's divorce and to speak in harmony with the
judgment of those universities which had declared Henry's first
marriage to be null. The great sheet with signatures and many lead
seals affixed to it, may still be seen in the Vatican archives. But
already Henry was himself actually reluctant to admit the authority
of the Roman court. Could he admit himself to be subject to
anyone on earth? In August for the first time a quite new phrase
appears in the English efforts on Henry's behalf: *"ne extra Anglicam
litigare."* The theory behind this was that no Englishman should
be cited to appear in and submit to a court of some foreign

jurisdiction. There is a parallel here with the German demand for a "Free Council in German land." There was talk now of demands for the case to be handed back to a court in England, or to allow Henry simply to proceed as he wished.

Privilegium Angliae was an ancient phrase also brought out for present and new use. Other vague phrases about a personal claim of Henry's to imperial status also began to appear, along with a request to his diplomats and others to find evidence for it. The theory that Christendom was only rightly ordered when ecclesiastical causes were forbidden to pass outside the boundaries of their own states, began now to be put about in propaganda provided by the king and Council. It would be summarized in *A Glasse of the Truthe,* published in 1532. In 1530 Henry had already ordered a search to be made in the Vatican archives on four matters: (1) For evidence of Henry's "authority imperial" within his realm. (2) For evidence of whether or not Henry, "having authority imperial," be under the Pope in any other matter than heresy. (3) Evidence as to whether jurisdiction in matrimonial causes belonged to the Pope from the earliest times or was something recent. (4) Evidence "after what sort the popes used emperors in cases of matrimony and chiefly in the realm of England." Henry's men had great difficulty getting access to the files. When they finally did, and managed to make notes surreptitiously, all they could report was evidence in the wrong direction on every count.

Late summer of 1530 Scarisbrick points to as crucial. For then Henry launched his claim to national immunity against Rome, announced a personal claim to imperial status, and began his first attempts at manhandling the clergy. At Michaelmas came the first citation of fifteen clerics, including Bishop Fisher, on Praemunire charges. But the attack was called off and Cromwell wrote to Wolsey: "There is another way devised." This was to be a Praemunire charge against the entire clergy of England. The charge eventually became that of having exercised the jurisdiction of the Courts Christian (the Church courts) in England, and within a few weeks the Praemunire charge against Wolsey himself went out.

Revolution was afoot, or at least vast transformation. For the Courts Christian had been part of the whole fabric of the national society for many centuries. The clergy sued for pardon.

Southern convocation agreed to pay a fine of £100,000. On January 24, 1531, Northern convocation at York agreed to pay £18,840. But it was all very strange. A clerical subsidy was due just at this time in any case. And the act of Parliament containing the pardon actually restored to the clergy those very Courts Christian which the charge had recently declared illegal. In 1532 the new Lord Chancellor Audley was to say openly, "Praemunire shall ever hang over your heads and so we laymen shall be sure to enjoy our inheritance by the Common Laws and Acts of Parliament." And now suddenly a further demand was made. Henry was to be called "protector and only supreme head of the English church." The clergy in agreeing added, "as far as the law of Christ allowed," and softened some of the other wording. And other criticisms were sent to the king, saying that he was threatening the unity of Christendom, from Cuthbert Tunstall, Bishop of Durham, and from southern convocation. All was in movement now. In trying to penetrate what was going on in Henry's mind about the Church as such, Scarisbrick says (p. 290): "Probably from late 1530 or early 1531 he was beginning to see the whole Christian world, as he believed it had been in the first centuries, as a federation of autonomous churches whose government was committed by God to princes, beyond whom lay no appeal, from whom the local church depended; and this is how the Church in England should be organised. He must restore what had been usurped, rehabilitate what had been trampled down."

Just over a year after the pardoning of the clergy Henry's attempt to get a divorce from Rome was still failing and conversely his determination to wipe away all competing sovereignty or jurisdiction was stronger, more mature and more articulate. The *Supplication against the Ordinaries* contained a long list of the usual grievances of the Commons and of the laity generally, against the Church, and at the same time served Henry's purposes. Things came swiftly to a new head in May 1532. Henry summoned a delegation from Parliament and held a copy of the oath of obedience to the Pope, sworn by all bishops at their consecration, saying: "well-beloved subjects, we thought that the clergy of our realm had been our subjects wholly, but now we have well perceived that they be but half our subjects, yea, and scarce our subjects." The bishops gave the king a document which set out the scriptural basis for their claim to legislative immunity. Finally, however, the bishops surrendered. In the text of *The Submission of the Clergy* it was agreed that no convocation would henceforth be assembled except by royal writ, no new canons enacted without royal assent, and all existing canons were to be examined by a royal committee. The following day, May 16, Sir Thomas More resigned the chancellorship. Earlier in this year an act was passed severely restricting payment of money to Rome. This *Submission* was, as More rightly saw, the end of the road for the old Church in England.

We are at the crossroads. Scarisbrick helps us to understand what was happening:

Henry's failure to get rid of Catherine drove him onwards to attack Clement (the pope) and his Church in England. But this was not the whole explanation of his actions. There were two ideas present in his mind: that he must procure a divorce; that kingship conferred on him a position in the Christian community that was not actually his, which had been usurped by others, which he must recover. The first was already a conviction; the second was already beginning to break the surface. They were indivisible and fed one another. The Royal Supremacy, Henrician Caesaropapism, call it what you will, grew with the divorce campaign, but was distinct from it. Had there been no divorce, or had Clement yielded, there would probably still have been a clash between the clerical estate and a prince who, in the name of reform, was beginning to claim new spiritual jurisdiction. The divorce did not directly beget Henricianism though it affected its growth profoundly. It may have carried incipient Caesaropapism to the breach with Rome when otherwise the latter might have halted at a stringent concordat; conversely, Henry's discovery of the true nature of Christian kingship gave a new thrust to the divorce campaign. But the divorce and the Royal Supremacy were not related exactly as cause to effect. Strictly speaking they were autonomous, though in complicated interplay—now accelerating, now hampering one another.

Scarisbrick says elsewhere: "Anticlericalism needed Henry if it were to succeed and Henry needed it."

In August 1532, Warham, the archbishop of Canterbury died.

While pondering this crucial appointment, Henry turned momentarily to foreign affairs and tried to win Francis I over to assist him in the divorce by a repetition of the Field of the Cloth of Gold. Henry sailed across the Channel in October, dangerously late in the year. But nothing was gained. In the same month Henry decided to have Cranmer appointed. Only twice in the last three hundred years had a man who was not already a bishop been appointed to Canterbury. Since his return from the Continent after his visit to Bologna and to the universities abroad, Cranmer had been at court, and had probably lodged with the Wiltshires, as their chaplain. In January 1532 Henry had appointed Cranmer ambassador at the emperor's court. On his way to Ratisbon, where the court was, Cranmer passed through Nuremberg and had his first experience of a town where the Reformation had occurred. He met the new Elector John Frederick, spoke with other Lutherans, including Spalatin and Fontanus. Cranmer had difficulty persuading either Lutherans or Catholics that Henry's first marriage could be nullified. Cranmer himself was subject for the first time directly to Lutheran influences, and received strong confirmation of the value he had already been putting on Lutheran theology. He took the remarkable step of marrying. As a priest, and ambassador, this was not likely to be readily condoned in England, as distinct from the taking of a mistress or concubine. Cranmer's wife was the niece of the reformer Osiander. On his return to England he kept the marriage extraordinarily quiet, and the myth arose that he took his wife about in a box. The king's decision to nominate Cranmer to Canterbury was publicly known by January 1533. By March Pope Clement had issued the necessary bulls for the appointment and sent the pall. He thought that if he could not give Henry a divorce, at least he could give him the archbishop he wanted. Cranmer took the usual oath of obedience to the Pope at his consecration but added a separate protestation that he did not intend this to be binding if it was against the law of God or against "our illustrious King of England," and that it was not to bind him against giving advice about the reformation of the Christian religion.

In January 1533 it was clear that Anne was pregnant. Very swift action was necessary if Henry's first marriage was to be nullified and his marriage with Anne regularized—he went through a secret marriage at this time, it is not known for certain who the witness was—and Anne recognized as queen, so that her child would be heir to the throne. A selected group of canonists decided, against Catherine's own witness, that her marriage to Henry's elder brother Arthur had been consummated. The houses of Parliament decided that in the case of a consummated marriage between Arthur and Catherine, Henry could not have contracted a legal marriage with Catherine. Cranmer was then granted a special license by the king to judge his marriage with Catherine. Henry had by now decided to have Anne crowned on Whitsunday. A succession of days on which the court of law might not sit, Rogation Days and Ascension Day, made Cranmer's task very trying. However, he managed it. He was assisted by Queen Catherine, who declined to accept the legality of the court and did not appear as a witness; she had appealed to Rome four years previously. The business was got through. Anne Boleyn was crowned queen. The populace knew what had been done. Men kept their caps on and remained silent as Anne passed during the coronation procession.

Jasper Ridley says, "by 1533 Cranmer believed in royal absolutism in its extreme form. He was probably influenced, not so much by Marsiglio's *Defensor Pacis* and Tyndale's *Obedience of a Christian Man* as by the political atmosphere in which he moved at Durham House and Hampton Court." It seems true that in the end Cranmer was prepared practically to do anything at all which his king commanded him. In April of the following year, when trying to persuade Thomas More to take the oath of succession submitted to him (including a reference to Henry's headship of the Church which was not in the act), Cranmer put the argument that if there is any doubt at all, then a man ought to obey his prince rather than decline to obey. More had said he did not blame others for swearing, and Cranmer pointed out that this must mean the matter was in doubt and that in such a case he should forget his unsure conscience and obey his prince. But for More this could not cancel out the final simplicity of the need to obey God first. He records the incident with a simplicity which provides an insight into the crucial nature of the decisions being taken at this time and the seriousness with which some people did take them. More says of Cranmer's argument: "This argument seemed to me suddenly so subtle, and namely with such authority coming out of so noble a prelate's mouth, that I could again answer nothing thereto, but only that I thought myself I might not well do so, because that in my conscience this was one of the cases in which I was bounden that I should not obey my Prince." More pointed out also that if Cranmer were right, then here was a simple way out of every perplexity, for a command from the king could settle it. To be fair to Cranmer we must remember that later in life he did act gravely to his own detriment on his conscience. But at this time his conscience seems to have been practically in direct equivalence with the king's command.

It has been said that men knew very well what they were doing, in the sense that they were making an absolute change in the Church. They were throwing off an allegiance, in religion, to the Pope which had been part and parcel of the Christian faith as far back as history could take them, an allegiance which had provided the Church with a proper polarity, setting it apart from the secular estates. Qualifications had been put on this allegiance, indeed such as the statute of Praemunire. But in practice the allegiance had continued and the Church had been a single communion and organization. Every bishop's appointment had been confirmed by Rome and needed to be. Every preacher, every doctrine, was under the ultimate control of the same one authority. England, perhaps more than any other country, had valued the communion with Rome and the authority of the Pope as the identification marks of the one Church.

But the implication that faithful Christians had a single Communion and organization needs to be justified. Since 1415 it was necessary to add "except in the case of Bohemia." And this exception was sufficiently destructive of the Catholic case that it was immediately adverted to as a prime example of an attack on the Church whenever Church unity was further threatened. Luther was accused immediately of being Hussite. Bishop Fisher's mind immediately turned to Bohemia when the Commons started their attack on abuses. But having named this one exception we have then to admit another, much bigger, so large that it was simply ignored in arguments of this kind. But it does hit at the heart of the Catholic theory. The schism between the Western and Eastern Churches had existed for about 450 years. It was seen to be sufficiently grave an attack on the Church's unity for Pope after Pope to be interested in trying to heal it. In the fifteenth century the Council of Florence superficially succeeded and in practice failed to heal it.

Then we have to look even yet again and admit that the widespread appearance of heretics throughout Europe for many centuries does not really allow the historian to speak in the somewhat romantic way still often used even by historians of high academic reputation about the unity of religion in Europe during the late Middle Ages—even though, in spite of the qualification, "Christendom" can still be recognized as a phenomenon which provided an initially credible basis for a claim that the papal Church was identical with Christ's Church.

Reformers like Tyndale, and his associates, and churchmen like Cranmer certainly knew what they were doing and intended it. That is to say, they intended, just as Luther and his followers did, to end the sovereignty, of perhaps a thousand years or more duration, of the papacy over local Christian churches. Equally the defenders, like More, like the emperor indeed, knew that they were defending this sovereignty. But it does not seem necessarily so clear that large numbers of other people saw the matter so clearly; and there appears to be good reason why they might not. It seems to have been only the holy (More, Fisher, Tyndale, the Carthusian monks) and/or the very intelligent (the same, sometimes) who recognized that a historical watershed was being passed. But it was not difficult perhaps for many others to argue in good faith that there had been battles between Pope and king before. And that decisions could be reversed, and often had been and were likely to be again.

This is not the place to argue the ethics of Cranmer's double oath, in obedience of the Pope, and in restraint of that obedience. At least the two were both made public. Nor the place to question how he could preside over the court which annulled Henry's marriage with Catherine—at the same time as communicating with Henry himself about its process. The significance for our purpose is simply that the old Church had been asking for trouble for some centuries. The trouble had now come.

Behind the Reformation Parliament stood the king's new first minister, Thomas Cromwell. Without him the rupture with Rome must still have occurred and the divorce, and the eventually strong flow of religious reformation. But Cromwell's own convictions, and his entirely exceptional administrative ability made of the parliamentary Reformation Acts one of the most important sequence of events in British history, and one of the fullest of Parliaments even by comparison with those of recent times. The whole achievement was organized with consummate ability.

During the first crucial half year of 1533 Cromwell had put through the Act in Partial Restraint of Annates (January), also the more famous Act in Restraint of Appeals. Its immediate purpose, passed in March, was to prevent Queen Catherine from again appealing, legally, to Rome. The act had an important preamble, which expresses Henry's growing obsession with his sovereignty, and Cromwell's approval of it, all taken up in the famous sentence: "this realm of England is an empire." It continued: ". . . governed by one Supreme Head and King having the dignity and royal estate of the imperial Crown of the same, unto whom a body politic, compact of all sorts and degrees of people divided in terms and by name of spirituality and temporality, be bounden and owe to bear, next to God, a natural and humble obedience." Cromwell had been reading Marsilius. During the following two years Marsilian doctrines were publicly used by Richard Sampson, Edward Fox and Thomas Starkey to provide good reason for the overthrow of papal jurisdiction in England. In 1535 Cromwell subsidized the publication of a translation of *Defensor Pacis*, the first English translation.

The break with Rome continued swiftly. The Pope excommunicated Henry, Anne and Cranmer, and deprived the latter of his see in the July immediately following the declaration of the nullity of Henry's marriage to Catherine, and the coronation of Anne—a mere four months after the arrival of the papal bulls for Cranmer's consecration as archbishop of Canterbury. Henry appealed against the Pope to a general council and instructed Cranmer to do the same.

Cromwell completed the establishment of Henry's absolute sovereignty and the break with Rome with six more acts of Parliament: the Acts of Dispensations; of Succession; in Absolute Restraint of Annates (which also instituted the process for the appointment of bishops that continues to the present day); of the Submission of the Clergy (the statutory form of the *Submission of the Clergy*); of Heresy (whereby it was no longer heresy to deny papal supremacy); and of Royal Supremacy. In December 1533 Cranmer was enthroned at Canterbury after walking barefoot through the town on streets which had first been spread with sand. In the meantime Cranmer had been dealing with cases of heresy. Doctrinally the Church in England remained formally orthodox. It was Cranmer who sent Frith to his bishop for sentence (death) in June 1533 for denying the Real Presence and purgatory.

Those who were worried by events but felt unable to resist were caught between the upper stone of Henry and his advisers, the need for a strong sovereign, the evidence of a continuing doctrinal orthodoxy (apart from papal supremacy), and the nether stone of anti-clericalism and the universally admitted need for reform of the Church. They were afforded no help from Rome; Pope Clement VII seems to have been largely unaware that the essential enabling events of an English Reformation were being enacted, just as Pope Leo X had been unaware of the importance of Luther. Traditionalists were caught also by fear; as Bonner said later: "Fear compelled us to bear with the times, for otherwise there had been no way but one." That way of martyrdom was in fact very difficult to choose. The arguments practically all seemed to go Henry's way. And even if they didn't entirely convince, fear and a hope that in any case rejection of the papacy might easily be reversed later, were sufficient to clinch the matter for nearly everyone. In the end only a few Carthusian monks, Bishop Fisher and Sir Thomas More and a few others stood out. The monks, Fisher and More were beheaded for treason in 1535.

For Fisher the matter was clear. He was an old-fashioned defender of the established Church. When things got desperate he even took the desperate step of appealing secretly in 1533 to the emperor to intervene. He received no answer. For More the matter was a very subtle matter both of legality and of conscience. A man of great spiritual sensitivity, he never wished to stand on the final ground of his own conscience if there was nearer ground in law or otherwise to withstand events. And his persecutors did in fact always provide him with that ground. When asking him to be Chancellor, Henry had promised never to bother him with the divorce matter, for More had immediately raised this as a reason for not accepting. In spite of this the Oath on the Succession was put to More. More was always prepared to swear to such a thing— if the king wished to make someone his heir that was his business, and he could demand obedience of his subjects. More's first refusal of the oath was to an oath put to him irregularly, containing added words about the king's sovereignty in spiritual matters, not specified by the act. Cranmer tried to persuade the king to let More swear only to the succession. But Henry was set totally now on complete victory on all fronts. The head of a queen or a friend or a Chancellor was nothing—just as More had foretold. More was eventually condemned to death on evidence certainly perjured. He was able the more easily to put his own real position with freedom after his conviction at the end of the trial. What was his position? The cruelty, irregularity and dishonesty of his accusers and judges make it the more difficult to look dispassionately at his conscientious position. But the irony of More's situation should be recognized. In 1522 More had cautioned the king about defending the sovereignty of the Pope as of divine ordering. Positions were now reversed. The king was having More executed for his loyalty to and faith in Christian unity as found in the single visible Church in communion with the Pope. More pointed to all the Councils of Christendom for over a thousand years—the same argument in principle as the young Emperor Charles had put fourteen years before at Worms. But More also stood quite simply for integrity and in a limited but real sense for freedom of religion and of conscience against tyranny.

In 1534 began Cromwell's spoliation of the monasteries. Again here was a matter crossed with ambivalence. Cromwell had closed twenty-nine religious houses in the twenties, on Wolsey's behalf and with Rome's consent, for the purpose of establishing a school at Norwich and a college at Oxford. Assets were turned from a doubtful to a very good use. The existing use was "doubtful" simply because of the state of affairs often to be found in religious houses, by which they became tepid in their religion, often ignoring much of the rule they were supposed to keep. Add to this picture Henry's wish to bring his whole realm firmly under his control, and his need for cash. A projection of the pilot scheme of the twenties might not seem unreasonable. The closing of small religious houses in order to found something else was in any case standard practice. Bishop Fisher himself had recourse to it in order to provide for his own educational foundation of St. John's College at Cambridge when Henry's promised contribution fell far short of what was needed.

Henry told the imperial ambassador Chapuys in 1533 that he was determined "to unite to the crown the goods which Churchmen held of it, which his predecessors could not alienate to his prejudice, and that he was required to do this by the oath he had taken at his coronation." English monasticism was a problem. It was easier to abolish it and take the assets than reform it. Knowles considers that its tepidity was in any case such that it was actually irreformable.

In 1535 Henry appointed Cromwell his vicegerent, vicar general and special commissary. His place was now something like that of Wolsey. He took official precedence over all the bishops, and had unlimited ecclesiastical jurisdiction. But it was a dangerous position for its holder. From such an elevated situation one is the more terribly toppled. But for the moment Cromwell was supreme. He proceeded with the dissolution of the religious houses. He would preside over doctrinal discussions sometimes too, normally taking the part of the progressive Lutheran viewpoint. By the time Cromwell had finished valuing and then annexing Church incomes, or taxing them, the Valor Ecclesiasticus was bringing in £40,000 a year to the monarch.

The dissolution was essentially Cromwell's work. He hated monasticism as parasitic, inefficient, often offensive religiously in its failure to live up to its own ideals. By the end of the dissolution Cromwell and his employees had themselves committed numerous offenses against justice and truth, against the ideals to which they were themselves bound as Christians. But they did not, generally, rival the brutality of either the Catholic Inquisition or of Protestant persecutors of Anabaptists. The dissolution proceeded as easily as the breakup of the religious communities had done in Germany. The great sums of money available as a result went to some small extent to endow grammar schools and colleges. About sixteen such schools and a few colleges, including Christ Church at Oxford and Trinity at Cambridge, and some regius professorships. The achievement was substantial but it could have been much bigger considering the assets available. The crown eventually sold off most of the property which came into its hands and used the cash in the forties to pay for Henry's final bout of warfare, principally in Scotland and France, and to help the government in a period of economic difficulty due to the inflow of cheap gold, the government's own adulteration of the coinage, rising population and static productivity.

The disowning of the Pope and the spoliation of the monasteries were resented by some of Henry's subjects, perhaps by very many, in spite of their anti-clericalism. It is impossible to assess the motives exactly. It is certain, however, that there was a large religious element in the only substantial challenge to the throne during Henry's reign. The time of its occurrence is significant. The so-called "Pilgrimage of Grace" was a northern revolt in 1536. The Northerners were still attached to their local leaders, the Percys. Henry had never extended the circuit of his travels to the North.

The Pilgrimage of Grace was the collective name given to various rebellions in the Northeast and in Cumberland in 1536. Partly religious, partly economic, partly a rebellion of feudal provincial lords, it attracted a very large army of followers, which could have seriously threatened the throne. It had the power at one stage to march and win; but it did not have the will. Like apparently everyone in England, the rebels did not dare to think in terms of defeating the monarch and substituting another. They wished only to insist on some economic demands, to oppose the reforms in religion, to ask for justice in their region. They feared, among many other things, that the dissolution of the monasteries would lead to money, actual coinage, going to new landlords in the South. Finally, they were deceived by promises of attention to their demands. Once dispersed, the leaders were arrested and executed, and no more was heard of the king's promises to attend to their demands.

As in Germany and Switzerland, though there was a core of Catholics who would resist the reforms to the death, whether at war or on the block, the majority even of those who objected to the changes were not sufficiently concerned to match the determination of those in the other camp. The dissolution of all religious houses was proceeded with in an opportunistic way. It was easy to do; it brought swift rewards in terms of cash; it fitted with Cromwell's beliefs and did not entirely outrage Henry's.

Cromwell also pushed on with the one thing which above all was likely to lead to a transformation of the character of the Church in England—the public reading of the Bible in English and the encouragement of the people to possess copies. Tyndale's work of translation, cut short by his death in 1536, had been carried on by two followers. Coverdale had completed the translation and published it as early as 1535 abroad, probably in Zurich, with a dedication to Henry VIII, a dedication which had not had Henry's authorization. Cromwell gave permission for its publication in England and in 1536 drew up ecclesiastical injunctions that every parson should provide a Bible in the church in Latin and in English, one that everyone could look at if he wished. This seems clearly to have had Henry's forthright support. But the injunctions were not sent out. Cromwell contented himself with pressing the bishops to request the parish priests to provide Bibles. Most of the bishops probably did so.

Another follower of Tyndale, John Rogers, used a pseudonym of Thomas Matthew in producing another English translation of the Bible, again following Tyndale's closely. This also Cromwell agreed to license for publication in England after Cranmer had brought it to him.

Cromwell found this a too haphazard way of going about things, and proceeded to arrange an official Bible, the Great Bible of 1539, whose composition in type, and possibly the printing, was done in France, only to be interrupted by the French inquisitor general, tipped off by English Catholics. Cromwell went to Paris to have the work done because he considered both print and paper better in that country. Gardiner was the English ambassador there till October 1538 and may have been responsible for the French intervention, as he was himself a consistent opponent of the open Bible. The Great Bible was a tremendous success, went through many editions, and in April 1540 was reprinted in a cheap edition for private reading. It again was basically Tyndale's version, as completed by Coverdale.

Cromwell had provided the organizational framework for the Reformation in the Reformation Parliament. Now he provided the real religious and cultural basis for the religious reformation itself in the vernacular Bible, eventually placed in every church in the country. And this religious reformation would very soon show that it was not just part of a political reformation. Within forty years Puritans were going to be nearly as much of a nuisance to the English sovereign as Roman Catholics. This English "dissenting" tradition, destined to flower in so many fruitful and various congregations and religious groups, from Quakers to Jehovah's Witnesses, from Congregationalists to Methodists, was in continuity with the Lollards and the medieval heretical traditions. It was fed by the same direct and simple response to the "plain sense" of

Scripture in its call to poverty, to worship in spirit, to a pure seeking after Christ and the Kingdom of God.

In his foreign policy Cromwell looked for some rapprochement between England and the Lutheran states. He was not a man ever to allow himself to be persuaded imprudently towards some political policy for religious reasons. All the same it must have been satisfactory to him to open negotiations with the enemies of the Pope and the Catholic emperor among the German states. As early as 1531 Robert Barnes was sent over to Germany to try to secure Luther's approval of the search for a divorce. But Luther and Melanchthon followed Tyndale's lead in denouncing the search. They considered that Henry's long association with Catherine could not be ended in this legalistic fashion. To get an heir it might be better to commit bigamy—a suggestion which was apparently made also even by the desperate Pope Clement at one point. Later Oecolampadius, Zwingli and Calvin came out on Henry's side, on the grounds that the Pope should never have given the dispensation, a conclusion based on a formula-type recourse to Scripture. In spite of the setback with Luther, delegations continued to pass to and from England and Germany, involving in particular the Hanseatic towns of Lübeck and Hamburg. In 1534 Henry appealed to them for help in an attempt to secure the vacant Danish throne for England. Bishop Bonner was dispatched to Denmark to see what the prospects were. But the Duke of Holstein got there first, and Denmark remained, shakily, part of the Empire.

In 1535 Melanchthon dedicated his *Loci Communes* of that year to Henry VIII, and received a reward of 200 crowns. It was suggested in England that Henry might become a formal ally of the Schmalkaldic League. But for this, formal assent to the Confession of Augsburg was required, and Henry was not prepared to go this far. In the following year, 1536, Henry thought that the doctrinal position of the Church in England should be clarified and the Ten Articles were adopted by convocation. These were strongly influenced by Melanchthon, parts being a verbatim translation of the Confession of Augsburg, but had crucial qualifications which stopped far short of a full Lutheran, let alone a full Zwinglian position. Only three sacraments are referred to, baptism, Eucharist and penance, but these are defined in an orthodox manner. Prayers for the dead are permitted, but without specific reference to purgatory. Justification is defined in one of Melanchthon's phrases, but watered down in a following phrase.

The next year the "Bishops' Book" was more orthodox still, including a reference to all seven sacraments. By 1539 the reaction, back to orthodoxy, assisted by a general political crisis, had gone further. The Six Articles Act of that date had a text of Henry's own making. It upheld transubstantiation, clerical celibacy, auricular confession, private Masses. Anyone speaking against these was to be burned. Cranmer opposed it as long as he dared. When it was passed he had to banish his wife, sending her over to her relations in Germany. But it is noticeable that in spite of the act, persecution of Protestants declined and pardons of them increased.

Thus the Reformation in England went forward in fits and starts. Nothing in it was consistent except the general trends among the populace at large. In spite of Henry's quite numerous points of agreement with the Continental reforms he was still a devotee of the Latin Mass and much of the traditional Catholic religious culture. Cromwell's enemies had seen this point of real differences between him and Henry and had waited their opportunity. It came with Henry's dislike for his fourth, German wife, the result of Cromwell's negotiations with the Protestant German states. After Anne Boleyn, Henry had married Jane Seymour and at last got himself an heir, in the baby Edward, born to Jane in 1537. But Jane died within weeks. The arrival of Anne of Cleves, fourth wife-designate, was the result of protracted negotiation. Henry took a sharp dislike to her, so much so that he found himself unable to consummate the marriage.

This was the opportunity for Cromwell's enemies—just as a failure in foreign policy and in Henry's marital life had been the opportunity for the enemies of Wolsey. In the case of Wolsey it had been his status as papal legate which had provided the way in to the charges against him. So with Cromwell it was also religion which provided the crucial cause, but this time in the opposite sense to that of Wolsey. Cromwell's enemies accused him of extreme heresy, of being an Anabaptist. Henry was persuaded to turn swiftly against him by means of a parliamentary act of attainder. Arrested on June 10, 1540, Cromwell was executed without trial on July 23. Of all his acts of cruelty this was one Henry certainly regretted later, considering that he had been misled. Two days after Cromwell's death three Catholics were hanged as traitors, and three Protestants, including Robert Barnes, were burned as heretics. This cluster of events is sometimes represented as symbolical of the Anglican *via media* in religion, the way down which the Church of England would march. In fact, however, it was more surely evidence of Henry's sense of insecurity and need to assert once again his sovereignty. Catholics sometimes say the Catholic Church must be divinely upheld, because only thus could it have survived the abuses and horrors perpetrated in its name by its members, and its authorities. Something similar might be said about the origin of the Church of England among these acts of thoughtless brutality perpetrated in the name of a monarch proud of his own theological ability and his own personal piety. It is true that the sheer absence of any consistent hard line or dogmatic identity during this decade does suggest the comprehensive future which was in store for the Church of England. But it seems macabre to take as the symbol of this the judicial murder of Catholics and Protestants alike at this time.

Although Henry was fascinated by theology, his position and arguments were entirely eclectic and had no inner coherence. Scarisbrick pinpoints anti-clericalism as the only consistent reference point. Henry prides himself on his traditionalism and orthodoxy, fiercely defending celibacy of the clergy, the denial of the chalice to the laity, and transubstantiation. But he is also a Renaissance-type reformer in that he would always support the closing down of shrines. Yet he approves prayer to saints as a form of mediation between man and Christ. He also wants to use Scripture as the reference point when arguments about the status and validity of each sacrament arise. Personally he does not cease to be pious and continues to attend Mass frequently and to take great personal interest in legislation on religious matters. His annotations on the Ten Articles, the Six Articles, the Bishops' Book together form a substantial corpus. But, as we have implied, little can in the end be deduced, because for the most part Henry has failed to attain any thorough grasp of theology. The last official doctrinal statement of the reign, the *King's Book* of 1543, has the same eclectic incoherence about it. His significance, beyond his anti-clericalism, which always meant support for the reforming movement, is that with him religion never becomes a side issue.

Through all this the most remarkable single fact is the survival of Cranmer from his consecration as archbishop of Canterbury in

1533 to the death of Henry. During the early 1540's, when the fairly conservative Six Articles were in force and Cranmer was forced to send his wife away, the aristocratic and Catholic faction tried to bring him down as they had brought Wolsey and Cromwell down. Superficially they seem to have been very near to success. It was, seemingly, only Henry's personal affection for Cranmer which finally led the monarch to say in no uncertain terms, "Leave my friends alone." Cranmer was pretty well the only friend he had ever said this about. But Henry's sixth and last wife, Catherine Parr, had a similar experience. She was a convinced Protestant and tried to convert Henry. The Catholic group at court sought leave from Henry to convict her of heresy when they heard him grumble at the way she lectured him. She only just survived. As in the case of Cranmer, Henry apparently agreed to her trial, but then relented and rebuked those who made the attempt.

Cranmer's was a remarkable performance. He never hesitated to appeal for others when he felt it was right. He appealed to the monarch to save Anne Boleyn in 1535, Thomas More a few months earlier in the same year, and Cromwell in 1540. Henry never bore a grudge against him apparently. Cranmer always made it clear that he would remain the King's good servant, but no other such servant ever dared to make such specific appeals to him. More would never have done so, because any appeals of this kind only reinforced the lion's knowledge of his own strength. "Ever tell him what he ought to do and not what he can, for if a lion were to know his own strength hard were it for any man to hold him," he advised Cromwell. Cranmer had an extraordinary lack of immediate finesse, legal, political or psychological, in his personal approach to the monarch—he would even often correct the theology of the monarch's marginal notes on religious documents, and once at least the royal grammar. But he would then revert, if he failed to persuade, to a loyalty so absolute that it often looks to be the purest opportunism. But through it all Cranmer succeeded very substantially in forwarding that moderate Lutheran reformation to which he had probably become committed during the years of private study in the twenties.

In the late thirties and the forties Cranmer turned to work on the liturgy, on those acts of public worship which were bound in the end to have a very great effect on the faith of a people if they took part in them Sunday after Sunday, especially if a large proportion of them were illiterate and even when literate only received a minute fraction of the written communications which we receive today. The sheer authority of the words spoken in church was great. During the last years of the reign this was the most fruitful line for progress. Cranmer's private work at this time enabled him when times were easier in the following reign to produce the basis of the liturgy to be used in worship in the churches of England for the next four hundred years, a liturgy which had much of Luther, something of Zwingli, Calvin and Bucer in it, but which was also Henrician, and in itself as a whole the unique product of Cranmer himself. He was to succeed in replacing a liturgy which was marked by very infrequent lay Communion and numerous private Masses with the liturgy of a regular congregational service.

The lineaments and new dimensions of a reformed Church were beginning to be seen. The sovereign part played by the Bible is well illustrated by one William Malden, describing his experience as a young man at Chelmsford soon after the Bible had begun to be read in church: "Divers poor men in . . . Chelmsford . . . brought the New Testament of Jesus Christ, and on Sundays did sit reading in the lower end of the church, and many would flock about them to hear their reading." He described a clash with his father and his attempt to persuade his mother not to "worship" the crucifix. He had Frith's book on the Eucharist. The Act of 1543 prohibited "women, artificers, apprentices, journeymen, servingmen, under the degree of yeomen, husbandmen and labourers" from reading the Bible. A shepherd near Oxford wrote in a copy of Thomas Langley's *Abridgement of Polydore Vergil:* "I bout thys boke when the Testament was obberagatyd [abrogated], that shepeherdys myght not red hit. I prey God amende that blyndnes. Wryt by Robert Wyllyams keppynge shepe uppon Seynbury Hill, 1546."

Scarisbrick comments: "By the 1540's heterodoxy had noticeably ceased to be merely an affair of pockets of Lollard weavers and husbandmen and merchants, or of individual clerics, but had penetrated and silently taken root in every level of society, including the Court. It had acquired powerful lay patrons; like Puritanism and Catholic recusancy later, it had won influential women to its cause who, more than any other persons perhaps, could allow it to come out of the universities and the avant-garde London churches to take possession of lay, domestic life." By the time of Henry's death the long-standing anti-clericalism, the desire for the Bible and resentment of foreign ecclesiastical influence had received massive encouragement. The basic structure of a state church had been erected by the acts of the Reformation Parliament. There was thus both the public sentiment and the shell of a structure which might be filled with Protestant teaching and worship. But, although in 1547 at Henry's death the Church of England was independent of Rome, many people thought it possible, or probable, that it would return to papal allegiance. While great numbers of people were inclined towards accepting some of the teaching of Protestantism and some of the "reforms"; yet the church services and the teaching generally given remained substantially orthodox from the Catholic point of view, only excepting allegiance to the Pope. Mass and all other official worship were still in Latin.

CHAPTER 6

France, Switzerland and
Calvin to 1542

During the late twenties and early thirties the Swiss and Rhineland towns continued to reform the Church in their various ways and speeds. In the van was Zwingli's Zurich. In the rear was Basel, where Oecolampadius gradually moved onward from Erasmus' position, favoring in his sermons Luther's side in the free will controversy. In between were Strasbourg, Berne, St. Gall and others. At Strasbourg Bucer was experimenting with liturgies and catechisms that were to exercise a great influence later on Calvin, and in England. All were in constant contact. Basel is of special interest in that Erasmus, although now openly refusing to associate himself with the full reforming position of Luther, remained in residence even while Oecolampadius, his own principal collaborator in the translation and editing of the early Fathers, was himself celebrating a reformed liturgy. Here Erasmus was strictly consistent. He had no objection in principle to reform of the liturgy. But while he saw such reforms as possible within a continuing loyalty to the old structure and to the papacy in particular, for Oecolampadius it was part of a new doctrine and a new form of the Church. In 1525 Oecolampadius published a piece on the controversy about the Eucharist. He interpreted the words "This is my body" in a "figurative" sense, relying on Tertullian, who took "body" to be *figura corporis.* Oecolampadius thought it best to have it printed in Strasbourg rather than Basel. The Lutheran Swabian preachers to whom he dedicated it rejected it, implying in their answer that the author was perhaps an even worse danger than Karlstadt. Bucer in Strasbourg wrote around, trying to mediate. Erasmus wrote very mildly in protest to the Council of Basel, making it clear that the book was opposed to the "teaching and consensus of the church." The University of Paris censured it.

Oecolampadius was not far from the position of Zwingli. He

simplified but did not entirely evacuate all sacramental affirmation from the Eucharist doctrine. "They speak well and religiously who say that they come to the Body of the Lord, or eat his Body; profanely and contemptibly, who declare that they only receive the bread and a sign . . ." By 1525 Oecolampadius was refusing to celebrate Mass when there were no communicants, and was using a simplified liturgy.

At the end of 1528 things began to come to a crisis in Basel. A petition demanding the abolition of Mass and an end to "divisive preaching" was sent to the magistrates by a meeting of 300 guildsmen in the Gardeners Guild—Oecolampadius had a connection with it through his wife, whom he, now aged forty, had married in March that year. Eventually a reforming ordinance was issued on April 1, 1529. It started with Romans 1:16, "I am not ashamed of the gospel of Christ." Coming later than in many towns, the reforms went through fairly quietly and without bloodshed. Erasmus was able to leave quietly and in full public view, when it was clear that the future of Basel was as a Protestant town, with Oecolampadius largely leading the religious initiative. Basel had come slowly to the point of crisis. It was faced all the more swiftly with the crucial disciplinary problems. Was the new Christian community to turn itself also into an organization which would discipline (or would join with the civil power to discipline) those whom it considered to be heretics? The answer was "yes." Within a year Anabaptists were being executed or drowned in Basel. By March 1531 none were left in the town.

As we have seen, in 1529 Oecolampadius was at Marburg with Zwingli controverting with Luther and Melanchthon. And in the following year or so Philip of Hesse began to bind the Protestants into an organization which could defend itself with force. In Switzerland that local confrontation of arms occurred which led to the death of Zwingli. Zwingli was succeeded in Zurich by the Englishman Henry Bullinger, a great disseminator of the Reformation through his typically English letter writing and quiet entertainment of visitors. In Basel Oecolampadius died in 1531. In 1534, of all people, the Basel authorities invited Karlstadt, now at Zurich, and undoubtedly dispensable as far as Bullinger was concerned.

At Strasbourg, as at the start, so later, things went particularly well. Bucer was one of the outstanding men of the Reformation. His Strasbourg became the principal city for everyone to take refuge in—not excepting Calvin himself, who went there when Geneva found their first dose of him too sharp. Although, like Luther and Calvin, Bucer had his prickly or tiresome side, it was he really who added the fourth word, "Love," as Rupp says, to the three dimensions of the Protestant Church—Word, Sacrament, Discipline. He was one for love in all senses. He managed to marry the reformer Capito off to Oecolampadius' widow, and then when he died, Bucer himself married this good lady, widowed as she was for the third time, for she was already widowed once when Oecolampadius took her at twenty-six. He found young Calvin a wife in 1540.

Bucer's strongest gift was in the liturgy. Influenced by Müntzer's liturgical innovations at Allstedt, he had set about creative liturgical experiment. For him as for the liturgical reformer of the twentieth century it seemed essential for the liturgy to teach, to mirror Christian belief. If the medieval church building had tried to teach with mural and statue, fresco and sculpture, the Protestant Church must teach in the language of worship, as indeed the early Church had done. With the same object in view Bucer introduced numerous hymns into his services. He became number four in the Reformation lists, after Luther, Zwingli and Calvin. Perhaps his strongest wish was for the unity of the Church, and he was foremost at Marburg, and at many later conferences, in trying to forge a common doctrinal basis for the Protestant Reformation. Yet he was never one for compromise. Not being able to accept Melanchthon's Confession at Augsburg in 1530, he became then the principal author of the Tetrapolitan Confession put forward by Strasbourg, Constance, Memmingen and Lindau. He was the architect of the Wittenberg Concord of 1536. Eventually, when the emperor brought Strasbourg and its master Jacob Sturm to their knees in 1548, Bucer could not go back on his Protestantism. He left for England.

The reforms of Berne and Geneva were linked. And of course they were linked in turn with the other cities. In 1528 there was a disputation in Berne to which Bucer and Capito came from Strasbourg. The result was the abolition of the Mass in that year. It was 1536 before the Reformation was formally proclaimed at Geneva on May 21. Two months later Calvin came, persuaded by Farel to come and help to ensure that the precariously achieved reform should put down roots.

Jean Calvin was born twenty-six years after Luther in Noyon. His father came from a family of boatmen and artisans, but managed to push his way up to a higher status. Five years before Jean's birth he became one of the town's registrars, and soon after that was appointed to various offices connected with the cathedral. The bishop was the ruler of the very churchy town, and one of the Twelve Peers of France. Young Jean used to mix with the family of the bishop of the time, Charles de Hangest, and contracted various aristocratic tastes and habits in this way. His early childhood was pious and conventional. His godfather was one of the cathedral canons. His mother, daughter of an innkeeper, had a reputation for piety, but we know very little about her, and she died while Calvin was young. At twelve years old Calvin's father obtained for him from the cathedral chapter part of the revenues of the chapel of Gesine, situated at the entry to the cathedral choir. They consisted of "a little wheat from Voienne and some barley from Espeville." The point of this was probably to enable him to go on to "higher studies" without too much cost to his father.

In 1523 there was an outbreak of plague at Noyon. Jean was sent with two other boys to Paris with a tutor. After being taught incompetently (Calvin says) for a short time by a master, he entered the Collège de la Marche and found a good teacher in Mathurin Cordier, who made such an impression on his pupil that Calvin always remembered him and invited him many years later, in 1559, to organize education at Geneva and Lausanne. Calvin went on to the Collège de Montaigu, a stronghold of orthodoxy. He was here for five years and only too little is known about them. He received the standard education. He could not have failed to have the opportunity to read Luther and the other reformers. He was friends with one Nicholas Kop, son of the physician of Francis I. Nicholas was friendly with humanists and budding reformers. Calvin's cousin, Pierre Robert, nicknamed Olivetan on account of the midnight oil he used so much of, was a disciple of the reformers. We have seen the atmosphere in which Farel and Lefèvre were attempting to further biblical scholarship and translation, with the king encouraging them a little and the Sorbonne, with its head Beda, opposing them, and the interval 1525–27, when Francis I was captive in Spain. Olivetan fled to Strasbourg in 1528. Farel had gone to Basel, then Strasbourg, a year or two before. This was the atmosphere of Calvin's education to the age of nineteen. Calvin himself apparently remained largely unmoved by whatever he may have read of the reformers, sticking to the Catholic ways of his upbringing.

These five years at Paris were followed by four at Orléans, Bourges and again at Paris, and they took Calvin to the age of twenty-three. He emerged as a very comprehensively educated young humanist. He had worked hard and read widely. He knew the Bible well. He knew the Fathers. He had read widely in the classic texts of Greece and Rome. He had studied the philosophical, theological and legal texts of his time. Halfway through this period, in 1528, he had just started "Theology," having completed "Philosophy," when his father decided to divert him from preparation for the priesthood as originally intended, to the study of law, at Orléans, with a view to a career as a lawyer. This change was due to a contretemps experienced by Calvin's father, a disagreement between him and the cathedral chapter which made his son's ecclesiastical future appear less rosy. Orléans was a very lively university and less subject than Paris to restrictive policies. Erasmus had taught there, likewise Aleander and Reuchlin. Pierre de l'Estoile was the most famous of the eight professors when Calvin went there. Calvin was greatly impressed by "his penetrative mind, his skill, his experience in law, of which he is the unchallenged prince of our epoch." It was at Orléans that Calvin learned Greek from Melchior Wolmar; also there and at Bourges that he overworked and while attaining a lifelong felicity of style contracted equally a lifelong stomach weakness, *imbecilitas ventriculi.* Wolmar was a teacher who remained a lifelong friend. He eventually obtained the chair of Greek at Tübingen and stayed there all his life. In 1546 Calvin dedicated to him his Commentary on II Corinthians.

In 1531–32 Calvin returned to Paris to a new college Francis I had founded in imitation of the Collège Trilingue (Latin, Greek, Hebrew) of Louvain. Calvin published his first book in 1532. It created no stir at the time and was widely considered evidence of a lack of appropriate humility. But the book tells us a lot about the man, his ability and his maturity. It was a commentary on *De Clementia,* (*Concerning Clemency*) of the ancient Roman author Seneca. Calvin's commentary on it is the work of a very accomplished humanist. Calvin was a Christian, a Catholic, but his quotations from the Bible are but three. While he refers fifteen times to Augustine's *City of God,* his method is the philological method of Valla, and the whole is an example of Renaissance scholarship, clearly in the same class as the work of Erasmus. The book shows us Calvin's serious, typically French logical intellect hard at work. It seems likely that his theory of providence, so marked in his later theology, is to be traced back to the philosophical concept of providence found in Seneca. Seneca insisted that government must submit to providence. Calvin comments, "this is also the teaching of our religion, that there is no power but of God and that everything is ordered by him, according to Romans 13." Here already we find a central theme of Calvin's theology. The fascinating thing is to find it set down in a more or less dispassionate context in this strictly humanist disquisition. Calvin had already set his intellectual sights and begun to map out a universal philosophy. But as yet he was lacking in any vital religious sense, or any apparent desire to follow it through in a strictly theological inquiry.

The religious ferment at Paris was still at its height. In 1533 in a new agreement with the Pope, King Francis I agreed to suppress heresy. But reformers were still in important posts in Paris. In the Louvre evangelical sermons were being preached at the request of Margaret of Navarre, the king's sister. On All Saints' Day Calvin's friend Nicholas Kop preached a sermon in the Church of St. Mathurins which praised reformers and expounded justification by faith. This was too much for the authorities, who tried to arrest him and fifty others. Calvin fled from the city to a friend at Angoulême, where he stayed under the pseudonym of Charles d'Esperville. From there he went on to the court of Margaret of Navarre, at Nérac, where Lefèvre was. The latter never joined the Reform but remained devoted to biblical studies in an Erasmian position. Sometime about now Calvin became convinced that he must abandon the communion of the papal Church and join the Reform. "God subdued and made teachable a heart which for my age was far too hardened in such matters."

Some years later Calvin described the experience of conversion of an advocate of the Reform in his letter to Cardinal Sadoleto, who had written against the reforms in Geneva. It seems almost certain that he was describing his own experience of a few years previous: "The more closely I considered myself, the more my conscience pricked with sharp goadings; so much so that no other relief or comfort remained to me except to deceive myself by forgetting. But since nothing better offered itself, I went on still in the way I had begun: then however there arose quite another form of teaching, not to turn away from the profession of Christianity but to reduce it to its own source, and to restore it, as it were, cleansed from all dirt to its own purity. But I, offended, by this novelty, could hardly listen to it willingly; and must confess that at first I valiantly and bravely resisted. For since men are naturally obstinate and opinionated to maintain the institutions they have once received, it irked me much to confess that I had been fed upon error and ignorance all my life. One thing especially there was that prevented me from believing in these people, and that was reverence for the Church. But after I had listened for some time with open ears and suffered myself to be taught, I saw very well that such a fear, that the Church might be diminished, was vain and superfluous."

Luther was smitten by powerful interior drives and could not deny the theology he saw forming itself in his mind and heart. In Calvin we find a kind of intellectual and logical complement to Luther. Not that Luther did not have a powerful mind, but the driving force was his own experience; as he says "*sola experientia theologum facit* [experience alone makes a theologian]." Calvin looks at everything in the light of the intellect. But until convinced by the reformers, although some of the teaching and other activities of the old Church increasingly failed to make sense to him, he thought it was better to tolerate them than to turn away altogether when there was nothing else to turn to. But then the teaching of the reformers suddenly came home to him, and he envisioned the possibility of "reducing" Christianity to its source. In the Bible it should be possible to identify the true heart of that which now seemed to the sensitive sixteenth-century scholar, with his newly polished Graeco-Roman perspective, such a bizarre amalgam, its failures and illogicalities all bitingly exposed by Erasmus. The thought which had struck so many reformers and heretics of the previous five hundred years now took root in the clean clear rigorous determined dispassionate mind of humanist Jean Calvin, classicist, Latin stylist, graduate of Orléans, Bourges and Paris. And immediately, it seems, the force of the Lutheran teaching conveyed itself to his mind. If he read the Bible in this frame of mind he found that it spoke to him of that simple doctrine of justification by faith which was destined to transform his approach to life as it was transforming that of so many others. The religious drive of Christianity, which in the thirteenth century had taken the form of desire to return to poverty and simplicity, found its most powerful outlet in the sixteenth century in the simple re-affirmation of that faith which is so often demanded of the questioner or aspirant in the New Testament. Luther had not only uncovered this signpost but had developed the necessary intellectual formula as well—justification comes to man by this faith which itself comes through the one channel of the Word, the Scriptures. *Sola fides, sola scriptura.* Once Calvin had become convinced that this was the proper interpretation of Christianity and this doctrine the true religious key to an understanding of life, he set to work to organize the insight and all accompanying insights. But first he must rearrange his life. He now understood what his friend Kop, and the other reformers he had met and heard in Paris, were about.

In May 1534 Calvin journeyed to Noyon to surrender his ec-clesiastical benefices. Enjoyment of them was no longer compatible with his religious beliefs. He returned via Paris, Poitiers and Angoulême to the University of Orléans for a short time. It was now that he wrote the first of his very numerous religious works. Already perhaps he felt the need to enter the lists on behalf of his newly fervent faith. And it may be significant that this work is not directed against the Church of his previous allegiance, nor is it concerned with any of the currently popular religious topics. It is written to controvert the thesis of some obscure Anabaptists, and it is written simply in the wish to scotch what Calvin sees to be an evident error. His book is entitled *De Psychopannychia* and seeks to contradict the idea that the souls of the dead go to sleep at death and remain so until the Last Judgment.

1534 was a climactic year. In October occurred the affair of the placards. All over Paris on the morning of October 17 people found placards denouncing the Mass. There was even one on the door of the king's apartment. This provoked a violent reaction from authority and it was no longer safe for Calvin to stay in the country. He went to Basel, one of the friendliest of the cities available for refugees, with the tolerant influence of Erasmus still strong in it. Here he helped his cousin Olivetan with his translation of the Bible, published in the following June 1535. And he now continued with and completed his own attempts to get his religious reorientation down in written form. He intended it originally as a means of organizing his own mind and of providing a statement he could show to others. Then he envisaged a wider use and added a preface addressed to Francis I, intended to persuade him to support the Reform. The opening pages of Chapter 2 of this book quoted from it. Calvin's book was the first version of the famous *Institutes of the Christian Religion,* which he continually revised and added to all his life. It represents his considered view of the Christian religion. Its final version occupies the twelve hundred very full pages of a modern book. Even this first version was not short, although some history books call it short. François Wendel, (in his *Calvin*) says of this first version that it was in one volume of 516 pages of small format, such as could readily be slipped into the vast pockets of the clothes then worn.

Before going on to consider these *Institutes,* which were published in the first year of Calvin's public work as a reformer, let us look once more at the year 1534 in Paris. It was not only the year of the placards, when Calvin had to leave Paris. It was also the year when the seed was sown in that town of a movement in the old Church, destined both to utilize and greatly to regenerate the religious drive and enthusiasm within it. A forty-year-old Spaniard, Don Iñigo López de Loyola (later to be called Ignatius), a man who must have seemed to be one of those never satisfied students, one of those obsessed students of the spirit, along with six companions who had gathered round him, dedicated their lives at Montmartre to the service of God. Of all the unpromising things, they swore, in the full medieval tradition, that they would make a pilgrimage to the Holy Land—Iñigo had already been once —or if this was denied them they would offer their services to the Pope. They took vows of poverty and chastity.

This was not just the quixotic asceticism of some Spaniard extremist, but the beginning of the end of a long pilgrimage of a man in his middle age. It was thirteen years since Iñigo had had his first religious experience, after being wounded in the defense of Pamplona against the French army. Reading the *Life of Christ* by Ludolph the Carthusian, he conceived then the idea of becoming a soldier of Christ instead of a soldier of a human army. He went up to the Benedictine monastery at Montserrat to try to understand, test and deepen the vocation which he seemed to think that he had. For thirteen years from that time he strove to deepen this

understanding, and to train himself spiritually. He took down notes
of his meditations and there gradually emerged *The Spiritual Exercises*, perhaps the most powerful single piece of writing in the
Roman Catholic Church for some hundreds of years, apart from
Scripture. Iñigo became suspect to the Inquisition—anything unusual was treated thus. He was in prison for a time. But he journeyed to Italy, and the Holy Land. Wherever he went Iñigo
attracted others of like spirit. In 1534 he was in Paris for the purpose of improving his own education—at the age of forty-three.

The only explanation of the life of Ignatius, as he came to be
called, was the religious drive. The religious order, the Society
of Jesus, known generally as the Jesuits, which was founded a
year later by him and his friends and which immediately flourished greatly, emphasized the virtue of obedience to their superior and fulfillment of the missionary task of the Church. But
the result of the emphasis which Ignatius had given in his own
life to the training of himself, to educating himself and his companions, led to the Jesuits founding colleges in Spain and Italy
particularly, and later all over Europe. Ignatius had taken from
the Benedictines of Montserrat something of the sober methodical
asceticism both of ancient Benedictine tradition but also something
of the *Innerlichkeit*, the inwardness of the late medieval traditions
of the Devotio Moderna in the Netherlands. His movement,
the Jesuits, eventually became both a place of supreme spiritual
discipline and fervor and also an order dedicated more than any
other to the work of converting men to Christ. Ignatius thus
continued the age-old tradition of the Church of inward spiritual
formation at the same time as undertaking new outward pastoral
tasks—only just managing to do it without being permanently
shot down by the Spanish Inquisition.

Calvin meanwhile was busy reformulating basic Christian theology, while assisting the establishment of Protestantism in Geneva
(1536–38), invited there by Farel, and in Strasbourg (1538–42),
where he went when there was irreconcilable disagreement between him and the Genevan magistrate. In towns where the Reform was becoming triumphant he felt the need and opportunity
to provide a total outline. Calvin produced a typically medieval
summa, a highly dogmatic system. Although the *Institute* had its
origin in Calvin's determination to find in Scripture the essence
or heart of Christianity, in practice it became a vast unfolding

of Christian doctrines often unrelated to Scripture except by the old medieval mechanical method of finding isolated texts to support them. At the same time no need was felt by Calvin to make the whole into a completely rigorous logical unity, for Scripture could never claim to be such. The individual parts were, however, logical and very clear, and often worked out in great detail. Both in its original Latin version and in its later French version it was a model of clarity, and the French version had a notable influence on the written French language.

Altogether, however, the influence of the *Institutes* was not due simply to its clarity or logic; it was due first rather to the practical power which Calvin wielded in Geneva and Strasbourg, the very severe discipline which he persuaded the church and the city council in those towns to wield over the citizens, and only thus to the great clarity and effect with which he wrote. These two things led to his having an influence on the reforms throughout France, and further afield. The *Institutes*, written first in Latin, translated by Calvin into French in 1541, provided a complete reference book of teaching for all those who felt they should ask advice from Calvin and try to follow his methods. Calvin is most easily understood as a scholastic or a "summist." His *Institutes of the Christian Religion* provide a complete guide to Christianity as he understood it. Until the end of his life he continued to add to it, to make it more completely an exposition of the Christian religion. His concern was to build a system. He was not at all worried that it was indeed simply another system, in many particulars identical with those of previous medieval summists. Indeed, with his understanding of history, and of the nature of the intellect, he found it natural to be in agreement with previous philosophers and theologians, and with previous interpreters of the gospel.

At the end of his opening "Method and Arrangement, or Subject of the Whole Work," Calvin sums up his intentions and thus also his understanding of Christianity: "Such is the arrangement of the Institutes, which may be thus summed up: Man being at first created upright, but afterwards being not partially but totally ruined, finds his entire salvation out of himself in Christ, to whom being united by the Holy Spirit freely given, without any foresight of future works, he thereby obtains a double blessing—viz. full imputation of righteousness, which goes along with us even to the grace, and the commencement of sanctification, which daily

advanced till at length it is perfected in the day of regeneration
or resurrection of the body, and this, in order that the great mercy
of God may be celebrated in the heavenly mansions throughout
eternity." It is noteworthy that neither Scripture is referred to,
nor is the "Word" of God mentioned. Equally it is noteworthy that
Calvin goes out of his way to express the essential Lutheran insights with all the emphasis he can give them, turning sharply
away from any possible Erasmian or humanist compromise: "not
partially but totally ruined, finds his entire salvation." No question
of any semi-Pelagianism! "Out of himself in Christ, to whom being
united by the Holy Spirit freely given, without any foresight of
future works. . . ."

The at first surprising absence of reference to Scripture is made
good in the "Epistle to the Reader." In this Calvin describes
his purpose, once again, very succinctly. He has given, he says,
"a summary of religion in all its parts, and digested it in an
order which will make it easy for anyone, who rightly compre-
hends it, to ascertain both what he ought chiefly to look for in
Scripture, and also to what head he ought to refer whatever is
contained in it." So Calvin's must not be taken simply as a summa,
or a final reference book. The reader must read Scripture, and
we do not give Calvin his due unless we make it clear that here
he was not in fact thinking of a mechanistic searching for texts,
but of a meditative reading, for he insists that the Spirit is the
final authority. And our reliance on Scripture itself is based on
faith—there is no rational demonstration, he says, why he should
believe in and rely on Scripture. "Our conviction of the truth of
Scripture must be derived from a higher source than human con-
jectures or reasons; namely, the secret testimony of the Spirit."
Again: "In vain were the authority of Scriptures fortified by argument, or supported by the consent of the Church, or confirmed
by any other helps, if unaccompanied by an assurance higher and
stronger than human judgment can give." "It is foolish to attempt
to prove to infidels that the Scripture is the Word of God. This
cannot be known except by faith." Aquinas would have agreed.

Calvin was the first major reformer to spend all his youth and
adult life in the atmosphere of the Reformation. He was nine
in the year when Luther was excommunicated. When he came
to set down his ideas it was not a matter of feeling an almost
obsessive or exclusive need to attack the old Church, and to

establish certain outstanding points and positions, as bridgeheads. Calvin felt able to set calmly about a complete exposition of Christianity in the context of the Reform. There was still a state of very acute tension between the reformers and the papal Church. But the humanist Calvin felt sufficiently confident to be able to attempt a complete exposé, virtually a medieval-style summa. "A comprehensive summary," perhaps a modern publisher or author might call it. It is the last written work of the Reform which we shall do more than refer to. For with it the Reform became a fully established part of the Christian scene. Luther had provided the essential drive to break away, and had provided, astonishingly, all the original insights, a great mass of detailed exegesis of Scripture; and he inspired numerous practical arrangements. Calvin wished to reduce all this to a single ordered scheme. Although to the reformers themselves their differences were large and great, in fact they only cover a very small area of the whole Christian revelation. On the whole they were in agreement with each other. And over very large areas they were also in agreement with the great theologians of the Middle Ages. A reader working his way through Calvin's *Institutes* will not find that he has to mark more than 5 per cent, probably less, of the work, as being unorthodox or "heretical" by medieval standards, or in disagreement, for instance, with Aquinas.

What stands out above all else to the objective historian of religion (as distinct from the religious polemicist, or the popular protagonist of Protestant or Catholic theory) is the continuity of Calvin with the past. Not only his theology, but the practice of Christianity is in many areas based on the same principles as that of the Middle Ages. At first this statement will leave many astonished. Surely the Mass has gone—and is not the Mass the center of it all? And surely the Church is now local instead of organized into a single centralized body—and again is not this centralization in the papacy at the heart of it? These assumptions will not bear extended examination. The center of the Christian religion is the revelation of Jesus Christ found in the text of the Bible, the adherence of men and women to this revelation in faith, and the acting out of it in a life of love. It is not possible to propound any theology of the Mass or any theology of the papacy without some such preliminary. What gives to them their importance is precisely the claim that the Mass and the papacy are parts of the organizational structure claiming to be rooted in this revelation.

There is not much emphasis on such structure in the New Testament, which is a record of revealing events and teaching. The early Church undoubtedly placed strong emphasis on the New Testament theme of worshiping God "in spirit and in truth" rather than, or at any rate as an essential conclusion of obeying the law. Yet it did gradually find itself requiring and setting up a structure. It grew eventually into the vast complicated structure of the late medieval Church, a structure which claimed for itself that unique validity, even a kind of holiness, which really belongs only to revelation itself, or to Christ himself. By extension this validity and holiness may, it can be said, belong to his Church, as seen ideally. But that Church is always present in the sinful men of the present generation. The achievement of holiness is never complete. The reformers found the organization gravely inappropriate to the religion, and the claims of its authority unsupported by Scripture. But Luther's original desire simply to reform that structure without breaking the visible unity of the Church was truly representative of the motive at the heart of all the major reformers. For none of them were millenarians or wished to adopt a virtually anarchist following of the Holy Spirit, as it might reveal itself— with the possible exception of Müntzer. All the others recognized that there must be objective norms and that there must be an organization, there must be a "Church" if the gospel was to be present to ordinary men, women and children day by day. Though they rejected the theory and practice of the papacy, they quickly substituted other authorities to assist the faithful in understanding the meaning of Scripture. Though they rejected the theory and practice of Mass as a sacrifice they substituted their own "scriptural" understanding of that celebration of the "Eucharist" which Jesus asked his followers to repeat. In the end what is really important is that both Catholics and Protestants were doing, as far as they could understand it, what Jesus had asked. Inevitably there was much more in common than not so. Thus the really noticeable thing, say to a twentieth-century Buddhist, is that these sixteenth-century reformers experienced just the same compulsions and needs as, and expressed doctrines very similar indeed to, those of the medieval theologians and the members of the medieval Church. They felt the need to gather together frequently to do what

Jesus had told his followers to do at the Last Supper. Of course they understood the meeting differently. And, culturally, they gave it a new orientation, with a new emphasis on the supper and the eating—an emphasis which had never been fully absent from the medieval Church. Aquinas' hymn for the feast of Corpus Christi has the food and the meal as its central theme: "*Laudis thema specialis, panis vivus et vitalis, hodie proponitur, quem in sacrae mensa coenae, turbae fratrum duodenae, datum non ambigitur,*" living and life-giving bread is laid on the table today for the sacred meal. . . .

This theme of continuity with the past is apparent in other spheres. Baptism remains the essential initiating sacrament. Marriage remains a sacred monogamous relationship specially blessed by God, in contrast with practice and theory in other continents. The emphasis is different, the essentials not.

Calvin dated his prefatory address to the King of France: "Basel, August 1, 1536." The address is some 9000 words long, and contains important doctrinal material. Calvin goes straight to the heart of Luther's teaching, showing he had accepted it entirely. He then goes on to the divisive issue at the heart of the Reformation, the nature of the Church. First, his Lutheran doctrine: "All prophecy ought to be according to the analogy of faith . . . What accords better and more aptly with faith than to acknowledge ourselves divested of all virtue, that we may be clothed with God, devoid of all goodness that we may be filled with him?" Calvin goes on to rejection of any kind of semi-Pelagianism, and perhaps of any kind of (Thomistic) doctrine of nature: "When these things, and others to the same effect, are said by us, they interpose, and querulously complain, that in this way we overturn some blind light of nature, fancied preparatives, free will, and works meritorious of eternal salvation, with their own supererogations added, because they cannot bear that the entire praise and glory of all goodness, virtue, and wisdom, should remain with God." He says no one was ever blamed for drinking too much of the fountain of living water, and asks: "What more agreeable to faith than to feel assured that God is a propitious Father when Christ is acknowledged as a brother and propitiator . . . ?" Calvin contrasts this faith with that demanded by the priests of the papal Church, which is submission to the "judgment of the Church, with what they call implicit faith." Calvin equates the "judgment of the Church" with "custom" (tradition) and rejects it as a possible norm: "Were the judgments of mankind correct custom could be regulated by the good. But it is often far otherwise in point of fact."

So Calvin turns to the nature of the Church—that area of theological discussion which had remained largely untouched by theologians but which had led many of those few who had turned to it into excommunication. Most theologians had ignored the subject because it had seemed to pose no problem. There really was not much difficulty in identifying the Church. Christendom was before them. But Calvin exposes the problem that had arisen when Marsilius and Wycliffe, Hus and Luther turned to this subject: "The hinges on which the controversy turns are these: first, in their contending that the form of the Church is always visible and apparent; and, secondly, in their placing this form in the see of the Church of Rome and its hierarchy. We, on the contrary, maintain, both that the Church may exist without any apparent form, and moreover, that the form is not ascertained by that external splendour which they foolishly admire, but by a very different mark, namely, by the pure preaching of the word of God, and the due administration of the sacraments. They make an outcry whenever the Church cannot be pointed to with the finger. But how oft was it the fate of the Church among the Jews to be so defaced that no comeliness appeared? What do we suppose to have been the splendid form when Elijah complained that he was left alone? How long after the advent of Christ did it lie hid without form? . . . Let us rather reverently admit, that as God alone knows who are his, so he may sometimes withdraw the external manifestation of his Church from the view of man . . . In opposition to the whole body of the prophets, Jeremiah is sent alone to declare from the Lord, that a time would come when the law would perish from the priest, counsel from the wise, and the word from the prophet."

Calvin, like Luther, finds important evidence and inspiration in the Old Testament. To a Christian today, entirely used to the idea that the Church as such was founded by Jesus Christ, it is strange to find the people of God in the Old Testament times referred to without apology as "the Church" so that they can be taken as an example of how the Church can be defaced. Calvin goes to pre-Christian history rather than to the words of the gospel or to the history of the Church proper, very much as the medieval theologians had always done. The reformer has not broken completely out of the world of formulas and definitions of the kind favored by the late Judaic church, just the legalistic approach which Jesus denounced in the Old Testament. However, it is already much that he propounds, the communitarian idea of the Church as primary and insists that the terrestrial organization cannot be identified just as it is with this community, this people of God, now those redeemed by Jesus. The crucial words in this description of the Church are: "pure" (preaching) and "due" (administration of the sacraments). The need for decisions as to when preaching was "pure" and when the sacraments were administered "duly" returns us directly to the central problem of Church structure. It is just as it was with the previous quotation about the authority and inspiration of Scripture and the Spirit. We still need a human regulator, a human sovereign. Even if the Church seen in its theological fullness may be invisible there remains the crucial problem of how the visible, known Church shall in fact carry on from day to day. Luther had already found he must either erect a whole set of new structures or use the old structures reformed. It was just that the need for reform of old structures or in some cases their rejection and the substitution of new structures seemed so extensive that Calvin felt the need to write this complete exposé of Christianity. This is the raison d'etre for the *Institutes*.

Calvin could not read German. But Luther published all his major works in Latin, and Calvin drew freely on them. The form and order of the *Institutes* followed Luther's Catechism, of which the form is an adaptation of traditional doctrinal forms, rather than anything revolutionary. The opening words are, however, highly characteristic of the age and remind us of Calvin the Renaissance scholar in their opening reference to "wisdom": "Our wisdom, as it ought to be deemed true and solid wisdom, consists almost entirely of two parts: the knowledge of God and of ourselves." This statement leads on into a first long section about man's knowledge of God, of his power and glory, seen and experienced in the created world. Calvin is constantly at pains to give full and proper weight both to the fact that this knowledge can be brought to man in a very full and wide-ranging way by the natural world, but also that this knowledge is not synonymous with any effective understanding of God's wish to save us, to draw us into his company, to deify us, and *a fortiori* is of no use in persuading man to make that act of living faith in God. This natural knowledge, though so extensive, is dead. But it also makes man guilty for not acting on it. So it was necessary to send his Son Jesus; or rather, as Calvin has it, "the light of his Word."

"Therefore, though the effulgence which is presented to every eye, both in the heavens and on earth, leaves the ingratitude of man without excuse, since God, in order to bring the whole human race under the same condemnation, holds forth to all, without exception, a mirror of his Deity in his works, another and better help must be given to guide us properly to God as Creator. Not in vain, therefore, has he added the light of his Word in order that he might make himself known unto salvation, and bestowed the privilege on those whom he was pleased to bring into nearer and more familiar relation to himself." Already at this early stage we begin to see the extremely austere side of Calvin's teaching. In shunning the legalistic severity of a man-controlled Church he ends up in the greater severity of a Church where God's majesty, not man-made canon law, leaves man more belittled. In going to the heart of the religious impulse he ends up in an extreme position typical of the medieval heresies, but now for the first time facing practical implementations. It was to lead to a very severe discipline in practice, first in Geneva, then in those countries which embraced his principles, particularly Scotland and parts of the Netherlands, France, Switzerland and North America.

At an early point in the *Institutes* Calvin introduces a reference to the predestination of the damned. This doctrine is not particularly significant for the Reformation, being a commonplace of medieval theology. But it occurs so frequently in the *Institutes* and clearly bothers Calvin so much that to omit it would be to omit a substantial part of that early history of the Reformation that we set out to describe. The idea of predestination of some men to hell is wrapped up with the attempts by Christians in the previous fifteen hundred years to produce a complete, watertight descriptive account of man and the world. Few Christians today defend the doctrine in its crude form as part of Christian revelation. Its acceptance during fifteen hundred years, and more, was due on the one hand to an overwhelming sense of God's overlordship and a desire to describe this adequately, and on the other hand to the desire to give adequate emphasis to the conviction of the impossibility of understanding him. At this his first reference, Calvin defends the doctrine in this way: "If at any time, then, we are troubled at the small number of those who believe, let us, on the other hand, call to mind, that none comprehend the mysteries of God save those to whom it is given." He returns to a systematic consideration later.

Calvin unfolds the traditional doctrine of the Trinity. Over the years he added greatly to this chapter, which in the first edition was quite short. Calvin's is the traditional Catholic doctrine, based on Augustine and the early councils. The doctrine of providence was another which only appeared fully in the later editions, but it came finally to occupy a prominent position; Calvin deprecated anything like what is sometimes referred to as the eighteenth-century idea of the "watchmaker" God, a creator who constructed the universe, wound it up and left it to run its way. On the contrary, Calvin's God is entirely involved in his world.

In Book II, Calvin comes to original sin, grace and free will. He had evidently studied the subject extensively both as it appears in Augustine and in the early reformers. As we remarked earlier, he had fully grasped the proposition of man's complete inability in the matter of salvation. It was not just that he, with Luther and the others, felt the need to oppose once for all the semi-Pelagianism of the fifteenth-century theologians. It was rather that they wished to disown forever any idea that Church authority could, as it were, act for God, could provide, more or less on demand, that initial grace which would enable man to reach his spiritual goal. They wanted to establish God's complete freedom and man's total enslavement to sin. So for thirty pages we have a catena of more or less extreme statements on these Lutheran lines from Calvin: "Free will does not enable any man to perform good works, unless he is assisted by grace; indeed the special grace which the elect receive through regeneration. For I say not to consider the extravagance of those who say that grace is offered equally and promiscuously to all." Calvin quotes Augustine widely: "I glory in nothing, for nothing is ours"; "Every good work in us is performed only by grace." These and numerous other statements are not meant to deny that a man may do many actions which have some immediately good result in the human community. They are meant to assert that unless they are actuated by sincere God-given spiritual motivation they have no value in God's eyes. As St. Paul put it: "If I give away all that I possess, piece by piece, and if I even let them take my body to burn it, but am without love, it will do me no good whatever." What the medievals hardly ever envisaged was that although this "supernatural" love does not seem in our experience to be simply part of man's natural endowment, yet there is no need in logic or in exegesis of Scripture to limit its offer by God only to some part of mankind; in fact the exact opposite is the case. They saw, with good reason in logic and exegesis, that one can only posit an outside source, that is, God, as the origin of this love. But they clung to a pre-Christian, perhaps partly Judaic, partly pagan idea that this love, this charity, must have something exclusive about it, and that the elect to whom it was offered had been chosen specially and that this was part of the unfathomable mystery of human life, which is in another sense the mystery of God.

A twentieth-century criticism of this doctrine should not be made from the point of view that every difficulty can be solved. Every attempt to answer all men's queries—other than by forbidding him to ask "unanswerable" questions in the manner of the linguistic analysts—ends up with insoluble mysteries of some kind. But at least we may try to specify the mystery more clearly. The twentieth-century theologian implies that grace is offered to all men; and many theologians now believe that every man gives some finally affirmative answer and that none is in a place of suffering for eternity. This brings the attention back to human failure on earth, to sin, malice, suffering and the failures of man to love here and now. Man is unable to answer this mystery in terms of the sciences of sociology, biology and psychology, which only give some account of the mechanism of this failure, of how the failure comes about. For the medieval, the mystery of sin was hardly a problem. He took the opening chapters of Genesis as a complete explanation. And this was true for Calvin also.

So we return to one more bout of quotations from Calvin, relying still on Augustine. He quotes the latter: "We know that Divine grace is not given to all men, and that to those to whom it is given, it is not given either according to the merit of works, or according to the merit of will, but by free grace; in regard to those to whom it is not given, we know that the not giving of it is just judgment from God." Calvin is more convincing when he describes the affirmative work of the Spirit: "God, therefore, begins the good work in us by exciting in our hearts a desire, a love, and a study of righteousness, or (to speak more correctly) by turning, training and guiding our hearts unto righteousness; and he completes this good work by confirming us unto perseverance." Again using Augustine (*De Correptione et Gratia*) very closely Calvin sums up Chapter 3 in Book II. He refers to Augustine: "He shows, *First*, that human will does not by liberty obtain grace, but by grace obtains liberty. *Secondly*, that by means of the same grace, the heart being impressed with a feeling of delight, is trained to persevere, and strengthened with invincible fortitude. *Thirdly*, that while grace governs the will, it never falls; but when grace abandons it, it falls forthwith. *Fourthly*, that by the free mercy of God, the will is turned to good, and when turned, perseveres. *Fifthly*, so directed, it *depends* entirely on the will of God, and not on any human merit. Thus the will (free will, if you choose to call it so), which is left to man is, as he in another place describes it, a will which can neither be turned to God, nor continue in God, unless by grace; a will which, whatever its ability may be, derives all that ability from grace." Calvin says that God works in his elect in two ways: "inwardly by the Spirit, outwardly by his Word. By his Spirit illuminating their minds, and training their hearts to the practice of righteousness, he makes them new creatures, while, by his Word, he stimulates them to long and seek for this renovation." In the reprobate the doctrine that none can come to God except those who the Father draws "is in them a savour unto death, it is still a sweet savour unto God." "In the matter of grace we give the first place to God, a secondary place must be assigned to our agency. If the only thing here insisted on were that good works are termed *ours*, I, in my turn, would reply that the bread which we ask God to give us is alone termed *ours*. What, then can be inferred from the title of possession, but simply that, by the kindness and free gift of God, that becomes ours which in other respects is by no means due to us."

We conclude this section of quotations from Calvin on the crucial issue of free will by returning to his opening of the whole discussion. It sets the discussion back in the contemporary humanist context, which was not friendly to these extreme statements about man's need of God. Calvin felt the need to make this opening apology:

I am not unaware how much more plausible the view is, which invites us rather to ponder on our good qualities than to contemplate what must overwhelm us with shame—our miserable destitution and ignominy. There is nothing more acceptable to the human mind than flattery, and, accordingly, when told that its endowments are of a high order, it is apt to be excessively credulous. Hence it is not strange that the greater part of mankind have erred so egregiously in this matter. Owing to the innate self-love by which we are all blinded, we most willingly persuade ourselves that we do not possess a single quality which is deserving of hatred; and hence independent of any countenance from without, general credit is given to the very foolish idea, that man is perfectly sufficient of himself for all the purposes of a good and happy life. If any are disposed to think more modestly, and concede somewhat to God, that they may not seem to arrogate everything as their own, still, in making the division, they apportion matters so that the chief ground of confidence and boasting always remains with themselves. . . . In considering the knowledge which man ought to have of himself, it seems proper to divide it thus, *first*, to consider the end for which he was created, and the qualities—by no means contemptible qualities—with which he was endued, thus urging him to meditate on divine worship and the future life; and, *secondly*, to consider his faculties or rather want of faculties—a want which, when perceived, will annihilate all his confidence and cover him with confusion.

Calvin now turns to the Ten Commandments, the Old Testament and the New, to Christ's work, and to his nature as both God and man. Many pages of magisterial exposition witness to Calvin's study of Scripture, of the Fathers and of reformers. One of the most important things to notice, Wendel tells us, is his determination to define and keep separate the divine and human natures of Christ. This mirrors the typical reformer's wish to guard the nature of religion itself as wholly "other." But Calvin is also balanced in this respect and a good example of Calvin's greatness as a theologian whose writing is still well worth reading is precisely when he is synthesizing: "The true substance of Christ is most clearly declared in those passages which comprehend both natures at once . . . His having received power from the Father to forgive sins . . . his bestowing righteousness, holiness and salvation . . . his being appointed judge . . . his being honoured even as the Father are not peculiar to his Godhead or his humanity, but applicable to both. In the same way he is called the Light of the world, the good Shepherd, the Door, the true Vine." Calvin goes on in this passage to an eschatology which is very close to Paul, yet picks up something of the millenarian feeling of the heretics and reformers who found the self-centered mechanistic attitude of some preachers so unsatisfying: "In the same sense we ought to understand the saying of Paul, that at the end Christ shall deliver up 'the kingdom of God, even to the Father.' The Kingdom of God assuredly had no beginning, and will have no end; but because he was hid under humble clothing of flesh, and took upon himself the form of a servant, and humbled himself, and laying aside the insignia of majesty, became obedient to the Father; and after undergoing this subjection was at length crowned with glory and honour and exalted to supreme authority, that at his name every knee should bow; so at the end he will subject to the Father both the name and the crown of glory, and whatever he received of the Father, that God may be all in all." In another passage we perhaps glimpse something of the inner life of Calvin, who generally is at the opposite end of the emotional spectrum from Luther, very disinclined to tell us anything: "He by whose aid we obtain favour must be a perpetual intercessor. From this again arises not only confidence in prayer, but also the tranquillity of pious minds, while they recline in safety on the paternal indulgence of God and feel assured, that whatever has been consecrated by the Mediator is pleasing to him . . . To this effect are the words of Christ: 'For their sakes I sanctify myself'; for being clothed with his holiness, inasmuch as he has devoted us to the Father with himself (otherwise we were an abomination before him), we please him as if we were pure and clean, nay even sacred."

Calvin moves on to discuss the modes of obtaining grace in Book III, and we come, then, again to Faith, and to repentance, and to prayer. In expounding the nature of faith Calvin is heir to all those heretics who had wished to deny the right of the papal Church to tell them precisely what they ought to believe. Calvin rejects, as we saw in the first quotation we made from him, on page 22, the scholastic teaching about "implicit faith"—an excuse, he says, for telling people they must believe whatever the Church says is true, and that this obedience does duty for any lack of understanding. Calvin insists on understanding. "Is it faith to understand nothing, and merely submit your convictions implicitly to the Church? Faith consists not in ignorance, but in knowledge, knowledge not of God merely but of the divine will. We do not obtain salvation either because we are prepared to embrace every dictate of the Church as true, or leave to the Church the province of enquiring and determining; but when we recognise God as a propitious father through the reconciliation made by Christ, and Christ as given to us for righteousness, sanctification and life. By this knowledge, I say, not by the submission of our understanding, we obtain an entrance into the kingdom of heaven. For when the Apostle says: 'With the heart man believes unto righteousness; and with the mouth confession is made unto salvation' (Rom. 10:10) he intimates that it is not enough to believe implicitly without understanding, or even inquiring. The thing requisite is an explicit recognition of the divine goodness, in which our righteousness consists." Faith involves a complete trust, without faltering, in all the promises of Scripture. This is beyond man, but Christ enables us. Faith, then, is "a firm and sure knowledge of the divine favour toward us, founded on the truth of a free promise in Christ, and revealed to our minds, and sealed on our hearts, by the Holy Spirit."

We move on to Calvin's consideration of repentance, and prayer. Calvin says we must experience conversion of our life to God, a transformation not only in external things but in the soul itself; and repentance which consists of mortification of the flesh and the quickening of the Spirit. Here Calvin reproduces Paul's thought exactly: "Both of these we obtain by union with Christ. For if we have true fellowship in his death, our old man is crucified by his power, and the body of sin becomes dead, so that the corruption of our original nature is never again in full vigour. If we are partakers in his resurrection, we are raised up by means of it to newness of life which conforms us to the righteousness of God. In one word, then, by repentance I understand regeneration, the only aim of which is to form in us anew the image of God, which was sullied, and all but effaced by the transgression of Adam." We come now to a number of particular points on which Calvin believed the Roman Church to have been mistaken. He deprecates much corporal penitence. It is surely from Luther that he gets the idea of saying that according to the old customs a man could never be sure he had really done full penance for his sins. He deprecates any ceremonial purging of sin, and animadverts particularly against the idea of "making satisfaction." Christ has done that. But, again like Luther, he does not wish to sweep "confession" away altogether. Private or public confession made to a pastor can be of great help to individuals, he says. But its purpose is to help the individual to reconcile himself and to give advice and comfort, not to forgive. Calvin gives it a high status, only just short of formal forgiveness: "It is no common or light solace to have an ambassador of Christ present, invested with the mandate of reconciliation, by whom she [the soul] may hear her absolution pronounced. The utility of the keys is justly commended when the ambassador is duly discharged with becoming order and reverence. . . . Nor is private absolution of less efficacy when asked by those who stand in need of a special remedy for their infirmity." Interestingly he says it is good for a whole Church sometimes to confess its sinfulness in public and ask forgiveness of God. Calvin instanced from the Old Testament the solemn confession made by the whole people under the guidance of Ezra and Nehemiah. Perhaps he was unaware of the gesture of Pope Adrian VI at the Diet of Nuremberg in 1522 (see p. 216) paralleled now by that of Pope Paul VI at the Second Vatican Council. What Calvin objects to is the idea of confession as obligatory and the idea of the pastor's part as necessary for the formal forgiveness of sin by God. He sees it, on the contrary, as a special remedy. "But when we treat of the keys we must always beware of dreaming of any power apart from the preaching of the Gospel . . . whatever privilege of binding and loosing Christ has bestowed on his Church is annexed to the word. This is especially true with regard to the ministry of the keys the whole power of which consists in this, that the grace of the Gospel is publicly and privately sealed on the minds of believers by means of those whom the Lord has appointed; and the only method in which this can be done is by preaching." It is here that Calvin goes on to speak against the practice of "making satisfaction," and so also of the concept of purgatory. On such occasions he does not hesitate to criticize Augustine, whom he elsewhere quotes so fully and enthusiastically. The idea of purgatory and of making satisfaction were specially to be castigated as the occasion for indulgences.

Calvin continues in Book II with pastoral concerns. In Chapter 6 he shows that Scripture aims at "love of righteousness" and "to prescribe a rule to prevent us from going astray while pursuing righteousness." We need an ideal, the ideal of holiness; we need to try to be holy because God is holy. We should progress a little every day. Here Calvin is very much in the atmosphere of late medieval devotion. We shall arrive at our goal "when relieved from the infirmity of flesh we are admitted to full fellowship with God." Chapter 7 speaks of self-denial. We "should put ourselves in the place of him whom we see in need of assistance and pity his misfortune" as if we felt it ourselves. He speaks of bearing the cross, and we seem to be in the world of the *Imitation of Christ*. Calvin the humanist then pulls himself up: "the contempt which believers should train themselves to feel for the present life must not be of a kind to beget hatred of it or ingratitude to God." He quickly sinks back, however, into the medieval style: "If departure from the world is entrance into life, what is the world but a sepulchre, and what is residence in it but immersion in death? If to be freed from the body is to gain full possession of freedom what is the body but a prison?" But he adds again straight away: "But we ought not to hate this life." Calvin finds the resolution to this ambiguity in a thoroughly traditional and biblical way in the resurrection: "The cross of Christ then only triumphs in the breasts over the devil and the flesh, sin and sinners, when their eyes are directed to the power of the resurrection." Calvin has a mystical approach worthy of the greatest of theologians: "To that union of the head and members, the residence of Christ in our hearts, in fine, the mystical union, we assign the highest rank, Christ when he becomes ours making us partners with him in the gifts with which he was endued." We are not at a distance from him; we have "put him on"; "been ingrafted into his body"; "he deigns to make us one with himself. We have a fellowship of righteousness with him." Justification has a central place in the scheme, with more than a hundred pages devoted to it. Calvin uses the Galatians theme with an effect specially his own though certainly inspired by Luther: the law does not give us justification, but still "it cannot be rightly inferred from this that believers have no need of the law. It ceases not to teach, exhort, and urge them to good, although it is not recognised by their consciences before the judgment seat of God." "The whole lives of Christians ought to be a kind of aspiration after piety seeing they are called unto holiness. The office of the law is to excite them to the study of purity and holiness, by reminding them of their duty." Consciences do not obey the law as if compelled by legal necessity, but being free from the yoke of the law. We voluntarily obey the will of God. Calvin uses a theme dear to Luther: "Servants dare not come into the presence of their masters until the exact amount of labour has been performed. But sons who are treated in a more candid and liberal manner by their parents, hesitate not to offer them works that are only begun or half finished, or even with something faulty in them, trusting that their obedience and readiness of mind will be accepted, although the performance be less exact than as wished." These concluding thoughts about justification come in a chapter on Christian liberty which is both original and owes something to Luther's own famous Reformation writing on liberty.

There follows a section on prayer, again pointing to the inner source of Calvin's power. Prayer is "that secret and hidden philosophy which cannot be learned by syllogisms, a philosophy thoroughly understood by those whose eyes God has so opened as to see light in his light." "To prayer then, we are indebted for penetrating to those riches which are treasured up for us with our heavenly Father." . . . Prayer is "a kind of intercourse between God and men, by which, having entered the upper sanctuary, they appear before Him and appeal to his promises, that when necessity requires, they may learn by experience, that what they believed merely on the authority of his word was not in vain."

Calvin goes into detail, giving rules for prayer. He makes the important preliminary and fundamental point that prayer is for our sake, not God's. In fact it is not our duty but something we need to do for our own sake. In a list of points he says: (1) Don't be distracted. But don't be scrupulous and worried if you do get distracted. (2) Ask for what you want and need, understanding that you only ask "in so far as it is God's will." All the same ask for what you really want. (3) Have humility. Discard all self-confidence. All the same, at the same time one must rest confident in God. Calvin refers often to saints but mostly to the holy men of the Old Testament; however, we pray to God only through our one mediator. But he is always intellectually scrupulous in defining exactly what he thinks to be the situation: "For though the saints are still permitted to use intercessions, by which they mutually beseech God in behalf of each other's salvation, and of which the Apostle makes mention; still these depend on that one intercession, so far are they from derogating from it." Calvin continues on the subject of prayer for many pages, 99 per cent of it acceptable to a Catholic.

Now Calvin comes formally to the doctrine which he himself described as "*horribile*," that of "Eternal Election," with its "election" of large numbers of men and women to eternal suffering. It is extremely difficult to be sure why Calvin did not succeed in breaking away from this doctrine, which in some ways offends viciously against the logic of Christian teaching in the New Testament, teaching of the redemption offered to all men. This is simply canceled out when some men have been in effect absolutely excluded from the beginning. A root idea in Calvin's theology, and probably that which made him sure of predestination, was the mystery of God's freedom and his actions, which are not to be fully understood by man. Calvin wrestles with this problem for many pages. Some fifteen thousand words after he has begun he is still repeating very much the same things as he has said at the start: "The refusal of the reprobate to obey the word of God when manifested to them, will be properly ascribed to the malice and depravity of their hearts, provided it be at the same time added, that they were adjudged to this depravity, because they were raised up by the just but inscrutable judgment of God, to show forth his glory by their condemnation." Calvin is doing no more than repeat in essence what Augustine and many other theologians had said. He was obsessed with the doctrine precisely because he had seen how offensive it was. But he cannot see how to dispense with it if God's freedom is to be fully asserted. Near the start of this Chapter 21 he writes: "We shall never feel persuaded as we ought that our salvation flows from the free mercy of God as its fountain, until we are made acquainted with his eternal election, the grave of God being illustrated by contrast—viz, that he does not adopt promiscuously to the hope of salvation, but gives to some what he denies to others."

Calvin's doctrine of the Church is essentially that of Luther. The preaching of the Word, and the administration of the sacraments are the signs of the presence of the Church. Calvin has a principle of wide tolerance. He emphasizes continually in this section that a man should not withdraw from any church if this sign is present even though "it may otherwise teem with numerous faults." He felt the need both for precision and for strong loyalty in this whole matter, which engaged him very closely in a personal way. He had taken the decision himself, in fact, to part from the Church of his upbringing. Throughout his stay in Geneva and Strasbourg, there was continuing argument about how the Church, that is, the new Protestant churches, should be established, how they should relate to the state. There was frequent need to take decisions about Anabaptists and others who would not accept the new reformed Church community any more than the old one. Calvin lays great emphasis on the seriousness of schism: ". . . there is no excuse for him who spontaneously abandons the external communion of a church in which the word of God is preached and the sacraments are administered." "Notwithstanding the faults of a few or of many, there is nothing to prevent us from there duly professing our faith in the ordinances instituted by God, because a pious conscience is not injured by the unworthiness of another, whether he be a pastor or a private individual; and sacred rites are not less pure and salutary to a man who is holy and upright, from being at the same time handled by the impure," a point which has often been made by Roman Catholic theologians.

Calvin turns again to the Old Testament for supporting illustrations, pointing to Isaiah, Jeremiah and Habakkuk. "If the holy prophets felt no obligation to withdraw from the Church on account of the very numerous and heinous crimes, not of one or two individuals, but almost of the whole people, we arrogate too much to ourselves, if we presume forthwith to withdraw from the communion of the Church, because the lives of all accord not with our judgment, or even with the Christian profession." "I deny not that it is the duty of a pious man to withdraw from all private intercourse with the wicked, and not entangle himself with them by any voluntary tie; but it is one thing to shun the society of the wicked, and another to renounce the communion of the Church through hatred of them." St. Paul did not withdraw from the Galatians, nor did he counsel others to do so.

Calvin understands the holiness of the Church in a sense acceptable to Catholic doctrine. ". . . the holiness of the Church: it makes daily progress, but is not yet perfect"; ". . . there is good reason for the Church being called holy, it is necessary however to consider what the holiness is in which it excells, lest by refusing to acknowledge any church, save one that is completely perfect, we leave no church at all." Calvin says the Donatists and the Cathari were both mistakenly looking for a "perfect" church. He says some Anabaptists make the same mistake. We, for instance, must not destroy unity of faith on account of minor differences of opinion, for instance, "if one, without any spirit of contention or perverseness in dogmatising hold that the soul on quitting the body is taken straight to heaven, and another, without venturing to speak positively as to the abode holds it for certain that it lives in the Lord," this latter presumably referring to the view that some souls are in Limbo or in purgatory, Calvin emphasizes that he does not condone even the smallest error. But these are not necessarily sufficient for a decision to leave a church. While deprecating schism, he praises unity—themes which seem odd to historians, who are not unnaturally inclined to regard the sixteenth-century reformers as at least the tools if not the very initiators of organic disintegration. But Calvin and Luther are both exceptionally self-conscious on unity: "By the unity of the Church we must understand the unity into which we feel persuaded that we are truly ingrafted. For unless we are invited with all the other members under Christ our head, no hope of the future inheritance awaits us . . ." Calvin says we are "made truly one by living together under the same Spirit of God in one faith, hope and charity, called not only to the same inheritance of eternal life, but to participation in one God and Christ. For although the sad devastation which everywhere meets our view may proclaim that no Church remains, let us know that the death of Christ produces fruit, and that God wondrously preserves his Church, while placing it as it were in concealment."

But Calvin sees in the Roman Church such a perversion of Scripture and of the true doctrine which Scripture puts before us that a Christian must separate himself. In the papacy instead of ministry he says there "prevails a perverted government, compounded of lies, a government which partly extinguishes, partly suppresses, the pure light . . . In place of the Lord's Supper, the foulest sacrilege has entered, the worship of God is deformed by a varied mass of intolerable superstitions; doctrine (without which Christianity exists not) is wholly buried and exploded, the public assemblies are schools of idolatry and impiety. Wherefore, in declining fatal participation in such wickedness, we run no risk of being dissevered from the Church of Christ."

However, Calvin is scrupulous in wanting to define the situation: "While we are unwilling simply to concede the name of Church to the Papists, we do not deny that there are churches among them." Calvin refers particularly to baptism as one valid element of Christianity which the papists retain. There is a direct and piquant parallel here, as the converse of this situation, in the selection of "baptism" by the Roman Catholic Church in the 1950's and 60's as a point on which they could find common ground with other Christians. But of course Calvin's point is not that there is common ground on which some new hoped-for union of Christians can be envisaged but rather that in spite of the iniquities of the papal system, something of true Christianity inevitably survives: "In one word I call them churches inasmuch as the Lord there wondrously preserves some remains of his people, though miserably torn and scattered, and inasmuch as some symbols of the Church still remain —symbols especially whose efficacy neither the craft of the devil nor human depravity can destroy. But as, on the other hand, those marks to which we ought especially to have respect in this discussion are effaced, I say that the whole body, as well as every single assembly, lacks the form of a legitimate Church." Calvin specifies his departure from the Church of Rome as a matter of standing by the truth. "The only cause of our estrangement is that they cannot tolerate a pure profession of the truth." The true Church is present where the sheep hear the voice of the Word. The union of charity depends on unity in faith. The formula is essentially medieval and Thomist!

Calvin turns in detail to the New Testament when setting out his teaching on the ministry. St. Paul, he says, names "Apostles, Prophets, Evangelists, Pastors, Teachers." Only the last two now have ordinary office. Of prophets he says, "by Prophets he means not all interpreters of the divine will, but those who excelled by special revelation: none such now exist, or they are less manifest." Calvin clearly does not want to be reckoned as a prophet; his teaching comes from Scripture, from logical exposition, and not from any special revelation. This was also essentially Luther's position, although there are passages in Luther which imply his own realization that if he is true to his own experience he can hardly deny the function of prophet to himself. But Calvin wants to keep all within strictly canonical and administratively intelligible bounds. So did Luther in principle. But Calvin is much more severely committed to it in theory and in practice; temperamentally it suits him and his humanist reasoning.

Pastors are to be elected, and that election must be by the Church itself, not the state: "Now we see that his [St. Paul's] custom was to appoint bishops by the suffrages of the people . . . Rightly, therefore, does Cyprian contend for it as of divine authority, that the priest be chosen in presence of the people, before the eyes of all, and be approved as worthy and fit by public judgments and testimony." "We see, then, that ministers are legitimately called according to the word of God, when those who may have seemed fit are elected on the consent and approbation of the people. Other pastors, however, ought to preside over the election, lest any error should be committed by the general body either through levity, or bad passion or tumult." It is a magisterial combination of most carefully worked-out doctrinal theory and practical directions borne of experience and knowledge of the world—levity, passion and tumult are to be suspected, even expected, and legislated for.

Calvin traces the historical process by which bishops, having been originally elected by the people and ordained by other bishops, at a later period were simply appointed by existing authority, a process which Roman Catholics have been widely pondering in the second half of the twentieth century with a view to a return to the ancient procedure. "Then in election, the whole right has been taken from the people. Vows, assents, subscriptions, and all things of this sort have disappeared; the whole power has been given to the canons alone." Calvin goes into detail and holds up to ridicule the question put, in the ordination service, to the congregation as to whether the candidate is worthy—a question not intended to be answered, but still surviving in this service in the twentieth century at the time of writing, when a new liturgy of ordination is expected shortly from the Roman Catholic Church authority. Calvin points out that ability to understand the Latin is not required and that nineteen out of twenty become priests through money and some other undue influence, that they are not ordained as ministers for a particular locality, but simply to offer the sacrifice of the Mass, and that the senior prelates normally collect many benefices in order to augment their income. And most priests have no true priestly task: "if it is the office of a presbyter to feed the Church, and administer the spiritual kingdom of Christ, all those priests who have no work or stipend, save in the traffic of Masses, not only fail in their office, but have no lawful office to discharge. No place is given them to teach, they have no people to govern. In short, nothing is left them but an altar on which to sacrifice Christ; this is to sacrifice not to God but to demons." Calvin deplores the failure of almost all bishops, and of great numbers of clergy, to preach.

Calvin gives a version of the doctrine of the inerrancy of the Church—that the Church cannot err in things necessary to salvation —which ties it to his overarching principle of deriving everything from the work of the Spirit and controlling everything by reference to the Word, while "they" (the Roman Church) make the Church infallible simply in its own right: "our meaning is that she cannot err, because she has altogether discarded her own wisdom, and submits to the teaching of the Holy Spirit through the word of God. Here then is the difference. They place the authority of the Church without the word of God; we annex it to the word, and allow it not to be separated from it."

The administration of the sacraments affords a central practical occasion to distinguish between the old Church and what Calvin sees must be the characteristics of a reformed Church true to Scripture. The crucial point is that to which we have already referred as the sense in which a sacrament achieves that which it signifies, to use Roman Catholic terminology, *ex opere operato*. That had come to mean "automatically" not only in practice but in the minds of some theologians. The survival of this attitude of mind among twentieth-century Roman Catholics is witness to the attraction of what, as a brief term, "white magic" is sometimes not an unfair description. Of course the great theologians, in particular Aquinas, never meant anything so stupid. The Christian is not just a dumb object, to be "marked" by the sacrament. He is a *fidelis*, a believer. And it was this, as Luther came to see, that ultimately must be of more importance even than the sacraments themselves. The sacraments were the occasions for the strengthening of that faithful man. They were indeed a visible symbol of an invisible grace, an indispensable grace. But they were a confirmation and a sanctification of a faithful life already there.

In the late Middle Ages, law, power, dogma, unity-uniformity all became so overstressed, that an exclusive emphasis on the *ex opere operato* aspect of the sacraments harmonized with the current understanding of the Church; and no one realized that it was indeed only the "current" understanding of the Church, as distinct from some permanent and exclusively right description— until Luther brought up that which had been ignored for so many centuries. And now here was Calvin reaffirming the Lutheran insight and putting it into further intelligible intellectual order. But this very ordering inevitably led to a new petrifaction, so that Calvin's *Institutes* became normative. And the Protestant churches in the end became as immovable and inflexible as that system which they replaced. But meanwhile what Calvin said was so obviously relevant to the daily practice that everyone who read it recognized it as a criticism which could not be just brushed aside. Either one must hope that the papal Church would take account of it and look more careful to its daily practice and its popular theology or one must join one of the new communities—but if so, which one? Here is Calvin:

A sacrament consists of the word and the external sign. By the word we ought to understand not one which, muttered without meaning and without faith, by its sound merely, as by a magical incantation, has the effect of consecrating the element, but one which, preached, makes us understand what the visible sign means. The thing, therefore, which was frequently done, under the tyranny of the Pope, was not free from great profanation of the mystery, for they deemed it sufficient if the priest muttered the formula of consecration, while the people, without understanding, looked stupidly on. Nay, this was done for the express purpose of preventing any instruction from thereby reaching the people: for all was said in Latin to illiterate hearers. Superstition afterwards was carried to such a height, that the consecration was thought not to be duly performed except in a low grumble, which few could hear. Very different is the doctrine of Augustine concerning the sacramental word. "Let the word be added to the element, and it will become a sacrament. For whence can there be so much virtue in water as to touch the body and cleanse the heart, unless by the agency of the word, and this is not because it is said, but because it is believed? For even

in the word the transient sound is one thing, the permanent
power another. This is the word of faith which we preach says
the Apostle (Rom. 10:8). Hence, in the Acts of the Apostles,
we have the expression, "Purify their hearts by faith" (Acts
15:9). And the Apostle Peter says, "The like figure whereunto
even baptism doth now save us (not the putting away of
the filth of the flesh, but the answer of a good conscience)"
(I Pet. 3:21). "This is the word of faith which we preach:
by which word doubtless baptism also, in order that it may
be able to cleanse, is consecrated" (August. Hom. in Joann.
13). You see how he requires preaching to the production
of faith. And we need not labour to prove this, since there
is not the least room for doubt as to what Christ did, and
commanded us to do, as to what the apostles followed, and a
purer Church observed. Nay, it is known that, from the very
beginning of the world, whenever God offered any sign to
the holy Patriarchs, it was inseparably attached to doctrine,
without which our senses would gaze bewildered on an un-
meaning object. Therefore, when we hear mention made of
the sacramental word, let us understand the promise which,
proclaimed aloud by the minister, leads the people by the
hand to that to which the sign tends and directs us."

What Calvin was saying has been to a great extent accepted by
historians of denominations today. Erwin Iserloh, a German Roman
Catholic, writes: "Late medieval theology and practice had destroyed the sign value of ecclesiastical penance and indulgences
by practically identifying them with what was signified, i.e., the
remission before God of punishment for sin."

Calvin feels strongly the need to defend the sacraments against
the Antinomians on the left in the tradition of the millenarians,
who looked for inspiration from the pure word of God and nothing
else at all. Calvin was particularly well suited to speak to them
since he was convinced that it was indeed the Spirit, the Holy
Spirit, alone, who could be appealed to by the Christian theologian
as the ultimate guarantor of his system, and that the Christian
must turn interiorly to him for the grace to believe and to live as a
Christian:

Wherefore, with regard to the increase and confirmation of
faith, I would remind the reader (though I think I have

already expressed it in unambiguous terms), that in assigning this office to the sacraments, it is not as if I thought that there is a kind of secret efficacy perpetually inherent in them, by which they can of themselves promote or strengthen faith, but because our Lord has instituted them for the express purpose of helping to establish and increase our faith. The sacraments duly perform their office only when accompanied by the Spirit, the internal Master, whose energy alone penetrates the heart, stirs up the affections, and procures access for the sacraments into our souls. If he is wanting, the sacraments can avail us no more than the sun shining on the eyeballs of the blind, or sounds uttered in the ears of the deaf. Wherefore, in distributing between the Spirit and the sacraments, I ascribe the whole energy to him, and leave only a ministry to them; this ministry, without the agency of the Spirit, is empty and frivolous, but when he acts within, and exerts his power, it is replete with energy. It is now clear in what way, according to this view, a pious mind is confirmed in faith by means of the sacraments—viz. in the same way in which the light of the sun is seen by the eye, and the sound of the voice heard by the ear; the former of which would not be at all affected by the light unless it had a pupil on which the light might fall; nor the latter reached by any sound, however loud, were it not naturally adapted for hearing. But if it is true, as has been explained, that in the eye it is the power of vision which enables it to see the light, and in the ear the power of hearing which enables it to perceive the voice, and that in our hearts it is the work of the Holy Spirit to commence, maintain, cherish, and establish faith, then it follows, both that the sacraments do not avail one iota without the energy of the Holy Spirit; and that yet in hearts previously taught by that preceptor, there is nothing to prevent the sacraments from strengthening and increasing faith. There is only one difference, that the faculty of seeing and hearing is naturally implanted in the eye and ear; whereas, Christ acts in our minds above the measure of nature by special grace.

But we should be content with the two sacraments which were instituted biblically, baptism and the Lord's Supper. He has a good piece on this, expounding man's need generally for a sacramental attitude to life, and how this is taken up for the Christian in Christ himself:

> With these two, therefore, let the Christian Church be contented, and not only not admit or acknowledge any third at present, but not even desire or expect it even until the end of the world. For though to the Jews were given, besides his ordinary sacraments, others differing somewhat according to the nature of the times (as the manna, the water gushing from the rock, the brazen serpent, and the like), by this variety they were reminded not to stop short at such figures, the state of which could not be durable, but to expect from God something better, to endure without decay and without end. Our case is very different. To us Christ has been revealed. In him are hidden all the treasures of wisdom and knowledge (Col. 2:3), in such richness and abundance, that to ask or hope for any new addition to these treasures is truly to offend God and provoke him against us. It behooves us to hunger after Christ only, to seek him, look to him, learn of him, and learn again, until the arrival of the great day on which the Lord will fully manifest the glory of his kingdom, and exhibit himself as he is to our admiring eye (I John 3:2). And, for this reason, this age of ours is designated in Scripture by the last hour, the last days, the last times, that no one may deceive himself with the vain expectation of some new doctrine or revelation. Our heavenly Father, who "at sundry times, and in divers manners, spake in time past unto the fathers by the prophets, hath in these last days spoken unto us" by his beloved Son, who alone can manifest, and, in fact, has fully manifested, the Father, in so far as he is of importance to us, while we now see him through a mirror. Now, since men have been denied the power of making new sacraments in the Church of God, it were to be wished, that in those which are of God, there should be the least possible admixture of human invention. For just as when water is infused, the wine is diluted, and when leaven is put in, the whole mass is leavened, so the purity of the ordinances of God is impaired, whenever man makes any addition of his own. And yet we see how far the sacraments as at present used have degenerated from their genuine purity. There is everywhere

more than enough of pomp, ceremony, and gesticulation, while
no account is taken, or mention made, of the word of God,
without which, even the sacraments themselves are not sacraments. Nay, in such a crowd, the very ceremonies ordained
by God cannot raise their head, but lie as it were oppressed.
In Baptism, as we have elsewhere justly complained, how
little is seen of that which alone ought to shine and be con-
spicuous there, I mean Baptism itself? The Supper was altogether buried when it was turned into the Mass. The utmost
is, that it is seen once a year, but in a garbled, mutilated,
and lacerated form.

This piece ends in French with a rhetorically impressive series
of adjectives: *"déschirée, découpée, départie, brisée, divisée, et
toute déformé."*

Of the sacrament of the Lord's Supper Calvin wants people to
partake much more often than the once a year at Easter which
had become common. He wants the emphasis to be on the meal,
the second covenant. "We have no wish to know how Christ is
hid under the bread; we are satisfied with his own words, 'This
is my body.'" But in fact he was inevitably drawn into the bitter
discussion about the nature of Christ's presence, and was caught
up in the fruitless analytic argument about terminology.

Calvin makes a strong case for saying that anointing, as it is
done in the Church of his time, cannot be solidly based on
Scripture and that one might just as well set up a second pool of
Siloam somewhere for people to dip themselves into for a cure, or
make a sacrament of our Lord's curing the blind man from clay
and spittle. He says: "James, in ordering that the sick be anointed,
seems to me to mean no other anointing than that of common oil."

A work of the size and of the range of the *Institutes* can hardly
be done justice to. In writing about it shortly or at length inevitably one emphasizes this aspect or that and gives an impression
which does not reflect the balance of the original. Calvin had read
immensely widely. He was standing on the shoulders of all past
theologians. Also he did not fear to use recent theologians extensively, for instance, Luther and Bucer. His great wish was to
find the heart of religion, the heart of Christianity, to expound
the overwhelming mystery of God, of his revelation in his Son,
and of his daily inspiration of Christians in his Spirit. He felt that

this mystery had been betrayed by the papal Church. In spite of his great desire for intellectual precision, he followed the current fashion of exaggerating the faults of an enemy. Like Luther, finding in Catholics little but the like exaggeration and an implacable belief in the infallibility of their own current doctrine, he accepted the necessity for schism.

In the twentieth century Protestants and Catholics find themselves usually in agreement, both in their rejection and in their acceptance of various parts of Calvin's teaching. But in the sixteenth century Calvin's great work was divisive, and definitive in its work of setting up a great new standard reference document for the reformed churches of the Calvinist allegiance. Calvin completed the final Latin edition of the *Institutes* in 1559, and then proceeded to translate it himself into French. Nowhere else in the whole corpus of Reformation events is there any book or even any event which finalized as this book did the achievement of the new separated reformed Protestant churches. The first French edition, Calvin's own translation of 1541, marks the beginning of something like a methodical attempt to found reformed churches in France.

CHAPTER 7

Europe 1532–64—from the
Peace of Nuremberg
to the Death of Calvin

Germany

The Peace of Nuremberg (see p. 238) led to a period of steady growth in conversions to Protestantism, both of institutions and of individuals. The Pope continued to delay the calling of a general council, which must now have the task of assessing the new teaching and the new Christian communities, as well as that of reforming the papal Church itself. The emperor continued to be taken up with administering his Spanish territories (away from Germany 1532–40) and with fighting the Turks and the French. The Protestants continued to take hold of the minds of ordinary people, and to establish the new, more simple ways of worshiping, a new Christian culture generally, over a steadily widening area—Württemberg from 1534, Brunswick, the Palatinate Neuburg and Regensburg from 1542, the Palatinate Electorate from 1546.

In 1534 Pope Clement VII died. This time the new Pope was a Farnese, the man recommended by Clement VII, an old man, brother of one of Alexander VI's mistresses, wealthy, the builder of the great Palazzo Farnese, still to be seen in Rome. His reign was expected to be neither long nor distinguished. Paul III's reign was both, in the event. Unlike his predecessor he was convinced that it was absolutely essential to call a council. It took him till 1545 to bring it about, due to the jockeying of the various parties involved, and the fear of many of his Curia that a council might make things worse for them in the everyday sense—it would almost certainly make it more difficult to appoint friends and relations to ecclesiastical positions. Even when the Council of Trent did finally open in 1545 it was by no means immediately obvious that sufficient bishops would come or that it would be able to get sufficiently satisfactory work done to be able to have much influence.

The Council of Trent opened in 1545; Luther died the following year; in 1555 the Peace of Augsburg institutionalized the situation recognized by the Peace of Nuremberg, and the emperor abdicated; in 1564 Calvin died. Lesser dates were the deaths of Francis I and Henry VIII in 1547; the death of Henry II of France in 1559. During these years, from 1532 till 1564, we have a kind of overture to the coming four hundred years, a prophecy of much that would happen between Catholic and Protestant communities in the following four hundred years. The political and military maneuverings of the emperor, the Pope, Francis I, the Protestant princes, and the Turks provided the political framework, and from time to time decisive influences.

Lortz concludes his great work on the German Reformation with a final part entitled "The Military and Political Struggle Settles the Issue." But it would be misleading if this were taken to mean that the sixteenth-century equivalent of politicians and generals imposed decisions on the regions and towns and villages of the empire, that is, roughly the German-speaking territories, regardless of religious factors. Catholicism remained dominant in some areas; Protestantism became dominant in others; the divisions may or may not have invariably reflected exactly the majorities in the respective areas who were firmly convinced in their adherence to the respective ideologies, doctrines and cultural patterns. But it could not be maintained that in most areas the will of a small minority was imposed by force. Where Protestantism prevailed, its followers were commonly more numerous and more firmly convinced than the Catholics on the one hand or than Anabaptists on the other. And so also where Catholicism prevailed, the Catholics were often more numerous. But in between the parties lay, as in England, a great number of ordinary people who, while not totally indifferent, were passive to the great public decisions—they had the old traditions in their bones, but they welcomed the vernacular worship and Scripture and the simple doctrine of faith. The details of the final preponderance of political power in favor of Catholicism or Protestantism were settled indeed by wars and negotiations, by the generals and politicians, by the "military and political struggle." These "generals" and "politicians" were incarnate in the Pope, the emperor, the Protestants princes, the Turks and the king of France.

The first two and the last were supposed to be committed to Catholicism, but in fact their policies sometimes militated strongly against the maintenance of the Catholic faith in substantial areas of Europe. In the end it was the reality of the strength of religious conviction which had to be respected and be taken account of by the "politicians." Thus the emperor, in spite of his personal commitment to the tradition of his fathers, always leaned to a compromise solution, at times almost on Erasmian lines, when year after year he was faced with the need to make decisions about policy. Like all statesmen—not only politicians—he had to face the facts.

Generally the relations between Catholics and Protestants during this time ran the whole gamut, from extreme mutual antagonism (often encouraged and exacerbated by Luther himself), which meant that each protagonist outlawed the other in the region concerned; through a tendency towards decisions to put up with each other, and to allow both traditions to be followed by their adherents, a sort of armed neutrality; to the other end of the spectrum, where positive efforts were made to realize some kind of reunion on the grounds that disagreements were not fundamental, and that something better than mere bare mutual tolerance was possible. All these are found, and all will continue through the following four hundred years.

It is generally thought, and with some considerable justification, that Luther deteriorated in these years. There is no doubt that he became more violently aggressive and that his language goes beyond what one could apologize for by simply comparing it with the language of his enemies or by the needs of the occasion. It became a kind of cliché, or expected style. But even so, his friends often tried to dissuade him from it. His last two best-known works are, however, replete with a more or less Rabelaisian anal vocabulary. That Rabelais has retained the respect of many indicates that this kind of vocabulary is not necessarily always out of place. It can be reassuringly robust. It is the bitterness and the apparent arrogance which goes with it in Luther's books that disturbs the reader. The edge is to some extent taken off this disturbance by the self-ridicule in which Luther sometimes indulges. He was far too sensitive and intelligent, altogether brilliant, not to know quite well what he was doing. And his practical achievement was in great measure a reason for him to think that what had happened was indeed the good thing which was God's will. He was in any case not unaware of how he appeared to others: "I acted the real Luther throughout at the late interview and addressed the legate in the most disconcerting terms," he wrote to Jonas after a meeting with the papal nuncio Paolo Vergerio in 1535, who had come to talk to Luther about the proposed council that the new Pope wished to call.

Luther had appealed more than once to a "Free Council in German Lands." He was beginning now not to be able to see much point in having one, and doubted whether one called by the Pope rather than the emperor would be likely to provide a sufficiently free context. He told the nuncio that Christendom perhaps might benefit from a council but one was no longer needed by the Protestants. The Protestant princes were emphatic that they wished for that which the estates had asked and the emperor had promised, a "Free Christian Council in Germany." This was reiterated in the interviews which led up to the Schmal-kaldic Articles drawn up by Luther and then modified by Melanch-thon when Luther was ill. The question of ultimate authority in matters of religion remained crucial.

The movement for reconciliation between the warring parties was led, among others, by Duke George of Saxony, who attended Catholic and Protestant services indifferently. From the papal camp a strong reforming and irenic party emerged, heirs of the century-long tradition of reformers within the papal Church. Cajetan, impressed by the Protestant achievement at Augsburg, looked for a way to keep the Protestants within the single ec-clesiastical organization. He turned towards a solution analogous to what could be envisaged in relation to the Eastern Orthodox Church—he suggested that married priests could be accepted, and Communion in both kinds, the two most public and contro-versial (if least "doctrinal," and in the end least significant) issues. He also proposed that there should be no "recantation," and that there should be some relaxation about the sense of the obligation on Christians to receive the sacraments and to keep feast and fast days. The new Pope encouraged the reformers at Rome, notably the layman Contarini, whom he soon made a cardinal, and Carafa (later elected Paul IV). A commission set up by the new Pope issued yet another reforming proposal *Con-silium de Emendenda Ecclesia* (signed among others by Reginald

Pole, the English cardinal, who had been in the running for the papacy). Contarini was himself convinced that Luther's theology of justification by faith was acceptable, the first of a thin line of Catholic theologians who have understood Protestant theology. At the Diet of Regensburg (1541) he took part with other Catholics and Protestants, including Bucer and Melanchthon in a long theological colloquium, which produced agreement on justification. But most people on each side simply did not want reunion.

Luther did nothing to help the irenic gestures. In 1541 he published *Wider Hans Wurst* (Against Hans Sausage) a diatribe against the Catholic duke of Brunswick. In 1545 came his final blast against the papacy, *Against the Papacy at Rome*, again full of extremely violent material; Luther had been roused by the Pope's reprimand of the emperor for his tolerance of the Protestants at the Diet of Speyer of that year. Although in a powerful military position at the time, the emperor had opted, from his position of power, for an immediate policy of toleration, the promise of a general council, and a "Christian Reformation." The religious question, it was now declared, was not to be solved by force but by goodwill and "Christian compromise." The estates voted for the emperor; a large force was voted to take the field against the Turk and be ready for use against France if necessary. One of the emperor's new supporters was none other than the originator of the Schmalkaldic League, Philip of Hesse, whose bigamous marriage, recently agreed to by Luther as a *pis aller*, had caused such scandal.

In 1545 the Pope at last managed to collect together sufficient officials local and central to get the long-promised council opened—at Trent, a place which could be thought of as German and Italian since both languages were (and still are) spoken here in the "no-man's-land" near the top of the Brenner Pass. To this council, destined, before its completion long after, to set the old Church on a path of reform, renewal, retrenchment and assertion of specific values and concepts for rather over four hundred years, came at first only a few of the Catholic bishops summoned to it—and no Protestants, for they were neither summoned, nor invited. Within a few months of its opening, Luther died. He had become almost perennially ill, worn out, one-eyed (as he said) and more irascible than ever, writing even to Katie his wife, during the final journey, which brought his death, in the same old cliché of grouse, criticism and faith: "Leave me in peace, you with all your worrying. I have a better one than you or all the angels to take care of me. He lies in the manger, and sits too at the right hand of God the almighty Father." He was on a journey to his old homelands to try to help to settle a dispute. He preached and kept up his normal life of preaching, praying, eating and drinking well. A heart attack killed him in an hour or so. Scribbled on a note on the table was: "We are beggars—that is the truth."

With Luther gone, the council begun and the emperor powerful militarily, Protestantism could, theoretically, have been crushed. It is true that the emperor was unable to trust the Pope whose military assistance might at any time be found working for the Protestant princes. And Francis I might be found encouraging the Turks to the east. And the Moslems were still a threat in the Mediterranean. Even so, the emperor was powerful. What really stopped him from crushing the Protestants was a prudent states-man's assessment of the extent to which many people had lost any wish to defend traditional Catholicism, for which he himself stood so firmly committed.

The result was that in 1548 the emperor issued what was called an "Interim" from Augsburg at his Diet there. It was a set of religious directives "for the meanwhile," that is, until the council should issue what the emperor supposed would be definitive con-clusions which would be widely regarded as binding and could be enforced by political authority. The Interim pleased no one. The Catholics considered it went too far. The wine was to be allowed at communion to the laity. Married clergy were to be permitted to remain married. The Mass was defined somewhat ambiguously. On the other hand the Protestants were to be restrained and Catholic rule maintained. So much so that a man such as Bucer considered that the essential liberty of conscience and the essential liberty to develop the new Christian communities as they should be was being removed. Meanwhile the wars and the negotiations went on.

Many times, even up to 1555, a superficial examination of the balance of forces might have led one to conclude that Protestantism was likely to disappear owing to the military superiority of the emperor. But although the whole foundation of his outlook was a view of Europe ruled in the name of a Christian magisterium, yet he never put specifically religious questions at the top of the agenda of his own accord. Equally he had the perspicacity to see that religious problems were not likely to be solved by force anyhow. So that his political and military maneuvering continued to be exercised in the name of political rather than religious realities. Unless he preserved the political reality of himself as emperor he would not be there to look after other matters. The view from the Protestant side had become equally muddy. The political concerns of the princes and other rulers who had become committed to Protestantism became overriding. But meanwhile religious realities continued to sort themselves out on their own account. Plurality was the only possible answer in the end. But the Thirty Years War of the following century showed that the lesson had not been learned. Even in the twentieth century the lesson has not been learned by all Christians everywhere.

In 1555 there occurred the first international agreement which was based formally on a pluralistic view. The policy, already foreshadowed, by which the particular type of religious uniformity in each region was settled by the ruler, was now enshrined in the Peace of Augsburg, a political peace treaty between the princes and the emperor. *Cujus regio, ejus religio.* All those who wished were to be allowed to move from one region to another, where their own religion was practiced. Although Charles had always tried to be the paternal "Peacemaker," this was really the end of his vision of a great Catholic Christian hegemony in Europe. He declined to come to the negotiations. His brother Ferdinand, crowned "king of the Romans" was to act. Equally Carafa, the new Pope Paul IV, would not go. But the reality was none the less. And the emperor underlined it by abdicating in the month following the announcement of the treaty. The next year he retired to a monastery in Spain. In 1558 he died. Not only had Protestantism won itself a permanent place in Europe, but it had also realized that, like the old Church, it must be willing to compromise. In the words of the old attitude, "Augsburg 1555 legalized a spiritual schism" (Lortz). The year 1532 had seen what was almost certainly an irreversible achievement, the establishment of a new orthodoxy. And 1555 saw the foreshadowing of pluralism, and even of the new kind of unofficial unity, which is growing in the twentieth century. By the time of the death of Calvin in 1564, the enormous growth of Protestantism in France together with the stable new Protestant communities in Switzerland and the Rhineland, and the newly official Protestant or at least non-papal communities in England and Scotland had made Protestantism into something like the equal of Catholicism.

France

France was no different from the German- or English-speaking countries in so far as the fundamental religious picture was concerned. Throughout northern and central Europe, with the exception perhaps of the Spanish Netherlands, there was the same suspicion of the clergy, the same desire to read Scripture, the same hunch that Christianity was at heart something essentially rather different from that presented by the existing ecclesiastical system and by the Pope, bishops and priests who worked it. In France disillusion with the official processes was common, from the refined humanist and evangelical Calvin, now in Geneva, to the peasants of Brittany, and the merchants of Lyons.

At first sight the political situation may look similar. Both in Germany and in France, as well as in England, the state had increasingly brought ecclesiastical activities into line with the state. We have seen the Statute of Praemunire passed in England at the end of the fourteenth century. We have noted the *Eigenkirche* in Germany, where the local civil authority exercised the right to visit and control the Church in various particulars. We have noted the rigid hold over Church appointments in France.

But we come now to a crucial difference. Germany was ruled by the emperor. The local princes, electors, and the emerging townships were none of them under the same kind of fairly direct and fairly strict control as were the local rulers in France and England. In German-speaking lands the drive towards some local autonomy coincided with the rise of Luther and the sudden major challenge to the religious fabric of society. The estates of the empire had been forever submitting their gravamina, serious matters of complaint, to the emperor, and against his officials. The estates were also forever complaining in the same breath of exactions made by Rome, of money going out of the country, with the implication that the emperor himself was not always entirely loyal to specifically German interests—although his anti-Roman interests were identical with those of the estates. Everyone with a grievance, from peasants to princes, and the old-style knights, quickly hitched their wagons to Luther's star. He did his best to unhitch them. And in his great theoretical works of 1520 he maintained the fundamental autonomy of the Church, of the spiritual authority. But as we have seen, the sheer difficulty of controlling the reform of the local religious church, and the difficulty of maintaining the impetus of reform, led him to rely on the "Godly prince." Political fragmentation and religious fragmentation inevitably threw prince and reformers into each other's arms.

In France there was nothing of this kind. The reform had either to convert the sovereign and his whole establishment, as it did in England under Edward VI and again under Elizabeth I, or else to establish an alternative Church and sue for toleration or be persecuted. Calvin addressed his *Institutes* to King Francis I in the hope of converting him, knowing his considerable sympathy with the general statement of the need for reform, similar to Henry VIII's, and knowing the conversion of his sister Margaret to the cause of the Reform. But in the end this was not successful. A mixed picture of persecution and tolerance emerged first under Francis I and then under Henry II, as increasing numbers of people and communities were in fact convinced that the gospel as proclaimed by the traveling representatives of Calvin was nearer to the truth than what they had been accustomed to. As in England, the medieval heresies had inured them to, and in some places thoroughly inoculated them against, a challenge to ecclesiastical authority. The Waldensians were still there, especially in the hills of the Southeast. The vernacular Scriptures had been increasingly in demand and increasingly produced. In some places, at least, there was an easy seedbed, just as elsewhere in northern Europe. But into that seedbed was sown the seed not of Luther's reform, but of Calvin's—although its theology drew very largely on Luther. The seedlings would grow not into established state Lutheranism, but into autonomous Calvinist churches, appropriate both to Calvin's religious theory with its logical insistence on the independence of the spiritual authority, and appropriate to the French situation, where in the end Catholicism remained the state religion, and the Protestants must gain tolerance from, rather than co-operation with, the state.

Calvin had been mistaken in thinking he could persuade Francis I. The affair of the placards (1534) seems to have been something like a turning point for the king. From that time on in matters religious he supported the orthodox policies of the Sorbonne and increasingly persecuted the Protestants. A preliminary amnesty was granted in 1535 giving six months to fugitives who wished to abjure. But thereafter steadily increasing measures were taken to destroy Protestantism. The Sorbonne published an index of forbidden books in 1542; and another one in 1544. In 1546 the translated Bible of Robert Estienne was added to it. In 1543 it published twenty-four articles of the Catholic faith, and Francis I accepted them. Executions resulted from the laws passed against the Protestants, most notably that of the "Fourteen of Meaux" in 1545 and the massacre that year of the Vaudois, as the Waldensians in southeast France were called. But none of this was sufficient to stem the swiftly mounting tide of Protestant conversions. Henry II succeeded Francis I in 1547, and intensified the persecution of Protestantism. But he merely prevented Protestantism from growing as fast as it would otherwise have done. For Calvin's influence was now very strong throughout France. In 1541 the French edition of the *Institutes* began to circulate; in 1551, his French translation of the Bible. From 1553 onwards trained preachers went into France from Geneva. They spread right across the country year by year. In 1559 they were sufficiently numerous to have decided to organize the first national synod in Paris. By 1561 Catherine de Médici reported that Admiral Coligny claimed there were 2150 Calvinist churches with ministers. For the first time a religious body had begun to make what the medieval lawyers had so often feared the papal Church might achieve—an *imperium in imperio*. This was the very thing that the Statute of Praemunire had been passed in England to prevent. Now the great medieval system was really breaking up. Here was what amounts to a typical medieval heresy or sect, grown to the proportion of a body which the state cannot fully control. One's mind goes back to a heretical assembly before the state or the Church had begun to think of methodical control, the first assembly of the Cathari in Bergamo, 1218.

Calvin was very far from being just the narrow-minded puritan which some of his activity in Geneva might lead us to suppose. He never lost the broad humanist approach imbibed in his early days and was able to write imaginatively helpful letters to the very numerous people who wrote to him for advice. There is a real sense in which his greatest work was the influence he was able to exercise elsewhere than in Geneva, particularly throughout the French-speaking countries and in England and Scotland. But of course he could not have achieved any of this if it had not been for his eminent position at Geneva.

On his return to Geneva from Strasbourg in 1541 Calvin thought he was returning only for a few days, considering that he would find it simply impossible to agree sufficiently with those in control. But Geneva was looking for discipline. They had a good house ready for the young master—Calvin was still only thirty-three—and a stipend twice that of any other preacher. So a twenty-four-year-long residence began. Calvin had already made his name in several international discussions with Catholics, in his *Institutes,* in his Bible. Standing at the top of the ladder built by Luther he proceeded to the tough daily task of converting a small city of about 13,000 people to Christianity, to Christ, as he understood the truth. Luther's theological vision of justification by faith stood at the heart of it, and many of Luther's other brilliant ideas. But Calvin was himself the greatest biblical scholar of his age, and a very accomplished student of the early Fathers. He proceeded, day in, day out, to preach and to advise, and to write. His commentaries on the books of the Bible include every book except Revelation—significant exception, one which points sharply away from the medieval approach always so enamored of that cryptic text.

As far as organization goes, Calvin worked out a fourfold system of pastors, teachers, elders and deacons, managed by a local consistory of pastors. In his own Geneva these worked in very close co-ordination with the magistrates. The mixture of co-operation, jealousy and contradiction which actually resulted was not unlike the medieval result—just as Calvin's theology was in many ways a direct descendant from the medieval world. The Reformation was the final maturing, within the same world as before, of forces of religious renewal which had been apparent for centuries.

Calvin's reign in Geneva, like Luther's coarseness, and like many other past good things, has become a caricature of itself in most histories. But Calvin was never the dictator, and only very gradually got his way. From the start he had to compromise—he wanted monthly celebration of the Lord's Supper, when all would communicate, intended specifically as a correction to the only annual communion of the majority of lay people under the old medieval Catholic convention. But he had to agree to a quarterly celebration. His rule, and that of his assistant preachers, and the magistrates with whom he worked, gradually extended, with the almost ludicrous logic for which it has become famous, to every moment of life, so that one thinks of it inevitably, and with some truth, as a totalitarian regime. The consistory at Geneva became famous for its pettifogging censures—of someone for singing a song defamatory of Calvin, of someone else for making a noise during a sermon, of a woman of seventy for marrying a man of twenty-five. But the examples are no different from those of any age in which those in moral and religious authority have been able to get free of supervision, criticism or public opinion.

The most distinctive thing, in the end, about Calvin's churches was, as with Luther's, their local autonomy. At the heart of them lay individual men and women living by an act of faith. They associated together to form a church locally. They owed no obedience to any other human community or organization. In the end it was the centralized papal system, with its canon law running through the whole extent of Western Europe that was being rejected. It was not exactly system qua system, so much as system qua a centralized uniformity in the name of Christ, that it was rejected. Luther was worried from time to time about having to set up a new system to replace the old; Calvin hardly at all. But neither wished to, or did, set up anything like a universal system to which all were supposed to be subject. The Bible was to remain the sole norm, and the preaching of the Word locally the principal task of the community. The Spirit would guide each individual and each local church in response to it.

"They always feared me more than they loved me," said Calvin on his deathbed. And there certainly was much to fear, and little on the surface in the human sense to love. Yet they missed him greatly when he was gone and they remembered his great devotion to all that was his duty. During the Strasbourg period Bucer persuaded him, after twice failing, to marry. His wife was the widow of an Anabaptist whom Calvin had converted. The twenty-four years at Geneva have been called a "marriage of convenience" between Calvin and his adopted city. Certainly there was little expectation of love—Calvin said he would "prefer a hundred other deaths to that cross, on which I should have to die a thousand times a day" when they were trying to persuade him to come back. The rational dominated on all occasions. Before he married he said, "I, whom you see so hostile to celibacy, have never taken a wife, and I know not if ever I shall marry. If I did so, it would be in order to devote my time to the Lord, by being the more relieved from the worries of daily life." But there is no doubt about the intelligence, and occasional dry wit, the iron will, the devotion, and when necessary the understanding of the practicalities of life, whether in his dealings with the magistracy at Geneva, or in writing advice to those in doubt. From time to time in his writing the spiritual man reveals the depth of his own inner experience.

Anabaptists and Others

Nothing perhaps reveals so clearly that the roots of the Reformation lay far back in history as the speed with which lesser breakaway Christian groups of every kind began to emerge, coalesce, form themselves, re-form themselves, excommunicate one another and generally proliferate all over the Northwest and center of Europe within a few years of Luther's first initiative. As we have seen, the earliest manifestation came from his own immediate colleagues, from Karlstadt, and then from Müntzer. All of them looked to Scripture in the regular manner of medieval heresy. All of them tended to demand a new kind of personal sincerity and commitment, a new application of that special commitment encouraged and catered for, till now, within the official structure by the religious orders. They did not theorize about justification by faith as much as demand from their members an explicit life of faith and loyalty.

Within a few years many of these groups began to crystallize their insight in terms of a rejection of infant baptism as typical of the old automatic type of religion, and to insist on adult baptism so that mature personal commitment could be explicit. The name Anabaptist came to be used and to cover a very great variety of communities, large and small, in a wide variety of locations. The likeness of the Anabaptists to the medieval heretic is very striking, in their simple reliance on Scripture and the fanatical commitment which went with it. Commonly groups of them rejected war and any military service, also ownership of property, the old Franciscan characteristics appearing once again, together with a promise of what we might now call anarchism. But where millenarian and apocalyptic tendencies became dominant, non-violence tended to give way to violence. The Peasants' War drew inspiration from Müntzer's apocalyptic religion. Anabaptists began to look as if they might even become a single movement when the Anabaptist Confession was signed at Schleitheim in 1527. It was in 1533–34 in the city of Münster that they had their first taste of power. John of Leiden, it was announced, was the king of New Zion. All goods were to be held in common, and the introduction of polygamy was illustrated by John's own nine wives, one of whom had her head cut off for impudence to him. To gain this position force had been used, and the Anabaptists remained in charge of the city for about fifteen months before being ejected. But most such groups did not aim at political power.

One group has survived into the twentieth century as a typical back-to-the-land, back-to-nature group. The Brüderhof had a farm community in England in the thirties and they can still be found in North America. The spirit is something like that of a self-sufficient monastery but expressed in terms of normal married and family life. This movement was founded, not surprisingly, in Moravia, by Jacob Hutter, and the official name of the group of Brüderhof is Hutterite. It was another Franciscan-type project: "Private property is the greatest enemy of love, and the true Christian must render up his will and become free from property if he would be a disciple." Everyone had to learn a craft. Another well-known Anabaptist group was the Mennonites in Switzerland, Germany and the Netherlands, with its liberal branch in the Netherlands called the Waterlanders.

Other groups sometimes loosely grouped under the name Anabaptist were not really so. The Socinians were a movement started in the years following 1580 by the Italian Socinus in Poland who denied the doctrine of the Trinity and founded the movement which became the Unitarian Church. He was a pacifist but not a millenarian. Then a whole further series of traditions began with the immigrants to America, most notably that which became Congregationalism. These had their roots in various separatist congregations in England which Queen Elizabeth's government had been trying to suppress, notably by the Act of 1593. The autonomy of each congregation, together with reliance on the Scripture was their most notable tradition.

CHAPTER 8

England 1547–59

The persons of Calvin and Luther, the volumes they had written and their practical achievements continued to dominate the scene throughout the mainland of Europe, in spite of numerous other minor leaders, much other literature, and many individual practical achievements. Luther's primary doctrine of justification by faith and Calvin's theocratic system together provided the two main springs, although in practice often raising up Protestant communities at enmity with each other, and gradually dividing the Continent between them. But in England there was no single dominant person, not even two or three, nor was there one single doctrine, nor even two or three dominating strands. It is impossible to generalize about the Reformation during the six years of the reign of Edward VI (1547–53), the five years of the reign of Mary (1553–58) and the long near half-century of Elizabeth I except to say that an enormous number of influences converged on England and that the national preference for a middle way meshed in easily with this pluralist situation and wound from it a very strong rope made up of strands so numerous as to be almost uncountable. England was at the receiving end of almost every Reformation influence. Just as the English language was made up from very numerous contributory languages, receiving wave after wave of influences in the course of a thousand years or so, and ended up with an exceptionally large vocabulary, in a similar sort of way England was a kind of terminus to which every Reformation train eventually came. All these different ingredients made up, along with many native initiatives, that idiosyncratic ecclesiastical pudding mixture from which were baked the Church of England, the various non-conformist churches, and indeed the peculiarly English type of Roman Catholicism.

Protestant influences had begun to gain some ascendancy at court once more during the last two or three years of Henry VIII's reign. With the accession of the boy king Edward VI, these influences won a total victory in the competition to advise him and to rule on his behalf during his minority. Within a few months of his accession the way was made open both for the wide range of moderate reforming Lutheran opinion already existing in England, to express itself, and for the more rigorous Calvinist influence to come into the country. The first important visible Reform event was the suppression of the guilds and chantries (endowed chapels for the offering of Masses for the dead) by the Council of State, a systematic suppression similar in method to that used by Cromwell in dealing with the monasteries. It has been suggested with good reason that this suppression of the guilds and chantries had a more immediate effect on the country than the suppression of the monasteries. The side chapels and chantries were no longer occupied day in, day out by priests offering Mass for the souls of the dead. And a wide variety of amenities, in terms of schools, hospitals, and almshouses, had their funds threatened; in the event only a small minority of such amenities disappeared, but this, along with the widespread suppression of the specifically religious activities, including prayer to particular patron saints and the festivity and holiday that went with it, meant that a substantial part of the old Catholic culture, of the pattern of daily life was excised.

Much the most important event of the reign was that of the Act of Uniformity of 1549. We saw that Cranmer had been working for many years at new versions of the liturgy. As archbishop of Canterbury he was now able to issue, with the assent of Parliament a new prayer book, the first and famous reformed Prayer Book of 1549. The Latin Mass was abolished. Everything was now in English. The new texts were a very skillful, sincere, profound weaving together of patristic, medieval and Reformation texts and insights. Cranmer had taken the English medieval Sarum rite (that used at Salisbury Cathedral) as his basis. He used much also from the new proposed reform of the Roman breviary, known as the Quignon breviary, particularly for his two new offices of Matins and Evensong. He was of course also very well acquainted with Lutheran usages and these again played a considerable part in his final versions.

Martin Bucer, who had fled from Strasbourg when the emperor was at its gates, was now professor of divinity at Cambridge. He was very well suited to working in England, being more tolerant than most of the Continental reformers. Dickens quotes his words: "Flee formulae, bear with the weak. While all faith is placed in Christ, the thing is safe. It is not given for all to see the same thing at the same time." Cranmer received him, old and ill, with great honor at Lambeth. He was only to live till 1551. Before then he completed his famous book *De Regno Christi*, which derives from his twenty-five years' experience in Strasbourg, and has been said to look forward to English seventeenth-century Protestantism. Bucer is interested in trying to understand Christian revelation within the whole context of world history, and is as worth reading today as any sixteenth-century theologian. His influence on Cranmer was to be considerable and he wrote at this time a *Censura* of the Prayer Book which led Cranmer to revise the second version of 1552.

Cranmer was moving rapidly away from the Catholic and Lutheran ideas about the Real Presence at the Eucharist and tending towards a Swiss Zwinglian emphasis on the Eucharist as memorial. But Cranmer's politic, comprehensive and synthetic approach led him to retain every traditional item that he could without offending what he believed to be the truth. So although the altar is now called a table, and although the sentence at Communion was changed in 1552 to "Take and eat this in remembrance that Christ died for thee, and feed on him in thy heart by faith, with thanksgiving," instead of the Catholic "The Body of our Lord Jesus Christ, which was given for thee, preserve thy body and soul unto everlasting life," still Cranmer continues to refer to the minister as a priest, and the people were to kneel to receive the sacrament. This kneeling was denounced by a Scottish minister, probably John Knox, and led to the insertion by the Council of State of the famous "black" rubric denying that this kneeling is intended to mean that "any adoration is done . . . unto any real and essential presence there being of Christ's natural flesh and blood." To the theologian the word "natural" really leaves the whole question open. At the Last Supper Christ was "naturally" present with his disciples when he fed them with bread and said "This my body" (to translate the presumably Aramaic original words as accurately as possible). Theologians of the Catholic tradition had been very careful, Aquinas in particular, to deny that this "body," this "presence," was a "local" presence—God could not in the form of the second person, be "confined" in a single place. It was a "sacramental" Real Presence—but to guard against this sacramental presence being watered down into something not real, the theory of the total transmutation of the inner substance of the bread was proposed. This was the famous "transubstantiation," which the Church then canonized as its official interpretation in the thirteenth century— though one should remember that the word substance was not a newcomer, it had already been in use in Christian theology for a thousand years.

We have already seen how this subject had become a typical center of regular medieval theological controversy. It was this rather highly sophisticated intellectual theological controversy which now engaged the interests of people generally and became a central Reformation topic—in many ways inappropriately. Luther had put at the heart of his reformation concern the denial of the idea of the Mass as a magical "work." There was no direct logical connection in the original Lutheran initiative between this denial and any specific definition of the eucharistic presence. But his denial of the Mass as a "work," and as a "sacrifice" supplementary to the sacrifice of Christ, now became tied in with attempts by other reformers to deny any kind of "real" presence. The common link was the implication of "white magic." Some reformers thought of "real presence" as something "magical," in fact "local" precisely in the sense always denied by many, though not all, Catholic theologians and to some extent encouraged by popular devotion to the blessed sacrament. In many ways all the discussion in the Middle Ages and in the modern times about the nature of the sacramental presence has been an intellectual game, often a desperately serious game but a distraction from the essential Christian message, and never more so perhaps than in the six- teenth century. In England people continued to worship in the church where they had always worshiped, with the same priests, doing what they had always done in the sense that bread was broken and eaten and wine poured out and drunk, in fulfillment of the "new Covenant" established by Jesus on the night before he died. But the belief or disbelief in "transubstantiation" was increasingly singled out as a symbol of what the old faith meant to one side and of what the Reformation denied on the other. So that eventually Cranmer died for his refusal to express such belief, the man least, of all sixteenth-century theologians, inclined to die for anything.

Cranmer had attempted in the early days of Edward's reign to silence public discussion on this matter as it had been silenced in the previous reign. He, and the Protector, Somerset, were of one mind here, and a royal proclamation of December 27, 1547 "prohibited all discussion about the nature of the Presence except by learned men in private. The people must believe that the body and blood of Christ is there; but no one must discuss, either in the pulpit or in the alehouse, whether it is there really or figuratively . . ."[1]

This was not an attempt to avoid crucial and difficult issues but to keep their discussion to those competent to discuss them. Cranmer broached, at this time, the other question about the Eucharist, in what sense it is a sacrifice. He formulated a number of questions to be answered by himself and other divines and bishops. Among them was: "What is the oblation and sacrifice of Christ in the Mass?" Cranmer's answer puts one in mind of discussion among Catholic theologians in the first half of the twentieth century: "The oblation and sacrifice of Christ in the mass is so called not because Christ is indeed there offered and sacrificed by the priest and the people (for that was done but once by Himself upon the Cross); but it is so called because it is a memory and representation of that very true sacrifice and immolation which before was made upon the Cross."[2] What does representation mean? Is it re-presentation? (See Appendix for further discussion.)

Three years later Cranmer published a book, his first since he had been made archbishop nearly twenty years before, in which he set out his own belief about the Eucharist. It was entitled *Defence of the True and Catholic Doctrine of the Sacrament of the Body and Blood of Christ* and amounted to a complete rejection of the orthodox Catholic teaching of transubstantiation, and an adherence to something like the teaching of Oecolampadius. The bread and wine derived their efficacy from the person receiving them. Christ is not there corporally. "Figuratively he is

[1] Quoted by Jasper Ridley in *Thomas Cranmer* (Oxford University Press, London, 1962), p. 275.
[2] Ibid., p. 274.

in the bread and wine, and spiritually He is in them that worthily eat and drink the bread and wine; but really, carnally and corporally He is only in Heaven, from whence He shall come to judge the quick and the dead."

Into the new national structure of the Church set up by Henry VIII, were being poured new habits of worship, in English, a steadily increasing acquaintance with Scripture, and a transformed understanding of Christianity based on the Lutheran and Calvinist models, as well as on earlier medieval heretical insight. An irreversible cultural process was taking place, and one which, while being imposed from above, was also welcomed by a few and found a certain indifference among a great many from below. The success of the Protestant element in gaining control of the Council of State and of the boy king, while certainly not representative of any large majority opinion, was an action flowing with the popular tide rather than against it. There was of course a strong minority opinion opposed to the innovations, and it soon showed itself.

Already in 1549 itself there was protest against the Prayer Book. But the violent opposition to it and to other reforms was ambiguous and as difficult to interpret accurately as were the protests in the reign of Henry VIII. The Cornish rebellion of 1549 objected to the new liturgy as to a "Christmas play," a term used as one of scorn for something not serious. The rebels demanded a ban on the English Bible, the restoration among other things of the Six Articles and of the Latin Mass with Communion only once a year. They said that as Cornishmen they couldn't all understand English in any case. Cranmer asked pertinently whether they understood Latin any better. They were defeated.

There was undoubtedly some economic motive in this western rebellion. The other substantial rebellion of the reign, Kett's in Norfolk, was largely against the enclosure of land, but had also a distinctive Protestant character to it. Other riots in Yorkshire were opposed to the reformers, and inherited some of the Catholic enthusiasm of the Pilgrimage of Grace. Two typical characteristics of Protestant Christianity were now apparent: the long-standing demand of heretics that the laity should communicate in the wine as well as the bread was accepted by the Prayer Book; the compulsory celibacy of the clergy was removed. Cranmer's wife began to appear in public in 1549, and many clergy began to marry.

Cranmer now set about the reform of canon law and the Church courts, and initiated a project for stating the essential beliefs of the Church in England. Once the reformed Church had a suitable form of public prayer and sacrament the next thing to do was to make sure it had a suitable legal structure, together with a form of belief. The latter project was the basis for the Thirty-nine Articles finally established in Elizabeth's reign, and still today the primary source document, after Scripture, for Christianity as understood by the Church of England. The articles were Cranmerian in several senses, not least in their ambivalent comprehensiveness. They run pretty well the whole gamut of the Reformation, enabling assent to them to run in most senses from high Lutheran (almost a non-papal Catholicism) to low Zwinglian. They reject Rome and communion with her. And, as emphatically, they reject the Anabaptists.

In this year 1549, all the essential lines of the Reformation in England were finally laid down. Given the legal enactions of Henry's reign and general popular sentiments, the achievement must be definitive. It may be useful to add at this point a comment on the Prayer Book by the twentieth-century historian to whom the sections in this book on the English Reformation owe most. The comment exhibits some of that self-criticism, sense of humor and British pragmatism which already began at times to show itself among adherents of the Church of England. A. G. Dickens has written: "Whatever further changes the future might bring, the new Church was henceforth furnished with a devotional asset ranking second after the English Bible. One Anglican at least is prepared to admit that for him the Prayer Book sometimes seems a shade over-felicitous. Intoxicated by verbal beauty, the feeble spirit can find a barrier—or invent a sub-Christian cult—as readily as when confronted by images and incense. Idolatry is a term with wider connotations than the early Reformers supposed!" That indicates the high respect in which Cranmer's English has been held in subsequent centuries. But at the time, of course, the language was simply good contemporary English.

The reign of Edward saw the origin in England of the great variety of belief and religious association which was eventually to be typical of Christianity in the British Isles and later in

America. It is beyond the scope of this book even to try to list all the variations. One name, however, needs to be mentioned, that of John Knox, the future Scottish reformer. He was already preaching an extreme Zwinglian Christianity, first at Berwick (1549), then in Newcastle-on-Tyne (1551), following on a period of service as a galley slave after capture by a Catholic, French and Scottish descent on St. Andrews in 1547. With the accession of Mary he would be one of the numerous exiles who fled to the Continent and in the following reign would return and help to ensure to Protestantism both in England and on the Continent the benefits of a thorough cross-fertilization. This process indeed began in England in Edward's reign with the arrrival there of numerous Protestants from the mainland, some of them specially notable. Bucer, as we have seen, became regius professor of divinity at Cambridge. His opposite number at Oxford was the Italian Peter Martyr Vermigli. Cranmer had always been impressed by the scholarship on the Continent and had strong links of friendship not least through his wife. He was pleased to bring these men over. There was much feuding between the proponents of various shades of eucharistic belief, and Cranmer found it difficult to welcome one and all. However, the only really sharp line was drawn against the Anabaptists. As many as 5000 foreign religious refugees seem to have settled in England, from the Netherlands and France, as well as from German towns where the Interim of 1548 had brought a renewed Catholic influence, as at Strasbourg. Letters to and from Bullinger, still the leading reformer in Zurich, provide much information as to the situation in England. Cranmer allowed a substantial degree of autonomy to the congregations established by these immigrants.

The parish clergy and their flocks in the English villages and towns had not as yet been much changed one way or the other by the various categories of official reform in Henry's reign. On the whole it is probably true that the rather decadent situation generally obtaining before the Reformation began, had been further worsened by the removal of funds. Recent research on an enthusiastic reforming bishop, John Hooper of Gloucester, shows that he found in 1551 of 331 parish clergy he examined, 168 could not repeat the Ten Commandments, thirty-four did not know where the Lord's Prayer came in the Bible, and thirty-nine did not know its author.

Before the end of Edward's reign Cranmer had composed the Ordinal, the rite for ordination of priests, which led Rome to conclude over three hundred years later that the Anglican clergy were not priests in the same sense as that of an ordained priest of the Roman Catholic Church. And the Revised Prayer Book had been issued, with its movement away from Luther further to the left.

Edward died. Mary, daughter of Catherine of Aragon, came to the throne in 1553. Even notably Protestant areas, in particular East Anglia, whither she escaped when Edward died, supported her wholeheartedly. The legal sovereign was not to be rejected for any reason, and the support for her rival, Lady Jane Grey, was minimal. England forthwith "became Catholic" again. But as it had never been at all certain which clergy accepted the Edwardine measures sincerely and which just put up with them, it was equally difficult to be sure which were pleased with the reversion to the papal Church and which were not. A great number must have begun to look with a certain passivity at the regular changes in theology and in the type of religion encouraged, several switches during Henry's reign, two during Edward's, now another major reversion. They went on with their tasks as best they could, many of them as inadequately as in the two previous reigns. A few monasteries were set up again, but not many. Mass was again in Latin. Vestments were worn if they had not been sold or some could be got from somewhere. Eventually papal supremacy was again acknowledged. Cardinal Pole took up residence at Lambeth Palace as papal legate. But Mary herself was not popular; she did the worst thing she could by emphasizing her Spanish descent, and in 1554 by marrying King Philip II of Spain, so bringing a whole train of Spanish courtiers into London, Catholic, proud and ostentatiously foreign. London did not like them.

The provincial rebellions were Protestant now, principally that of Thomas Wyatt. Three others, in Devon, the Welsh Marches, the Midlands, were economic in origin, and only quite partially religious. Motives were mixed and perhaps the principal common complaint was objection to foreign influence.

Mary, a strict and scrupulous Catholic, began to persecute Protestants. The wealthier kind fled abroad, about 800 of them. It was largely the poorer people, unable to emigrate, who are found in the list of those burned for heresy. The married clergy were

formally parted from their wives. Some commentators noted that
some clergy seemed to be disillusioned with wedlock and parted
willingly. Others, however, certainly didn't, and came together
again with their wives in the following reign.

The most important event of the reign was perhaps the
burning of Cranmer. For so long had he retained his position,
based on his belief in the overriding need to obey the sovereign.
He had managed to accommodate his conscience to the several
changes of front by Henry, and to the varying demands of the boy
Edward and his two masters, first Somerset, then Northumberland. But in the end it was this belief in obedience to the
sovereign that was his undoing. Before he died, Edward had been
persuaded to sign a "device" whereby both Henry VIII's children, by
Queen Catherine and Queen Anne Boleyn, the princesses Mary
and Elizabeth, were declared to be bastards and put aside in
the succession in favor of Lady Jane Grey, daughter of Henry's
niece and recently married to Northumberland's son. Cranmer was
very loth to sign his agreement to this "device" and only did so
when the boy king challenged him specifically with the need
to obey his king. This obedience was the key to all Cranmer's
political life. But his faithfulness to it at this point provided
Queen Mary with the basis for a charge of treason. When this
was finally brought to bear on him, Cranmer was drawn into
stating his religious views, and therefore into speaking what was
heresy by Catholic standards. He set the government a problem,
in that an archbishop of Canterbury must first be stripped of his
office before being declared a heretic. The legal process which
must go through Rome took time. Cranmer had the special agony
of many months in prison to start with, for the one crime which
he above all abhorred, that of treason, one that he would never
willingly have committed.

To the historian, the burning of Cranmer is something of a
reductio ad absurdum of the whole business of burning or executing
a man merely for his religious opinions. The policy only began
seriously in England in the early fifteenth century, with the act
De Haeretico Comburendo. The burnings, accompanied now by
executions, went steadily on into the sixteenth century, maintained
by Cranmer himself, though increasingly balanced out by the
capital punishment of Catholics too. In Edward's reign the burning
of heretics of the extreme left continued in principle, though in

practice only two actually suffered, Joan Bocher for denying the incarnation, and a Dutch surgeon, George van Parris, a Unitarian. The leaders of the "Catholic" western rebellion suffered capital punishment, but so did Kett and the others. There were the expected political deaths for "treason" when Northumberland ousted Somerset. Now in Mary's reign, from having dwindled to a trickle, the persecution of heretics swiftly swelled again, and included not only Anabaptists but Protestants of all kind; so that eventually it included the man who for twenty years and more had been the nation's first bishop, the archbishop of Canterbury. He had, of course, been moving quite slowly but very steadily into a more and more Protestant position.

If to the historian, who knows of the switch back yet again in the following reign, the burning of Cranmer must seem futile, no doubt very little of this attitude can be attributed to the view of the ordinary man at the time. But something of this cynicism is beginning to be seen. There is always popular sympathy with the man being burned, whatever his opinion—and the populace usually manages to grasp whether the man is specially worthy of respect. Cranmer's death was preceded by those of Ridley, Latimer, Hooper and others. But Cranmer's was a more crucial affair, just because here was a man who would never die for a theological formula if he could avoid it. This had been true of Thomas More as well, a man who understood that of which T. S. Eliot, in the context of Thomas Becket, was to say in our day, "the last temptation is the greatest treason, to do the right thing for the wrong reason"— the temptation to court martyrdom. But certainly such a temptation never entered Cranmer's mind. There is no room here to retell all the detail of his lengthy stay in prison, his considerable suffering there, and his lengthy defense of himself. Eventually, by just exactly what sort of psychological process we do not know, he was persuaded to recant and to swear to the Catholic faith. Mary and her advisers, however, were determined to have him, and in the full medieval tradition it was decided that he should burn even though he had recanted. This seems to have given Cranmer the strength to disavow finally what he surely had not begun to believe fully again, the papal supremacy, transubstantiation, the Mass as sacrifice. His Protestant theology was now perhaps thirty years old, and his slowly developing eucharistic theology had only reached its final stage in his book of 1550 after long careful and scrupulous thought. The final scenes were all the more impressive. When expected to read out his recantation in St. Mary's Church, Oxford, he read instead a disavowal of it. This had been preceded by other doubtful incidents, a first partial disavowal and further recantations in the face of the threat of a terrible death by burning. The final shocking disavowal was confirmed in the fire itself, Cranmer holding out into the flames his right hand, guilty of writing the recantations. None of it, in the end, did the Catholic cause any good at all. Protestantism profited from this strange and famous martyrdom.

Meanwhile the émigrés were busy abroad. As many as eight separate towns had English congregations formed in them. These were Emden, Wesel, Frankfurt-am-Main, Strasbourg, Zurich, Basel, Geneva and Aarau. From these towns, and especially from presses at Emden, came Protestant pamphlets into England, from the pen of John Knox and others. Above all, they produced a new version of the Bible, with an introduction by Calvin, the famous "Breeches" Bible—breeches being the word to describe the covering Adam and Eve made for themselves. This version of the Bible was to be used more than any other during the coming reign. There was a new version of the Psalms as well—and then a version of Psalm 100 which had the now famous "Old Hundredth" tune composed for it. There were many disagreements, notable among these being at Frankfurt, where for a time was John Knox until he was expelled and went to Geneva. Others went too, and it was due to this mass migration that the Bible translation already mentioned, and other literary work was undertaken, and a general compaign inaugurated against Cranmer's Prayer Book, of which the 1552 version was still considered to have too many unbiblical elements remaining in it. However, on the whole, the large band of moderates remained dominant.

It has been said, unkindly, that Queen Mary left England more Protestant than she found it. Precise criteria and sufficient evidence would hardly be available to make such a statement feasible. A generalization that seems nearer the mark is that when Elizabeth came to the throne at the end of 1558 the pluralistic nature of the religious situation in England could not be reversed. Maybe nearly half the population had not known any time of settled religion—it had always been change and change again. As we have already noted, a certain cynicism, whether overt or unconscious, was inevitable. Policies come and policies go—and the ordinary people go on going to their church. They adapt their behavior, as does the local priest or clergyman, to the demands currently made by authority. Within this situation may be found signs of strong traditional Catholic faith and many elements of strong approval of new Protestant teaching. Among the former will be a belief in the Real Presence, a secret doubt about the real authority of the throne in religious matters, a hankering for some of the externals of the old order, in terms of candles, vestments and maybe the Latin language. Among the latter will be a strong delight in hearing, and reading where possible, the Bible, through the availability of new translations or the paraphrases of Erasmus in the parish churches, in worshiping in a language known to them, in a reasonable and open-minded affirmation of the status and responsibility of lay people, and of the family. Common to both is a strong faith in God and an attachment to prayer.

But of really militant Catholics who wished to restore papal supremacy or of militant Protestants who wished to establish a Calvinist regime only small groups existed in the capital, and individuals or tiny groups in thin networks across the country. The great majority of people did not wish to be involved in any such campaigns. But as the forty-five years of Elizabeth's reign unfolded, the security which they brought, in their turn provided the occasion for many people to take up increasingly individual and partisan attitudes. Both the committed Catholic party, and the Puritan party or parties, grew in numbers and in strength of organization. In the former case, as the committed Catholics grew in numbers and activity, so also did the campaign against them, for in their case, there was a real threat to the throne. International politics were involved. The Spanish Armada witnesses to that. There was also some increasing threat involved in the developing "nonconformism" of the Puritan movements. Like the Catholics, they had a sense of history and a confidence in their own doctrines, for their roots went strongly and continuously back into the Lollard past. However, it is not the intention of this book to go methodically forward beyond that point where the Reformation is essentially irreversible. We take that point to be the Elizabethan Settlement of 1559. It is this we must now summarize.

Elizabeth was consciously pragmatic, but also consciously following in the steps of her father. She deliberately avoided theories and polemics, as far as possible whether Catholic or Protestant, although in order to follow some kind of a middle road her first actions inevitably involved expression of dislike of the specifically Catholic ways which she inherited from her half sister. So within the first months, she requested a bishop to cease elevating the Host at Mass; she told the abbot and monks at Westminster to take away their ceremonial candles because she could see well enough; she put up a Protestant to preach at Paul's Cross. If she was following her father in some sense, it was not in terms of any well-defined reformed orthodoxy, which was really the mark of his reign. But equally she did not want to encourage the extreme Geneva émigrés. She chose as archbishop of Canterbury Mathew Parker, her old tutor, who had managed to ride out Mary's reign without emigrating, a retiring scholar, not unsuited to take up the reins laid down by Cranmer.

The Elizabethan Settlement comprised two principal acts of Parliament, those of Supremacy, intended to re-establish the sovereign as head of the Church, and of Uniformity, to provide for uniformity in worship, of 1559, together with various other lesser acts. The bill for the Supremacy was at first transformed in the Commons into a thoroughgoing act for re-establishing Protestantism. To achieve this a very active Protestant minority in the Commons persuaded their colleagues to vote with them. This was remarkable evidence of the extent to which Protestantism was now favored, accepted or tolerated. The newly elected House of Commons was not packed; a third of its members had been in Queen Mary's Parliament. The Lords reformed this Bill of Supremacy so that it was again the simple bill for re-establishing the supremacy of the sovereign, instead of the Pope. On March 22 this received the assent of the queen, who issued on that day also a proclamation allowing Communion in both kinds to the laity. A week later a disputation was held in the choir at Westminster Abbey between Protestant and Catholic divines. Although the queen did not much love the émigrés, from whose company the Protestant speakers came, Dickens says there was no real intention of giving the Catholics a fair hearing, but only of depriving them of the chance of claiming they had been suppressed without a hearing.

John Jewel, the bishop of Salisbury, right-hand man of the archbishop of Canterbury, listed the three articles for debate as follows: "Our first proposition is, that it is contrary to the word of God, and the practice of the primitive church, to use in the public prayers and administration of the sacraments any other language than what is understood by the people. The second is, that every provincial church, even without the bidding of a general council, has power either to establish, or change, or abrogate ceremonies and ecclesiastical rites, wherever it may seem to make for edification. The third is, that the propitiatory sacrifice, which the papists pretend to be in the mass, cannot be proved by the holy Scriptures."[3]

The queen did not want to exacerbate relations between Catholics and Protestants, and wished to go slowly with the very moderate, more or less Lutheran Protestantism which was roughly the direction of her own inclinations. When the Commons tried at this time to reinstate the clergy dispossessed by Mary, she almost certainly approved the opposition to it of the Lords. Another moderating event during the middle part of 1559 was the queen's decision to change the description of her own supremacy over the Church to that of "Supreme Governor" instead of "Supreme Head." An important distinction. She did not wish to run the Church, but only to be its first governor; although later she insisted that her position was just the same as that of her father. Another moderating change was the comprehensiveness introduced into the words at the Communion in the Act of Uniformity. The words of the 1549 Prayer Book—"The Body of our Lord Jesus Christ, which was given for thee . . ."—were reinstated as a prefix to the "Take and eat this in remembrance" of 1552. And the black rubric inspired by Knox's protest was removed.

Knox was personally triumphant in Scotland in the following year, where his policy came to effective power following on Elizabeth's military victory there in 1560. This was a kind of pointer to the steadily increasing Protestant character of the following forty years of the reign. Another symbolical event was the publication in 1563 of the *Acts and Monuments* of John Foxe. This book of the English Protestant martyrs became a source document for the piety and outlook of the whole of the new non-papal Christianity which was to develop in English-speaking lands.

"Pluralism" and "complexity" are the keynotes to religion in

[3] A. G. Dickens, *The English Reformation* (Batsford, London; Schocken Books, Inc., New York; 1966).

English-speaking countries from now on. The drive towards religious uniformity within a given territory, canonized at the Peace of Augsburg, is shown to be strong by the very titles of the English Parliamentary Acts of Uniformity. And there is no doubt that government felt its safety and efficiency to depend on a certain minimum uniformity. Yet within this context the note of tolerance of a certain diversity is increasingly struck: "The Catholic gentleman with his circle of Catholic friends, his relationships by marriage, his Catholic servants and tenants, his private chapel and his private chaplain, often regarded his religion as his own business and not a matter in which the central government ought to interfere. His attitude was admirably expressed by Lord Vaux who when he was presented for not coming to church in 1581, together with 'his household and familiars and divers servants,' justified himself on the ground that he 'did claim his house to be a parish by itself.' A very similar situation existed in the households of many Puritan gentry where the family, their guests, and their servants assembled for prayers, and where a chaplain or local minister preached to the assembled company, catechised the dependants and children, and co-operated with the master of the house in organising a 'godly life' for the whole establishment."[4]

The same writer goes on to point out that this picture is itself somewhat contradicted by the missionary fervor of the Catholic priests who came into England with its "conversion" as their single aim, and who of course met martyrdom in substantial numbers. Complexity again! There is no doubt that we now have a kind of religious pluralism throughout Europe which reaches its climax in England. The limits put on it are the limits put on it by the need to prevent revolution or threat to government. But the religious drive itself is running fiercely in numerous directions, potentially hostile to or competitive with one another. Yet as it is all inspired by the same sources, by the Bible and the fifteen centuries of Christian practice, so also eventually these different practices have the possibility of convergence and of the suppression of mutually hostile or competitive emphases. Already in the second half of the sixteenth century perceptive men were beginning to see that the different religious traditions could nourish one another. Theoreti-

---

[4] Patrick McGrath, *Papists and Puritans under Elizabeth I* (Blandford Press, London, 1967).

cally Protestantism and Catholicism were utterly opposed the one to the other. In practice everywhere the two had very large areas in common, and individual men and women in both camps began to see they could draw profit from one another. Robert Parsons, the Jesuit leader of attempts to reinstate Catholicism in England, published in 1582 his *The First Booke of the Christian Exercise, appertayning to Resolution. Wherein are layed downe the causes and reasons that should move a man to resolve hym selfe to the service of God,* later known as *The Christian Directory.* By the time of his death in 1610, there had been at least fifteen Protestant editions of it, in addition to the four known Catholic editions. Equally of course Catholics were enormously influenced by the Reformation. Justification by faith brought a renewed understanding of the primary part played in all religion by the act of faith. Catholics took the doctrine, without being much aware of it, into their own armory at the Council of Trent. The translations of the Bible by Tyndale and Coverdale had a great influence on the Rheims and Douay versions by Catholics and equally those versions also influenced the Authorized Version of King James' reign. At these fundamental levels of communication and inspiration a practical community of interest was already being revealed.

CHAPTER 9

Twentieth-century Outcome

The impetus of the sixteenth century continued almost unchecked for three centuries. The seventeenth and eighteenth centuries and much of the nineteenth century saw a proliferation of both the Protestant and the Catholic traditions. In the Protestant churches men and women continued to arise who went out from them and founded new Christian communities and traditions, such as the Quakers in the seventeenth century and the Methodists in the eighteenth century. There were very many other less well-known examples. The Church of England maintained both a Protestant and a Catholic tradition and spread them throughout the English-speaking world which was itself rapidly increasing in size. The Roman Catholics retained and hardened their emphasis on uniformity and on their claim to be the one true church. In practice they also reflected the growing complexity and differentiation of European, and later American, Asian and African, society, but the dominant features of the Roman Catholic Church continued to be "unity" in the sense of visible uniformity, the absolute sovereignty of the Pope, and an overriding emphasis on the grace-giving efficacy of validly administered sacraments.

Towards the end of the nineteenth century the Reformation gale seemed at last to be blowing itself out. The churches based in Europe, still fragmented, and embattled one against another, were presented with growing missionary challenges not only in Europe but in all the other continents. Pastoral and missionary pressures began to produce a reversal of the trends towards ever greater fragmentation. Although individual response to the gospel inevitably continued to lead to the founding of new religious communities, particularly in parts of Africa and North America, the majority of larger Protestant and non-Roman Catholic bodies ceased to spawn great new schisms. A slowly increasing minority of their members began to regret the divisions between them and to ponder the possibility of reunion. The beginning of a convergence was to be seen. It became definite, with a more or less measurable curve, when the first ecumenical meeting was held in Edinburgh in 1910.

Along with practical challenges to the Church's mission, abroad and at home, went another deeper trend towards unity in terms of an increasingly scientific examination of the Bible and of the other first-, second- and third-century source documents of Christianity. This was in fact a continuation of that philology which had itself been one of the root drives behind the Reformation events. Bit by bit agreements and disagreements between biblical scholars across denominational frontiers came to be more important than their denominational allegiances. This process began to involve biblical scholars within the Roman Catholic Church as well. The unitary nature of truth effected, and still continues to effect, a tendency towards union. And biblical research began to show that many of the Reformation insights were well based. Roman Catholic theologians began to take notice of the historical and biblical researches of their Catholic and non-Catholic colleagues. The drift of their researches seemed to harmonize with the drift of practical answers beginning to form in the minds of Catholic pastors and missionaries faced with problems similar to those facing Protestant ministers. A crisis point was reached, and to the astonishment of those who had supposed it to be unchanging, the old Church signified its intention of taking into itself many of the reforms of the sixteenth century, albeit appropriately updated, and tailored to fit. If 1910 was the beginning of the end of the Reformation gale, the opening of the Second Vatican Council was the hauling down of the Counter-Reformation ramparts put up against that gale. A new Christian era had certainly begun.

The individual items of reform which the Roman Catholic Church decreed at Vatican II are important, also the way in which they were mutually integrated. Most obvious, to begin with, was the change, permitted and very widely welcomed, to worship in the vernacular, instead of Latin. Of equal importance, and well integrated into the liturgical reform, was the new fundamental emphasis on Scripture, not only in church, but in personal prayer and group social application. Along with these two went another typically Reformation emphasis, the importance of the local church. This latter meant a measure of decentralization, and so a break on the, until then, all-pervading influence of the papacy. Along with this went a revival of the early Church emphasis on the community as "the people of God," and so on the responsibilities of all baptized members and their full participation in the worship and life of the Church. Consultation became more frequent at all levels. It was realized that a greater measure of participation of laity and clergy was required in the appointment of bishops. These reforms were the actions of the Church as a whole, the Pope, the bishops, the clergy and people. Historically it is interesting and important that Popes Pius XI, XII, and John XXIII, also their predecessors Benedict XV and Pius X, in lesser measure, all issued policy documents which strongly supported the young movements at the grass roots that led up to these decisions of Vatican II. The local church was again to be accorded its rightful status; but no one wanted, as a corollary, anything like the disappearance of the papacy.

The theology of the Church to be found in the central document of Vatican II, on "The Church," and implications of this worked out in the texts entitled "The Laity" and "Declaration on Religious Freedom" and in the very long and idiosyncratic text "The Church and the World," all point away from that exclusive interpretation of the phrase "the true Church," outside which a Catholic might expect to find only some very problematical kinds of goodness, truth or spiritual authenticity. This is in some ways the crux of the whole matter. It was the hard definition of the Church which made "heresy" inevitable throughout the Middle Ages, and the occasion of virtually all the practical abuses that in turn gave rise, in the immediate sense, to the Reformation itself. Vatican II prepared the way for Roman Catholic theologians to discuss with their Christian colleagues in the other communions the technical detail of Reformation theology, justification by faith, the nature of the Church, and the way in which God saves all those whom he came to save, but to whom man has not yet brought the gospel and the visible Church.

Of other highly controversial Reformation topics, two stand out as being in the forefront of current Roman Catholic reform, or discussion. The Roman Catholic laity now take Communion in the wine as well as the bread, on certain occasions. Much more important is the matter of clerical celibacy. For many years the celibacy of the clergy had been described, for aspiring Roman Catholic converts, as "only a matter of discipline—it could be changed." The married clergy of the Eastern rites in communion with Rome were pointed to as evidence of this. In the 1950's, Pius XII agreed to the ordination to the Catholic priesthood of a small number of married ex-Lutheran pastors. Now, as everyone knows, a very strong movement, supported by a large minority of both clergy and laity, but opposed by the Pope, most bishops and many priests and laity has arisen within the Catholic Church for celibacy to be voluntary for the secular clergy, as distinct from the regular clergy, who, wishing to take vows of celibacy, poverty and obedience, have joined a religious order. The last breezes of the Reformation are blowing freshly into the open windows of the old Church.

The most central controversial topic, after Scripture, in medieval heresies, in the Reformation, and in current Roman Catholic discussion, is the character of the priesthood, or the ministry. Today Roman Catholic theologians are beginning to agree that the medieval understanding of priesthood and ministry as the profession of an ordained sacramental priesthood had much in it that was simply attributable to the cultural ethos of the time, and much that cannot be defended on a basis of the New Testament and the primitive Church. They begin to see that one of the essential points of the medieval heretic and of the sixteenth-century reformers was correct. All baptized Christians are committed to a priestly task; on the other hand, the sacramental ways of grace open to men through the sacraments administered by the ordained priesthood are not exclusive in the sense that those who do not partake of them are necessarily in a spiritually dangerous position— St. Augustine had already made this clear, although it was often forgotten by those who had to oppose heretics and reformers.

The movement away from an elite theology is common to both Protestants and Catholics. Medieval Catholicism and Tridentine Catholicism had built a legalist intellectual barrier around membership of the Church. All those who would or could not make public expression of belief in the formulas were excommunicate. The Protestant churches inherited and accepted the same approach in spite of the strong objections of reformers precisely to medieval legalism and its idea of a visible Church organization understood as virtually identical with the community of the "saved." Although in theory an important point in the sixteenth-century reforms was the insistence that the Church was essentially invisible, in practice the new churches erected even higher membership barriers than the medieval Church had done. The theory of election inherited from the medieval system was developed by Calvin into an emphatic assertion that God had mysteriously chosen some men and rejected others. The persecution of those not prepared to yield assent went along with an elitist theory and practice, even more strict than the medieval pattern, just because the Protestant communities had to identify themselves by contrast with, and set apart from, the Roman Catholic communities and other Protestant communities, and indeed to some extent the world at large. This exclusive, legalist, intellectual definition of the Church, of Church membership and of lived Christianity is now seen to be out of harmony with the gospel and any possible understanding of Christianity. And it is seen to be entirely inappropriate to a society with areas of high rates of literacy, and areas of high sensitivity and response to individual needs and inspiration.

Are the churches tending then towards a solution simply of introducing a greater practical flexibility about membership of the Church, and its expression in worship and in behavior? In many ways, yes. But at the same time they are seeing a need, all the greater, to distinguish on the one hand between the spiritual heart of the revelation of Jesus, the loving committed life which it demands, and on the other hand the intellectual implications of this which it may not be easy for anyone to grasp at first, or to express, or honestly assent to, implications about the proper way to describe the nature of man, Jesus, God. If it is felt that the intellectual verbal expression of the faith of a man or woman must be given space to grow, it is felt equally strongly that the challenge to express care and love for others in immediate practical personal terms must be presented more immediately. If the churches are likely to be less demanding about the assent required to theological doctrine and so also to doctrine about the nature of the Church and its organization, they may perhaps be more demanding on anyone who wishes to be a Christian, in the realm of such personal commitment.[1]

The old cry of the medieval heretic and the medieval reformer for a Church which follows the gospel exhortation to poverty is taken up today in the practical terms of insistence that Christians

---

[1] Cf. comments in many places in *The Foolishness of God* by John Austin Baker, Darton, Longman and Todd, London, 1970.

should share their wealth systematically with the rest of the world —and that the churches themselves should be as demonstrably poor as possible. Along with the call to poverty in the Middle Ages tended to go an apocalyptic or millennial approach, also a genuine desire for union with God. Within the organized Church, to a great extent these drives were channeled into the religious orders. Disciplined by the vows of obedience, poverty and celibacy, those who wanted to act in both the letter and the spirit of the gospel exhortation to take no thought for the morrow and live a life without possessions, were thus enabled to live the life of prayer and contemplation which they desired. Incidentally, they often contributed substantially to society in terms of farming, or education or what we today might call "culture," in that their liturgy provided the occasion for great achievements in architecture, sculpture, painting and music.

These religious orders were of course creations of their own age and time and entirely characteristic of them. Although the vows of obedience, chastity and poverty play the part we have described and are the fruit of wise Christian reflection on human nature, it is important to understand the sense in which they were specially characteristic of medieval culture. The vow of obedience reflected the world of feudalism, the world of threatening nomadic tribes, of incipient civilization. The medieval religious order was the product of its age as well as of wise reflection on human nature. Reliable organization, the conditions of trust necessary for any human community, were hardly to be found without rigorous sanctions. The vow of celibacy reflected that distrust of the sexual and emotional aspect of human nature which was partly a reaction to Greco-Roman civilization, partly an expression of Christian asceticism rooted back perhaps in the ascetic movement of the Essenes, illustrated in the lives of St. Paul, St. John the Baptist and indeed of Jesus himself. We have seen the emphasis it was able to attain among the Manicheans. The vow of poverty was perhaps more closely rooted in the gospel text itself than the other vows. Symbolizing the purity of spirit, it made possible a real detachment from worldly goods, and was a protest against the luxurious living of prelates and kings.

Altogether, the three vows freed a man or woman from the insistent demands of human society at large, demands on his compassion, his interest, his self-seeking, his need or desire for a family, his desire for the sexual and total companionship of marriage. He was freed for the primary tasks of contemplation, prayer, public worship, care for others. Today the religious drive is running strongly in similar directions. The reaction to and protest against a world organized on the basis of the profit motive is not just a reaction. It is a genuine drive to seek deeper into the nature of man. The desire to contemplate is simply and precisely a desire to contemplate truth. The desire to find fulfillment in love, and particularly in self-giving and care for others is just that. The Christian gospel has these things at its heart. There is a growing realization among Christians that not only must they not try to make "heretics" of those numerous bands of people who are turning towards contemplation and a committed life of caring for others but that new ways must be set up to encourage and make possible this "committed" Christian life of caring for others, of personal "poverty," of contemplation. It must be done without demanding a lifelong commitment, vows for life.

As yet there is also a great gap at the sexual level, in that an immense opportunity awaits the Church for setting forth the ideals of celibacy on the one hand and of married life on the other, fully human, and sacramental ideals. The twentieth century treats sex as a plaything; and then finds that this capacity and all the emotions which it involves becomes the center of mental, or rather human, breakdown. This takes us out beyond the proper subject of this book, for the medieval world still held the sexual life so entirely within conventions and taboos that its indulgence, idealization, sacramentalization were all severely structured, and the Reformation in the end had little new to say about it, except in so far as Luther further emphasized the value of family life, and took the general cynicism about the celibate life to a final conclusion by denying that as a lifelong commitment it was a proper Christian ideal in any kind of regular way. A comprehensive Christian grasp and expression of the sexual life has had to wait on the development of the human sciences.

But in all these series of challenges and opportunities it is being seen that it is necessary to avoid setting up a great legalistic framework, and to avoid insisting on a commitment for life. Here, as in every other sphere of Church life, it is seen that flexibility is going to be a prime need, and that there is now an opportunity to avoid past mistakes. In the Middle Ages the first Cistercians lived a life of very great poverty and asceticism and a life of prayer which attracted thousands of monks. St. Francis attracted tens of thousands by the sublimity and simplicity of his ideal. Church authority decided that in both cases the achievement must be closely monitored, and the ideals protected. The attempt at organization and canonical protection was a failure. Abuses set in precisely with the organization. New movements had to keep on arising to reform the rotting communities. In practice they degenerated precisely because their ideals achieved for them far greater security than ever existed in the world, such is the irony of life. Something similar happened with the Church as a whole. The whole priestly and sacramental machine, articulated in theory down to the last detail, is due in some sense to an obsession with perfection. It was all something of a self-deception. But it is true that the circumstances of the time made organization very difficult to achieve efficiently. The sheer difficulty of communication was paramount. Suddenly today this difficulty has disappeared almost overnight. We have a quite new set of situations, for which the old structures are often inappropriate.

Flexibility of structure in response to the very rapidly changing demands of individuals and societies is one of the crucial needs of our time throughout the human community. The phrase "global village" has been coined to describe the ease with which we can now communicate with one another, the proximity into which we are all put with one another. The information and data required for taking decisions are able to be collected swiftly. Computers are able to give us answers to problems incomparably more speedily than ever was possible even twenty years ago. Organizational structures designed to allow for the difficulties of gathering people together, consulting them and communicating decisions to those concerned are now often quite inappropriate. There is no absolute need to fix a policy and stick to it for a considerable time, for purely organizational reasons. It is easy to consult people, easy to communicate and administer the decisions, to a far greater extent than ever before. The human task now is often that of framing the right questions; human groups no longer need to spend time in hazarding, on the basis of personal opinion, answers to many questions, because the machines can provide quick and certain answers.

In our global village, it is no good pretending anyone can do anything without others knowing. We are in a kind of totalitarian situation. We do not need to turn this universal mutual awareness into formal tyranny, even though we can all monitor each other all the time. In this situation of potentially total information, old-fashioned centralization is no longer sensible. It is no longer in any way necessary to have at all a high degree of uniformity. We now have the opportunity for flexibility far greater than ever before. While in the past we could tolerate the occasional eccentric or very eccentric individual, we could now tolerate eccentric or very eccentric groups, movements—only so that they do not do damage to other groups. So, as always, in the Church the great movements have come up from below.

It will be clear that issues are being sorted out today in such a way that the continuing division of Christians into the communions established at the time of the Reformation, committed to doctrinal formulations worked out then, and in the subsequent two hundred years, in a total balanced European system of mutual contradiction, is no longer accepted by many theologians and many members of these bodies. The only reason that many continue to profess their Christianity within their chosen traditions is simply that they recognize on the one hand the ineligibility of either anarchism, or of a new syntheticism as options; on the other hand they recognize the particular values of their chosen traditions and the importance of continuity. They trust the Spirit to lead them on into the new ways. These ways are thought of as assisting the continued movement of every man towards God, enabling him to begin to perceive, accept, rejoice in and spread the knowledge of the perpetual movement of God towards him. All Scripture, all Christian tradition is seen as a service toward that end.

We see then that in some senses the individual inspirations of the sixteenth-century reforms have run their full course. They no longer inspire specifically separate Christian churches, and their insights are becoming, like all other Christian insights, part of the total Christian tradition, part of that total body of contemplation of, meditation on, and praxis around the Bible, which has always made of Christian writing a further "Scripture," gloss of those "Scriptures" originally selected by the Church. But if the reformers have run their course, Christianity is still the religion of reformation. Current "Scripture" illustrates this. We began with the Bible, and St. Augustine. We end by commending the reader to the modern reformers.

My book has attempted to be relevant history. I now invite the reader to project an examination of history through current trends into the future. It is impossible to impose generalizations on current events. It is also the nature of this book not to want to provide a final summing up, to have the last word or to end with a satisfactory resolution in a reassuring diatonic chord. We are in a historical continuum. If we would help to mold the events in it, we must be patient to them. So I take leave of the reader by putting him in the hands of contemporary theologians, who should help him to make his own further projection and to decide on his own action within history.

Appendix

The Theology of the Eucharist

In recording controversies about eucharistic theology it is useless for the historian simply to record the variety of opinion about transubstantiation and the nature of the Mass as sacrifice, memorial, etc. Without giving some idea of the mental context and the general assumptions, and without some attempt at evaluation he does not provide a record of any significance historically or theologically. I have tried to provide some evaluation in the text of the book, but inevitably a great deal of it is merely implied. In this Appendix I take the evaluation a step further, by providing what I hope will prove to be illuminating quotations from Cranmer, from the historian A. G. Dickens, followed by an extended theological comment from the theologian Louis Bouyer. The point, as will be seen, is that to attempt to pose and solve a theological problem of this kind exclusively in an analytical or logical framework is not likely to be successful. Bouyer suggests that a return to the original Jewish language and event may be enlightening.

Cranmer wrote at a disputation in April 1555: "The soul is fed with the body of Christ, the body with the sacrament . . . so one thing is done outwardly, another inwardly; like as in baptism, the external element, whereby the body is washed, is one; so the internal element whereby the soul is cleansed, is another . . . Outwardly we eat the sacrament; inwardly we eat the body of Christ." Dickens comments on this: "These ostensibly simple phrases concealed a multitude of metaphysical and historical problems; some theologians think them not far from Zwinglian symbolism while others regard them as closely related to pre-medieval Catholic tradition and as presenting a genuine *via media*, quite distinct from transubstantiation or consubstantiation or the radical teaching of Zwingli and the other Swiss Reformers.

"Everyone who has studied the growth of Cranmer's convictions must sometimes have shared the feeling of Cardinal Gasquet, who found it 'difficult to determine with precision, at any given time, the exact phase of a mind so shifting.' Yet if we go on to imply that a man was a fool or a knave to move from one position to another, especially in relation to this particular doctrine, we misunderstand the enquiring spirit of these years, the doctrinal maelstrom which caused even the unimaginative Gardiner to show uncertainties and Tunstall, the most conservative of Henry's bishops, to regret Innocent III's rigid definition of transubstantiation while accepting it as a loyal son of the Church."

There is a case for saying that the whole analytical approach to the Eucharist is mistaken, and that Christians should return to that single-minded, comprehensive, Hebrew approach, which is to be found at the origins of Christian worship. It may well be answered that you can neither ignore history nor stop it. However, there is certainly a strong case for saying that Christians might find the best key to a further understanding and exposition of their eucharistic worship by examining the Jewish approach. Louis Bouyer makes out a strong case for trying to cope with the theological problems of the eucharist in this way: "Let us notice three important problems which Christian antiquity never seems to have posed. They have, however, been a bone of contention ever since theologians who did pose them lost sight of the fundamental ideas of Jewish thought on the berakah. First, the problem of knowing whether the eucharistic consecration results from the recitation by the celebrant of the words of institution, or from an "epiclesis," a special invocation (a problem argued between east and west); second, the problem of knowing whether the celebration of the Eucharist ought to be considered as being in itself sacrificial, or as being only the memorial of the sacrifice of the cross (a problem argued between Catholics and Protestants); and third, the problem of the relation between the eucharistic symbols, the broken bread and the cup, and the presence, whether it be a matter of the simple presence of the body and blood of Christ under these symbols, or of the presence of his action (of his "mystery") underlying the liturgical action (a problem argued today among Catholic theologians themselves).

"The first problem seems the more insoluble because we can find texts in Christian antiquity, at first sight at least, in favor of either solution. For example, St. John Chrysostom says as categorically as possible that the eucharistic consecration comes from the words of the Lord, while St. Cyril of Jerusalem is no less categorical in saying that the consecration is accomplished by the invocation (epiclesis) of the Church. However, when we look at the matter more closely, it appears very doubtful whether either saint meant by these expressions what we understand by them. St. John Chrysostom did not mean simply that the consecration is achieved by the words of institution pronounced *hic et nunc* by the priest, but rather that it results from the will Christ expressed in saying them originally. In the same way, it is at least doubtful that St. Cyril was thinking, when he wrote epiclesis, of a particular formulary, isolated from its context: what he meant by this word was the whole eucharistic prayer. We must in fact say that such opposition, as we can now see it, has hardly any meaning for one who preserves a living sense of what the original Eucharist was, so like the berakah from which it came. It was essentially a prayer, *the* prayer *par excellence*, but a set prayer of adherence in an exulting faith to the divine Word, to that Word expressly conceived as offering itself to us in an act both creative and saving. Looking at it in this way, the opposition between 'words of institution' and 'epiclesis' has no meaning: the eucharistic prayer is an indivisible unity; each aspect demands the other.

"Exactly the same is true in the case of the opposition between the 'eucharistic sacrifice' and the 'memorial of the sacrifice.' In Jewish religious thought, as Jeremias very clearly shows, far from the 'memorial' being opposed to reality, it is the evocation of it, the representation in the most literal sense. Again, as we can see particularly from the Qumran texts and those like them, the berakah of the community's feasts had already become, for the Jews of the time of Christ, something equivalent to but higher than all sacrifices, since the community, thereby making the 'memorial' of the history of their salvation, at the same time dedicated themselves with all the strength of their being as the community of the people of God. Once again, the opposition disappears when it is placed in the context of the transition from Judaism to Christianity.

"Now we may be entitled to predict from what has just been said that the same will be true for our third problem, that of the presence beneath the symbols. Is it the presence of the whole mystery, or simply that of the body and blood of our Savior? Now the idea of liturgical 'memorial,' far from being opposed to that of a presence, real but mysterious, is a way of approaching it. The Eucharist, like the berakah and following it, makes a 'memorial' of the *mirabilia Dei* precisely so far as they become in some way sharable, assimilable by us. In the Eucharist, God recalls them for us, we commemorate them before him in such a way that they come through to us and we are rapt by them. To which we should add all the Jewish thought on the Shekinah, the particularized presence of God with his people, at first localized in the Holy of Holies, which became as it were the focal point of the covenant. This idea was the forerunner of the Christian idea of the Incarnation. But we can also see, in the rabbinical idea that the Shekinah was present wherever a few faithful Jews were assembled to meditate liturgically on the Torah, in the still more precise idea, but equally rabbinical, that in saying the berakoth over all things pious Israelites prepared there a dwelling place for the Shekinah; we can see in these ideas the beginnings of a richer and more balanced idea of the sacramental presence of the incarnate God, itself destined to be only the means for the final presence of the God who is 'all in all.'

"These few remarks have only been put forward as hints for research. They are only intended to call attention to the so far practically unexplored riches to be found, first, in a comparative study of the liturgies of synagogue and church, and then in the possible deepening of our liturgical and sacramental theology which would come from such a study, which is really the study of the origins of Christian worship." (*True Worship*, edited by Lancelot Sheppard, London; and Helicon Press, Inc., Baltimore; 1963.)

Bibliographical Notes

Introduction and Chapter 1

The terms "law" and "gospel" which I use to characterize the papal Church on the one hand and Protestantism on the other have been used very often by Protestant authors. They summarize accurately the central theme of Luther and most of the other reformers. In the middle of the nineteenth century Karl Heinrich Ullmann wrote, "broadly seen the Reformation is the reaction of Christianity as Gospel against Christianity as 'Law,'" in his book REFORMERS BEFORE THE REFORMATION. H. A. Oberman discusses the concept of the "forerunner," and the opposing concept of radical discontinuity at the Reformation in his book FORERUNNERS OF THE REFORMATION (see bibliographical note to Chapter 3). My work stands on the shoulders of past works, and I have taken account of Oberman's discussion. All history must have some ongoing continuity. The pressure for reform was growing for three centuries before the Reformation, but the probable nature of the resulting actual Reform changed as the pressure became both stronger and more various. The character of the historical Reformation presented a kind of discontinuity in that it proceeded from the inner experience of a particular man.

The Introduction and Chapter 1 have drawn on a very large number of works, and it seems pointless to attempt to draw up an undifferentiated list of histories of the Reformation which I have consulted. But I select the following as being among the more important or interesting books which do not occur in the bibliographies to the other chapters. THE NEW CAMBRIDGE MODERN HISTORY. Vol. I, *The Renaissance, 1493–1520.* Cambridge University Press, Cambridge, 1964. Vol. II, *The Reformation 1520–59.* Cambridge University Press, London, 1965. Dickens, A. G. REFORMATION AND SOCIETY *in Sixteenth Century Europe.* Thames and Hudson, London; Harcourt, Brace, Jovanovich, New York; 1966. A very well illustrated, readable, well-informed summary.
Hughes, Philip. THE REFORMATION, *A Popular History.* Burns and Oates, London, 1957; Hanover House, Garden City, N.Y., 1957, under the title *A Popular History of the Reformation.* A Roman Catholic scholar's summary. Chock full of useful information. It is also a work of Roman Cath-

olic polemic, and in this sense "dated," but this animus does not render the book useless.

Leonard, Emile G. A HISTORY OF PROTESTANTISM. Vol. I, *The Reformation*. Nelson, London, 1965. This has a fundamental approach to the subject from a French "reformed" but ecumenical point of view. Enlightened, very fully informed, its author has produced an exceptionally valuable book. It confirmed several general and particular conclusions which were forming in my mind as I planned my own book. Sometimes, as with all summaries which attempt to produce precise statements, it presents a too clear-cut picture. It is excessively unfortunate that the last sentence of the book is the most absurd of these: ". . . in the economic sphere, Calvin is the founder of our civilisation."

Trevor-Roper, H. R. RELIGION, THE REFORMATION AND SOCIAL CHANGE. Macmillan, London, 1967. A collection of essays by a well-known scholar. A stimulating book, with interesting facts often appearing in its pages. The essay on witchcraft has been criticized by other scholars.

Many of the books listed in the bibliographical notes on subsequent chapters also helped me in the writing of this introductory material.

Chapter 2

THE CAMBRIDGE HISTORY OF THE BIBLE. Ed. G. W. H. Lampe. Vol. II, *The West from the Fathers to the Reformation*. Cambridge University Press, Cambridge, 1969. There is much valuable information in this book, not previously easily available to the general reader. Its authority lies behind a few of my statements and quotations. The book serves to highlight our ignorance about the origins of the vernacular Bibles in Europe; there is great scope here for further research. At the moment we have only a hypothesis, a very strong probability, that Waldensian heretics were the first methodical translators of the Bible into two, perhaps three, four or even five European languages.

Deanesly, Margaret. THE LOLLARD BIBLE. Cambridge University Press, London, first edition, 1920; new edition, 1966. This book provided more material for Chapter 2 than any other book. A very remarkable work, it is highly significant that for its reissue in 1966, forty-six years after its first publication, the author added no more than a page and a half at the beginning. I have taken from it the citations of a number of original documents. The author's use of More's *Dialogue against Tyndale* led me to look again at the original, and to concur with her that the references in this polemical piece by Thomas More provide a witness of exceptional importance to the state of Bible reading and related matters in England in the late 1520's. *The Lollard Bible* covers a far greater range of material than its title indicates.

Hall, Basil. THE TRILINGUAL COLLEGE OF SAN ILDEFONSO AND THE

MAKING OF THE COMPLUTENSIAN POLYGLOT BIBLE. *Studies on Church History*, No. 5. E. J. Brill, Leiden, 1969.

Smalley, Beryl. THE STUDY OF THE BIBLE IN THE MIDDLE AGES. Basil Blackwell, Oxford, 1952. The author's detailed researches bring us the authentic facts and atmosphere of Bible study in the five hundred years preceding the year 1300.

Chapter 3

Aston, Margaret. THE FIFTEENTH CENTURY. Thames and Hudson, London; Harcourt, Brace and World, New York; 1968. An excitingly written, very well-illustrated brief survey.

Augustine. THE CONFESSIONS. F. J. Sheed. Sheed and Ward, London, 1944.

AN AUGUSTINE SYNTHESIS. Erich Przywara. Sheed and Ward, London, 1936. Here are two ways into the writings of Augustine himself for the general reader who lacks the time or the necessary preparation to read more difficult original texts.

Chaucer, Geoffrey. THE CANTERBURY TALES. Penguin, London, 1951.

THE CLOUD OF UNKNOWING. Translated into modern English. Penguin, London, 1961.

Cohn, Norman. THE PURSUIT OF THE MILLENNIUM. Granada, London; Harper and Row, New York; 1970. Along with Leff's book this is essential reading for anyone studying the medieval heresies. Its subtitle is: "Revolutionary millenarians and mystical anarchists of the Middle Age." It shows how very often "a particular outbreak of revolutionary millenarism took place against a background of disaster," the major example being at the time of the Black Death.

Dawson, Christopher. THE MAKING OF EUROPE. Sheed and Ward, London, 1939; New York, 1934. This book, first published in 1932, is still to be found on the lists of university lecturers. It remains one of the best descriptions of the new Christian unity which gradually grew up in Europe between the years A.D. 400 and 1000.

Deanesly, Margaret. A HISTORY OF THE MEDIEVAL CHURCH 590–1500. Methuen, London, 1969. This is a useful brief student's handbook, published in Methuen's University Paperback series.

Hay, Denis. EUROPE IN THE FOURTEENTH AND FIFTEENTH CENTURIES. Longmans, London; Holt, Rinehart and Winston, New York; 1966. The best guide to these centuries in a single volume. I have relied on it quite often. The author is aware of the importance of the religious dimension, but stops short of any attempt to deal methodically with it: ". . . one meets the problem of what men and women believe in and how far their beliefs influence their actions. It is an impenetrable question in our own day and no easier in earlier centuries. One is left with external evidence only." My own work is based on the supposition that one must treat life as a whole and assume that the public religious dimension relates precisely and essentially to an inner life, and that this latter private dimension is not just something we may pretend to be non-existent. It is of significance historically, and we can know something about it.

Julian of Norwich. REVELATIONS OF DIVINE LOVE. Penguin, London, 1966.

Kempe, Margery. THE BOOK OF, A Modern Version. Oxford University Press, London, 1954.

Knowles, David. THE EVOLUTION OF MEDIEVAL THOUGHT. Longmans, London; Helicon Press, Baltimore; 1962. A standard guide to the evolution of philosophy and theology, showing the main trends from Plotinus to Ockham.

——. THE MIDDLE AGES. Vol. II of The Christian Centuries. Darton, Longman and Todd, London; McGraw-Hill, New York; 1969. Probably the most balanced and reliable guide to Christianity in these 900 years. I have relied on it at many points. Its least satisfactory parts are those dealing with heresies.

——. THE RELIGIOUS ORDERS IN ENGLAND. Vol. III. Cambridge University Press, London, 1959. Essential.

Langland, William. PIERS PLOWMAN. VISIONS FROM. Translated into modern English by Nevill Coghill. Phoenix House, London, 1949. One of several modern editions of the famous medieval work. It is specially prepared for the reader without special knowledge.

Leff, Gordon. HERESY IN THE LATER MIDDLE AGES; The Relation of Heterodoxy to Dissent c.1250–1450. 2 vols. Manchester University Press, Manchester; Barnes and Noble, New York; 1967. I refer to this book in the text. It provides much more detail than was easily available to the general reader prior to its publication. It is crammed with information. Certain items have been challenged by other historians, but these do not amount to more than a small proportion of the whole of this immensely full and detailed work.

Nolthenius, Helene. IN THAT DAWN; The Thirteenth Century in Italy. Darton, Longman and Todd, London; McGraw-Hill, New York; 1968. A scholar's popular book on the Duecento (the title of the original Dutch version), from which I have taken the two verse quotations early in Chapter 3.

Oberman, Heiko Augustinus. THE HARVEST OF MEDIEVAL THEOLOGY; Gabriel Biel and Late Medieval Nominalism. Harvard University Press, 1963.

——. FORERUNNERS OF THE REFORMATION; The Shape of Late Medieval Thought Illustrated by Key Documents. Lutterworth, London; Holt,

Rinehart and Winston, New York; 1967. These two books are simply
invaluable for anyone wishing to come to grips, first hand, with late
medieval theology, but without the time for systematic study. In the
second book a typical section is that entitled "The Church." It has
often been remarked that there is no thesis, in Aquinas, *De Ecclesia*.
It was only in the fourteenth century that others than canonists began
to look at "ecclesial" problems and see them whole. After a lucid
introduction, Oberman provides substantial excerpts from the text of
Hus's crucial text *De Ecclesia*, and the complete text of the papal
bull *Execrabilis*. The excerpt from Hus ends with a very significant
summarizing sentence that has almost a post-Vatican II feel about it:
"Thus the pope is not the head nor are the cardinals the entire
body of the holy Catholic and universal Church. For Christ alone is
the head of that Church and all predestined together form the body,
and each alone is a member of that body, because the bride of Christ
is united with him." THE FORERUNNERS is a work of history, with a
stimulating long opening chapter defending the concept of the "Forerunner."

    THE HARVEST is more specifically a work of theological research.
It also has the purpose of defending the late medieval "nominalists"
as truly "Catholic." But the value of the book is in enabling us to
read a thorough exposition of Biel's theology, the theology which
Luther read as a student; Biel was perhaps the best-known late
fifteenth-century theologian. It is from Oberman's important chapter
"Christ and the Eucharist" that I quote Oberman's judgment on Biel's
exposition of the dual nature of the Eucharist as sacrifice.

Poole, Reginald Lane. MEDIEVAL THOUGHT AND LEARNING, Society for
the Propagation of Christian Knowledge, London, 1920. It is well
worth reading this famous book of a scholar from a previous age.
It is not a big book. Its full title is *Illustrations of the History of
Medieval Thought and Learning*.

Runciman, Steven. THE MEDIEVAL MANICHEE; *A Study of the Christian
Dualist Heresy*. Cambridge University Press, Cambridge, 1947.

Russell, Jeffrey Burton. DISSENT AND REFORM IN THE EARLY MIDDLE AGES.
University of California Press, Berkeley, 1965. The factual basis of the
book is meager for the early centuries of the Middle Ages, and the
book is not as useful as its title and length at first suggest. But his
use of the researches of those who went before him is suggestive at
times.

Southern, R. W. THE MAKING OF THE MIDDLE AGES. Hutchinson,
London; Yale University Press, New Haven; 1953. A modern classic.
Ripe, beautiful and scholarly picture of the intellectual foundations.
Written from an intense and wide knowledge and love of the subject
matter.

Tavard, G. H. HOLY WRIT OR HOLY CHURCH; *The Crisis of the Protestant Reformation.* Burns and Oates, London, 1959; Harper and Row, New York, 1960. A valuable short study of the sources, from the fifteenth century to Trent and the Elizabethan Settlement.

Thomson, J. A. F. THE LATER LOLLARDS, 1414–1520. Oxford University Press, London, 1965. An important detailed description, discursive and statistical, all based on original research.

Tierney, B. FOUNDATIONS OF CONCILIAR THEORY. Cambridge University Press, London, 1957. Essential reading for study of this subject.

Trevor-Roper, Hugh. THE RISE OF CHRISTIAN EUROPE. Thames and Hudson, London; Harcourt, Brace, and Jovanovich, New York; 1965. A brilliant description of the rise of Christianity up to c.1500, in a short text, heavily and excitingly illustrated. It omits any analysis of the Christian drive at the heart of the events so brilliantly selected and described.

Ullman, Walter. THE INDIVIDUAL AND SOCIETY IN THE MIDDLE AGES. Methuen, London, 1967; John Hopkins Press, Baltimore, Maryland, 1966. An exceptionally valuable book for understanding the development of a sense of responsibility in the individual Christian citizen, and its contrasting absence in the layman in the Church.

Chapter 4

When we reach the sixteenth century itself, we find that today there is a variety of editions and of selections available of works written in that century. Of all the authors there is no doubt that Erasmus is the most easy to read today. A man of quite exceptional gifts, his writings cover a very wide range, and we have many of his letters. There are many editions available of his various writings. Luther wrote a vast quantity and again there is a considerable variety available, either in new editions or in older editions in libraries. Tyndale, Thomas More, Calvin and many of the other names which occur in this and the following chapters wrote works which are available to the twentieth-century reader. The bigger bookshops and libraries are always ready to advise and recommend, and I leave readers to them or to the services of individual teachers and tutors under whom they may be working, restricting myself to more recent secondary works about the Reformation and the sixteenth century generally.

Atkinson, James. MARTIN LUTHER AND THE BIRTH OF PROTESTANTISM. Penguin, London, 1968. A readable and reliable middle-length account of the history and theology, written with fervor by a protagonist of Luther.

Bainton, Roland, H. ERASMUS OF CHRISTENDOM. Collins, London, 1970;

Charles Scribner and Sons, New York, 1969. A very good popular biography.

Bouyer, Louis. ERASMUS AND THE HUMANIST EXPERIMENT. Chapman, London; Newman Press, Westminster, Maryland; 1959. A very useful little work, with links to Bouyer's final chapter in Vol. II of *The Cambridge History of the Bible*.

——. THE SPIRIT AND FORMS OF PROTESTANTISM. Harvill Press, London; Newman Press, Paramus, New Jersey; 1956. A translation of Bouyer's famous *Du Protestantisme a l'Eglise*, this was a climactic work of exceptional importance. From the influence of its author and his thesis came Hans Küng's more detailed works along similar lines. Not to be compared with that fact, I may, however, mention that the reading of this book led me to undertake reading which led in its turn to my book JOHN WESLEY AND THE CATHOLIC CHURCH (Hodder and Stoughton, London, 1958), and thence to my MARTIN LUTHER (Newman Press, Westminster, Maryland, 1964), and then the present work.

Campbell, W. E. ERASMUS, TYNDALE AND MORE. Eyre and Spottiswoode, London; Bruce, New York; 1949. An old-fashioned book which, however, contains a good deal of useful material, and is easy to read. In the tradition of R. W. Chambers, with whom the author worked on a new edition of More's works.

Chadwick, Owen. THE REFORMATION. Penguin, London, 1960. Probably the best short account. Extends well beyond the usually designated end of the Reformation.

Chambers, R. W. THOMAS MORE. Jonathan Cape, London; Harcourt, New York; 1935. The great biography which is the exemplar of many later studies by other authors. Still essential reading for an understanding of one aspect of the Reformation.

Dickens, A. G. THE ENGLISH REFORMATION. Batsford, London; Schocken Books, Inc., New York; 1966. The standard work on this subject, based on the author's original research. This work is indispensable for an understanding of the Reformation in England, and I have used it more than any other. An obvious admirer of the Church of England he works very hard to be fair, only occasionally betraying a bias, whose light shading shows up against the marked detachment of most of the text. At one point, hard put to it by the activities of Cromwell and Cranmer, he writes: "Amid the enormous psychological pressures of the period who save men of heroic simplicity could occupy high office and yet emerge with a record of consistent belief and profession?" Thomas More can hardly be judged as simple; yet he does surely stand out as a man of integrity with a stature far above that of his fellows, without having to be merely "simple." But Dickens tends perhaps to be over-kind to everyone. I quote a greatly generous commendation of other Catholics from his excellent THE

COUNTER REFORMATION (a book in the same series as his REFORMATION AND SOCIETY; see bibliography to Chapter 1): "In its saints many of us have found the permanent significance of the Catholic Reformation. They are indeed too good to remain the exclusive possession of the Church which bore and nourished them. In some sense their message serves not Catholics alone, but all men of good will: by such spiritual graces their exalted origins and destinies stand universally proclaimed."

——. MARTIN LUTHER AND THE REFORMATION. English Universities Press, Ltd.; Harper and Row, New York; 1967. One of several good brief studies.

Ebeling, Gerhard. LUTHER; *An Introduction to His Thought*. Collins, London; Fortress Press, Philadelphia; 1970. A theological study by a famous Protestant theologian. Serious exposition by a loyal follower.

Erikson, Erik H. YOUNG MAN LUTHER; *A Study in Psychoanalysis and History*. Faber and Faber, London; W. W. Norton, New York; 1958. A famous psychologist's study of Luther's youth and early manhood. There is some very useful material here, along with some speculation which is perhaps not too firmly based in historical fact.

Fransen, Piet. INTELLIGENT THEOLOGY, Vol. III. Darton, Longman and Todd, London; Franciscan Herald Press, Chicago; 1969. In this book is a dialogue between the author and the well-known Scottish theologian T. F. Torrance on the subject of "Grace and the Sacraments." Covering the early Church, the medieval theologians, Luther, Calvin and Trent, but written from a twentieth-century standpoint, this essay provides a helpful introduction to the theological problems really at issue between Catholics and Protestants.

Green, V. H. H. LUTHER AND THE REFORMATION. Batsford, London; Putnam, New York; 1964. A very good middle-length study.

Hughes, Philip. THE REFORMATION IN ENGLAND. Burns and Oates, London; Macmillan, New York; 1963. The very lengthy lifetime's work of a great scholar. Written in a spirit of apologetic, often of polemic. At a later date, already in sight, when emotions will no longer be so easily engaged, its value may well be rated higher than by many today.

Huizinga, J. ERASMUS OF ROTTERDAM. Phaidon Press, London, 1952; Charles Scribner, New York, 1924. A famous biography which is still well worth reading.

Iserloh, Erwin. THE THESES WERE NOT POSTED; *Luther between Reform and Reformation*. Chapman, London; Beacon Press, Boston; 1968. The author maintains with great cogency that Luther acted prudently in the early years of his lectureship at Wittenberg. He gives useful background about indulgences. The title of the book refers to the detailed argument in its last part. The author maintains that Luther sent the Theses out to his superiors, but did not post them up publicly;

the argument seems to be convincing and certainly reflects ill on the lack of proper examination of the facts by historians in the past.

Jedin, Hubert. A HISTORY OF THE COUNCIL OF TRENT, Vols. I and II. Nelson, London; Herder and Herder, New York; 1957. Essential reading for the historical background to the opening months of the council. Vol. I records the long prehistory of the council. Vol. II reaches to 1547.

Küng, Hans. JUSTIFICATION. Burns and Oates, London, 1964; Thomas Nelson and Sons, Camden, New Jersey, 1965. The crucial book for understanding how the definitions of the Council of Trent are in tune with Protestant doctrine.

Lortz, Joseph. THE REFORMATION IN GERMANY. 2 vols. Darton, Longman and Todd, London; Herder and Herder, New York; 1968. A translation of the classic work of the Roman Catholic German historian. It enters more thoroughly into the spirit of the times, and quotes more liberally from Luther and other contemporary authors, than any other recent book. I rely on it frequently.

McSorley, Harry J. LUTHER: RIGHT OR WRONG? *An Ecumenical-Theological Study of Luther's Major Work* THE BONDAGE OF THE WILL. Newman Press, New York, 1969. This is an exceptionally successful work of theology, essential reading for anyone who wishes to go into the theology and history of this topic in detail. McSorley rejects Oberman's defense of Biel.

Palmer, Paul F. SACRAMENTS AND FORGIVENESS; *History and Doctrinal Development of Penance, Extreme Unction, and Indulgences* (SOURCES OF CHRISTIAN THEOLOGY, Vol. II). Darton, Longman and Todd, London, 1960; Newman Press, Westminster, Maryland, 1959. Contains essential texts.

Pelikan, Jaroslav. SPIRIT VERSUS STRUCTURE; *Luther and the Institutions of the Church*. Collins, London; Harper and Row, New York; 1968. A very valuable little work. The author writes with great care and perception to examine Luther's criticism of priesthood, monasticism, baptism, law, the sacraments and their Protestant replacements.

Preus, James Samuel. FROM SHADOW TO PROMISE; *Old Testament Interpretation from Augustine to the Young Luther*. Harvard University Press, Cambridge, Massachusetts, 1969. A very useful book of original research and exposition. Difficult and rather abstract, but intellectually rewarding.

Roper, William, and Nicholas Harpsfield. LIVES OF SAINT THOMAS MORE. Edited with an introduction by E. E. Reynolds. J. M. Dent and Sons, London; Dutton, New York; 1963. The first biographies of More, written in the sixteenth century. Essential reading.

Rupp, Gordon. PATTERNS OF REFORMATION. Epworth, London, 1969. A detailed exposition of the life and thought of Oecolampadius, Karlstadt, Müntzer and Vadianus. A very valuable study of Reformation events from the points of view of four lesser but very important figures. I have used detail from this book from time to time, when the first three are referred to in my text.

————. THE RIGHTEOUSNESS OF GOD. Hodder and Stoughton, London, 1953. This great work has been superseded in some respects by more recent research. It remains, however, a classic of Luther interpretation.

Scarisbrick, J. J. HENRY VIII. Eyre and Spottiswoode, London; University of California Press, Berkeley; 1968. A new biography which has made all previous biographies largely redundant. It sticks closely to the monarch himself, his actions and his writings, and as a result provides a more convincing picture of the man himself than has been available before.

Schwiebert, E. G. LUTHER AND HIS TIMES. Concordia, St. Louis, Missouri, 1950. A mine of information, and invaluable as a kind of encyclopedia on the "times" and the "life," rather than on the theology.

Tauler, Johann. SIGNPOSTS TO PERFECTION; A Selection from the Sermons of Johann Tauler. Ed. and tr. Elizabeth Strakosch. Blackfriars Publications, London, 1958. A useful selection which enables us to understand what attracted Luther to this representative of the central medieval mystical tradition.

Todd, John M. MARTIN LUTHER; A Biographical Study. Burns and Oates, London; Newman Press, Westminster, Maryland; 1964. An attempt at a study of the man and the theologian, which understands both the Catholic friar and the Protestant leader.

Wicks, Jared, S.J. MAN YEARNING FOR GRACE; Luther's Early Spiritual Teaching. Corpus Books, Washington, D.C., 1968. I consider this the best work on the subject. Written entirely from original research, it provides a very readable text, and many imaginative suggestions, as well as massive notes giving the references for the statements.

Chapters 6 and 7

Many of the books already mentioned continued to be of assistance for the period covered by these chapters, for instance, THE NEW CAMBRIDGE MODERN HISTORY and Lortz's THE REFORMATION IN GERMANY. Although I do not list the works of the reformers themselves, it is worth pointing out that in the case of Calvin, the situation is more or less the opposite of that of Erasmus, whose output is so various and is available in various editions of greatly varying date. Calvin intended to produce one book as a guide to Christianity. His Institutes of the Christian Religion, in contradistinction to the work of all the other reformers, provides in one lengthy but coherent text virtually the whole of his thought. The expert must read his biblical commentaries, his sermons, his letters, but the student of theology whose time is limited can find the essential here. References and quotations in this book are to the translation by Henry Beveridge (reprinted 1962) published by James Clarke and Co., U.K. I add three more titles:

Evennett, Outram. THE SPIRIT OF THE COUNTER-REFORMATION. Cambridge University Press, London, 1968.

Jedin, Hubert. A HISTORY OF THE COUNCIL OF TRENT, Vol. II. Nelson, London, 1961; Herder, New York, 1962.

Wendel, François. CALVIN. Collins, London, 1956.

I quote a remarkable paragraph from Evennett's book, which is relevant to the purposes of the present book: "There has been an insufficient liaison, so to speak, between the historians of the Church and the historians of religion—between the ecclesiastical historians proper and all those authors who in the last fifty years or so have done so much to explore, map and illuminate something that, for the Christian believer, is basic to the inner life of the Church, and should therefore be basic to Church history, namely the history of spirituality—devotion, prayer, mysticism . . . In the better integration of the history of spirituality into ecclesiastical history on the one hand, and on the other the fuller recognition of the necessary organic similarities in the evolution of ecclesiastical and secular societies . . . lie the way to a new and perhaps more fruitful mode of ecclesiastical history."

Chapters 5 and 8

In the list of books for Chapter 4, I have already included a number of those which are useful for the subjects of these chapters, most notably Scarisbrick's biography of Henry VIII and Dicken's History of the English Reformation. In addition to these needs to be listed the most recent and invaluable biography of Cranmer:

Ridley, Jasper. THOMAS CRANMER. Oxford University Press, London, 1962.

Another very useful recent book which covers the last years covered by Chapter 8 is:

McGrath, Patrick. PAPISTS AND PURITANS UNDER ELIZABETH I. Blandford Press, London, 1967.

Chapter 9

For this last chapter it is impossible to begin to list all the books which have influenced it or which might enable an interested reader to follow it up. I restrict myself to indicating the book which I regard as the best short guide to the theology of the Second Vatican Council:

Butler, Christopher. THE THEOLOGY OF VATICAN II. Darton, Longman and Todd, London, 1967.

And to quoting from a note (p. 285) in MAN YEARNING FOR GRACE by Jared Wicks (see bibliographical note on Chapter 4): "Reflection on the situation of Catholic theology after Vatican II suggests that Luther, especially in his response to the *via moderna* of scholasticism, has an added relevance for today. Theologically, Vatican II embodies the option of the teaching Church not to speak in the technical language of the neo-scholastic theological manuals. Instead of the highly conceptualized preparatory schemata, the Council gave us documents filled with biblical images, enlivened by pastoral immediacy. Theological work after the Council is already marked by these same characteristics. Thus, it should prove instructive to review Luther's theological venture in order to assess the gains and losses of his very influential biblical-pastoral work."

INDEX

Abelard, 84
Adelmann, 196
Adiophora, 204
Adrian of Utrecht, Pope Adrian IV,
215–16
Aelfric, St., 33
Albert, Elector, archbishop of Mainz,
146, 154, 164–65, 208
Albert of Prussia, 213, 218
Albigensians, the, 68
Alcuin, 33
Aldebert, 69
Aldus Manutius, 118, 120
Aleander, 94, 120, 137, 178, 188–89,
279
Alexander V, Pope, 90
Alexander VI, Pope, 13, 99
Alfred, king of England, 33
Amsdorf, 208
Anabaptists, 211, 234, 244, 276, 335–
36, 339
  Confession of the, 327
Anfechtung, psycho-physical attack of
depression, 110, 113, 127, 195, 232
Annates, Act in Partial Restraint of,
263
Anne of Bohemia, Queen, 40, 89
Anne Boleyn, Queen, 241, 251–52, 254–
55, 259–60, 272
Anne of Cleves, 270
Antichrist, the, 59, 69, 85, 98, 168, 247
Anti-clericalism, 63, 95, 105–6, 118, 140,
222
Appeals, Act in Restraint of, 263
Aquinas, Thomas, 77, 84, 135, 289, 331
Arnold of Brescia, 71
Audley, Sir Thomas, Lord Chancellor,
257
Augsburg, Confession of, 237–38, 277
  Apology of, 236–37
  Diet of, 99, 235–39
  Interim of, 319
  Peace of, 315, 319–20, 344
Augustine, St., 58–62, 82, 124–28, 134–
35, 278, 293–95, 353
  his *The City of God,* 124
  a Manichee, 65–66
  and mysticism, 76
  his *The Trinity,* 124
Augustinian Canons, the, 78, 119–20
Augustinian Hermits, the Order of, 72,
110, 125, 201
Authority, 45–46, 73–81, 86, 124, 156,
159, 164, 188, 233–34, 241–42, 286–
88
Averoës, 178
Avignon, the papacy at, 79–81, 99

Baptism, 75, 289, 305, 310–12, 326

Barnes, Robert, 219
Basel, Council of, 92, 99, 217, 222,
275–76
Beda, Nicholas, 221, 278
Beguines and Beghards, 37
Bergamo, Waldensian conference at, 75,
323
Bernard, St., 70, 156
  and Abelard, 84
  and mysticism, 76–77
Bernardino, St., 26
Bernhardi, Bartholomew, 134
Bible, the
  "Breeches," 340
  Calvin's translation, 323
  the control of translations, 28–29
  Cromwell and Coverdale and the
    Great Bible, 219, 241
  Czech translations, 40
  Erasmus' New Testament, 49–50
  in the fifteenth century, 43–44
  the first printed bibles, 43–44
  Lefèvre and French translations, 117,
    143, 221
  licensed reading of, 40, 45–46
  Luther's Bible, 199, 205
  many European translations, 44n, 49n
  and the ordinary Christian, 25–28
  as reformers' norm, 21–22
  and the scholars, 22–25
  in Spain, 31–34, 44n, 47–49
  translations not outlawed, 33–38
  translations outlawed, 30–33, 40–47
  Tyndale's translation and derivatives,
    50–51, 219, 241, 267
  Wycliffe's translation, 39–40
  Ximenes' polyglot, 47–50
Bible, Books of the
  Ecclesiastes, 123
  Epistles, 119
  Galatians, Letter to the, 127–31
  Gospels, 35, 81, 119, 121
  Hebrews, Letter to the, 127
  Isaiah, 303
  Jeremiah, 123, 303
  Job, 35
  John's, St., Gospel, 67
  Matthew's, St., Gospel, 174
  Pentateuch (first five books of Old
    Testament), 51
  Psalms, 45, 113, 127, 131
  Revelation of St. John, 45
  Romans, Letter to the, 127, 128, 174,
    276
  Tobit, 35
Bible Historiale, of Guyart des Moulins,
35
Biel, 103, 114, 127, 134
Bilney, Thomas, 214, 235–36